William Blake

Essays in honour of Sir Geoffrey Keynes

Sir Geoffrey Keynes by Peter Wardle

William Blake

Essays in honour of Sir Geoffrey Keynes

Edited by Morton D. Paley and
Michael Phillips

OXFORD
AT THE CLARENDON PRESS
1973

Oxford University Press, Ely House, London W.1

GLASGOW   NEW YORK   TORONTO   MELBOURNE   WELLINGTON
CAPE TOWN   IBADAN   NAIROBI   DAR ES SALAAM   LUSAKA   ADDIS ABABA
DELHI   BOMBAY   CALCUTTA   MADRAS   KARACHI   LAHORE   DACCA
KUALA LUMPUR   SINGAPORE   HONG KONG   TOKYO

© *Oxford University Press 1973*

*Printed in Great Britain
at the University Press, Oxford
by Vivian Ridler
Printer to the University*

PREFACE

WITH this collection of essays we pay an affectionate and, we hope, appropriate tribute to Sir Geoffrey Keynes. It would, at this time, appear unnecessary to attempt even an encomium to his work in the field of Blake scholarship. Having established Blake's text and, with untiring efforts, identified and recorded his work as an artist in word and picture, Sir Geoffrey has provided students with the prerequisites for their serious consideration of this major English artist. Nor have Sir Geoffrey's achievements been limited to Blake. He has published bibliographies of Donne, Browne, Harvey, Boyle, Evelyn, Ray, Hazlitt, Jane Austen, Brooke, Sassoon, and others, in addition to editing the works of many of these and other writers. In 1966 his *Life of William Harvey* received the James Tait Black Memorial Prize for biography. A further testimony to his scholarship and to his perseverance and taste is his splendid collection of rare books and manuscripts, which has often formed a basis for his bibliographical studies and whose details are recorded in *Bibliotheca Bibliographici*. It is proper that this collection should, by way of conclusion, present in detail the wide range of his contribution to Blake studies. His achievement is the more remarkable when we remind ourselves that his professional career has not been that of a literary scholar, but that of a distinguished surgeon. His profession, however, might well be an index of the humanity and warmth that has always accompanied his literary interests and inspired all those who have been privileged to enjoy his correspondence, academic hospitality, and company. This man of such extraordinary abilities and accomplishments has always found time to assist and encourage the beginner: we are all his students.

The essays in this volume range in subject-matter from the earliest of Blake's writings and art to the works and friendships of his last years and the vicissitudes of his posthumous reputation. The contributors themselves have an equally varied approach, ranging from close analysis of the language of Blake's poetry, individual poems, and plates to thematic studies encompassing the greater part of his poetry and associated visual content. All these essays are explorative. Not all of their authors are Blake specialists, and those who are range from academics with established reputations to young scholars. In wishing to include a varied approach, which would disclose the work of new and talented Blake students as well as those of authority, we hope we have composed a volume in keeping with the spirit of Sir Geoffrey Keynes and the nature of his interest in Blake. We offer it, at least, hoping that it will be accepted as a tribute to his involvement with a man the full significance of whose writing involves us all.

vii

Preface

We wish to thank the following individuals and institutions for their generous help and encouragement. For permission to quote from Samuel Palmer's correspondence, Yale University Library, John E. A. Samuels, Paul Mellon, A. H. Palmer II, Anthony W. Richmond, the Victoria and Albert Museum, Joan Linnell Ivimy, and Sir Geoffrey Keynes. Permissions to reproduce pictures are given in the List of Illustrations; we would like to thank all these for their courtesy and also A. C. Cooper, Fine Art Photographs Limited, London, for pictures formerly in the W. Graham Robertson Collection. F. R. Leavis's lecture at Bristol University first appeared in *The Human World*. It is a particular pleasure to express our gratitude to David Piper, A. L. N. Munby, Reginald Williams, the staff of the Clarendon Press, and the many contributors to this volume and others who have given generously of their time in helping one another and the editors.

Morton D. Paley and
Michael Phillips

Berkeley and
Edinburgh
March 1973

viii

CONTENTS

LIST OF ILLUSTRATIONS

List of Illustrations

List of Illustrations

List of Illustrations

ABBREVIATIONS

Bentley, *Records*	G. E. Bentley, Jr., *Blake Records*, Oxford, 1969
Bibliography	G. E. Bentley, Jr., and M. K. Nurmi, *A Blake Bibliography*, Minneapolis, 1964
Blake Studies	G. L. Keynes, *Blake Studies: Essays on his Life and Work*, 2nd ed., Oxford, 1971
Blunt	A. Blunt, *The Art of William Blake*, New York, 1959
E	D. V. Erdman, ed., *The Poetry and Prose of William Blake*, New York, 1965
EG	*The Everlasting Gospel*
GA	*The Ghost of Abel*
J	*Jerusalem*
K	G. L. Keynes, ed., *The Complete Writings of William Blake*, Oxford, 1966
Keynes, *Bible*	G. L. Keynes, *William Blake's Illustrations to the Bible*, London, 1957
MHH	*The Marriage of Heaven and Hell*
Separate Plates	G. L. Keynes, *Engravings by William Blake: The Separate Plates: A Catalogue Raisonée*, Dublin, 1956
VDA	*Visions of the Daughters of Albion*
VLJ	*Vision of the Last Judgement*

I

BLAKE'S EARLY POETRY

Michael Phillips

THE self-inquiry and progress that Blake urges each of us to undertake in the later works, especially in the *Songs*, *Milton*, and *Jerusalem*, appears to exist at a personal level in the poetry of his youth—the poetry that he composed before he was twenty-one. Perhaps as a result of possessing relatively little knowledge of this period and because of our preoccupation with the overtly complex works of his maturity, we have underestimated the importance of these years, and in particular their significance for Blake himself.[1]

As he tells us in his letter to Flaxman (12 Sept. 1800) it was during this period that Milton 'shew'd me his face' and 'Ezra came with Isaiah the Prophet', that Shakespeare 'gave me his hand' and 'Paracelsus and Behmen appear'd to me'.[2] We know from Benjamin Heath Malkin that Blake's taste in artists such as 'Raphael and Michael Angelo, Martin Hemskerck and Albert Durer', and his 'Gothicised imagination' were largely acquired and confirmed during this time.[3] His marginalia disclose that he carefully read and annotated 'Burke's Treatise on the Sublime . . . Locke on Human Understanding & Bacon's Advancement of Learning',[4] works which antithetically prompted his intellect to question and clarify fundamental premisses regarding the nature of language and mind. He was also occupied with the business and skills of his apprenticeship under James Basire and with writing his first poems, *Poetical Sketches*.[5]

---

[1] This essay discusses in abbreviated form one of the themes of my full-length study of Blake's early life and writings, which is near completion.

[2] K, p. 799. [3] Bentley, *Records*, pp. 422–3. [4] K, p. 476.

[5] Select bibliography of critical discussion of *Poetical Sketches*. T. S. Eliot, 'Blake', *The Sacred Wood*, 1920, pp. 137–43; S. Foster Damon, *William Blake, His Philosophy and Symbols*, 1924, pp. 253–63; Mark Schorer, *William Blake: The Politics of Vision*, New York, 1946, pp. 401–6; Northrop Frye, *Fearful Symmetry*, 1947, pp. 177–86; Cleanth Brooks [on 'My silks and fine array'], *CEA Critic*, xii. 9 (Oct. 1950), 1–6; David V. Erdman, *Blake: Prophet against Empire*, Princeton, N.J., 1954, 2nd ed., 1969, esp. pp. 15–23, 27–9, 63–85; Harold Bloom, *Blake's Apocalypse*, 1963, pp. 13–22; Robert F. Gleckner, 'Blake's Seasons', *Studies in English Literature*, v (Summer 1965), 533–51; John Holloway, *Blake: The Lyric Poetry*, 1968, pp. 9–20; Geoffrey H. Hartman, 'Blake and the "Progress of Poesy"', *William Blake: Essays for S. Foster Damon*, ed. A. H. Rosenfeld, Providence, R.I., 1969, 57–68; William K. Wimsatt, 'Imitation as Freedom—1717–1798', *New Literary History*, i. 2 (Winter 1970), 215–36; L. C. Knights, 'Early Blake', *Sewanee Review*, lxxix (1971), 377–92; F. R. Leavis, 'Justifying One's Valuation of Blake', in the present volume, pp. 66–85; see also, Margaret Ruth Lowery, *Windows of the Morning*, New Haven, Conn., 1940; and John W. Ehrstine, *William Blake's Poetical Sketches*, Washington State University Press, 1967.

Poetical Sketches were composed between 1769 and 1778. When the opportunity came for the poems to be printed privately in 1783 Blake had kept his most recent compositions in manuscript for approximately six years, and the earliest for fourteen. Clearly they were of importance to him. I have discussed the care with which Blake emended copies of *Poetical Sketches* immediately following their printing and thereafter, and—significantly—that he continued to present copies to friends and acquaintances until his death.[6] I wish to show here what was particularly personal about the contents of the volume: to trace in the poems themselves the record of self in relation to its increasing sense of poetical vocation. We can recognize in the early poems, and in particular *An Imitation of Spencer*, *Mad Song*, and *Samson*, Blake's moments of crisis and doubt and isolation as the nature and implications of his vocation became more clearly defined. His experimenting in idiom, which nowhere else in his writings is so abundant and diversified, is but one reflection of this progress and search.

The subject is not unrelated to what T. S. Eliot identified as the 'peculiar honesty' of Blake's poetry, 'which, in a world too frightened to be honest, is peculiarly terrifying'. Eliot was referring to the demands which Blake makes upon us, upon our sense of integrity and our perception of the world. In Blake there is no place for compromise; compromise is left for us to make, and in doing so it is made with a heightened awareness gained from our knowledge of the man and his writings. Before Blake could make these demands upon us he had to exercise a profound honesty with himself—with regard to the nature of his identity and the role he felt called to fulfil. It is in his early poetry that these demands upon himself and their eventual acceptance are mirrored.

1

An Imitation of Spencer[7] has remained all but unnoticed by students of Blake. It is of peculiar importance in that it is perhaps the poet's most explicit statement regarding the literary predicament he felt himself to be in during the 1770s. When reading the poem we first notice an extraordinary density of classical allusion; but this does not betray Blake as writing in the Augustan line. Together with his contemporary reader we are alerted by the title and form.

In view of the writings on *The Faerie Queene* by Thomas Warton and Richard Hurd and previous and contemporary use of the stanza in the eighteenth century by Thomson, Beattie, and others, a poem in imitation of Spenser composed in stanzas following the Spenserian model would have identified a sympathy on the part of the poet with *native* tradition—what Blake, Hurd, and their contemporaries

---

[6] 'Blake's Corrections in *Poetical Sketches*', *Blake Newsletter*, iv. 2 (Fall 1970), 40–7.

[7] Blake's spelling of Spenser's surname was not exceptional; see Edward Bysshe, *Art of English Poetry*, 1702, p. 33, which he studied.

would also have recognized by the term 'Gothick'. Significantly, by the 1770s the imitation of Spenser had also established an expectation of another kind (particularly in view of the wide popularity of James Beattie's *The Minstrel*, 1771, 1774): it indicated a personal, often introspective subject-matter which was made tolerable by the distancing effect of the form and style. John Upton, with his famous edition of *The Faerie Queene* (1758), was perhaps instrumental in the development of this personal element within the convention when he drew attention to levels of 'historical allusion' in Spenser's poem—levels at which the allegory became intelligible when related to the author and his contemporaries. Upton's remark concluding his commentary to Book I typifies the new focus of attention. 'Spenser in his letter to Sir W. R. tells us his poem is a continuous allegory: where therefore the more allusion cannot be made apparent, we must seek (as I imagine) for an historical allusion; and always we must look for more than meets the eye or ear; the words carrying one meaning with them, and the secret sense another.'[8] With regard to Blake's stanzas one's initial observation may be that of John Sampson (1905), that they are 'all different and all wrong'.[9] But beginning with Prior's *Ode* to the Queen (1706) there had been ample precedent during the eighteenth century (and the seventeenth) for writing an irregular stanza.[10] What we are witnessing in the stanzas of *An Imitation of Spencer* is further exploration— a variety of attempts to modulate the form in new ways. However, we can also recognize in the perversity of variation Blake's evident disquiet within the convention.

An Imitation of Spencer takes us a stage beyond the condemnation of contemporary poetry that is made in *To The Muses*, where a delicate, 'melodious' rhythm and the use of conventional measure and diction play artfully and ironically against the poem's statement. *To The Muses* epitomizes and confirms the final epode of Gray's *Progress of Poesy* and as such laments the dearth of truly inspired poetry. In 1773 another *Progress of Poetry* was published and in its concluding lines the author also paused to reflect, but significantly with less optimism and without the element of autobiographical presumption that one can find in Gray.

> Fain would I now th'excelling bard reveal,
> And paint the seat where all the muses dwell,
> Where Phoebus has his warmest smiles bestow'd,
> And who most labours with th'inspiring God![11]

To the author of these lines the landscape of contemporary poetry appears barren

---

[8] *Spenser's Faerie Queene*, ed. John Upton, 1758, ii. 428.

[9] *Poetical Works of William Blake*, Oxford, 1905, p. 21 n.

[10] E. P. Morton, 'The Spenserian Stanza in the Eighteenth Century', *Modern Philology*, x (Jan. 1913), 365–91.

[11] Anon., *Annual Register . . . For the Year 1772*, p. 230.

and the search for a truly inspired poetry vain. But if one genuinely claimed to be writing poetry of divine or prophetic quality the response of the age would be equally dispiriting, as the opening stanzas of *An Imitation of Spencer* make clear.

> Golden Apollo, that thro' heaven wide
>   Scatter'st the rays of light and truth's beams!
> In lucent words my darkling verses dight,
>   And wash my earthy mind in thy clear streams,
>   That wisdom may descend in fairy dreams:
> All while the jocund hours in thy train
>   Scatter their fancies at thy poet's feet;
> And when thou yields to night thy wide domain,
> Let rays of truth enlight his sleeping brain.
>
> For brutish Pan in vain might thee assay
>   With tinkling sounds to dash thy nervous verse,
> Sound without sense; yet in his rude affray,
>   (For ignorance is Folly's leasing nurse,
>   And love of Folly needs none other curse;)
>
> Midas the praise hath gain'd of lengthen'd ears,
>   For which himself might deem him ne'er the worse
> To sit in council with his modern peers,
>   And judge of tinkling rhimes and elegances terse.

By his invocation Blake identifies himself with a divinely inspired or prophetic poetry. The corresponding imagery of light and illumination dispelling poetic and mental darkness, and oblique allusion to *The Faerie Queene*, give definition to the nature and tradition of the poetry that he desires to write.

It is in the second stanza that Blake makes his first use of classical myth in order to develop with precision the allegory and implications of his own poetical progress. The myth is derived from Ovid (*Met.* xi), but Blake may also have recalled its use by Smart in his masque *The Judgement of Midas* (*Poems on Several Occasions*, 1752) as both Smart and Blake similarly depart from Ovid in representing Midas as judge, and Blake omits Tmolus altogether. In Blake's stanza the indictment is conveyed with accuracy and wit. In Pan's contention with Apollo that the flute is preferable to the lyre, and Midas' subsequent judging in favour of Pan, the taste of the literary establishment is confirmed. The inspired, 'nervous verse' of Apollo is dismissed in preference to the 'tinkling sounds' of Pan; and Midas is portrayed as indeed fit company to 'sit in council with his modern peers' and judge of 'tinkling rhimes, and elegances terse'. In concluding his stanza with the use of epithet, 'tinkling rhimes', followed by periphrasis 'elegances terse' (presumably for the heroic couplet), Blake turns the diction of convention against itself and tags the judgement of his day as effectively as Apollo dealt with Midas.

In the first two stanzas Blake has made his own position clear and, in relation to it, that of his age. The third stanza is the first of three that Blake devotes to Mercury and in each instance the manner is sufficiently detailed and particular to alert us to other forms of literary allusion; in the third stanza it is to Virgil.

> And thou, Mercurius, that with winged brow
>   Dost mount aloft into the yielding sky,
> And thro' Heav'n's halls thy airy flight dost throw,
>   Entering with holy feet to where on high
>   Jove weighs the counsel of futurity;
> Then, laden with eternal fate, dost go
>   Down, like a falling star, from autumn sky,
>   And o'er the surface of the silent deep dost fly:

The allusion made here, read together with the first line of the fourth stanza, 'If thou arrivest at the sandy shore', derives ultimately from Homer (*Il.* xxiv. 339–48; *Od.* v. 1–87), but its more immediate association is with the famous passage in *Aeneid* iv. Following the appeal to Jove by King Iarbas, Jove instructs Mercury to reveal himself to Aeneas. Mercury descends to earth and in dramatic terms reminds and encourages Aeneas to observe and fulfil his destiny; to continue his journey from Troy and found the new province and seat of civilization at Rome. The development of Blake's allegory is clear. Characteristically, the progress of poetry moves from Greece to Italy, from Italy to England, and then from Chaucer to Spenser, Shakespeare, Milton, Dryden, and Pope. It is for Blake to complete a journey typologically similar to that of Aeneas: the poetry of his day is lifeless and in ruins, and it is for him to persevere in breaking with the poetry of the Roman line that has usurped native tradition and to establish a new poetry of vital authority. The mythology of progress and quest had evidently appealed to Blake from an early age, as it can clearly be recognized in the subject of his first independent print, *Joseph of Arimathea among the Rocks of Albion*—'Engraved when I was a beginner at Basires' (1773),[12] which portrays the mythological founder of Christianity in Britain who journeyed to Glastonbury from the scene of the crucifixion where he had received the blood of Christ in the holy grail.

---

[12] The first state of this engraving, discovered by Sir Geoffrey Keynes, is reproduced in *Blake Studies*, 2nd ed., Oxford, 1971, Plate 14.

The fourth stanza of *An Imitation of Spencer* develops the quest theme, and in terms of allusion it moves from Virgil to Spenser.

> If thou arrivest at the sandy shore,
>> Where nought but envious hissing adders dwell,
> Thy golden rod, thrown on the dusty floor,
>> Can charm to harmony with potent spell;
>> Such is sweet Eloquence, that does dispel
> Envy and Hate, that thirst for human gore;
>> And cause in sweet society to dwell
> Vile savage minds that lurk in lonely cell.

Reference here is made initially to the *caduceus*; an example is reproduced as a tailpiece in Jacob Bryant's *New System* (1774–6), which Blake possibly engraved at the time.[13] Its use as described by Blake is found in Spenser where it is the essential device which enables Sir Guyon and his Palmer to 'charm to harmony with potent spell' Acrasia's victims, men who have been changed into savage beasts, and thus they successfully overcome the final obstacle in their journey to the Bower of Bliss (*Faerie Queene* II. xii. 37–42). In terms of Blake's contemporary situation, similar obstacles stand in the way of the poet and it would seem that only a magical, civilizing device (representing divine protection) will bring the 'hissing adders' and 'vile savage minds' of his contemporaries into 'harmony' and 'sweet society', thus enabling the poet to continue his vocational journey without further hindrance or distraction. Blake's reference to 'Envy and Hate . . .' also gives this stanza an element of almost morbid introspection, reminding one of Cowper, and in particular of the passage in *Lines Written During a Period of Insanity*—

> Hatred and vengence, my eternal portion,
> Scarce can endure delay of execution,
> Wait, with impatient readiness, to seize my
>> Soul in a moment.

—though these lines would not become known to Blake until years later.

In the penultimate stanza Blake invokes Mercury's aid in obtaining divine assistance so that his inspiration, symbolized by the Pindaric eagle as in Gray and Collins, can attain a height and intensity associated with the source itself, 'Sol's palace high'; the 'chambers of the sun' that were described in *To The Muses*.

> O Mercury, assist my lab'ring sense,
>> That round the circle of the world wou'd fly!
> As the wing'd eagle scorns the tow'ry fence
>> Of Alpine hills round his high aery,
>> And searches thro' the corners of the sky,

---

[13] Reproduced in Keynes, *Blake Studies*, Plate 11.

Sports in the clouds to hear the thunder's sound,
    And sees the winged lightnings as they fly;
Then, bosom'd in an amber cloud, around
    Plumes his wide wings, and seeks Sol's palace high.

In the final stanza of *An Imitation of Spencer* the thematic structure of the allegory is given a new and poignant coherence. In this instance Blake turns to the original for both Aeneas' journey and Sir Guyon's quest—Homer's *Odyssey*.

And thou, O warrior maid invincible,
    Arm'd with the terrors of Almighty Jove!
Pallas, Minerva, maiden terrible,
    Lov'st thou to walk the peaceful solemn grove,
    In solemn gloom of branches interwove?
Or bear'st thy Egis o'er the burning field,
    Where, like the sea, the waves of battle move?
Or have thy soft piteous eyes beheld
    The weary wanderer thro' the desert rove?
    Or does th'afflicted man thy heav'nly bosom move?

In describing Athene, Blake carefully distinguishes between the *Iliad* and the *Odyssey* with regard to the nature of her relationship to Odysseus; the order in which he indicates her attributes follows precisely the shift from the earlier to the later work of Homer.[14] Blake acknowledges her prowess in war, but his desire is for the quality of personal sympathy and affection which is first introduced at the beginning of the *Odyssey* when she pleads on behalf of Odysseus that he be allowed to continue his journey back to Ithaca. In turning in his invocation from Athene 'maiden terrible' to the goddess of 'soft piteous eyes'—who is asked to look upon the poet as 'the weary wanderer' roving the poetic desert of his day—Blake associates himself with Odysseus and the occasion of Homer's second poem. The exactness with which the allusion is placed, locating Odysseus at his loneliest and most forsaken hour, discloses in an unobtrusive manner the extent of the poet's own feeling of isolation. The use of the interrogative in the final lines compounds this feeling, and leaves the last of the poet's unanswered questions lingering in the mind long after the lines have been read.

It is significant that the progress of Blake's allegory moves from Aeneas distracted at Carthage to Sir Guyon entering the Bower of Bliss, and then to Odysseus on Calypso's isle before the outset of his journey home. The final stanza clarifies the progress in that like Aeneas at Carthage following his confrontation with Mercury, Sir Guyon entering Acrasia's garden, and finally Odysseus, Blake has

---

[14] A full discussion of the change in relationship between Athene and Odysseus is given in W. B. Stanford, *The Ulysses Theme*, 2nd ed., Oxford, 1968, pp. 25–42.

rejected the inducements to submit and conform or merely remain content with things as they are; and again like Aeneas, Sir Guyon, and Odysseus, but with a mounting emphasis as we move from stanza to stanza, Blake is aware that in another sense his journey is only just beginning. Having identified himself in the opening stanzas with a divine or prophetic inspiration, in his final line Blake acknowledges that his contemporaries will look upon him as 'afflicted', probably in the same way that they patronized the affliction of Collins, Smart, and Cowper; the Pindaric association in the penultimate stanza anticipates the implication to be drawn here. In the next poem that I wish to discuss we can recognize that Blake also intended a second and even more exacting meaning in his suggestion of journeying alone 'afflicted' by prophetic inspiration and calling.

2

Gilchrist's remark on Blake's *Mad Song*, 'the daring expression of things otherwise inarticulate', is still apposite in that it begs the obvious but essential interpretive question. Clearly the poem is concerned with madness, but of what kind? And there is the evident verbal allusion 'a-cold'; as James Thomson ('B.V.') commented in an unjustly neglected essay, '*Mad Song* immediately reminds us of the character assumed by Edgar in *Lear*.'[15] But what is the significance of the relationship between *Mad Song* and *King Lear*? And in the poem's final lines we find an apparently unresolved paradox: the 'east' is the source of both 'comforts' that have increased and the 'frantic pain' that seizes the brain of the singer. Nearly every writer on Blake has recorded his admiration, and brief commentary on *Mad Song* exists in relative abundance. But these central questions and the poem's paradox still seem to have been skirted.

In his essay Thomson also drew attention to Blake's poem in relation to the tradition of Tom o' Bedlam songs, having been prompted by Isaac D'Israeli's chapter on the subject in *Curiosities of Literature* (1859). D'Israeli in turn had written in response to the publication of six such songs—three original and three in imitation—in Percy's *Reliques* (1765), a copy of which Blake owned and studied.[16] In his discussion D'Israeli notes that the tradition originated with the harmless lunatics of Bethlam Hospital who were turned out as a result of lack of support and overcrowding. Miserable and unattended they wandered the country chanting wild ditties dressed 'all over with rubins (ribands), feathers, cuttings of cloth, and what not'. Here are the first two stanzas and chorus of the genuine mad song which D'Israeli quotes in full. They offer the best description of their circumstances, and sound the authentic note of their cries.

---

[15] 'The Poems of William Blake', *The National Reformer*, N.S. viii (14 Jan. 1866), 23.
[16] The autograph copy is in possession of Wellsley College, Mass.

From yᵉ hagg and hungry Goblin,
Yᵗ into raggs would rend yee,
and yᵉ spirit yᵗ stand's by yᵉ naked man,
in yᵉ booke of moones defend yee
That of your fiue sounde sences,
you neuer be forsaken,
Nor wander from selues with Tom,
abroad to begg your bacon,
while I doe sing any foode any feeding,
feedinge—drinke or clothing,
Come dame or maid, be not afraid,
poore Tom will iniure nothing.

Of thirty bare yeares haue I
twice twenty bin enraged,
and of forty bin three tymes fifteene
in durance soundlie caged,
On yᵉ lordlie loftes of Bedlam
with stubble softe and dainty,
braue braceletts strong, sweet whips ding dong
with wholsome hunger plenty,
and nowe I sing etc.[17]

It was not long before beggars and mountebanks adopted the dress and manner of the genuine Tom o' Bedlam in order to take advantage of what charity they were given. Edgar in *Lear* similarly adopts such a disguise and feigns their chant and song, though the sincerity of his intention is not in question.

Poor Tom; that eats the swimming frog, the toad, the todpole, the wall-newt, and the water; that in the fury of his heart, when the foul fiend rages, eats cow-dung for sellets, swallows the old rat and the ditch-dog; drinks the green mantle of the standing pool; who is whipp'd from tithing to tithing and stock-punish'd and imprison'd; who hath had three suits to his back, six shirts to his body,

Horse to ride, and weapon to wear,
But mice and rats and such small deer
Have been Tom's food for seven long year (III. iv. 132–43).

This raises the first important question with regard to Blake's poem.

Mad Song

The wild winds weep,
And the night is a-cold;

---

[17] I quote the original text printed in *Loving Mad Tom, Bedlamite Verses of the XVI and XVII Centuries*, ed. Jack Lindsay, 1927, repr. 1969, p. 23, whose unacknowledged source is British Museum, Giles Earle Additional MS. 24665 (1615).

Come hither, Sleep,
 And my griefs infold:
But lo! the morning peeps
 Over the eastern steeps,
And the rustling birds of dawn
 The earth do scorn.

Lo! to the vault
 Of paved heaven,
With sorrow fraught
 My notes are driven:
They strike the ear of night,
 Make weep the eyes of day;
They make mad the roaring winds,
 And with tempests play.

Like a fiend in a cloud
 With howling woe,
After night I do croud,
 And with night will go;
I turn my back to the east,
From whence comforts have increas'd;
For light doth seize my brain
With frantic pain.

Harold Bloom (*Blake's Apocalypse*, 1963)[18] appears to accept that the madness is not genuine, being the product of a 'self-deceiving' singer of the poem whom he clearly distinguishes from Blake. In this sense, Bloom sees the poem as anticipating Blake's genius for 'intellectual satire' and, thus extends the view of Northrop Frye (*Fearful Symmetry*, 1947) that the singer 'is mad because he is locked up in his own Selfhood or inside, and cannot bear to see anything'; *Mad Song*, according to Frye, being 'the germ of Blake's whole conception of "Spectres"'. This interpretation of the poem, which apparently evolved from Yeats's brief remarks in his *Muses Library Edition* of Blake (1893), would seem to be held in general acceptance in view of the absence of alternative readings. But the reading is inadequate as it clearly places any admitted burden of seriousness on the singer and locates Blake at an objective remove from the evident emotion that the poem expresses.

 L. C. Knights (*Sewanee Review*, 1971) seems to be alone in considering this element of seriousness and evident immediacy of tone which the poem presents.

The total effect is a half-pitying definition-by-expression of a particular kind of pain—

[18] See also *The Visionary Company*, 1962, pp. 14–15.

but only half-pitying: for with the return of basic rhyme pattern and a more insistent, less broken rhythm in the final stanza, Blake brings out how much of this distressed and distressing consciousness is in fact willed. The speaker exults in his desperate attempt to keep ahead of the dawn, to prevent the flooding in of light—

> I turn my back to the east,
> From whence comforts have increas'd . . .

The madness is not less poignantly expressed for containing this implicit criticism; it is as though the poet said: this frantic pain, which is real and wounding, is one with the turning of the back on 'light' and 'comfort'; see how, in refusing life, human beings can so desperately maim themselves.

Knights does not identify the singer as Blake, but he does admit a much closer singer–author relationship in terms of the poem's emotional focus—though critical of the action, Blake emotionally involves himself in it. And in noticing the return of basic rhyme pattern in the final stanza, indicating that the distress of the singer is 'in fact willed', Knights alters our attitude toward him in an important respect from the 'self-deceiving' figure which Bloom observed: for Knights the singer is fully aware of his action, and in the fullness of his awareness has chosen to retreat into night. However, in suggesting that the singer 'exults' in his desperate attempt to keep ahead of the dawn, turning his back on the 'light' and 'comfort' of life, I believe Knights goes astray.

What he appears to have neglected is the manner in which the pattern of rhyme and rhythm complement the poem's cycle and its development. In the opening lines of the poem the rhyme and rhythm are unbroken and at the same time we are introduced to a scene set in night in which the singer is attempting to invoke Sleep to 'infold' his misery—to bring unconsciousness. (Blake was specially careful in correcting 'unfold' to 'infold' in *Mad Song* before presenting copies of *Poetical Sketches*; the emended verb is crucial in making the poem's cycle explicit.) But the invocation fails as dawn approaches and the rustling 'birds' (also consistently emended by Blake) race before the approaching storm. Correspondingly, the rhyme pattern becomes broken with the approach of light and heightened consciousness. Rhyme and rhythm become even more jarring and erratic in the second stanza where the singer appeals to heaven to bring relief and fails; the storm rages now and becomes the reflection of the singer's distress. In the opening lines of the final stanza the singer becomes one with the storm—'like a fiend in a cloud', howling woe. The storm will become abated only as the singer escapes from light and the consciousness that it brings. The singer 'crouds' into night, and as he re-enters darkness, and presumably gains the relief that comes with unconsciousness, the rhyme and rhythmic pattern return to normal. The singer has come full circle from night to day and back into night;

logically we have returned to the opening scene of the poem, and with the probability of the cycle recurring the singer's dilemma intensifies.

Blake's word-play in *Mad Song* takes us further in exploring the poem's meaning. Winds 'weep'—nature has been humanized and is in misery witnessing the singer's misery. Morning 'peeps', it would seem maliciously, but the 'eyes of day' are weeping in the second stanza and retrospectively we realize that dawn was evidently in fear of what was about to take place. In the second stanza, where rhyme and rhythm are most discordant, the 'notes' of the singer's song are 'driven' against the 'paved' vault of heaven, they 'strike' against the ear of night— the rhyme and rhythm are broken just as the singer's song, which then ironically becomes the 'play' of tempests. As the singer hears his notes broken, and his song twisted into the storm, he can no longer sing—now he howls his woe. In the succeeding line Blake dramatically transforms the noun *croud* into a transitive verb, but in doing so retains the resonance and metaphorical significance of its primary usage: the singer 'crouds' into night to lose himself and any sense of identity which remains. It is in the final lines that we realize that the inability to sing was the singer's all along—the destruction was self-destruction. In the final four lines the singer attempts an explanation of what has been described. The 'east', the source of light, has brought 'comforts' and these have 'increas'd': presumably there has been a growing sense of fulfilment as consciousness and perception of the world have become heightened; now the perception has become too great and the singer must turn away. The paradox of *Mad Song* is of a kind with Ecclesiastes (I: 18)—'For in much wisdom is much grief: and he that increaseth knowledge increaseth sorrow'—which Blake himself echoed years later in his remarks recorded by Crabb Robinson, 'Though he spoke of his happiness he spoke of past sufferings and of sufferings as necessary. "There is suffering in heaven, for where there is the capacity of enjoyment there is the capacity of pain."'[19]

This returns us to *Lear*. The verbal allusion that has been discussed does not preclude our thinking merely of Edgar; in the atmosphere and imagery of *Mad Song* it is Lear himself who is brought to mind during his progress over the heath into madness. In returning to *Lear* I wish to address the question regarding the nature of the madness in Blake's poem—is it feigned, and if not in what sense is it genuine? The essential concern of Shakespeare's play is with appearance versus reality—with the paradox of sight: Lear sees, but does not perceive; Gloucester perceives but only in blindness; each of the characters views Lear differently, recognizing a facet or facets of his character, but none sees the man in the round; Lear himself, only when stripped of all worldly acquisition and garbed in weeds, recognizes truth and then only in the lightning flashes of madness and in the

[19] *Henry Crabb Robinson on Books and Their Writers*, ed. E. J. Morley, 1938, i. 327–8.

company of a half-mad fool and of a friend who pretends madness; only the mute spectator is allowed to observe the whole, and in doing so recognizes the paradox of his own position—the little world of the stage is but a reflection of the larger world of which he is a part: he too is blind, though in his awareness (gained from the play) there is hope.

The vision of Blake's poem is essentially the vision of *Lear*. The madness of the poem is itself paradoxical: in seeing, the singer ultimately sees too much too deeply. This is sanity to a degree and as such exists on the edge of madness. To stand and accept the revelation continuously and in its totality—to face the light—demands inordinate courage and a vocational, willed determination. The experience in *Mad Song* is initially and increasingly fulfilling, until the sense of vocational purpose and corresponding determination weaken as the perception becomes too intense. In a famous letter (23 Oct. 1804) Blake reflects upon the period of his youth during which he composed *Poetical Sketches*, a period during which he was 'enlightened' with 'light' and which ended with the commencement of twenty years of 'darkness'.

Suddenly, on the day after visiting the Truchsessian Gallery of pictures, I was again enlightened with the light I enjoyed in my youth, and which has for exactly twenty years been closed from me as by a door and by window-shutters. . . . Dear Sir, excuse my enthusiasm or rather madness, for I am really drunk with intellectual vision whenever I take a pencil or graver into my hand, even as I used to be in my youth, and as I have not been for twenty dark, but very profitable years. I thank God that I courageously pursued my course through darkness.

Blake's letter enables us to comprehend more fully the significance of *Mad Song*. The 'light' which seizes the brain of the singer of the poem is that of visionary illumination—the bardic illumination of Homer blind; of Matthew (6: 23) 'If therefore thine eye be single, thy whole body shall be full of light'; of Milton in his descriptions of his blindness and, as Gray described, 'blasted with excess of light'. The especial poignancy of the poem, however, is in its element of defeat: the singer does not stand, and in turning into night weakens in the face of his calling. If we recall the historical associations for the singer of a mad song—a man outcast, wandering alone, mentally afflicted—their relevance is perhaps no less disturbing for the singer of this brilliant revival of an earlier lyric form.

In the final poem in *Poetical Sketches*—significantly the only Biblical poem in the volume—Blake indicates his acceptance and willingness to take up the mantle of the last poet–prophet of England. In so doing he stands as the figure in the pencil drawing (1780) and the later engraving of *Albion rose* (Plates 1 and 4)—which probably originated from his study of Albrect Dürer at this time (cf. Plate 5)—and,

1. Pencil drawing for *Albion rose*, 1780.
Victoria and Albert Museum

2. *Blake aged 28*.
Pencil sketch by Catherine Blake,
c. 1827–31.
Fitzwilliam Museum, Cambridge

3. *Albion rose*. Engraving: enlarged detail.
Lessing J. Rosenwald Collection,
National Gallery of Art, Washington, D.C.

Albion rose from where he labourd at the Mill with Slaves
Giving himself for the Nations he danc'd the dance of Eternal Death

4. *Albion rose*. Engraving.
Lessing J. Rosenwald Collection, National Gallery of Art, Washington, D.C.

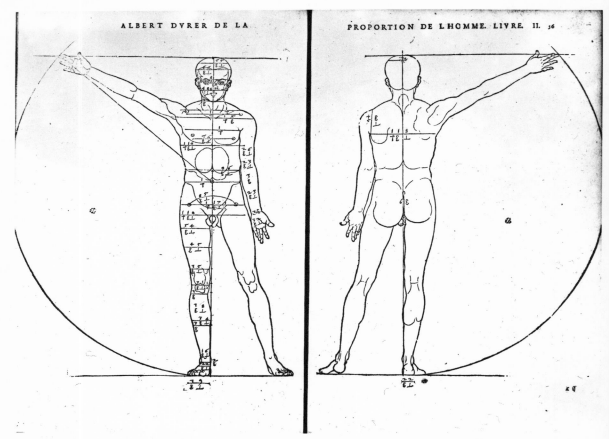

5. Albrecht Dürer: *De la proportion des corps humains* (1614), Book II. Engraving.
Edinburgh University Library
(First published, Nürnberg, 1528)

unlike the singer of *Mad Song*, embraces the light of prophetic illumination. But similarly with the paradox of the final lines of *Mad Song*, the Blake-like face of both the pencil drawing and engraving (cf. Plates 1, 2 and 3) register deep concern, knowing—at the same time accepting—what the perception will bring. In *Samson* we can recognize Blake leaving the mental storm and anguish which indecision had wrought, and accepting, hesitatingly, to 'write with iron pens the words of truth'.

3

Samson has traditionally been considered a fragment and of little intrinsic merit. During the nineteenth century critical opinion of the poem was rare and when discussed at all it was usually together with the other 'prose fragments' contained in *Poetical Sketches*; recent opinion has not altered in its estimation. In 1940 Margaret Ruth Lowery, who offered interesting remarks on Blake's treatment of Dalila, wrote of *Samson*, 'There is no action. Nothing is concluded. Blake had made merely a beginning.'[20] And in 1967 John W. Ehrstine, drawing upon David Erdman's remarks that Samson was a precursor of the deliverer–revolutionary figure which would be developed in Blake's later, more politically thematic works, concluded, 'As a piece of literature, *Samson* achieves relatively little. It is incomplete, and the portraits of Samson and Dalilah suffer accordingly.'[21] Upon closer reading, however, *Samson* is a highly integrated and specially significant work, the success of which is largely dependent upon our recognition of the degree of familiarity with Judges 13–16 and *Samson Agonistes* which Blake evidently assumed on the part of his contemporary reader.

In using the story from Judges to form a tragedy 'according to ancient rule' Milton began his narrative *in medias res* and confined his action to one particular time and place expecting his reader to be aware of the preceding events of Samson's life. Blake may have been partly influenced by Milton's application of the unities but in terms of the conventions which his poem observes he looked to the epics of Homer and Virgil, and particularly the Milton of *Paradise Regain'd*, in order to write a 'brief epic', or *epyllion*—such as the Book of Job, or Catullus 64. In accordance with these conventions Blake opens his poem by stating its theme. 'Samson, the strongest of the children of men, I sing; how he was foiled by woman's arts, by a false wife brought to the gates of death!' He then invokes the muse to inspire and instruct him.

O Truth, that shinest with propitious beams, turning our earthly night to heavenly day, from presence of the Almighty Father! thou visitest our darkling world with blessed feet, bringing good news of Sin and Death destroyed! O white-robed Angel, guide my timorous hand to write as on a lofty rock with iron pens the words of truth, that all who pass may read.

And remaining in strict accordance with epic convention Blake begins his narrative *in medias res*. '—Now Night, noon-tide of damned spirits, over the silent earth spreads her pavilion, while in dark council sat Philista's lords; and where strength failed, black thoughts in ambush lay.' Blake has been precise in adopting the opening structure of classical epic. Further examples of his adherence to convention can be recognized in Samson's closing speech, where he gives a narrative recapitulation of events which preceded the point at which the poem began, and in the ironic prophecy of future history (of Samson) in the lines of the Angel which conclude the poem. Blake's choice of Samson was also a viable one in the tradition.

[20] *Windows of the Morning*, p. 78; see also pp. 72–82.
[21] *William Blake's Poetical Sketches*, p. 42.

C

Convention required that the progress and fate of the hero implicated, and at least in part represented, the progress and fate of his people. Blake shows through his imagery that the fate of Israel rested with Samson; it is Samson who has ravaged the enemy of his people—'Desolation spread his wings over the land of Palestine; from side to side the land groans, her prowess lost, and seeks to hide her bruised head under the mists of night.' Blake's Samson is also of heroic stature: 'he seemed a mountain, his brow among the clouds', his 'thoughts rolled to and fro in his mind, like thunder clouds, troubling the sky'. And in Blake's poem Samson's legendary significance in representing the deliverer of an oppressed people is enforced, as in his recollection of his father's prayer.

'O Lord, thy flock is scattered on the hills! The wolf teareth them, Oppression stretches his rod over our land, our country is plowed with swords, and reaped in blood! The echoes of slaughter reach from hill to hill! Instead of peaceful pipe, the shepherd bears a sword; the ox goad is turned into a spear! O when shall our Deliverer come? The Philistine riots on our flocks, our vintage is gathered by bands of enemies! Stretch forth thy hand and save.'

Samson is at the emotional centre of this passage, and throughout the poem he bears the weight of his people's oppression and their hope of deliverance.

After the opening lines the poem turns sharply from narrative to dramatic poetry without a subsequent return to narrative. Homer and Milton had formed their epics out of a series of dramatic episodes. Blake may have followed their model, particularly that of the dramatic units of *Paradise Regain'd*, in so far as he constructed his poem out of a single such episode. Blake also maintains an elevated style, its diction and diversity of rhythm resembling the blank verse of *Samson Agonistes* but with distinct Biblical intonation and a variation in cadence similar to that of Isaiah. William Butler Yeats and Edwin John Ellis remarked in 1893 that it was in *Samson* (and *The Couch of Death*) that 'the great symbolic language in which the prophetic books were to be written, is indicated'.[22] It is important to recognize here that in *Samson* Blake is making a conscious attempt at achieving a syntax and diction of an inspired or prophetic character. In *Samson* we can notice clearly that Blake is knowingly moving toward the tradition and modes of Hebraic prophecy, which will be the principal inspiration for his later prophetic poems.

In the Book of Job Milton found his 'brief model' of the epic poem, as Blake would have been aware from the famous passage in *The Reason of Church Government*.[23] Blake would have recognized for himself the influence of the Book of Job

---

[22] *The Works of William Blake*, i. 184.
[23] *Complete Prose*, Yale, 1953– , i. 813. Milton's prose would have been available to Blake in John Toland's edition (1698), which was often reprinted.

in *Paradise Regain'd*. For both poets Job presented the principal Old Testament source for the portrayal of spiritual trial with the Samson of Judges offering a counterpart, the degeneration and regeneration of physical strength. Both Milton and Blake drew upon the two sources equally portraying a Job-like Samson—both let us share Samson's inmost thoughts.

We follow the story of Samson in Judges from the foretelling of his birth to his death; in *Samson Agonistes* we first encounter Samson as a prisoner at Gaza on the festival day of Dagon, the last day of his life. In Blake's *Samson* the concentration is greater still. Succeeding Milton Blake chose the hour of Samson's fall. Blake ends his poem the moment before Samson finally reveals his secret to Dalila and consequently is taken away by the Philistines as their prisoner. In effect, the next dramatic episode in Samson's life is that portrayed in *Samson Agonistes*. Presumably Blake expected that his reader would establish the link between his own account and Milton's, as well as the account in Judges; just as Milton relied (to a lesser extent) upon his reader being aware of the circumstances which brought about Samson's fall as they were given in the Bible.

The dramatic poetry in Blake's poem begins with Dalila's attempts to secure Samson's secret and concludes with a long speech of Samson which is very closely based upon Judges 13: 2–18. In this concluding speech Samson recalls to Dalila every particular of the events which occasioned his birth as they are given in the Bible: the circumstances of his parents and of Israel, the two visitations of the Angel, the prophecies, all but the crucial warning of the Angel to Manoa's wife as related in Judges.

Now therefore beware, I pray thee, and drink not wine nor strong drink, and eat not
    any unclean thing:
For, lo, thou shalt conceive, and bear a son; and no razor shall come on his head.

(13: 4–5.)

Blake has had Samson progress through nearly the whole of the thirteenth chapter of Judges with the omission of the end of verse 5 becoming increasingly conspicuous—indeed, it becomes allusion by conspicuous omission. All that remains for him to retell is the warning of the Angel to Manoa's wife, but Blake ends his poem with the angel's request for an offering. By having Samson recall the events recorded in Judges in detail Blake has had Samson waver before his fall with dramatic effect. We already know from the poem that Samson had given himself entirely to Dalila. For Blake to have had Samson disclose the secret of his strength would have produced anticlimax. Instead, Blake abandons the anticipated and ends his poem, not in gloom and despair over Samson's fall, but in an unexpected atmosphere of hope. 'The Angel answered, "My name is wonderful; enquire not after it, seeing it is a secret; but, if thou wilt, offer an offering unto the

Lord."' In these final lines Blake has blended irony with prophecy, for the offering of Manoa and his wife will ultimately be their son at the festival of Dagon. The irony of these final lines is positive, for it is at Gaza that Samson will be inspired to fulfil his destiny. From Blake's close attention to detail we can see that *Samson* is not a fragment but an allusively complex poem, apparently modelled upon 'brief epic' or *epyllion*. That Blake accomplished what he set for himself may be seen from his statement of theme: Samson is 'foiled by woman's arts' and thus 'brought to the gates of death'; though the fall itself is eluded.

Blake's poem depicts Samson just before the scene of *Samson Agonistes*, where his spiritual trials will take place and where his mind will eventually become illuminated by divine knowledge and the true purpose of his life will become clear. By giving himself entirely to Dalila, 'Hear, O Dalila! doubt no more of Samson's love', the fundamental change that will take place in the course of his life is set in motion. As the blind prisoner at Gaza he will become free to recognize and to accept the true import of the prophecies of his birth.

We may ask why Blake chose to follow Milton by writing a poem on Samson. By determining the attitude toward Milton's tragedy which prevailed at the time we can obtain a better understanding of the influences which encouraged his choice. The significance of this question relates not only to the poem under discussion but also to the nature of Blake's subsequent development as a poet and the influence that the figure of Milton evidently exercised so profoundly upon his thought and sense of vocation.

During the latter half of the eighteenth century the identification of Milton with the Samson of *Samson Agonistes* was a critical commonplace.[24] This is reflected, for example, in the remarks of the first editor to annotate Milton's drama, Thomas Newton, as well as in the unpublished remarks of others which he incorporated in his notes—'Here Milton in the person of Samson describes exactly his own case, what he felt, and what he thought in some of his melancholy hours. He could not have wrote so well but from his own feeling and experience.'[25] In his *Life* of Milton, prefixed to his variorum editions of *Paradise Lost* and *Works* which from the 1750s until the appearance of Todd's great edition in 1801 were considered standard, Newton remarked, with regard to *Samson Agonistes*, 'We may suppose that he was determined to the choice of this particular subject by the similitude of his own circumstances to those of Samson blind among the Philistines.'[26] This

[24] Published *critical* opinion was nearly non-existent before Johnson's *Rambler* essays of 1751 (139–40), which were written in response to the 'celebration' of the tragedy 'as the second work of the great author of *Paradise Lost*' and with the exclusive view of examining it 'according to the indispensable laws of Aristotelian criticism'. Handel's adaptation of the chorus from *Samson Agonistes* (1740) helped to give the drama wider popular attention, although it had been readily available in editions since its first appearance.

[25] *Paradise Regain'd* A Poem in Four Books. To which is added Samson Agonistes . . . A New Edition, with Notes of various Authors, By Thomas Newton, 1752, p. 235. See also notes on pp. 203, 214–15, 233, 242, 261, and 286.   [26] *Paradise Lost*, 1753, vol. i, p. lxiii.

identification with Samson would have been originally inspired by Milton's own remarks and poetry which referred to his loss of sight, especially the long passage in the *Second Defense*,[27] his letter to Emeric Bigot, 1656, sonnet xxii beginning 'Cyriack, this three years' day', and of course the invocation to Book III of *Paradise Lost*.[28] Following Milton's own writings, Andrew Marvell was apparently the first to associate the poet with the figure from Judges[29] in his poem *On Paradise Lost* (line 9), which was prefixed to the second edition of Milton's epic (1674) and often reprinted.

The view was soon adopted that it was evidently as a result of his blindness that Milton was enabled to see beyond the visible realities of the physical world. In the conclusion to his brief but highly regarded *Account* of Milton's life first published in 1725, Elijah Fenton remarked,

Perhaps the faculties of his Soul grew vigorous after He was depriv'd of his sight: and his Imagination (naturally sublime, and enlarg'd by reading Romances, of which he was much inamor'd in his youth). when it was wholly abstracted from material Objects, was more at liberty to make such amazing excursions into the Ideal World when in composing his Divine Work He was tempted to range *Beyond the Visible diurnal sphear*.[30]

In 1734 Jonathan Richardson discussed the subject at length. 'Blindness (God knows) is Terrible', but ''tis a Common Observation', continued Richardson, 'that a Loss or Defect in One Faculty is Compensated with Advantages to the rest.'[31] In Richardson's ensuing remarks the common belief was again indicated that as a result of his loss of sight Milton obtained a visionary faculty with which he was able, as Fenton had remarked, to 'make such amazing excursions into the Ideal World'. 'Nor is it Unnatural to a Good Mind, call'd off from Worldly Enjoyments by Some Disastrous Circumstance, to Raise it Self, with More Vigour than Otherwise it would Ever have Exerted, Thither where are hid the Treasures of Wisdom, Unattainable in this Atmosphere, the Cares and Joys of Sense in which the Generality of Us are Envelop'd.'[32] In concluding his remarks Richardson turned to Milton's writings in order to illustrate his own and the belief of his age.

but I love as often as I can, to bring Him to tell my Reader what I would Say if I were able. be pleas'd then to turn back to pag. lxiii; to which add what he says in a Letter (Ep. 21.) to Emeric Bigot Anno 1656———*I rejoice then that you have a just Sense of the Transquility of my Mind in This so Great a Loss of my Sight———as for the being bereav'd*

[27] *Complete Prose*, Yale, IV. i. 584–91.

[28] Cf. *A Complete Collection of the Historical, Political, and Miscellaneous* WORKS *of John Milton, Both English and Latin*. To which is Prefix'd The Life of the Author . . . (by John Toland), Amsterdam (London), 1698, i. 41.

[29] And with Tiresias; cf. Milton's *De Idea Platonica*, lines 25–6.

[30] *Paradise Lost*, 1725, pp. xxvii–xxviii.

[31] *Explanatory Notes and Remarks on Milton's Paradise Lost*, 1734, p. cxxiii.   [32] Ibid.

of my Sight wherefore should I not bear it with Patience since I hope 'tis not so much Lost,
as call'd Inward, and Added to the Vigour of my Mental Sight.   as III. 51.

> *So much the rather thou Celestial Light*
> *Shine Inward, and the Mind through all her Powers*
> *Irradiate, There plant Eyes, all Mist from Thence*
> *Purge and Disperse, —————[33]*

The following translation from Milton's *Second Defense* is the one which Richardson referred to his reader. It deserves being given in full.

To End, As for my Blindness, I prefer It, if I Must have One either to that of Salmasius, or Your's. Your's is Sunk into your Deepest Senses, Blinding your Minds, so that You can See nothing that is Sound and Solid; Mine, Takes from Me only the Colour and Surface of Things, but does Not Take away from the Mind's Contemplation, What is in Those Things of True and Constant. Moreover, how many Things are there which I would Not See? How many which I can be Debar'd the Sight of without Repining? How Few Left which I Much Desire to See? But neither am I Disheartened that I am Now become the Companion of the Blind, of the Afflicted, of Those that Sorrow, and of the Weak; Since I Comfort my Self with the Hope, that These Things do, as it were, make Me Belong still more to the Mercy and Protection of the Supream Father. There is, according to the Apostle, a Way through Weakness to the greatest Strength; Let me be the Most Weak, Provided that in my Weakness that Immortal and Better Strength Exert it Self with more Efficacy; Provided that in my Darkness the Light of the Face of God Shine the Clearer; So shall I prove at the same time the Most Weak and the Most Strong; Dark-Blind and at the same time Clear-Sighted; O Let Me be Consummate in this Weakness! in This, Perfected! Let Me be Thus Enlighten'd in This Darkness![34]

Blake's response to this moving passage in Milton can be easily imagined. Commentary continued on the topic of Milton's blindness and on the corresponding biographical associations of *Samson Agonistes*,[35] but in 1746 John Upton stated what had become and what was to remain the acknowledged view of *Samson Agonistes* in the eighteenth century. 'Samson imprison'd and blind, and the captive state of Israel, lively represents our blind poet with the republican party after the restoration, afflicted and persecuted.'[36] We can see that the notes incorporated in Thomas Newton's editions of *Samson Agonistes*, together with the remarks in his *Life*, merely reflected established opinion in the eighteenth century with regard to the way in which Milton's tragedy was viewed.

The early lives of Milton, beginning with those of Antony à Wood (1691),[37]

[33] *Explanatory Notes and Remarks on Milton's Paradise Lost*, p. cxxiv.   [34] Ibid., p. lxiii.
[35] See Thomas Birch, *A Complete Collection of the Historical, Political, and Miscellaneous* WORKS *of John Milton*, 1738, vol. i, pp. xxxii, xxxiv; and Frances Peck, *New Memoirs of the Life and Poetical Works of Mr John Milton*, 1740, p. 85.
[36] *Critical Observations on Shakespeare*, 1746, p. 162.
[37] Wood's Life was first published in *Fasti Oxonienses*, 1691, pp. 880–4.

Edward Phillips (1694),[38] and John Toland (1698); and continuing in the eighteenth century with those of Elijah Fenton (1725), Jonathan Richardson (1734), Thomas Birch (1738), and Thomas Newton (1753), portrayed Milton as a man who very early in life recognized his vocation and then religiously trained and stored up his mind in preparation for its fulfilment; as a man who also wrote in defence of domestic, civil, and religious liberty and was then ostensibly repaid with blindness and ultimately with political chastisement and isolation following the Restoration. But it was the common belief of nearly all eighteenth-century writers on Milton that his great 'Compensation' for his loss of sight and isolation was that he was enabled to see into worlds of the imagination further and with less hindrance than any of his predecessors in the language. From 'Dark-Blind' his mind became 'Enlighten'd' in ways which few men had experienced.

Milton's life, as it was presented in the eighteenth century, offered Blake a model from which he could obtain inspiration and guidance with regard to his own sense of poetical vocation. Blake would also have been aware of the current identification of the poet with the Samson of *Samson Agonistes*. Thus the choice of subject for the one Biblical poem in his earliest volume may have been determined by two factors. First, in writing on Samson, Blake could identify himself, indirectly, with Milton. Secondly, the eighteenth century's biographical reading of *Samson Agonistes* would have indicated to Blake a similarity between his own position and that of the central figure of his poem.

Blake evidently recognized that there was a correspondence between himself with reference to his vocation and the particular stage in Samson's life which he chose to depict. In his poem Blake has concentrated upon the turning point in Samson's life. From this point Samson will go on to fulfil his destiny. He will become the prisoner of the Philistines, he will be blinded; but in his blindness he will achieve divine illumination, and as a prisoner he will deliver his people from oppression. In having Samson recall the prophecies of his birth, his father's prayer for his people's deliverance, and the corresponding visitation of the angel which concludes the poem, Blake has dramatically transformed the hour of Samson's fall into one of promise and wonder.

The parallel between Blake's own position with regard to his vocation and the position of Samson depicted in his poem is further suggested by his invocation, where a new beginning is also suggested. The first part of Blake's invocation follows in full: 'O Truth, that shinest with propitious beams, turning our earthly night to heavenly day, from presence of the Almighty Father! thou visitest our darkling world with blessed feet, bringing good news of Sin and Death destroyed!' This first part of Blake's invocation anticipates the symbolic implications of the

---

[38] Edward Phillips was the author of the anonymous Life prefixed to *Letters of State, written by Mr. John Milton*, 1694.

poem's prophetic element, for it suggests the Second Coming, the banishment of Sin and Death which entered the world of man at his fall, and lastly, apocalypse, the rebirth of man into the eternity of vision. This is an appropriate preparation for Blake better to enable his reader to recognize the associations and allusions in the second part of his invocation, which are of a far more particularized and personal nature: 'O white-robed Angel, guide my timorous hand to write as on a lofty rock with iron pens the words of truth, that all who pass may read.' This is Blake's earliest overt statement regarding his vocation. He has recognized, and it would appear accepted, what he has been called to do. Uniting his two creative abilities into one mode of expression he will take up the graver's 'iron pens' and etch his poetry of 'truth'.

The phrasing of Blake's invocation is in other ways significantly appropriate. The phrase 'guide my timorous hand' links Blake's statement with the opening lines of *Samson Agonistes*, 'A little onward lend thy guiding hand / To these dark steps, a little further on', which echo through Milton's drama alluding to the guiding hand of God which will lead Samson to his ultimate fulfilment. The allusion to *Samson Agonistes* is then complemented and enforced by an allusion to the *Book of Job*. The line 'to write as on a lofty rock with iron pens the words of truth, that all who pass may read' closely paraphrases the prelude to the prophecy of a forthcoming redeemer who will bring truth and light into the world of fallen man as it occurs in Job:

Oh that my words were now written! Oh that they were printed in a book!
That they were graven with an iron pen and lead in the rock for ever!
For I know that my redeemer liveth, and that he shall stand at the latter day upon
the earth.

(19: 23–5.)

In the two parts of his invocation Blake has arranged literary allusion in a most subtle but determined manner. The suggestion in the first part of the Second Coming and apocalypse is carried and enforced by the paraphrase of Job's prelude to his famous prophecy of a forthcoming redeemer. Correspondingly, the advent of truth and light entering the world of fallen man is shifted from the universal and time future to the particular and time present, from the personification of 'Truth' to Blake, 'guide my timorous hand to write . . . the words of truth'. The immediate fulfilment of the prophecy is left firmly with the poet. But Blake also discloses by his allusion to the opening lines of *Samson Agonistes*, and by the symbolic implication of his poem as a whole, that his task has only just begun. The burden of the perception of truth, and of providing his fellow man with that perception, will incur a spiritual struggle of a kind similar to that portrayed in Milton's drama; indeed, to that of Milton's own life as it would have been read by Blake.

24

In concluding my discussion of Blake's first attempt in the mode of symbolic biography of Milton, I should remark briefly on its relationship to his last—one of the supreme achievements of his poetical maturity. In *Milton* the protagonist must 'go to Eternal Death!' (14. 14) before he can begin his spiritual ascent and regeneration—his paradoxical 'morning of the grave' (14. 20)—and 'Annihilate the Self-hood of Deceit and False Forgiveness' (16. 1), represented by his wives and daughters. In *Samson* we have essentially the same situation and subject—Samson must fall, seduced by Dalila, in order to rise and fulfil his destiny; and in doing so overcome the spectre of female will and deceit which Dalila represents. In both poems also Blake himself is an integral figure: oblique in the former, and manifest in the latter; but in the two poems their roles are significantly reversed. In his early poem Blake looks to Milton for spiritual guidance and example, while in his later work Milton is guided by Blake's example. In both, however, they become one and as one voice; Milton's lines are as fitting for the conclusion of the final work in *Poetical Sketches* as for *Milton*.

> I come in Self-annihilation & the grandeur of Inspiration
> To cast off Rational Demonstration by Faith in the Saviour
> To cast off the rotten rags of Memory by Inspiration
> To cast off Bacon, Locke & Newton from Albion's covering
> To take off his filthy garments, & clothe him with Imagination
> To cast aside from Poetry, all that is not Inspiration
> That it no longer shall dare to mock with the aspersion of Madness
>
> (41: 2–8.)

The importance of the thematic relationship between the two works has been indicated, if only briefly. There is also a second similarity that has not been recognized—that of their structural conceptions of time.

Milton presents us with perhaps the boldest advance in the history of English literature in terms of narrative structure. Although in one sense it is anticipated by conventions of epic poetry—time past and future being reviewed and foretold during a narrative time present as the scenes in the garden of Eden in *Paradise Lost*; in another sense, and one more faithful to Blake's poem, it anticipates innovations of narrative structure that have only recently evolved in twentieth-century fiction, beginning, most obviously, with Proust; though both Fielding and Sterne can be recognized as harbingers of future development. Blake's conception stems from his experimenting in idiom in *Poetical Sketches* in terms of both syntax and mode. As one turns the pages of his first volume it is evident that Blake has progressed from lyric to dramatic to an essentially Hebraic idiom—with a corresponding progress in terms of variations in verse and syntactic forms. Blake will incorporate nearly all to a greater or less degree in his later poetry;

but with his first major work in illuminated printing, the *Songs of Innocence*, to his last, *Jerusalem*, he will write essentially in either the Hebraic mode of the hymn of praise, the psalm, or that of the prophetic book. His practice in Hebraic parallelism is first evidenced in the 'prose fragments' concluding *Poetical Sketches* and reflect a profound study of varieties of syntactic structure found only in the Bible; almost certainly aided by studying Robert Lowth's 'Preliminary Dissertation' to his translation of Isaiah (1778) or Lowth's earlier classic work, *Praelectiones de Sacra Poesi Hebraeorum* (1753, trans. 1787). Blake's experiments in breaking with conventions of syntax, diction, and punctuation, in attempting to write an 'inspired' language of poetry—and by so doing counterpoint the empiricist premisses of Locke (*Essay*, esp. bk. iii) and others with regard to the nature of language—should not obscure the fact that he would have been equally interested in and in need of antithetical concepts of structure. Again, those he located were essentially Hebraic; though he would call upon other conceptual modes and even employ tactics characteristic of the Augustans—e.g. his 'tragic (vs. comic) inversion' of Milton's *Nativity Ode* as conceptual structure for *Europe: A Prophecy*.

Basically there are two kinds with regard to concepts of time: *kairos*, the moment in which 'time is fulfilled' (as in Mark 1 : 15); and *chronos*, passing time.[39] It is the former that we can clearly recognize as unifying *Milton*:

> Every Time less than a pulsation of the artery
> Is equal in its period & value to Six Thousand Years.
> For in this Period the Poet's Work is Done: and all the Great
> Events of Time start forth & are concievd in such a Period
> Within a Moment: a Pulsation of the Artery.
>
> (28. 62–3, 29. 1–3.)

We find a similar moment in *Samson*, though one not fully realized in the sense of being articulated—a balance between time past and time future, a verbal wavering on the moment of fall which is one with the moment of rebirth. It is less easy to recognize other forms of structural and stylistic innovation in *Poetical Sketches* without engaging in detailed discussion; though in Blake's experimenting in syntactic parallelism one can see the origin of the arrangement of *Jerusalem*, where it has been expanded to form (for example) the poem's antiphonal chapters, Christians-Jews; mythic figures, Albion-Los; and personalities, Blake-Hayley. These instances suggest how Blake's early poetry reveals his profound struggles with form, language, and self, and how these struggles relate to his later works.

---

[39] For discussion of the concepts of *kairos* and *chronos*, as related to modern fiction, see Frank Kermode, *The Sense of an Ending*, Oxford, 1966, esp. pp. 44–64. For background on the Hebraic element in the eighteenth century, see Murry Roston, *Prophet and Poet*, London, 1965.

4

In conclusion I wish to look briefly at a poem which is outside the frame of *Poetical Sketches*—the *Introduction* to the *Songs of Innocence*—but which provides a retrospect of the subject of this essay and as such epitomizes the progress that has been traced.

> Piping down the valleys wild
> Piping songs of pleasant glee
> On a cloud I saw a child.
> And he laughing said to me
>
> Pipe a song about a Lamb:
> So I piped with merry chear.
> Piper, pipe that song again—
> So I piped, he wept to hear.
>
> Drop thy pipe thy happy pipe
> Sing thy songs of happy chear,
> So I sung the same again
> While he wept with joy to hear
>
> Piper, sit thee down and write
> In a book that all may read—
> So he vanish'd from my sight.
> And I pluck'd a hollow reed.
>
> And I made a rural pen,
> And I stain'd the water clear,
> And I wrote my happy songs
> Every child may joy to hear

In defining what he terms 'objective syntax', Donald Davie writes that the term expresses the fidelity with which the syntactic development of a line of poetry, or an entire poem, 'follows a form of action'; such as 'the movement of destiny' through a man's life.[40] In other words the syntactic progress of a line or poem parallels the progress of the event or the logical development of thought that is being expressed. Davie's observation is, I believe, exactly the case with Blake's *Introduction*. The syntactic progress of the poem serves as a paradigm for the action—there are no grammatical inversions or confusions resulting from simile or metaphor; the progress is recorded as it occurred—each subject/verb/object construction that makes up each line signifies a single event in its respective order in the development from beginning to end, from the initial point in time past to

[40] *Articulate Energy*, London, 1955, p. 79.

time present. The progress is recorded as it occurred, and the simplicity is such that it is allusively deceptive.

In the first stanza the piper is responsible for his piping; he wanders carefree and his songs are correspondingly light and cheerful—essentially he is performing for his own pleasure. He then has a vision of a child who speaks to him—it is a poetic inspiration which in its personification defines the poetry that it is to inspire. The child addresses the piper and asks him to pipe a song about a 'Lamb'— defining further the nature of his inspiration—which the piper does; again the piper is cheerful and significantly the child is silent. The child asks again, and again the piper agrees but this time the child weeps—there is no indication that he weeps for joy here and we assume that the piper must not be responding as the child wishes and therefore the child is saddened.

The child then responds and addresses the piper sternly, 'Drop thy pipe, thy happy pipe'; and with equal insistence, 'Sing thy songs of happy chear'. The request is significant: the pipe being the instrument traditionally associated with secular pastoral, and the song—the hymn of praise—traditionally indicating religious pastoral. The transformation of mode and subject-matter from the poetry of Blake's youth to that of his maturity has been quietly announced. Now the child weeps 'with joy to hear'; and addresses the piper again.

> Piper, sit thee down and write
> In a book that all may read—
> So he vanish'd from my sight . . .

As the child disappears he in fact becomes one with the piper; Blake has alluded to his own invocation in *Samson* which announced his acceptance to write 'with iron pens the words of truth, that all who pass may read'. The child's disappearance signifies the piper's comprehension and acceptance of the inspiration and calling; and now it is for him to share with his fellow man the vision of childhood—the vision of the Lamb—that his inspiration has revealed. As the poem reaches its conclusion Blake maintains the privileged distance between reality and fiction which pastoral provides—'I pluck'd a hollow reed, / And I made a rural pen'—his graver; 'And I stain'd the water clear'—his water colours to illuminate; 'And I wrote my happy songs / Every child may joy to hear.' The poem ends in the past tense—where all of the events that it records have taken place; in opening the *Songs of Innocence* and having read the last line of the *Introduction* we enter the present and begin our own progress and search.

II

BLAKE'S 'GOTHICISED IMAGINATION' AND THE HISTORY OF ENGLAND

David Bindman

It has been generally assumed that Blake's contact with Gothic works of art in Westminster Abbey, which he engraved for the Society of Antiquaries during his apprenticeship to Basire from 1772 to 1779, was decisive for his early development as an artist, and that his recognition of the qualities of Gothic sculpture, in particular the tomb effigies in Westminster Abbey, was both spontaneous and precocious at such an early date. Eudo Mason compared Blake's raptures in Westminster Abbey with Goethe's reaction to Strasbourg Minster in 1770 as the first whole-hearted expressions of feeling for the Gothic in the eighteenth century.[1] We have Blake's own testimony that he admired Gothic sculpture as an apprentice, but Gilchrist, Blake's first biographer, writing about 1860, translated this early appreciation into an anachronistic expression of Victorian ideas of the Gothic: 'He pored over all [the Westminster Abbey tombs] with a reverent good faith, which, in the age of Stuart and Revett, taught the simple student things our Pugins and Scotts had to learn a century later.' Blake, therefore, in Gilchrist's account, by the force of a simple faith akin to that of the medieval sculptors themselves, had apprehended the true qualities of the Gothic tombs in the face of their neglect by Blake's blindly rational contemporaries.

There is, however, nothing in the early accounts of Blake's apprenticeship to suggest that he was a Ruskinian *avant la lettre*, and Blake's supposed 'reverent good faith' has no earlier source than Gilchrist. In the time of Blake's youth the Gothic style was not normally associated with piety and the Middle Ages were not necessarily seen as an Age of Faith. In the words of Gilchrist 'a fervent love of Gothic' was something of 'an originality' at the time of Blake's apprenticeship; Gothic buildings were primarily to be seen as gloomy, solemn, and occasionally sublime places whose main purpose was to commemorate the dead buried within. Horace Walpole writes of the 'gloomth of abbeys and cathedrals',[2] and in *Blair's*

---

[1] Eudo C. Mason, *The Mind of Henry Fuseli*, 1951, p. 222.

[2] H. Walpole to H. Mann, 27 Apr. 1753. (Quoted R. W. Ketton-Cremer, *Horace Walpole*, 1940, p. 157.) Walpole suggested that Gothic was appropriate to domestic buildings but not to gardens because 'Gothic is merely architecture; and as one has a satisfaction in imprinting the gloomth of abbeys and cathedrals on one's house, so one's garden, on the contrary, is to be nothing but riant, and the gaiety of nature'.

Grave, a poem that Blake may have begun to illustrate at an early age, Gothic churches are showplaces of vanity, mortality, decay, and melancholy:

> the gloomy ailes,
> Black plaister'd, and hung round with shreds of scutcheons
> And tatter'd coats of arms, send back the sound,
> Laden with heavier airs, from the low vaults,
> The mansions of the dead.

Thomas Maurice in the introduction to his poem *Westminster Abbey*, first published in 1784,[3] justifies using the Abbey as a poetic subject on similar grounds: 'This mighty dormitory of the illustrious dead cannot fail to awaken in the mind the most awful reflections on the transitoriness of human glory, and the vanity of all sublunary distinctions.' The tombs are to be seen as reminders of the vanity of human power and ambition:

> Senseless to glory as their marble shrines,
> The jasper columns that their ashes shade,
> Low in the dust each mighty chief reclines,
> In mail no more but mantling shrouds array'd.

Blake's own account of his work in Westminster Abbey is to be found in the introductory letter by Benjamin Heath Malkin to *A Father's Memoirs of his Child*, published in 1806.[4] The account is derived from conversations with Blake himself, who is quoted directly elsewhere in the same introduction. According to Malkin, 'He was employed in making drawings from old buildings and monuments, and occasionally, especially in winter, in engraving from those drawings. This occupation led him to an acquaintance with those neglected works of art called Gothic monuments.' Blake saw in Gothic monuments 'the simple and plain road to the style of art at which he aimed, unentangled in the intricate windings of modern practice'. Gothic art, then, did not impress Blake by its piety, as Gilchrist implied, but by simplicity and purity of style, which, even as a young apprentice, he had felt to have been lost by the masters of his own day. This nostalgia for a style 'unentangled in the intricate windings of modern practice' was characteristic of contemporary Neoclassicism, but Blake was probably the first to find it embodied in English Gothic sculpture as well as in Greek and Early Renaissance art. A comparable enthusiasm for the work of hitherto despised Italian 'Primitives' can be found in a report from Italy by George Romney, a painter with strong leanings towards Neoclassicism, whom Blake may have known at this time. In 1775 Romney wrote from Venice: 'I met with great

---

[3] Thomas Maurice, *Westminster Abbey: an Elegiac Poem*, 1784.

[4] Benjamin Heath Malkin, *A Father's Memoirs of his Child*, 1806, pp. xvi–xxxvii and xxxviii–xli. *Bibliography*, No. 391.

entertainment from the old masters, in particular Cimabue and Masaccio; I admired the great simplicity and purity of the former, and the strength of character and expression of the latter. I was surprised to find several of their ideas familiar to me, till I recollected having seen the same thoughts in M. Angelo and Raphael, only managed with more science.'[5] In the late eighteenth century a taste for Gothic art was perfectly compatible with a belief in the artistic supremacy of the Greeks; indeed Neoclassical artists and theorists in the 1770s and 1780s were the first to rescue the Italian 'Primitives' from oblivion.

Blake very occasionally uses Gothic motifs in his early works, but they are largely confined to 'period' detail, and hardly set him apart from his contemporaries. *The Ordeal of Queen Emma* water-colour (Private coll.)[6] is perhaps the most interesting example. The scene is from the life of Edward the Confessor who, according to legend, falsely accused his own mother of adultery and forced her to submit to an ordeal. Edward was regarded by eighteenth-century historians as the archetype of the tyrannical medieval monarch who attempted to falsify history into commemorating him as a saint. He was also known in Blake's time as the builder of the first church of Westminster Abbey;[7] therefore a 'Gothic' setting was appropriate to Queen Emma's ordeal, which Blake may have understood to have taken place in the Abbey. Blake seems also to have derived the shape of the draperies and something of the stiffness of the postures from his study of Westminster tombs. A praying figure in the background is certainly modelled on the tomb of Aveline of Lancaster, particularly in the enveloping piece of drapery, which is open in the front like that on the tomb.[8] Blake also seems to have deliberately avoided contrapposto in the figures, and the gestures are curiously hieratic, strengthening the feeling that they are tomb-effigies come to life.

Medieval tombs were a particular subject of interest to the Society of Antiquaries, which had commissioned James Basire to make the illustrations to *The Sepulchral Monuments of Great Britain*,[9] written by its president Richard Gough. The Society was concerned at the decay of these monuments, more because they could be dated with some precision[10] than for their artistic qualities. The Society's attitude towards the past was rigidly antiquarian; it was bitterly reproached by Horace Walpole because, despite his constant prompting, it ignored questions of taste: 'The antiquaries will be ridiculous as they used to be; and since it is impossible to infuse taste into them, they will be as dry and dull as their predecessors.'[11]

[5] J. Romney, *Memoirs of the Life and Works of George Romney*, 1830, p. 107.
[6] K. Preston, ed., *The Blake Collection of W. Graham Robertson*, 1949, No. 66, p. 167.
[7] Maurice, op. cit., pp. 2–3.

[8] Blunt, p. 5.
[9] *Blake Studies*, ch. III, 'The Engraver's Apprentice', pp. 14–30. P. Miner, 'The Apprentice of Great Queen Street', *Bulletin of NYPL*, lxvii. 10, pp. 639–42.
[10] Joan Evans, *A History of the Society of Antiquaries*, 1956, p. 154.
[11] Letter to W. Cole, Sept. 1778. Evans, op. cit., p. 155. He also wrote in 1780, 'I endeavoured to give the antiquaries a little wrench towards taste—but it was in vain.' Ibid., p. 169.

6. *The Ordeal of Queen Emma.* Water-colour.
Private Collection

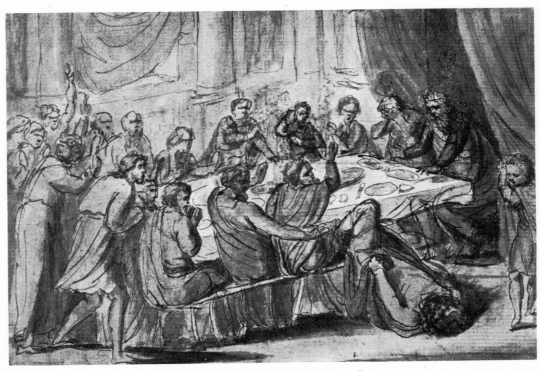

7. *The Death of Earl Godwin.* Water-colour.
British Museum, Department of Prints and Drawings

Richard Gough, in the preface to the first publication of *Archaeologia*, the society's periodical, in 1770 noted that the Society was concerned with 'British Antiquities' and that it was interested above all in an accurate record of the past. 'The arrangement and proper use of facts is HISTORY—not a mere narrative taken up at random and embellished with poetic diction, but a regular and elaborate inquiry into every ancient record and proof, that can elucidate or establish them.'[12] Although a number of papers read to the Society were concerned with Gothic architecture, its field of activity was 'British antiquity' in general, and it was not especially concerned with the Gothic period or style.

Blake's experience of the tombs in Westminster Abbey gave him a direct and sustained contact with English Gothic art that was unique amongst the artists with whom he was associated, although Flaxman, for one, was to become interested in Gothic sculpture at about the same time.[13] In common with artists like John Hamilton Mortimer and Angelica Kauffmann, Blake painted a number of medieval subjects in the years of his apprenticeship and later, but it is apparent that, with the exception of *The Ordeal of Queen Emma*,[14] they do not seem to have been affected by his experience of Gothic tombs or architecture. Nor can one define the context of Blake's early historical water-colours as 'medieval' even in the widest sense, because surviving examples encompass the history of England from its mythological foundations to the fifteenth century, with no particular emphasis on the Gothic ages.

Malkin's account of Blake's youth mentions that Blake began making drawings from the history of England while he was still an apprentice: 'Such was his employment at Basire's. As soon as he was out of his time, he began to engrave two designs from the History of England, after drawings which he had made in the holiday hours of his apprenticeship. They were selected from a great number of historical compositions, the fruits of his fancy.' Thus, Blake began engraving his designs after he had completed his apprenticeship to Basire in 1779, approximately at the time he was entering the Royal Academy School. One of the engravings can almost certainly be identified with *Edward and Elenor*, which, although dated 1793, is in the rather mechanical style of his early work; the other has disappeared without trace. Ruthven Todd has suggested[15] that it might have been based on the water-colour of *The Penance of Jane Shore* (Tate Gallery), but *The Ordeal of Queen Emma* corresponds more in size and shape to the *Edward and Elenor* engraving. The date of 1793 on the address of the *Edward and Elenor* engraving is explained by the fact that it appears for sale in Blake's *Prospectus* of 10 October 1793, in the company of his large engraving of *Job*, dated 1793 as well,

[12] Evans, op. cit., p. 146.
[13] W. G. Constable, *John Flaxman 1755–1826*, 1927, pp. 22–3.
[14] For a list of all medieval subjects exhibited at the Royal Academy in the years 1769–79, see Blunt, p. 7.
[15] R. Todd, ed., *Gilchrist's Life of William Blake*, 1945, p. 369.

which also exists in a first state completed some years earlier.[16] In addition Blake exhibited at the Royal Academy in 1780 a water-colour of *The Death of Earl Godwin* which was mentioned in a review in the *Morning Chronicle and London Advertiser*[17] by his friend George Cumberland, and there is a description of an early water-colour of *The Penance of Jane Shore* in the *Descriptive Catalogue* of 1809 which Blake describes as having been 'done above Thirty Years ago' (K, pp. 585–6). *The Death of Earl Godwin* is known through a water-colour sketch in the British Museum, formerly in the Gould Weston and Graham Robertson collections.[18] Erdman assumes it to be a sketch for the water-colour exhibited in 1780, rather than the water-colour itself, but in the absence of a larger version, it may itself be the one that was exhibited. In any case, this sketch must date from the years 1779–80, as can be confirmed by the immaturity of the drawing, and the insensitivity of the colouring, remarked upon by Cumberland in his review.

The Penance of Jane Shore exists in two water-colour versions and a pencil drawing. The Tate Gallery version has been generally assumed to be the one exhibited in the 1809 Exhibition, but the smaller and less accomplished version (Sir Edmund Verney collection) has a better claim to a date of *c.* 1779. Blake's reference to a date of 1779 or earlier, for the version in the 1809 Exhibition, then, may refer to the date of conception rather than of execution. The smaller version corresponds closely to *The Death of Earl Godwin* in size, technique, and drawing style, while the Tate Gallery version may even be as late as the early 1790s.

The small water-colours of *The Death of Earl Godwin* and *The Penance of Jane Shore* provide a firm basis for dating a number of other water-colours of English historical subjects, most of which have emerged from the Gould Weston collection formed in the mid nineteenth century. They clearly form a series with the two water-colours, corresponding in size, technique, handling, and, in most cases, provenance. They can be arranged as follows in chronological order of historical events:

SUBJECT	COLLECTION	PROVENANCE
1 *The Landing of Brutus*	Robert H. Taylor Princeton, N.J.	Gould Weston sale, Christie's 15 July 1957 (Lot 26)
2 *Lear and Cordelia*	Tate Gallery (Butlin cat. No. 2)	bt. by Mrs. Samuel Smith and Miss Julia Smith from Mrs. Blake *c.* 1828–9
3 *The Landing of Caesar*	Robert H. Taylor Princeton, N.J.	Gould Weston sale Christie's 15 July 1957 (Lot 25)

[16] *Separate Plates*, Nos. III, IV, and K, p. 207.

[17] 'No. 315, the death of Earl Godwin by Mr. Blake; in which, though there is nothing to be said of the colouring, may be discovered a good design, and much character.' (Bentley, *Records*, p. 17.)

[18] Preston, op. cit., No. 67, p. 170.

SUBJECT	COLLECTION	PROVENANCE
4 *St. Augustine converting Ethelbert of Kent*	Lady Melchett	Gould Weston sale Christie's 15 July 1957 (Lot 27)
5 *The Death of Earl Godwin*	British Museum	Gould Weston family W. Graham Robertson (Preston cat., No. 67)
6 *The Finding of the Body of Harold*	Present whereabouts unknown	Gould Weston family bt. in Christie's 28 June 1904 (Lot 10)
7 *The Making of Magna Carta*	Robert Essick	Gould Weston family W. Graham Robertson (Preston cat., No. 68)
8 *The Keys of Calais*	Beinecke Library, Yale	Gould Weston family W. Graham Robertson (Preston cat., No. 69)
9 *The Penance of Jane Shore*	Sir Edmund Verney, Claydon, Bucks.	Sir Harry Verney, exhibited Carfax Gallery 1905

Gould Weston bought works by Blake at the Tatham sale of 29 April 1862 and from Joseph Hogarth (Southgate & Barrett, 7 June 1854), who probably acquired his collection from Tatham, whose collection in turn came from Mrs. Blake. The series, perhaps including No. 9, whose provenance is unknown, but excluding No. 2 which did not belong to Gould Weston, could possibly have been part of Lot 1095 in the Joseph Hogarth sale, 'W. Blake Historical Subjects 13 items', or part of the residue of Lot 172 in the Tatham sale, Sotheby's 29 April 1862, which is described as follows: 'The Black Prince introducing John of France to his Father [now Harold Macmillan coll.]. Sacrifice of Manoah [Lady Melchett coll.], and others in colours, in colours and indian ink, 9 items', sold to Weston for 19s. 0d.

The Gould Weston series is clearly incomplete, and either it was left unfinished or several of the group are lost. A clue to Blake's intentions is to be found in a list of historical subjects on f. 116 of the Notebook (K, p. 208). Sir Geoffrey Keynes has connected this list with the announcement in the 1793 Prospectus of 'The History of England, a small book of Engravings. Price 3s', which has disappeared without trace, if it was in fact executed. The connection with the lost book is given weight by the deleted word 'frontispiece' next to No. 5 on the list, which suggests that Blake was considering publication of the designs in book form. There is no doubt that Blake was taking stock of his previous attempts at English historical subjects in 1793, but it is likely that only the *Edward and Elenor* engraving was issued, as an independent large plate. In any case the list must

8. *The Landing of Brutus.* Water-colour.
Collection of Robert H. Taylor

9. *Lear and Cordelia.* Water-colour.
Tate Gallery, London

date from after 1787, when Blake acquired the Notebook on the death of his brother Robert.[19]

The Notebook list itself contains numerous deletions and alterations that suggest that Blake had failed to find a satisfactory order. Some of the subjects in the Gould Weston series reappear, but not all; *St. Augustine converting Ethelbert of Kent*, *The Death of Earl Godwin*, and *The Finding of the Body of Harold* are absent.

The list reads as follows:

1. Giants ancient inhabitants of England
2. The Landing of Brutus
3. Corineus throws Gogmagog the Giant into the Sea
4. King Lear
(5 del) The Ancient Britons according to Caesar (The frontispiece—del.)
6. The Druids
7. The Landing of Julius Caesar
8. Boadicea inspiring the Britons against the Romans
   (The Britons distress & depopulation
   Women fleeing from War
   Women in a siege)
9. Alfred in the countrymans house
10. Edwin & Morcar stirring up the Londoners to resist William the Conqr
11. W the Conqr Crownd
12. King John & Mag Charta
   (A Famine occasioned by the Popish interdict)
13. Edward at Calais
14. Edward the Black Prince brings his captives to his father
15. The Penance of Jane Shore
(17 The Reformation by HVIII—del.)
(18 Ch. I beheaded—del.)
(16, 17 del.) 19. The Plague
(17, 18 del.) 20. The Fire of London
(18 del.) 16. The Cruelties used by Kings & Priests
(19 del.) 21. A prospect of liberty
(20 del.) 22. A Cloud.

The page containing the list also has in pencil, very rubbed, a list of the plagues of Egypt. At the bottom, upside-down, is the word 'Fronti', which presumably is the beginning of the word 'Frontispiece' and perhaps was intended to be the beginning of a revised list of English historical subjects which Blake never completed.

Blake also made a number of larger water-colours, of varying sizes, of English historical subjects, which were probably not intended to form a clearly defined series, and were not necessarily painted at the same time. They are more mature

[19] *Blake Studies*, pp. 13–22.

10. *The Landing of Caesar*. Water-colour.
Collection of Robert H. Taylor

11. *St. Augustine Converting Ethelbert of Kent*. Water-colour.
Collection of Lady Melchett

12. *The Making of Magna Carta.* Water-colour.
Collection of Robert N. Essick

13. *The Keys of Calais.* Water-colour.
Beinecke Library, Yale University

in style than the Gould Weston series and, with the exception of *The Penance of Jane Shore*, they can be dated to the early 1780s. Some of them may, however, be later reworkings of earlier designs. The group contains, in addition to *The Penance of Jane Shore*, *The Ordeal of Queen Emma*, *The Black Prince introducing John of France to his Father*[20] (Harold Macmillan coll.), and *Gregory and the British Captives* (Victoria and Albert Museum). The predominantly dramatic rather than historical nature of the subjects suggests that they were meant to be independent works. Even so, it is significant that the range of subjects is not confined to the 'Gothic' period, but also looks back to the period before the conversion of Britain.

Both the Gould Weston series and the Notebook list begin with a subject or subjects from 'British Antiquity'. British Antiquity is the name used by Camden and later historians for the period, called by Milton the 'Region of Smooth or Idle Dreams', from the mythological foundation of Britain by Brutus the Trojan, the apocryphal grandson of Aeneas, and his dynasty, to the landing of Caesar. The story of British Antiquity was first told in Geoffrey of Monmouth's *Historia Regum Britanniae* of *c.* 1135.[21] The existence of British Antiquity was the subject of much argument amongst antiquarians in the sixteenth century, but it was generally regarded by the seventeenth century as an invention by Geoffrey himself, and at best containing 'somewhat of truth in it under a mighty heape of monkish forgeries'. As scholarly and rational history gained ground, so the legend of British Antiquity was correspondingly discredited. Poets like Michael Drayton, who wrote *Poly-Olbion*, helped to keep the Brutus legend alive, and Milton who was well aware that it was a fabrication of 'the monkish historians' nevertheless claimed in his *History of Britain* that it contained 'the footsteps and reliques of something true' and that it was suitable for 'English poets and rhetoricians who, by their art, will know to use them judiciously'.[22]

Although British Antiquity had been virtually forgotten by the early eighteenth century, and Milton's *History of Britain* was scarcely read,[23] Blake expressed a strong belief in it and allied himself defiantly with his poetic predecessors against the rational historians, whose scholarly attitudes were represented pre-eminently in his own day by the Society of Antiquaries. He wrote in the *Descriptive Catalogue* of 1809, describing his painting of *The Ancient Britons*, 'in this picture, Believing with Milton the ancient British History, Mr. B. has done as all ancients did, and as all the moderns who are worthy of fame, given the historical fact in its poetical vigour so as it always happens, and not in that dull way that some historians pretend, who, being weakly organised themselves, cannot see either miracle or prodigy' (K, p. 578).

[20] Keynes, *Bible*, No. 56, where it is identified as *Saul and David*.
[21] The definitive work on British Antiquity is T. D. Kendrick, *British Antiquity*, 1950.
[22] John Milton, *The History of Britain, That part especially call'd England*, 1st ed., 1670, p. 3.
[23] There are no reprints after 1719 recorded in the catalogue of the British Museum Reading-Room.

Milton's *History of Britain* was, therefore, almost certainly the source of Blake's knowledge of British Antiquity, but that work goes only as far as 1066, and the most readily accessible source for Blake's illustrations to the later period, such as *The Keys of Calais* and *The Penance of Jane Shore*, was Rapin's *History of England*. Rapin's book was first translated into English in the years 1725–31, and the illustrations by Hayman and Blakey, first published 1751–2, were forerunners of the later genre of English historical painting. Rapin's immense chronicle in its illustrated form was a great success and, according to Pye, opened the way to the massive engraving programmes of Boydell and others. This work gives little credence to British Antiquity, and, according to a contemporary reviewer, Rapin had 'shown that the people have their rights as well as kings their prerogatives; that our monarchy was not absolutely hereditary'.[24] Rapin, then, reiterated the standard Whig view that the history of England was the story of British liberty, which had existed since the earliest times, and which it was the duty of government to maintain against tyranny on the one hand, and against fanaticism on the other. As Blake noted, it was a work of rational history, which applied a certain scepticism and caution to medieval chronicles, in particular to those parts which proclaimed miracles and prodigies. Blake, in 1809 in the *Descriptive Catalogue*, described Rapin as a 'reasoning historian, [a] turner and twister of causes and consequences', classifying him with Voltaire, Echard,[25] Plutarch, and Herodotus.

Blake's water-colour of *The Landing of Brutus* in the Gould Weston series is apparently the only attempt at the subject in the eighteenth century; it is significant also that the water-colour identified as the *Landing of Caesar* is in a similar style, thus emphasizing the parity of mythological and historical events in Blake's mind. *The Death of Earl Godwin* is also an unique subject in the period; it derives from a story in Rapin that does not appear in Milton's *History of Britain*, but Rapin casts doubts on its credibility: 'But this circumstance, had it been true, was too remarkable to be omitted by the Historians of the best credit, who make no mention at all of it. They agree, Goodwin died suddenly, as he sat at Table with the King, but say not a word of the above-mentioned Circumstances, which probably were invented to blacken the Memory of the Earl and his Family.'[26] Although the story of King Lear, represented in the Gould Weston series by *Lear and Cordelia in Prison*, properly speaking belongs to British Antiquity, it is a special case because of Shakespeare's play, which was frequently performed in the seventeenth and

---

[24] Quoted by C. Mitchell in 'Benjamin West's Death of General Wolfe and the Popular History Piece', *Journal of the Warburg and Courtauld Institutes*, vii (1944), p. 27.

[25] Echard is presumably the Laurence Echard (1670?–1730) whose chief work was *A History of England*, 1707–18. According to Erdman, one of the compilers of Thomas Hollis's *Memoirs* contrasted historians who write 'for the use of kings or rather tyrants' including Hume, Echard, and Smollett, with those like Rapin who write 'for the use of the people'. D. V. Erdman, *Blake: Prophet against Empire*, rev. ed., 1969, p. 67.

[26] P. de Rapin-Thoyras, *The History of England*, trans. by N. Tindal, 1725–31, ii. 75–6.

eighteenth centuries. The subject is the reconciliation of Lear and Cordelia, which takes place in a tent in Shakespeare's play, and not in a prison, as in the water-colour. Blake has presumably gone back to the story in British Antiquity as recounted in Milton's *History of Britain*, in which Lear appears as the last of the line from Brutus of Troy, and, after being released from prison and regaining his kingdom, is succeeded by his daughter Cordeilla or Cordelia.[27] The so-called 'happy ending' of Nahum Tate's version of Shakespeare's *King Lear* is in fact a reversion to the earlier legend, which Shakespeare had altered to give the play a tragic conclusion.

All the subjects in the Gould Weston series, apart from *The Landing of Brutus* and *Death of Earl Godwin*, have precedents in the work of other painters of the period, in particular that of John Hamilton Mortimer, who had been one of the earliest English painters to specialize in English historical subjects. These became popular with painters from the 1760s onwards and had become emancipated from the genre of book illustration. This development dates essentially from the foundation of the Society for the Advancement of the Arts, Manufactures and Commerce, which began to give premiums for paintings of English historical subjects from 1760 onwards.[28] In the words of William Hayley, Blake's future patron, in the notes to his *Epistle to Romney*, 1788: 'The great encouragment given our painters to select subjects from English history, has of late years been very observable. Many individuals of rank and fortune have promoted this laudable plan with spirit and effect; and the society of arts and sciences have confined their premiums to subjects taken from the British annals.'[29]

The first premium of the Royal Society of Arts, Manufactures and Commerce was won in 1760 by Robert Edge Pine for the *Surrender of Calais to Edward III* and his own pupil John Hamilton Mortimer won a premium of 50 guineas from the same society in 1763 for *Edward the Confessor despoiling his Mother*, a subject that, like Blake's *Ordeal of Queen Emma*, illustrates the cruelty of Edward the Confessor. Blake's admiration for Mortimer is well known: 'While Sir Joshua was rolling in Riches Barry was Poor and Unemployd except by his own Energy Mortimer was calld a Madman and only Portrait Painting applauded and rewarded by the Rich and Great' (K, p. 445). He is referred to by Blake as a genuine history painter, like Barry and Fuseli, who was thwarted by the domination of Sir Joshua Reynolds and the portrait painters. He died in 1779, but there is a possibility that Blake could have known him. Mortimer was associated with the academy in the Duke of Richmond's gallery of casts which was attended by students of Pars's drawing school,[30] to which Blake had belonged before he started his apprenticeship to Basire in 1772. Mortimer had a considerable reputation as an

[27] Milton, op. cit., pp. 17–20.   [28] H. T. Wood, *A History of the Society of Arts*, 1913, pp. 151–61.
[29] W. Hayley, *Life of George Romney*, 1809, p. 413.
[30] W. T. Whitley, *Artists and their Friends in England, 1700–99*, 1928, i. 237.

imaginative artist, and Blake saw Reynolds's attack on artists who wait 'for the inspirations of Genius' in *Discourse II* delivered in December 1769 as 'A stroke at Mortimer' (K, p. 457). Mortimer and Reynolds certainly disagreed on the role of imagination in art and Mortimer's romantic 'genius' was of precisely the kind that Reynolds regarded as a dangerous example to the students who made up his audience for the *Discourses*. Hayley, in his *Epistle to Romney*, describes him as follows:

> The rapid Mortimer, of spirit wild,
> Imagination's dear and daring child,
> Marks the fierce ruffian, in the dungeon's gloom,
> Stung with remorse and shuddering at his doom.[31]

Although Mortimer and Reynolds had been on terms of friendship, Mortimer was one of the most important artists to hold out against the monopoly of the Royal Academy in its early years. Mortimer was President of the Incorporated Society of Artists in 1774, and in 1775 he signed a letter to Romney in Italy urging him to exhibit at the Incorporated Society. Mortimer eventually relented and agreed to join the Royal Academy in 1778, shortly before his death, and the Royal Academy Exhibition of 1779 contained a posthumous exhibition of his work. George Romney remained irreconcilable, and exhibited the majority of his paintings at the Free Society of Artists until it decayed into obscurity after 1783.[32] It is not clear why Mortimer and Romney refused to join the Royal Academy; it may have been due to a desire to keep artists free of royal 'tyranny' but there is little evidence of their political opinions except that they were, like Blake, admirers of Milton, whose *Paradise Lost* had acquired republican connotations in the late eighteenth century. The choice of subjects from English history, however, could have political implications; Benjamin West, the King's painter, for example, exhibited at the Royal Academy in 1779 a painting entitled *Alfred divides his Loaf with a Pilgrim*, which showed England's most popular king committing an act of saintly virtue, whereas Mortimer's painting of *King John delivering the Magna Carta to the Barons* provided a lesson to one contemporary, William Hayley, of the dangers of royal tyranny:

> Yet still to nobler heights his [Mortimer's] genius springs
> And paints a lesson to tyrannic kings:
> In his bright colours, see the fields appear
> To freedom sacred, and to glory dear,
> Where John proud monarch baffled on his throne,
> Hears the brave chief his lawless pow'r disown
> And for an injur'd nation nobly claim
> The glorious CHARTER of immortal fame![33]

[31] Hayley, op. cit., p. 369.   [32] Whitley, op. cit., i. 329.   [33] Hayley, op. cit., pp. 369–70.

Mortimer does not seem to have contemplated a series of paintings or engravings on the theme of History of England, but his historical paintings were frequently exhibited. In addition to *Edward the Confessor despoiling his Mother* and *King John delivering Magna Carta to the Barons*, he painted *Lear and Cordelia*, *The Landing of Julius Caesar*, and *The Battle of Hastings*.[34]

The Notebook list, although it is tentative in parts, gives a view of Blake's interpretation of the whole panorama of English history from its mythological origins to the apocalyptic future. According to the legend of British Antiquity, Brutus drove out the giants who were the original inhabitants, and Gogmagog was a survivor who, after attacking the camp of Brutus, was defeated in combat by Brutus' companion Corineus and thrown over a cliff.[35] The last subjects in the list bring the narrative to Blake's own time, and after *The Plague* and *The Fire of London*, real events of the seventeenth century, and *The Cruelties used by Kings and Priests*, there is *A Prospect of Liberty* followed by *A Cloud*. *A Prospect of Liberty* and *A Cloud* remain puzzling, as neither is a pictorial subject in the same vein as the foregoing, nor is it clear why *A Prospect of Liberty* should be followed by *A Cloud*.

The engraving known as *Glad Day* may provide a clue to Blake's intended conclusion of both the Gould Weston and the projected Notebook series. It is signed 'WB in 1780' but the surviving impressions cannot be earlier than the 1790s. As in the case of the print of *Joseph of Arimathea*, which, although it is in Blake's mature engraving style, is dated 1773, the year of its initial conception, it is likely that the date of 1780 on the *Glad Day* engraving refers to a lost first state, or at least the date of Blake's original idea.[36] The inscription on the uncoloured impression of *Glad Day* must belong to the period of the reworking, possibly as late as 1810, but the identification of the exultant figure as Albion points to the theme of national regeneration. According to Milton, Britain was called Albion by the Greeks and Romans, and Albion is used in that sense in the 'Prologue to King John' in the *Poetical Sketches*. Albion is seen there as an allegorical female, but her sons also participate in her exultation. It is possible, then, that the original design for the engraving was to provide a culmination to the series of illustrations to the *History of England*, showing in allegorical form the nation exulting in liberty after freeing itself from 'The Cruelties used by Kings and Priests'.

Unlike Milton who showed disdain for the ancient Britons, Boadicea in particular, and praised the civilizing efforts of Titus, Blake, in adding to the Notebook list the subjects of *Boadicea inspiring the Britons against the Romans* and *The Britons distress & depopulation* following her defeat, implicitly takes the side of the Britons against the Romans. The story is recounted by Milton, but with the emphasis of his Roman sources on the hideous cruelty done to the Romans and

---

[34] G. Benthall, 'John Hamilton Mortimer, A.R.A.', MS. in the Victoria and Albert Museum.
[35] Milton, op. cit., pp. 13–14. This incident is not mentioned by Rapin.   [36] *Separate Plates*, pp. 3–5.

their just revenge against the savage Britons. The subjects of *The Druids* and *The Ancient Britons*, Blake's designs for which are known only through the Notebook list, are hardly mentioned by Milton in his *History of Britain* except to suggest that the former spoke Greek and forbade any records to be kept of their history. Rapin discussed the society of the ancient Britons at some length, partly to show the enduring nature of 'British liberties' in the face of continued invasion by foreign conquerors, including the Romans and the Normans.[37] Other subjects in the Notebook list also contribute to the theme of resistance against the foreign tyrant, for example, *Edwin and Morcar stirring up the Londoners to resist William the Conqueror*, while *A Famine occasioned by the Popish interdict* shows also the consequence of priestly wrath.

The apocalyptic role given to *The Plague* and *The Fire of London* and the fact that *A Prospect of Liberty* follows immediately after *The Cruelties used by Kings and Priests* suggest that liberty will be achieved by revolution arising from despair and not by steady ordered progress. *The Plague* and *The Fire of London* may be intended as visitations of divine wrath to follow the tyrannical excesses implied in the preceding subjects in the list. *The Cruelties used by Kings and Priests* also continues the underlying theme of *The Penance of Jane Shore*, *Edward at Calais*, and *King John and the Magna Carta*, which show monarchs as either merciless or tyrannical.

The Penance of Jane Shore was a subject made popular by Rowe's play of 1714 of the same name, which was reprinted several times in the eighteenth century; Edward Penny, who was a visitor in the painting school of the Royal Academy in 1780, also attempted the subject.[38] The story of *Gregory the Great and the Captives*, which exists only as an independent water-colour and is not mentioned in the Notebook list, can be seen as a necessary incident in the conversion of Britain, but in Blake's water-colour the emphasis seems to be on the righteousness and beauty of the British captives compared to their Roman captors. The figure of Pope Gregory is the familiar white-bearded tyrant who later emerges as Urizen in the Prophetic Books, and his astonishment at the beauty of the British captives may be seen as having encouraged him to impose his priestly will on the British people.

The Notebook list also enables one to bring into a relationship with a proposed *History of England* series some other works by Blake. In 1784 Blake exhibited at the Royal Academy *A Breach in the City, the Morning after the Battle*, with *War unchained Fire, Pestilence, and Famine* following. Erdman has suggested these two paintings depict in allegorical form the consequences of Edward III's invasion of France.[39] *A Breach in the City*, however, is more likely to be connected with the

---

[37] Rapin, Vol. i, *Introduction*, pp. i–xi.
[38] The painting is now in Birmingham City Art Gallery. [39] Erdman, op. cit., p. 75.

three subjects in the Notebook list which show the depredations of the Romans after the defeat of the Britons: *The Britons distress & depopulation*, *Women fleeing from War*, and *Women in a siege*. In the Notebook list, *The Plague* and *The Fire of London* appear to be the consequences of the Reformation and the Civil War respectively, i.e. as divine judgements on relatively recent events, while *A Famine* follows 'the Popish interdict' on King John. Blake may, therefore, have intended, when he was compiling the Notebook list, to bring into the *History of England* series early water-colours of *Fire*, *Plague*, and *Famine*, which exist in a number of versions.[40] Later versions of the three water-colours were brought into the Butts series of Biblical illustrations, and related to the Seven Plagues of Egypt, but the existence of comparable subjects in the Notebook suggests that they were conceived initially within the context of English history, and were only later adapted for use as illustrations to Exodus.

Further background to Blake's conception of the *History of England* can be found in the *Poetical Sketches*, which were first published in 1783, but according to the anonymous introduction were 'commenced in his twelfth, and occasionally resumed by the author till his twentieth year', i.e. between the years 1769 and 1778. The shorter historical fragments, the 'Prologue to King Edward the Fourth' and 'The Prologue to King John', are unmistakably concerned with the destructive effects of war, which is coupled with tyranny; 'Tyranny hath stain'd fair Albion's breast with her own children's gore' (K, p. 34). 'The Prologue to King John' is passionately anti-war, and presumably was intended to be for a play on King John whose tyrannical excesses were curbed by the Magna Charta, as in Blake's illustrations of the subject. Erdman also sees an implied comment on George III's attempt to supress the American rebellion. Despite his horror at the excesses of war, Blake foresees a time when the tyrant will be humbled, and national regeneration can take place:

Beware O Proud! thou shalt be humbled; . . . O yet may Albion smile again, and stretch her peaceful arms, and raise her golden head, exultingly! Her citizens shall throng about her gates, her mariners shall sing upon the sea, and myriads shall to her temples crowd! Her sons shall joy as in the morning! Her daughters sing as to the rising year! (K, p. 34.)

Edward III's opportunistic and brutal campaign in France was, as Erdman has pointed out,[41] the real subject of the play 'King Edward the Third' in the *Poetical Sketches*, and one example of his cruelty was his treatment of the burghers of Calais, whom he spared only after the entreaties of his wife. An attempt was made by Benjamin West, at the instigation of George III,[42] to create a patriotic

---

[40] Keynes, *Bible*, Nos. 37, 38, 39.

[41] Erdman, op. cit., p. 63.

[42] According to Galt, West complained to the King of Italian painters that 'many of their noblest efforts [were] devoted to illustrate monkish legends, in which no one took any interest, while the great events in the history

46

Edward III in a series of large paintings for Windsor Castle, but it was generally agreed amongst those associated with the Society of Antiquaries that the Norman kings were bloodthirsty, tyrannical, and philistine.[43] Blake exhibited a painting of *The Bard* from Gray at the Royal Academy in 1784 (now lost) and also a later version now in the Tate Gallery, at his own exhibition of 1809.[44] The Bard is more an agent than a prophet of doom, who is able to weave 'the winding sheet of Edward's race by means of sounds of spiritual music and its accompanying expressions of articulate speech' (K, p. 576). The Bard's oppressor was Edward I, and his curse was visited on his descendants including Edward III, who was drawn by Blake from his effigy in Westminster Abbey.

Although Blake probably read Milton's *History of Britain* at an early age, he would also have found a precedent for his interest in British Antiquity and medieval history in the work of Thomas Chatterton. Chatterton claimed that the Rowley manuscripts were written in the fifteenth century, but in the poetic dialogues he ranged over all periods of English history, including the mythological origins of Britain. In a poem by Thomas Chatterton that Blake must have read, *A Bristowe Tragedie : Or the dethe of Syr Charles Bawdin*,[45] Blake could have found the archetype of his tyrant king, the vengeful Edward who determines to kill the brave Sir Charles Bawdin despite the entreaties of the latter's family. Chatterton's *The Englysh Metamorphosis* is about the mythological origins of Britain, and tells the legendary story of the creation of Snowden following the conquest of England by Brutus of Troy, the grandson of Aeneas. *Goddwynne, A Tragedy* is a verse drama that claims to redeem Earl Godwin's reputation from the harm done to it by Edward the Confessor's chroniclers because 'he gifted ne the churche'; it depicts him as a patriot who defied the tyrannical and weak Edward the Confessor, who had virtually surrendered to the Normans. The incident of Godwin's death from choking on a morsel of bread does not appear, for it must have smacked to Chatterton of a monkish fabrication.

Flaxman exhibited at the Royal Academy in 1780 a *Sketch for a monument to Chatterton*, which has been convincingly connected with a number of early drawings by Flaxman on the theme of *Despair offering a bowl of poison to Chatterton*.[46] Chatterton was still a major topic of controversy in literary London at the time.

of their country were but seldom touched . . . and the King, recollecting that Windsor Castle had, in its present form, been erected by Edward the Third, said that he thought the achievements of his splendid reign were well calculated for pictures, and would prove very suitable ornaments to the halls and chambers of that venerable edifice.' J. Galt, *Life of Benjamin West*, 1820, p. 44.   [43] Erdman, op. cit., p. 65.

[44] M. Butlin, *William Blake (1757–1827): A Catalogue of the Works of William Blake in the Tate Gallery*, 1957, No. 42.

[45] M. Lowery, *Windows of the Morning*, 1950, p. 178.

[46] I. A. Williams, 'An Identification of some Early Drawings by John Flaxman', *Burl. Mag.*, 1960, pp. 246–50. The original monument seems not to have been executed, but in 1812 Flaxman made a slight sketch for a tablet to Chatterton to go in St. Mary Redcliffe, Bristol, but this was also not executed. The sketch is reproduced in John Britton, *Autobiography*, 1850, ii. 68.

He had died in 1770, and the question of the authenticity of his work remained alive until the 1780s, although few people doubted that the *Rowley Poems* were forgeries by Chatterton. Blake and Flaxman shared an appreciation of Chatterton's genius, and it is likely that the enthusiasm for Blake's youthful poetry that resulted in the printing of the *Poetical Sketches* was due to the conviction amongst the Mathew circle that he was another Chatterton.

The home of the Mathews, whose meetings both Flaxman and Blake attended in the early 1780s, was something of a showplace of Gothic taste, and Flaxman was commissioned to design a room in Gothic style.[47] The attitude of the Mathews seems to have been relatively light-hearted and quite unsympathetic to Blake, as J. T. Smith implies in his account of Blake's reception there. Flaxman at that time was attracted to the Middle Ages as an age of chivalry through reading Thomas Percy's *Reliques of Ancient English Poetry*, first published in 1765. He wrote in 1780 to his wife a letter accompanying a copy of Percy's *Reliques* in which he praised 'the heroic virtue, the constant love, and every noble quality which exalts the human soul, which is expressed in a way so simply cannot fail of pleasing you'.[48] Two drawings in pen and grey wash, almost certainly of the same period, by Flaxman of *Sir Cauline and the Fair Christabelle* (C. Powney coll.)[49] and *Lord Cobham going to his Execution* (York Art Gallery) are examples of the same interest in medieval chivalry. While Blake himself was immune to the appeal of knightly virtue, his brother Robert seems to have been more susceptible to it, if in an ironical sense, as can be seen in his drawing of a knight in armour apparently pursuing a lady in a forest, in the Notebook, f. 9.

Blake seems also to have been immune in his early years from the artistic influence of 'Gothick Horror', made fashionable by Horace Walpole. Although there are a number of close parallels between the language of the poem 'Fair Elenor' in the *Poetical Sketches* and passages in Horace Walpole's *Castle of Otranto*,[50] Blake seems not to have responded in this period to the lone master of the 'Gothick' in painting, Henry Fuseli. Fuseli exhibited his masterpiece in this genre at the Royal Academy in 1780 (at which Blake was also an exhibitor), *Ezelin Braccia-ferro, musing over Meduna, destroyed by him for disloyalty during his absence in the Holy Land*.[51] There is no record of Blake's reaction to the painting, but its basic frivolity found no echo in his early work, although Fuseli was later to become a friend and mentor.[52]

[47] J. T. Smith, *Nollekens and his Times*, 1828 (Bentley, *Records*, pp. 456–7).
[48] D. Irwin, *English Neoclassical Art*, 1966, pp. 88–9.
[49] An illustration of the ballad in Percy's *Reliques*, 1765, i. 40–56, entitled *Sir Cauline*.
[50] Lowery, op. cit., p. 167.
[51] There is a version in the Sir John Soane Museum.
[52] The assumption that Fuseli and Blake were on terms of friendship in the early 1780s cannot be substantiated. In the brief verse autobiography in the letter to Flaxman of 12 Sept. 1800 (K, p. 799) Blake states that 'when Flaxman was taken to Italy [i.e. in 1787] Fuseli was given to me for a season'.

In conclusion, then, Blake by no means confined his attention to the 'Gothic' period in English history, or had a particularly strong conception of its historical place. He was profoundly distrustful of the study of history that was being carried out by his employers at the Society of Antiquaries, and his choice of subjects for illustration shows that he regarded mythology as a fitter subject for a poet's attention than deeds that he felt had been purged of meaning by 'reasoning historians'. Blake saw in the tombs of Westminster a simpler and purer form of art, but an art that was forced to serve tyranny by giving to it a false aura of sanctity. Malkin claimed that Blake saw the heads as portraits, but this cannot have been regarded by Blake as a worthy purpose for art; the fact that Gothic artists were forced to reproduce the features of their masters is an indication of the tyranny of the kings and of the enforced servility of the artist. If Blake went so far as to have a conception of the Gothic period in his early years, it was a notably bleak one. It was the age of 'Kings and Priests', the latter protecting the former by distorting history. On the other hand, Blake had ambivalent feelings towards the 'monkish fabrications' of the medieval historians. History was frequently used by tyrants to deceive posterity about their characters and deeds, but the chroniclers still gave 'the historical fact in its poetical vigour'; what the rational historians of the eighteenth century saw as credulity, Blake admired as the ability to see 'miracle or prodigy'. The chroniclers preserved the mythological content of the past and thus a higher truth than mere facts. Blake may also have had in mind at this early date a distinction between true and false poets; between those like the Minstrel in the play 'King Edward the Third' in the *Poetical Sketches*, who flatter kings by a vision of material and military power, and the artists of the Westminster Abbey tombs, whose honesty reveals the truth about their inhabitants despite the latter's attempt to conceal it by a display of pomp and splendour.

Blake's choice of subjects of an anti-tyrannical nature, like *Magna Carta* and *Edward III at Calais* was not unusual in the artistic milieu in which he worked; but from his earliest moments as an independent artist Blake implicitly rejected the 'reasoning historians' by choosing subjects that were not sanctioned by earlier precedent. Malkin gives a clue to Blake's youthful personality in recounting his difficulty with his fellow apprentices 'who were accustomed to laugh at what they called his mechanical taste'. It is clear that he was a lonely and withdrawn youth, taking a cynical view of conventional beliefs. His first series of water-colours of the history of England can be regarded almost as a turning upside-down of the accepted views of the Society of Antiquaries. Blake deliberately flaunts the anecdotal and mythological side of history against the 'regular and elaborate inquiry into every ancient record and proof', which was the express purpose for which he was employed in Westminster Abbey and elsewhere.

III

THE ALTERING EYE
BLAKE'S VISION IN THE *TIRIEL* DESIGNS

Robert N. Essick

BLAKE composed and illustrated *Tiriel* at a crucial point in the development of his skills as a poet, painter, and engraver. The first books in relief etching, *There is no Natural Religion* and *All Religions are One*, very probably appeared in 1788, one year before *Tiriel*, and both *Songs of Innocence* and *The Book of Thel* are dated 1789 on their title-pages.[1] Given this milieu, *Tiriel* appears to be something of an anomaly. While the poem itself looks forward to the symbolic narrative, rhetoric, and versification of the later prophetic books, the accompanying designs are very clearly not intended as preliminaries for a work in relief etching. These wash drawings, typical of preliminaries for line engravings, and their physical separateness from the manuscript text point towards a conventional means of publication, with the text in letterpress and the designs as full-page engraved illustrations. Thus, as a work of composite art, *Tiriel* seems to be a step backwards, an abortive experiment in a form contrary to Blake's vision, and later achievement, of a medium uniting word and picture. Although this assessment is difficult to dispute, it has had the unfortunate consequence of drawing attention away from *Tiriel* as an illustrated work. Except for Bentley's careful descriptions of the designs in his edition of *Tiriel*, and occasional brief references to them in the midst of essays on the poem, recent criticism remains under the influence of S. Foster Damon's comment that 'only one [design] seems to cast any light by its symbolism upon the meaning'.[2] More recent studies have been centrifugal, spinning off from the poem itself to find sources for characters, plotting, and themes in Aeschylus,

---

[1] For the dating of *Tiriel*, reproductions of the nine extant illustrations, and the text of the poem used for this study, see William Blake, *Tiriel, Facsimile and Transcript of the Manuscript, Reproduction of the Drawings, and a Commentary on the Poem*, ed. G. E. Bentley, Jr., Clarendon Press, Oxford, 1967. For the dating of the other works mentioned here, see 'Blake's Chronology', *Bibliography*, pp. 31–8.

[2] *William Blake, His Philosophy and Symbols*, Houghton Mifflin, Boston, Mass., 1924, p. 309. The 'one' design in question is the last, but Damon's interpretation is wrong, as I argue below (see note 21).

The Altering Eye: Blake's Vision in the Tiriel Designs

Sophocles, the Bible, *King Lear*, Cornelius Agrippa, Swedenborg, William Stukeley, *The Poems of Ossian*, Mallet's *Northern Antiquities*, D'Hancarville, *The Book of Enoch*, Jacob Bryant, and Edward Davies (whose book, *Celtic Researches*, did not appear until some fifteen years after the composition of *Tiriel*).[3] But a closer look at all the designs can tell us much about *Tiriel*, particularly in the ways it embodies, in rudimentary form, some major themes and motifs of the illuminated books and later writings on art.

Modes of vision are a central concern in *Tiriel*. As Gleckner has pointed out, 'there is something wrong with the vision' of all the characters in the poem.[4] The illustrations contribute substantially to the visionary theme. Tiriel's blindness is the most apparent motif of limited perception both in the text and in seven of the nine extant designs.[5] But he is also one of Blake's travellers, particularly as represented with his staff in the sixth drawing and being led by Hela in the tenth drawing. In *All Religions are One* Blake writes that 'as none by travelling over known lands can find out the unknown, So from already acquired knowledge Man could not acquire more. . . .'[6] These lines on the seventh plate are illuminated with a tiny figure striding forward with a staff much like Tiriel's. Both are imper-cipients who learn nothing of spiritual wisdom from the lands they physically visit. On the ninth plate of *All Religions are One* Blake pictures a man groping in the dark, arms outstretched, almost tripping over the long robes covering his lineaments. In similar fashion, the child of 'A Little Boy lost' in *Songs of Innocence* reaches out for an ever-retreating vaporous light while wandering in the dark forest of experience. In spite of their obvious differences in age, all three of these wanderers share with Tiriel perceptual limitations. They are the contraries to the travellers of expanding perception found in the later prophetic books, such as the figure of Los—Blake on the frontispiece to *Jerusalem*. The dark environment

---

[3] See particularly Kathleen Raine, 'Some Sources of *Tiriel*', *Huntington Library Quarterly*, xxi (1957), 1–36; id. *Blake and Tradition*, Princeton University Press, Princeton, N.J., 1968, i. 34–66 (a revised version of the preceding article); John Beer, *Blake's Visionary Universe*, Manchester University Press, Manchester, 1969, pp. 60–7, 336–42; Nancy Bogen, 'A New Look at Blake's *Tiriel*' and Mary S. Hall, 'Blake's *Tiriel*: A Visionary Form Pedantic', *Bulletin of NYPL*, lxxiv (1970), 153–76. Although he only refers to the existence of the illustrations in a footnote, Robert F. Gleckner's chapter on *Tiriel* in *The Piper and the Bard*, Wayne State University Press, Detroit, Mich., 1959, pp. 131–56, remains the most sensitive and sensible reading.

[4] *The Piper and the Bard*, p. 156.

[5] The present ownership of the designs is as follows (numbered according to Bentley's arrangement throughout this essay): 1, Paul Mellon; 2, Fitzwilliam Museum, Cambridge; 3, untraced; 4, Department of Prints and Drawings, British Museum; 5, untraced; 6, Robert N. Essick, Pasadena, California; 7, Victoria and Albert Museum, London; 8, Sir Geoffrey Keynes; 9, untraced; 10, Mrs. Louise Y. Kain, Louisville, Kentucky; 11, Sir Geoffrey Keynes; 12, formerly in the collection of T. Edward Hanley, Bradford, Pa., present location not known. The untraced drawings Nos. 3, 5, and 9 are known only through the descriptions in W. M. Rossetti's 'Annotated Lists of Blake's Paintings, Drawings, and Engravings' in Alexander Gilchrist, *Life of William Blake*, Macmillan, London and Cambridge, 1863, ii. 253–4, Nos. 156a, d, g. The descriptions are repeated, with identifications of the characters pictured, in the second edition of Gilchrist (1880), ii. 273–4. There are no known preliminary sketches for any of these designs.

[6] K, p. 98.

of the little lost boy and of the figure on plate nine of *All Religions are One* has its internal equivalent in Tiriel's blindness.

Har and Heva, as presented in the second and eleventh designs, continue the theme of narrowed vision. Perhaps Kathleen Raine's observation that they 'are immersed in the waters of hyle—matter—for their philosophy is unspiritual'[7] over-states the case, but the water surrounding the pair in the second drawing does suggest one of those tepid baths which relaxes the body and dulls the senses. This drawing does not illustrate any passage in the poem, but a similarly drowsy setting is described in a 'Song' in *Poetical Sketches*:

> Memory, hither come,
>   And tune your merry notes;
> And, while upon the wind
>   Your music floats,
>
> I'll pore upon the stream,
> Where sighing lovers dream,
> And fish for fancies as they pass
> Within the watery glass.
>
> I'll drink of the clear stream,
>   And hear the linnet's song;
> And there I'll lie and dream
>   The day along:
>
> And, when night comes, I'll go
>   To places fit for woe,
> Walking along the darken'd valley
>   With silent Melancholy.   (K, p. 8.)

The sensibility of this song, with its shadows, water, dreams, and closing note of melancholy, finds its pictorial expression in the second *Tiriel* design. Har and Heva, with their faces in a position almost identical to that in James Barry's 'Jupiter and Juno on Mount Ida',[8] seem hypnotized as they press their foreheads together and stare into the 'watery glass' of each other's eyes. This odd con-figuration, and the retention of a close face-to-face posture even in sleep (drawing No. 11), suggest a limited perspective, shrunken to total self-involvement or lulled

---

[7] *Blake and Tradition*, i. 53.

[8] Barry's painting in the Sheffield Art Gallery is offered as a possible source for the eye-to-eye position in David Bindman, ed., *William Blake: Catalogue of the Collection in the Fitzwilliam Museum, Cambridge*, Heffer, Cambridge, 1970, p. 8. The painting is reproduced in Frederick Cummings and Allen Staley, *Romantic Art in Britain: Paintings and Drawings 1760–1860*, Philadelphia Museum of Art, 1968, p. 117.

14. *Har and Heva Bathing* (*Tiriel* drawing No. 2). Wash drawing.
Fitzwilliam Museum, Cambridge

into sleep. This portrayal of Har and Heva in the *Tiriel* designs anticipates their even more limited and frightful condition described in *The Song of Los* (1795):

> Since that dread day when Har and Heva fled
> Because their brethren & sisters liv'd in War & Lust;
> And as they fled they shrunk
> Into two narrow doleful forms
> Creeping in reptile flesh upon
> The bosom of the ground;
> And all the vast of Nature shrunk
> Before their shrunken eyes.   (4. 5–12.)

Ever since Damon's study of Blake in 1924, Har and Heva have been taken as symbols for poetry and painting in a weak and degenerate state.[9] It is difficult to find specific passages in *Tiriel* to substantiate this interpretation, but the second and eleventh drawings tend to support this allegorization of their role. As representatives of the arts or the faculties which produce art, Har and Heva have contracted their vision to a transfixed gaze at each other or at their own reflection in a way that could only produce the sleep of the eleventh drawing, the 'fancies' of the melancholy lover in the 'Song' from *Poetical Sketches*, the 'doleful forms' of *The Song of Los*, a beguilement like Jupiter's on Mount Ida, or an equally limited art. The lost fifth drawing, described by Rossetti as 'Har and Heva, playing Harps' (Gilchrist, 1880 ed., ii. 273), could possibly lend further support to Damon's interpretation, but since we know nothing of the background, disposition of figures, or other crucial matters, further speculation about the design would have little merit.

As the guardian of 'the vales of Har' (line 56), Mnetha is necessarily implicated in the shrunken perception of those who dwell there. As several critics have pointed out, her name is based at least in part on 'Mnemosyne', the Greek goddess of memory and mother of the muses.[10] Mnetha's watchful, protective role in the three designs in which she appears underscores a motherly relationship to Har and Heva, while her costume baring one breast in the second and eleventh drawings adds a Greek note to her portrait. In the second design Mnetha appears to be as transfixed as her dependants, staring blankly off into space, or into her memories. Har and Heva are 'waited on' (line 58) by Mnetha, and thus if we follow Damon's allegorical reading the result is Art nourished by Memory, the faculty called upon for inspiration in the 'Song', quoted above, with its tone so similar to

---

[9] *Blake, His Philosophy and Symbols*, p. 307. Bentley, ed., *Tiriel*, p. 16, states that the interpretation of Har and Heva as representatives of the arts 'is by no means clear from the poem, but it is a fair extension of Blake's meaning in *Tiriel* in the light of his later ideas'.

[10] See Bentley, ed., *Tiriel*, p. 16, and Raine, *Blake and Tradition*, i. 52.

15. *Har and Heva Asleep* (*Tiriel* drawing No. 11). Wash drawing.
Collection of Geoffrey Keynes

16. *Har Blessing Tiriel* (*Tiriel* drawing No. 4). Wash drawing.
British Museum, Department of Prints and Drawings

17. *Age Teaching Youth.*
Water-colour. Tate Gallery, London

the atmosphere of the second design. These tentative iconic possibilities in the *Tiriel* designs are harbingers of Blake's mature commentaries on the 'Daughters of Memory' ('Annotations to Reynolds', K, p. 452) and the limitations of an aesthetic based on memory rather than imagination.

The leaf and tendril pattern on Mnetha's dress in the fourth drawing and on the counterpane in the eleventh drawing stands in bold contrast to the simplicity of all other clothing in the design series. Blake used this elaborate motif, reminiscent of the decoration in medieval manuscripts, in four other designs in ways that illuminate its significance in *Tiriel*. In an illustration for Gray's 'A Long Story', Blake clothes the 'imp' who frightens the neighbourhood children and animals in a patterned gown like Mnetha's.[11] The context is playful, and the imp is Gray himself, but the costume does suggest the robe of a sorcerer with magical influence over man and beast. Given Blake's usual iconographic consistency, this meaning

[11] Reproduced in *William Blake's Water-Colours Illustrating the Poems of Thomas Gray*, with an Introduction and Commentary by Sir Geoffrey Keynes, J. Philip O'Hara, Chicago, 1972.

developed years later in the Gray illustration may be latent in the earlier use of the same basic motif in *Tiriel*. In the eleventh drawing, Har and Heva are quite literally 'under' Mnetha's spell, covered by the pattern emblemizing her powers. A drawing in the British Museum associated with the *Tiriel* illustrations in date and style shows a bearded man and dark-haired woman embracing, their faces pressed together almost exactly as in the second *Tiriel* design.[12] Behind is a curtain decorated with the leaf and tendril pattern. This combination of motifs underscores the link between Mnetha's dress and restricted vision. The motherly protector of youthful innocence becomes an enchantress when she maintains a world of hypnotic suspension and the consequent limited perspective of the sort displayed in both the British Museum drawing and the second *Tiriel* illustration.

A fourth appearance of the leaf and tendril motif is in the water-colour drawing 'Age Teaching Youth' dating from the same period as *Tiriel*.[13] Here an old man with prominent knees drawn almost to his chest sits on the left, his posture and large book suggesting the repression and false wisdom symbolized by Urizen in the illuminated books of the 1790s. He shows his book to a young girl who points towards the sky as if to contradict with spiritual insight the letter of the ancient man's code. Before them sits a youth of indeterminate sex wearing a shortened model of Mnetha's dress, fully absorbed in writing or drawing on a tablet. The concept most readily suggested by the leaf and tendril pattern is, simply, nature.[14] In 'Age Teaching Youth', the costume thus completes a triad of motifs representing law, spirit, or imagination, and a mind limited to nature and its imitation. In another early design, 'An Allegory of the Bible',[15] a figure also wearing the patterned dress leads a child towards a figure gesturing in welcome. Behind this foreground group two rows of steps rise towards some children presumably learning from the holy writ radiantly hovering above and behind them. Nature leads only to the foot of the stairs; then other guides must take over to bring the child to spiritual truths. And thus it is in *Tiriel*, with the telling difference that Har and Heva are not children and there is no one to point to heaven or lead them to realms of light. The etymology of her name and the iconography of her dress suggest that Mnetha is both memory and nature, a Vala-like female will and prototype for those 'destroyers of Jerusalem' in *Milton* 'Who pretend to Poetry that they

[12] For a discussion and reproduction of this drawing, and another associated with *Tiriel* showing a man and woman warming themselves before a fire in a forest, see Michael J. Tolley, 'Some Blake Puzzles—Old and New', *Blake Studies*, iii (Spring 1971), 107–28 and Plates 1, 3. None of the figures in these drawings can be positively identified with characters in *Tiriel*.

[13] Described and reproduced in Martin Butlin, *William Blake: A Complete Catalogue of the Works in the Tate Gallery*, Tate Gallery, London, 1971, p. 29.

[14] Mary Hall (op. cit., p. 170) relates the motif to Harmonia's 'patterned dress with figures of the earth, heavens, stars, seas and rivers', but none of these is pictured on Mnetha's dress.

[15] Described and reproduced in Butlin, op. cit., p. 25. Butlin dates this water-colour drawing in the early or mid 1780s.

may destroy Imagination / By imitation of Nature's Images drawn from Remembrance' (41. 21, 23–4). Mnetha's nature–mother–enchantress portrait in the designs shows her to be, like Tiriel himself, a creature of limited and limiting vision.

Several motifs running through the designs underscore the waning vitality—artistic, political, and moral—of Tiriel's world. Other than Mnetha's protective dominance over Har and Heva, the female principle is everywhere shrunken or cursed. Myratana dies, 'shrinking in pangs of death' (line 20) as Tiriel curses his sons in the first design. Later, Tiriel's daughters huddle together for protection in the seventh drawing and finally are brought to their knees, 'weeping with cries of bitter woe' (line 261), in the eighth drawing. Hela is reduced to terror in the tenth and twelfth drawings, while Heva's face is marked with a similar emotion as she seeks protection from Tiriel in the fourth and sixth drawings. Tiriel's own diminished state is imaged not only by his blindness but also by his baldness, mentioned six times in the poem, and square-cut beard. Even Har has luxuriant hair and a full beard, although they are white like Tiriel's. Mnetha's bound hair and feet enclosed in slippers in the fourth drawing emphasize her restrictive character. In the first drawing, Heuxos's hair is turning grey as he begins to assume his father's role as king. In contrast to the images of baldness and white hair are the dark locks of Myratana (drawing No. 1) and Hela (drawings Nos. 8, 10, and 12). Ijim's luxuriant hair and powerful body mark him as a Samson figure, while the bearing of Tiriel on his shoulders suggests the story of Aeneas and Anchises. But Tiriel's wife dies at the very beginning, Hela's hair becomes a snake-filled emblem of her father's curses (drawing No. 11 and lines 317–22), and Ijim becomes a confused beast of burden for the man of fallen vision. Traditional emblems of physical strength and motifs suggesting the vital myths of the past are twisted and weakened in the text and designs of *Tiriel*.

Although the drawings are, like the poem, dominated by dramatic confrontations between characters, the backdrops for these events have their own role to play. The poem insists that Har and Heva live in tents, but the heavy, rectilinear walls of their dwelling in the fourth and sixth designs are only slightly less monolithic than the walls of Tiriel's palace in the seventh and eighth drawings. These oppressive enclosures, at once both massive in their substance and abstract in their geometry, mirror the drama of closed vision taking place before them. Rossetti's description of the lost ninth design, showing 'richly-sculptured columns',[16] holds out tantalizing possibilities for a contrasting architectural motif. But if, as Bentley suggests in his convincing analysis of Rossetti's comments,[17] these columns are part of the 'lofty towers' (line 256) of the houses belonging to Tiriel's dying sons, then these works of art are presented only to be cursed and destroyed. In the first design the cold severity of the undecorated columns of

---

[16] Gilchrist, *Life of William Blake* (1863), ii. 254, and (1880), ii. 273.   [17] Bentley, ed., *Tiriel*, p. 43.

18. *Tiriel Carried by Ijim* (*Tiriel* drawing No. 7). Wash drawing.
Victoria and Albert Museum

Tiriel's palace filling the middle distance is matched by the mathematical proportions of the pyramid in the distant landscape. The opening scene of the pictorial drama is thus placed within a classical and Egyptian setting. The disposition of architectural motifs in the middle ground and background may have been meant to suggest a temporal, rather than simply spatial, recession, with Tiriel and his family standing in the foreground as the less than magnificent inheritors of the Egyptian and Grecian cultures behind them. The Platonic concept of the transmission of ancient wisdom from Egypt to Greece suggested by the first design is implicit in Blake's later attacks on the Neoclassical values of his own time. In the 'Laocoön' inscriptions, the 'Gods of Greece & Egypt' are jointly condemned as 'Mathematical Diagrams' (K, p. 776) and in 'On Homer's Poetry & on Virgil' Blake announces that 'Sacred Truth has pronounced that Greece & Rome, as Babylon & Egypt, so far from being parents of Arts & Sciences as they pretend, were destroyers of all Art' (K, p. 778). Given Blake's own early classical tastes, it is doubtful that this sort of strident denunciation is even implied in *Tiriel*. As late as 1800 Blake wrote to Cumberland in praise of 'the immense flood of Grecian light & glory which is coming on Europe' (K, p. 797). The first clearly anti-classical statements do not come until 1804 when Blake wrote to Hayley that he had thrown off a 'spectrous Fiend' identified as 'the Jupiter of the Greeks' (K, pp. 851–2). But even here the spectre is, like Tiriel and his destructive curses, the 'ruiner of ancient Greece' rather than the embodiment of a classical civilization antithetical to true art. Blake's shifting reactions to classicism are difficult to pinpoint with certainty,[18] but the first *Tiriel* design does suggest that as early as 1789 Blake was beginning to ponder, and embody in his art, his own views on history and culture.

The costuming and arrangement of Tiriel's sons offer another portrayal of cultural history. Given the Greek setting of the first design, the vines in the hair of the third son call to mind an early, Bacchic culture, the second son's laurel wreath a heroic age, and Heuxos's spiked crown the present kingship he will inherit from his father. The increase in the amount and luxuriance of clothing among the sons matches the progress and final decadence imaged by the three types of headgear, lending visual support to Gleckner's statement that 'the sons and daughters of Tiriel revolt, it is true, and this is good; but their assumption of the very authority, material wealth, and power they deny to Tiriel constitutes an assumption of his error as well.'[19] Like the movement from Egypt to Greece to Tiriel suggested by the spatial arrangement of the entire design, the line of Tiriel's sons is at once both a historical progression from past to present and a fall into accusation, weakened vision, and tyranny. In 1793 Blake modelled his line engraving of 'Our End is

---

[18] The best study of Blake's classicism is David Bindman's unpublished doctoral dissertation, 'The Artistic Ideas of William Blake', University of London, 1971.   [19] *The Piper and the Bard*, p. 156.

19. *Tiriel Supporting the Swooning Myratana* (*Tiriel* drawing No. 1). Wash drawing.
Collection of Mr. and Mrs. Paul Mellon

Come', which in a later version became 'The Accusers of Theft Adultery Murder', after Tiriel's sons. As Sir Geoffrey Keynes has pointed out, a preliminary drawing for the engraving with another group of figures similar to those on the left in the eighth *Tiriel* design firmly establishes a link between the two compositions.[20] The appearance of Heuxos and three other sons in this eighth design is particularly close to 'The Accusers', for the faint outline of a rejected arm position for the last son in the row of three is the same as the gesture of despair used for the middle figure in the engraving. These later versions of Tiriel's sons in Blake's graphic art fulfil the prophecy implied by their presentation in the *Tiriel* designs.

The landscape backgrounds in the second, fourth, sixth, and tenth designs seem at first glance to offer little commentary on foreground events, but when seen in contrast to the pastoral settings of *Songs of Innocence* their iconic dimensions become apparent. *What* is represented in these landscapes is of secondary importance; the *style* in which they are presented is most significant. In *Songs of Innocence* outlines are clear and lighting is for the most part direct and complete, as if every object were self-illuminated. In *Tiriel*, outlines tend to merge and a pervasive murkiness weakens all light. In the second design the landscape is only a pattern of deep shadows, just as its inhabitants are described in the poem as 'But . . . the shadow of Har' (line 59). Behind Mnetha's head is the 'tent of Har' (line 68), or perhaps only the base of the oak beneath which Har and Heva find protection. The viewer's inability to define forms and identify objects is a basic quality of this landscape. Even though Har's land is described in the poem as 'pleasant gardens' (line 62), in the drawing it is only a dark clearing in an even darker forest—the perfect setting for muses with impaired powers of vision. In the eleventh design a tapestry replaces the usual landscape, but this backdrop is also murky and ill defined, its leaping child a mere shadow of those happy, youthful dancers in *Songs of Innocence*. Mnetha's garden, the garden of memory, turns out to be only a forest which becomes for Tiriel the wilderness of experience in which he wanders. In *A Father's Memoirs of His Child* (1806), Benjamin Heath Malkin quotes Blake's commentary on drawing styles that calls to mind the decadent pastoral world of *Tiriel* and two of its leading inhabitants: 'Had the hand which executed these little ideas been that of a plagiary, who works only from memory, we should have seen blots called masses; blots without form, and therefore without meaning. These blots of light and dark, as being the result of labour, are always clumsy and indefinite; the effect of rubbing out and putting in, like the progress of a blind man, or of one in the dark, who feels his way, but does not see it' (K, p. 439). The landscape in the tenth design is clearer than the 'blots of light and dark' of the second design, and far less frightening than the scenes it illustrates in the poem (lines

---

[20] See Keynes, *Pencil Drawings by William Blake*, Nonesuch Press, London, 1927, Plate 10, and *Separate Plates*, p. 21.

20. *Tiriel Leaving Har and Heva* (*Tiriel* drawing No. 6). Wash drawing.
Collection of Robert N. Essick

321–2, 327, 341–4), but its very gentility bespeaks a lack of energy exemplifying the visionary limitations of its inhabitants. The *Songs of Innocence* designs have a vital presence, created by a harmonious combination of pictorial simplicity and conceptual intensity, completely absent from the *Tiriel* illustrations. Blake's final commentary on such a landscape, and the aesthetics which it represents, appears in the last design. Tiriel lies dead at Hela's feet, as rigid and lifeless as a fallen column from his own palace or one of the sepulchral effigies Blake studied in Westminster Abbey while an apprentice engraver. The forest behind him is now a cage of trees shutting out all open vistas, while amongst the branches 'black berries appear that poison all around' (line 385). The iconography of the forest landscape and the story of Tiriel's life of curses unite in the image of this bitter fruit.[21]

The style of the *Tiriel* designs forms a significant part of their total meaning. Many of the motifs in these drawings are repeated in the illuminated books of the 1790s; it is primarily the style of the drawings which sets them off from Blake's other illustrations to his own poetry. The artist has altered his own eye and hand to produce a style consonant with the limited vision portrayed in the poem and designs. Their very conventionality—an amalgam of Barry's monumentality and the softer lighting and shading of Stothard—exemplifies and implicitly comments upon a tradition of book illustration as restrictive as the perceptions of Har, Heva, and Tiriel. The second and eleventh drawings are particularly significant in this regard. Both are executed in a freer style and on a considerably larger scale than the other extant designs, and both picture Har, Heva, and Mnetha in scenes hardly mentioned in the poem. These may have been produced sometime later than the other designs, for they suggest that Blake was attempting to move away from literal illustration and develop the Har and Heva story into a pictorial commentary on eighteenth-century aesthetics bound to the imitation of nature and to the memory of a once glorious but now decayed classical tradition. While these two designs are the most ambitious in the series, they also underscore the failure of *Tiriel* to realize fully Blake's intentions. Their very existence suggests a dissatisfaction with the other, earlier designs and even with the entire project of writing a 'prophetic book' with separate illustrations based closely on the text. Blake had set for himself an extremely difficult task—to portray and comment upon fallen vision without placing his own style and point of view beyond the artistic limitations imposed by that vision. It was not until years later, in the Job engravings, that Blake created a form of illustration at once both conventional in its medium and expansive in its imaginative perceptions.

[21] Damon, in *Blake, His Philosophy and Symbols*, p. 309, writes that 'the vines of the ecstasy of true feeling spring up around him', while Bentley in his edition of *Tiriel*, p. 49, and Harold Bloom in *Blake's Apocalypse*, Doubleday, New York, 1963, p. 27, both identify the berries as grapes. The text of the poem clearly indicates something far less palatable.

IV

JUSTIFYING ONE'S VALUATION OF BLAKE[1]

F. R. Leavis

BLAKE is for me—has long been—a challenge and a reproach. He is a reproach because the challenge remains still untaken. To take it would mean a very ambitious self-commitment. I think one ought to have the courage to plunge, knowing that the upshot could hardly be the kind of success that would, by satisfying it, justify the ambition, which is a strong sense of the need. The compelling power of this motive, then, is inseparable from a realization of the problem it faces one with. In saying these things I am postulating that Blake is a major value, and one of peculiar importance for our time. That conviction, as I hold it, is unaccompanied by doubts, but how is one to enforce it? There you have the problem. To justify and enforce such a conviction would be not only to explain what it means and why one is compelled to hold it, but to show that it is reasonable to believe that Blake might be effectively current as a value of that order.

Everyone knows the kind of difficulty I am thinking of. But that is too easily said. Even when there was an educated public, I mean one capable of supporting an intelligent contemporary performance of the function of criticism, the 'everyone' it comprised was a minority; and it was a minority of a minority that could be looked to as capable of forming, positively and decisively, the kind of conviction now in question. Those considerations don't dispose of the importance of *having* an educated public—an assumption it wouldn't be in place to argue now. What *is* in place is to remind you (this is a university audience) of the context of pre-, occupations involved in my discussion of Blake—to my sense, necessarily involved; that is, not accidentally or arbitrarily. Think of me, then, as what I am here and there known to be—much concerned for the idea of the university as having for its constitutive function to be a creative centre of an educated public—the educated public society so desperately needs. It is an idea that emphasizes the co-presence of the major studies and disciplines as a necessary condition; emphasizes therefore the distinctive nature of the English School as a liaison-centre that is in an

---

[1] A lecture given at Bristol University 15 Nov. 1971. I accepted the invitation of Bristol University because I knew that only by being committed to such an 'occasion' (for Blake was the specified subject) should I be able to make the attempt that I had long thought I ought to make, and of which I had so vivid a realization of the difficulties.

important sense non-specialist—a liaison-centre in the way in which a focus of humane consciousness must be.

The question I have in mind, then, when I speak of Blake as a challenge may be thought of as this: what kind of approach should one make it one's aim to develop in working with students in a university English School? One certainly can't, if at all responsible, say 'Get the Blake in the Oxford Standard Authors and read it through', or 'Dip pertinaciously, sample copiously, and you'll soon begin to find your bearings, and before long have notes for the organized and really repaying study.' There isn't any book one can recommend as a guide, either on Blake in general, or even on *Songs of Innocence and of Experience*. In fact, it is one's responsibility to warn the student against being hopeful of light and profit to be got from the Blake authorities and the Blake literature. More than that, he should be told unequivocally that none of the elaborated prophetic works is a successful work of art.

It is because Blake was a great artist that he matters; the principle that should govern one's dealings with him is implicit in that truism. I use the word 'artist' as it was used by Blake himself, whose genius manifested itself in two arts—the poet's and the artist's in our narrower sense of the word. I shall concern myself only with the poet. It is obviously improbable that anyone studying the work of the poet at all profitably won't develop a decided interest in his visual art, and I see in Blake an opportunity, should there be anyone at hand both informed and intelligent, to foster such an associated interest in a way not normally to be expected in 'English Studies' and hardly likely to stop short at Blake. Associated, and immediately relevant, but an interest in a different art—I find support, or countenance, for this emphasis in a sentence from Eliot's essay on Blake[2] in which he dwells on the genius as a 'peculiar honesty'.—'And this honesty never exists without great technical accomplishment.'

'Technique' in an art of language is necessarily so different a kind of thing from technique in any of the visual arts that one doesn't expect a critic who is qualified for intelligent discussion of the engravings and paintings to be very helpfully articulate about the poetry—the inverse of which proposition is equally true. Further, the nature of Blake's genius and of his importance to us favours adequate discussion very much more in terms of the poetry than in terms of line, colour, and visual design.

I had better add at once that 'technique' is not a word I myself, with the point in mind that I had to make, should have chosen to use. What it portends in Eliot's sentence is clear enough because of what one knows of Eliot. In any case, the context makes it plain. The essay, indeed, considered as a whole, offers, for my purpose, which is to convey my notion of the right critical approach to Blake,

---

[2] 'Blake', *The Sacred Wood*, London, 1920, pp. 137–43.

a rare kind of help—not the less so for also presenting, while it is one in which Eliot's distinction as a critic appears strongly, his distinctive limitations and weaknesses.

He means by the 'honesty' he stresses in Blake that rare capacity to recognize and seize in his art the personal thisness of his experience which is the mark of great creative genius—that thisness in which significance inheres. Such 'honesty', then, entails uncommon percipience, intelligence, and self-knowledge. Throwing incidentally and unconsciously a good deal of light on himself, Eliot says:

It is important that the artist should be highly educated in his own art, but his education is one that is hindered rather than helped by the ordinary processes of society which
constitute education for the ordinary man. For these processes consist largely in the
acquisition of impersonal ideas which obscure what we really are and feel, what we
really want and what really excites our interest. It is of course not the information
acquired, but the conformity which the accumulation of knowledge is apt to impose,
that is harmful. Tennyson is a very fair example of a poet almost wholly encrusted with
opinion, almost wholly merged into his environment. Blake, on the other hand, knew
what interested him, and he therefore presents only the essential, only, in fact, what can
be presented and need not be explained. And because he was not distracted, or frightened,
or occupied in anything but exact statements, he understood. He was naked, and saw
man naked, and from the centre of his crystal.

Defined here, we have the force of 'technique' invoked when Eliot says: 'This honesty never exists without great technical accomplishment.' When we ascribe great technical accomplishment to Tennyson, 'technique' has a different force. People who met him, Henry James, for instance, commented on the surprising contrast between the unsmooth, unemollient, and formidably masculine actual person and the person asking to be divined as the poet of Tennysonian poetry. Tennysonian technique, that is, answered to a specialized poetic sensibility that excluded from creative expression all but a narrow range of conventionally poetic interests, or elements of experience. Since it suffered no surprises, but worked only in the familiar, it could achieve and maintain a kind of perfection. When on the other hand, Eliot says of such honesty as Blake's that it 'never exists without great technical accomplishment' he means what he says but is not always recognized to mean. It is of course obviously true that if the poet hadn't had the skill to communicate the 'peculiar honesty' in his poetry we couldn't have known that it existed. But Eliot means more than that. What he has in mind, he being himself in his paradoxical way a major poet, is that a great creative writer, a truly and significantly *creative* writer, doesn't just think out what he has to say and then develop and refine the procedures for communicating it. It is true that his struggle with technique and the problems in general of procedure is the business of *making communicable*; but that is, at the same time and inseparably, the process of dis-

68

covering, or arriving at, what communication his profoundest sense of his theme insists that he shall make. Technique, as Eliot uses the work, is heuristic. The point I have made in explaining its use is important in its bearing on Blake's situation and circumstances and the problems they faced him with, and on the nature of his defeats.

In speaking of Blake's struggle with technique I use Eliot's word, which, I have avowed, I would rather have avoided, since it doesn't, for my purpose, point with the needed specificity. That requisite some phrases thrown out by Eliot himself (though not in the same essay) supply. They occur in a place that has a lively general relevance: a later introduction to a limited edition of Johnson's satires. There he says: 'Sensibility alters from age to age in everybody, whether we will or no, but expression is only altered by a man of genius.' The sentence that follows completes the effectiveness of the pointer: 'A great many poets . . . are second-rate just for this reason, that they have not the sensitiveness and consciousness to perceive that they feel differently from the preceding generation, and therefore must *use words* differently.' We have there an implicit account of the 'honesty' that 'never exists without great technical accomplishment'. Eliot avoids the word 'sincerity', no doubt for the obvious reason that, being the first word to hand and the more commonly resorted to, it tends, as 'honesty' in Eliot's dictum hardly does, to pass for self-explanatory and hiding no problems.

Blake was the man of genius who in the eighteenth century 'altered expression'—altered it in a fundamental way. Eliot doesn't say that, but he unmistakably attributes genius to Blake; and the great technical accomplishment he credits him with was a matter of using words. What we have in front of us, in fact, is what, when we come to Wordsworth, who at the end of the century was again faced with 'altering expression' (Blake's work having gone unrecognized), we are taught to discuss as the problem of 'poetic diction'.

Not much profit, I think, has ever, since Wordsworth's 'Preface' provided an academic text for it, come of such discussion, though Wordsworth himself in the 'Preface' is wrestling with real problems. And a major profit of considering the Blakean genius will be a new realization of the vital human issues that, for Wordsworth, were implicit in that curious, enlightening, and certainly not unintelligent document, which deserves a better fate than its conventional status represents. Different as Blake was from Wordsworth, the same issues were involved in Blake's achievement of 'technical' sufficiency.

In Eliot's recognition of the magnitude of the achievement there is something paradoxical and contradictory. Thus he can say of the century in which Blake was born: 'So positive was the culture of that age, that for many years the ablest writers were still naturally in sympathy with it; and it crushed a number of smaller men who felt differently but did not dare to face the fact. . . .' That is

69

a classical statement of the hostility of the Augustan climate to the highest kind of creativity. It was not only that the empiricist ethos evoked by Blake with the names of Newton and Locke prevailed, in its absolutist confidence, as the reigning common sense—asserting itself in the strongly positive stylistic conventions, so that nothing, it was felt, existed for serious expression if not capable of being *stated*, explicitly, rationally, and conventionally. Augustan civilization was also polite, which means that the cultural code was, among other things, a code of manners: the assumption conveyed in the conventions was that nothing worthy of literary expression could be at odds with an implicit context—insistently present in tone, gesture, and movement—of overtly social circumstance. But if the truism that man is a social being is to mean this, then the human spirit is doomed to sicken in rebellious inertia. It was Blake's genius to be certain of that with fierce creative intensity, and to live his protest.

The tribute that Shelley, criticizing Wordsworth in 'Peter Bell the Third', paid him as the great liberating creativity of the age applies with equal felicity to Blake:

> Yet his was individual mind
> And new created all he saw . . .

Mind is necessarily individual mind, and individual minds necessarily imply individual persons who have unique histories and can't be aggregated with others or moulded to standard or generalized. Life is *there* only in individual lives, whence alone the vital creativity can come without which culture, civilization, society, decay. The need for insistence on that truth didn't cease with the 'Romantic' revolution in literature. Eliot's way of registering his sense of Blake's genius—'He was naked, and saw man naked, and from the centre of his crystal'—shows how he realized the force of that need in the days (around 1920) when he himself achieved a 'technical accomplishment' that involved a major 'alteration of expression'. And yet he can write: 'His philosophy, like his visions, like his insight, like his technique, was his own. And accordingly he was inclined to attach more importance to it than an artist should; this is what makes him eccentric and makes him inclined to formlessness.' What, one is inclined to ask, *could* a Blake's philosophy have been but his own? 'Philosophy', however, is a word that may mean a diversity of things, and, if one had not been familiar with Eliot's own peculiar weakness, his paradoxical and habitual deep-seated self-contradiction, one might, at this point in the essay, have passed the criticism as intellectually respectable. But well before the end of the essay it has become quite impossible not to make a drastic comment on Eliot. After a brief and con-descending sentence summarizing in large quasi-cliché terms what he sees as the gifts that give Blake a right to be remembered, he writes: 'Had these been controlled by a respect for impersonal reason, for common sense, for the objectivity of science, it would have been better for him.' That in its gratuitousness is surely just absurd, and tells us more about Eliot than it tells us about Blake. Seeing what respect (which prevailed) for impersonal reason, for common sense, for the objectivity of science meant in the 'positive culture' against which the genius that conceived Urizen had, of its very nature, to wage life-long war, it amounts to saying that it would have been better for Blake (and for us) if he had escaped having genius. Born in the mid eighteenth century, genius such as Eliot has described had necessarily an intense belief in human creativity, and was dedicated to its vindication.

But Eliot, though himself a major poet, couldn't believe in it; he hadn't the wholeness, with the courage it brings, which *is* belief, and at the best was equivocal. We have the essential paradox in his most sustained and impressive work, *Four Quartets*, where, offering to achieve the assurance he needs by creative means, he reveals his inveterate underlying will to discredit creativity. In that early essay on Blake, continuing his verdict, he goes on: 'What his genius required, and what it sadly lacked, was a framework of accepted and traditional ideas which would have prevented him from indulgence in a philosophy of his own, and concentrated his attention upon the problems of the poet.' What, we ask, *are* the 'problems of the poet'? The problems of a poet that are worth any intensity of study are the problems of a man—one open to being profoundly disturbed by experience, and capable of a troubled soul: Eliot in the 1920s declared his readiness to regard poetry as a 'jeu de quilles'. *Four Quartets* is hardly that, but the writer of this self-contradictory criticism is still there in the religious poet. The question, however, prompted by Eliot in the same place, that really needs answering, and answering with some care, is: what *was* this philosophy of Blake's that Eliot is referring to? Or rather, the prior question is: just what is he thinking of— what kind of thing—when he refers in that ironical way to Blake's 'philosophy'? The care is needed because the answer doesn't readily present itself, as the established tradition of Blake exegesis brings out: Eliot's phrase and his irony call our attention involuntarily to possibilities, even (it is fair to say) probabilities, of confusion in a matter that is of great importance. In fact, these considerations have so much behind them, and so much is at stake, that I don't myself think of attempting to supply an immediate answer. Yet the need to have supplied one will be a dominant and directing presence in my mind through the critical argument that must follow.

My use of Eliot is a means of economy; with its rare distinction the context of the prompting phrase I quoted gives the question, as it arises out of his critique, an impelling significance for critical thought it wouldn't otherwise have had. That is not the only reason for bringing in Eliot, our major modern poet, whose difference from Blake enhances the relevance. This observation of mine implies, of course, that I think them both, in what they communicate, highly important to us all who are troubled, as we have reason to be, about the way our civilization is going. I think also that the great importance of Eliot—to my sense of which I have, with some care, more than once testified—is inseparable from the 'no' that must, it seems to me, be one's response to the basic attitude conveyed by his work; and I think the correlative antithesis, the approvable positive, the x implicitly postulated in the 'no', is represented by Blake. That is, I think that Blake, who died in 1827, should be a major living force today, and that his attitude to life and civilization has a validity, a salutary and inspiring rightness, that Eliot's hasn't.

The problem, as I've said, is to suggest cogently, within a reasonable compass, how such a conviction can be justified; and to do that would be to intimate with persuasive force how one would proceed to put it, as a conviction the accepted validity of which was grounded in perception and understanding, into effective currency. Eliot himself, with his observations about the significance of Blake's early published work, *Poetical Sketches* (1783), the contents of which were written when Blake was between twelve and twenty, points us to the right and obvious starting-place. His particular remarks, however, I don't find very helpful. He says, after a generalization about boys of real promise: 'So with Blake, his early poems are technically admirable, and their originality is in an occasional rhythm.' Actually the originality strikes me, and should, I think, strike every reader, all the way through, and one might spend with a student group a profitable hour discussing a number of diverse pieces, some of which look at first sight like exercises in contemporary modes, but most of which give proof of an insistent rhythmical preoccupation—one significantly uncontemporary.

I must for the present occasion confine myself to the absolutely essential. I will quote then from Eliot this, which enables me to make the necessary points with economy.

But his affection for certain Elizabethans is not so surprising as his affinity with the best work of his own century. He is very like Collins, he is very eighteenth-century. The poem, 'Whether on Ida's Shady Brow', is eighteenth-century work; the movement, the weight of it, the syntax, the choice of words:

> The languid strings do scarcely move!
> The sound is forc'd, the notes are few!

This is contemporary with Gray and Collins, it is the poetry of a language that has undergone the discipline of prose. Blake up to twenty is decidedly a traditional.

This summing-up seems to me decidedly perverse. It is also very misleading. That 'To the Muses' as a whole answers to the description, 'contemporary with Gray and Collins', is certainly true, though, if there were time, I could say what it is that makes the poem, for me, Blake's, and not by either of the others. As things are, I will merely remark that if 'To the Muses' is placed side by side with the 'song' printed half-a-dozen pages earlier, 'How Sweet I roam'd from Field to Field', the latter, with its subtly transmuted eighteenth-century quality (which is paradoxically personal and unpolite, the transmutation being only brought out by the lapse into 'diction': 'And Phoebus fir'd my vocal rage') is seen to come from the same sensibility, and yet could obviously not have been written by either Gray or Collins—or (I will add) by anyone but Blake. But a good deal more remarkable is that Eliot should have ignored the poem that comes next:

> My silks and fine array,
>   My smiles and languish'd air,
> By love are driv'n away;
>   And mournful lean Despair
> Brings me yew to deck my grave;
> Such end true lovers have.
>
> His face is fair as heav'n
>   When springing buds unfold;
> O why to him was't giv'n
>   Whose heart is wintry cold?
> His breast is love's all-worship'd tomb,
> Where all love's pilgrims come.
>
> Bring me an axe and spade,
>   Bring me a winding sheet;
> When I my grave have made
>   Let winds and tempests beat.
> Then down I'll lie as cold as clay:
> True love doth pass away!

That also is called 'Song' and is, in its utterly un-eighteenth-century way, unmistakably inspired by the songs in Shakespeare. Eliot perhaps felt that this point was covered by his reference to Blake's 'affection for certain Elizabethans'— 'not so surprising', he says, 'as his affinity with the very best work of his own century'. Surely it is much more surprising and incomparably more significant than the alleged 'affinity'—a word that itself seems to me a misdirection. In any case, the explicit and specific reference to Shakespeare is wholly necessary; for what makes the poem so remarkable is not merely the song-like rising and lapsing flow, but the nature of the relation to *Hamlet*. When we ask what lies behind the effect of poignant pregnancy we find both the tragic Ophelia and the grave-diggers' scene. What is so significant is the spontaneous, uncalculated, inward nature of the relation. For it is the nature and the essential necessity of Blake's liberation from the eighteenth-century *literary* and the eighteenth century in all its modes that we should be studying; and how revealing an index the 'Song' is we realize when, turning the page, we read out (as we have to—if only in imagination) another Shakespearian poem:

> Memory hither come
> And tune your merry notes . . .

Again we have that unique Blakean relation to Shakespeare. There are, we know, songs in *As You Like It*, and this, in its movement, is Shakespearian song. But it is not, for all the element of specific reminiscence, mere mimicry in the form of a variation; it is not inspired Shakespearian pastiche. The indebtedness to Shakespeare is a Blakean response to that constituent mood[3] of the play which we associate with the melancholy Jaques.

I call it the unique Blakean relation to Shakespeare because, if it were a question to be settled by the producible evidence, we could reasonably say that the only man who in the first age of bardolatry could read Shakespeare was Blake; for in general the 'positive culture' acted as a transmuting 'screen'; it stood between the eighteenth century and the revered poet-dramatist. A condition of the advantage Blake enjoyed, or another aspect of it, is to be seen in the very different poem printed immediately before:

> I love the jocund dance,
> The softly-breathing song,
> Where innocent eyes do glance,
> And where lisps the maiden's tongue.

I won't say that this is popular art, for we recognize it as a poem by William Blake. But no one will question that it is related to popular tradition. The movement— a kind that recurs a good deal in Blake—is the movement of children's rhythmic games, or of dance. There is, in fact, in Blake plenty of evidence that a traditional popular culture of a kind that could, and did, affect his poetic use of the English language was strongly alive in the London in which he grew up. It was perverse of Eliot, or (putting it perhaps more justly) an expression of a characteristic basic ignorance in him, to call the young Blake a 'traditional' by reason of an 'affinity' to be discerned in *Poetical Sketches* with Gray and Collins. Actually, we see Blake to be far more deeply rooted than either of those two—a perception that entails a challenge, a dismissive one, to the peculiarly shallow and inadequate conception of the 'traditional' that enfeebles Eliot's thought (both as critic and poet).

Talking with a discussion group, I might—thinking of Eliot's avowal of two starting-points for the development of his own poetic—have said that Blake also

---

[3] See James Smith's essay on *As You Like It*, reprinted in *Selections from Scrutiny*, vol. i, Cambridge, 1968.

had two starting-points: one in traditional popular culture and the other in Shakespeare. These are clearly observable as such in *Poetical Sketches*. Yet, in that, here and here, we have to recognize that they are both *present* but are not altogether distinct from one another, they are not really separable. It was a mark of Blake's genius—a manifestation of his significance in the cultural history that intelligent literary students, repudiating distinctive 'literary values', inevitably find them-selves studying—that he successfully, and very early, abrogated for himself the insulation established at the end of the seventeenth century between the recognized culture (now polite) to which literature belonged and cultural tradition as maintained at the popular level. The parallel and contrast between Blake and Wordsworth, who came later and succeeded in becoming an influence, repays study. Blake's own success had no influence—unless, as I have suggested in dis-cussing *Little Dorrit*, it is manifested in Dickens, the last major creative writer who was able to be that and at the same time to draw on a culture that was both traditional and popular (and Dickens too owes an immeasurable debt to Shake-speare).

I turn now to a poem in *Poetical Sketches* that I haven't yet mentioned, and about which it seems to me remarkable that Eliot says nothing: 'Mad Song'. Eliot surely can't have missed seeing its relation to Shakespeare, and its success (to me very impressive) as an intensely Blakean poem makes his omission, in commenting on those early performances in general, to take account of the kind of significance it so clearly has remarkable indeed. 'Mad Song' starts with a hint (recalling 'Poor Tom's a-cold') that it comes from a genuinely mad Edgar, madly inspired; but it gives us too, with the distraught anguished Lear, the human tempest of passion, self-assertion, jealousy, cruelty, and murderous hatred that gets its focal evocation in the scene on the heath:

> The wild winds weep
>   And the night is a-cold;
> Come hither, Sleep,
>   And my griefs infold:
> But lo! the morning peeps
>   Over the eastern steeps,
> And the rustling birds of dawn
> The earth do scorn.
>
> Lo! to the vault
>   Of pavèd heaven,
> With sorrow fraught
>   My notes are driven:
> They strike the ear of night,
>   Make weep the eyes of day;

> They make mad the roaring winds,
>   And with tempests play.
>
> Like a fiend in a cloud,
>   With howling woe
> After night I do croud,
>   And with night will go;
> I turn my back to the east
> From whence comforts have increas'd;
> For light doth seize my brain
> With frantic pain.

The strongly Blakean character of this response to Shakespeare's *Lear* has, for us, an emphasized significance when we read in *Songs of Experience* the two quatrains of 'Infant Sorrow':

> My mother groan'd, my father wept,
> Into the dangerous world I leapt;
> Helpless, naked, piping loud,
> Like a fiend hid in a cloud.
>
> Struggling in my father's hands,
> Striving against my swaddling bands,
> Bound and weary, I thought best
> To sulk upon my mother's breast.

This is pure Blake, with no hint that would have made one say 'Shakespeare!' My 'emphasized' regarded the way in which Blake's profound indebtedness to Shakespeare is made manifest. His sense of the dangerous complexities of life and human nature is his own; but we see that the education of his powers of expression that went with his addiction to Shakespeare was, inseparably, an education of his power to perceive, to recognize, and to imagine—and 'imagine' lays the stress on the heuristic aspect of creative expression; that is, on the perception that is, or that becomes, discovery.

The range and diversity of human life over which Blake's perception and intuition played was immense; hence the incomparable value to him of Shakespeare. Eliot, having remarked that the *Songs of Innocence and of Experience*, and the poems from the Rossetti manuscript, are the poems 'of a man with a profound interest in human emotions and a profound knowledge of them', says: 'The emotions are presented in an extremely simplified abstract form.' That, in the right context (which the reader should supply), is not misleading; both 'simplified' and 'abstract' are words that embrace more than one possibility. Of one obvious kind of simplicity—it represents an attitude that simplifies—he is a master: I am thinking of the 'Introduction' to *Songs of Innocence* and of the poem that follows, 'The

Echoing Green'. The touch in these poems is so sure because, while what each communicates is presented as an actuality of human experience that is for Blake a genuine and important value, he has his vivid knowledge of what they exclude, and knows that he has it in him to write 'The Tyger'.

The emotions and intuitions informing that poem belong to 'experience' in inverted commas—to 'experience', then, in a sense that doesn't suggest the reassuring. The unreassuringness is not a mere matter of the power with which the fearful menace of the tiger is evoked; and what we so unmistakably get also is not only the intuition of the cruel potentiality as having an awe-inspiring beauty; these carry with them the unquestioning realization that what the tiger symbolizes is a fact of life, and necessary. The 'necessary' is a recognition that a fact is a fact; it is a recognition that entails a troubled sense of the nature of energy—which life cannot do without. There is no protest. The essential attitude—one neither of protest nor of acceptance, but of constatation—is given in a question that is not so much interrogative as an utterance of profound awe:

> Did he who made the Lamb make thee?

'The Tyger', then, though no doubt there is some sense in which it might be called the product of a labour of simplification, exhibits marked complexity. It is complexity of a kind that couldn't have been achieved in a poetry describable with Eliot's intention as 'contemporary with Gray and Collins'. For, to arrive at the 'great technical accomplishment' that Eliot credits him with, Blake had to escape from the 'positive culture'. That is, to become the poet his genius meant him to be, to free his genius, he had to escape from the language that had 'undergone the discipline of prose'. That discipline—about which Eliot shows a paradoxical naïvety when he says: 'To have the virtues of good prose is the first and minimum requirement of good poetry'—makes the map the reality. It implies that, essentially, there is only the one mode of literary expression: you have your ideas; you get them clear; you find *les mots justes* to fit them with from among the large words fixed by definition in the dictionary; and you put these words together according to the rules of grammar and logic.

This prescription holds for all purposes that could belong to literature. But the major poet's creativity is heuristic; it is concerned with discovery, or new realization, such as the discipline precludes; with apprehensions and intuitions that of their nature can't be *stated*. That is his importance. I called Eliot's dictum paradoxical because one way of intimating the nature of the originality that gives him importance in history is that he created, and justified, a poetic that makes nonsense of the dictum. That is why in the 1920s Dean Inge, Platonist, scholar and gentleman, called Eliot a 'literary Bolshevik'. What the charge meant was, among other things, that Eliot's poetry didn't make sense—that it didn't lend itself in the ordinary way to paraphrase of the prose sense. It was unintelligible, or offensive, to persons educated in terms of Victorian or Edwardian taste and expectation.

The complexity of 'The Tyger' means that it encourages the idea that it could be paraphrased almost as little as 'Marina' does (I take an obvious but comparatively simple Eliotic example). The poem, of course, is one of those of Blake's which make an immediately compelling imaginative impact. I have said that it conveys no protest; it constates. But what it constates is a fact that is a value, and the problem constituted by the fact that there are other values gets its recognition in the poem itself:

> Did he who made the Lamb make thee?

That might have stood as an epigraph to *Songs of Innocence and of Experience* printed as one creative work—which it is as surely as *Four Quartets* (for all the differences between the modes of Eliot's unity and of Blake's). The problem pointed to in the pregnant epigram of the question is formidably complex; it is presented by the inclusive whole, which insists implicitly that there can be no pointing with epigrammatic neatness to any solution. The constituent 'Songs' vary immensely in kind, convention, and poetic quality, in a way that makes it important not to forget that what they form is more than a pair of parallel aggregations, and that one must not see them or try to see them as merely illustrations of an antithesis or pair of opposing themes.

Some of them, like 'The Tyger', are, standing by themselves, poems of a high order—for instance, 'London', 'The Sick Rose', 'Ah! Sunflower', 'The Echoing Green'. On the other hand (I take my examples from *Experience*, in the arrangement that Blake once prescribed) we have, with the pregnant two-stanza concentration of 'Infant Sorrow' between them as a foil, 'A Little Boy Lost' and 'The Schoolboy'. No one would think of picking either of those six-stanza poems, with their developed explicitness, for an anthology of the Blakean strength. Indeed it is common, I think, to feel some uneasiness, even if in comment this is half-suppressed, at—'A Little Boy Lost' being in question (to take that)—the implausibility of the utterance ascribed to the child:

> 'Nought loves another as itself,
> Nor venerates another so,
> Nor is it possible to Thought
> A greater than itself to know:
>
> 'And, Father, how can I love you
> Or any of my brothers more?
> I love you like the little bird
> That picks up crumbs around the door.'

78

But the tendency to charge Blake with implausibility, banality, too direct and simple explicitness, and sentimentality, can hardly survive the realization, verified and confirmed in the reading and re-reading, that the inclusive work *is* the essential whole that Blake intended. For though, when we revert to the comparison with *Four Quartets*, there isn't a close parallel to be invoked, there *is* an essential analogical bearing. The great diversity of mode, method, and attack is necessary to what is undertaken—and achieved. The poems to which one would not grant anthological status don't stand single, alone, and apart. Nor, it can be added, perhaps not altogether unnecessarily, do those which convey Blake's basic intuitions and reactions, whether of positive certainties or of abhorrence, in terms of the creatively evoked, uncommented, and unquestionable immediate. And the diversity is really diversity; it is not reducible to the difference between the poetically strong and the less irresistibly poetic; that is, to the difference between 'The Schoolboy' and 'London', which follows it.

If we look at 'A Little Boy Lost', we see that immediately before comes 'The Garden of Love', one of those simpler poems of 'Experience' which, while they are not bait for the anthologist, we appreciate at once as playing acceptably their part in the thematic build-up. Before 'The Garden of Love' comes the emblematic quatrain called 'The Lily', which follows 'Ah! Sunflower'. And that is one of those miracles of Blakean pregnancy ('The Sick Rose' is another) which need to be discussed. I shall not discuss it now; under these conditions there isn't time. I ought to read out, as leading back to it from 'The Schoolboy', 'Infant Sorrow', 'A Little Boy Lost', 'The Garden of Love', and 'The Lily'. But there isn't time, and, in any case, to stop at 'Ah! Sunflower' would be arbitrary. As things are, with my case to enforce about the nature of *Songs of Innocence and of Experience*, I can only hope to have suggested to some effect how one would proceed with a student-group that is devoting a number of meetings to Blake.

In that work he offers no solution of the problems it presents. But one mustn't suggest that he does no more than convey his sense of the complexity. He does that with an insight and a power that make it plain why he should have incurred his indebtedness to Shakespeare: no other writer could have served him, in his formative years, so well. For, as Eliot puts it, he had a 'profound interest in human emotions', and the 'profound knowledge' of them that Eliot credits him with was inevitably a profound insight into the complexity of human relations. In 'Innocence' these are a simple matter, and love is trust and security. But in 'Experience' love involves the complexities of sex; it is the 'rose', and the rose is the prey of the invisible worm that flies in the night, in the howling storm. Love, and not merely sexual love, tends in its diverse forms to possessiveness, and jealousy is for Blake an inexhaustible theme; it plays a major part in the 'howling storm' that one thinks of as raging through the prophecies. Blake, nevertheless, who sees that belief in energy, which is dangerous, goes necessarily with belief in life, stands up with angry spontaneity for desire, the anger being directed against priests, their religion, and moral codes in general.

Songs of Innocence and of Experience does indeed present human life as a frightening problem. What, then, can one say to enforce one's judgement that the effect of the poetry is very far from the inducing of an acceptance of human defeat? One can testify that the poet himself is not frightened, and, further, that there is no malevolence, no anti-human animus, no reductive bent, in his realism: nothing could be more unlike the effect of Swift. The answer is to be found *there*. Blake believes in human creativity, as Eliot in *Four Quartets* so paradoxically—and significantly—does not. His belief is not a mere matter of explicit affirmation; it is implicit in the art. There is explicitness, too, again and again, in that—in the poetic presentation; the implicit and the explicit confirm and enforce one another. So there need be no hesitation about invoking the explicitly formulated as, in the collected volume, one finds it in other than creative forms.

Though Eliot says '*The Marriage of Heaven and Hell* is naked philosophy', the comprehensive statement of Blake's 'philosophy' I might be expected to conclude with couldn't be drawn from what is found there—a summary of the substance wouldn't provide it. I put 'philosophy' in quotation marks because I don't like the word in this use of it: Blake is peculiarly exposed to falsifying expectations and wrong-headed cults that it may very well encourage. Let me say bluntly that I am not grateful to Yeats for inaugurating the kind of Blake research of which Miss Kathleen Raine is the recognized high-priestess in our time. Blind to Blake's genius, it generates blindness, and perpetuates a cult that, whatever it serves, doesn't serve Blake or humanity. The notion that by a devout study of Blake's symbolism a key can be found that will open to us a supreme esoteric wisdom is absurd; and to emphasize in that spirit the part played in his life's work by Swedenborg, Boehme, Paracelsus, Orphic tradition, Gnosticism, and a 'perennial philosophy' is to deny what makes him important.

He was very intelligent and kept his mind constantly informed and in training, showing more than competence in relation to what was then modern thought—the thought of his time, as well as mastery of his own, which was astonishingly—and centrally—original. His habitual use of the names of Newton and Locke was not the expression of *une manie*; it was an insistence on human creativity—the creativity of life; a necessary insistence that is not less in place today. He insisted in an age of Lockean common sense that perception was not passive, and that there was a continuity from the inherent creativity of perception to the creativity, trained and conscious, of the artist. 'Jesus was an artist,' he says. That remark implies, of course, a conception of art different from either Pater's or T. S. Eliot's—a conception that seems to me sound; at any rate, I share it. It implies a conception of human creativity that is at the same time a conception of human responsibility; and one aspect of Blake's living importance is that he compels us to realize fully and clearly what 'human responsibility' means.

I must here refer to the distinction he makes between the 'identity' and the 'selfhood' in the individual human being. He was never in danger of forgetting that only in the individual being is life concretely 'there'. The 'selfhood' is that which asserts itself and seeks to possess from within its self-enclosure. The 'identity' is the individual being as the disinterested focus of life; it was as 'identity' that Lawrence's Tom Brangwen 'knew he did not belong to himself'. Blake was voicing the same recognition when he said of his paintings and designs: 'Though I call them mine, I know that they are not mine.' The reply made to Crabb Robinson's inquiry 'in what light he viewed the great question concerning the Divinity of Jesus Christ' is a parallel formulation: 'He said—*He is the only God*— But then he added—"And so am I and so are you".'[4] Crabb Robinson goes on: 'Now he had just before (and that occasioned my question) been speaking of the errors of Jesus Christ.' Blake, who knew he wasn't infallible, had no tendency to mistake himself for God.

It was in this combined clarity and intensity of conviction that the sense of human responsibility he so signally represents was manifested. There is no paradox here—or in what follows: it is a question of giving the due force to the phrase 'human responsibility'. The conviction was a creative drive, and it led him, in his most ambitious attempts, the major prophecies, into difficulties that defeated his art. He takes up in them a challenge so formidably presented in the totality of *Songs of Innocence and of Experience*. He commits himself to what it is customary to describe, with a good deal of reason, as epic treatment, although Shakespeare counts for essentially more in it than Milton does: it is not merely the verse that is positively un-Miltonic.

There is a book—one of the few guides to which one can concede a certain credit balance of usefulness—called *Blake's Humanism*.[5] The word 'humanism', at any rate at Cambridge, suggests a form of hubristic enlightenment ('Cambridge Humanism'), but what the author intends by it is to emphasize (rightly) the characteristic of Blake's thought expressed in his insistence that Man, concretely 'there' only in the individual human being and governed by his knowledge that he doesn't belong to himself, is responsible for determining what his responsibility is. That is indistinguishable from determining what he himself is in relation to what he ought to be (according to the *ahnung*, the divination, he at the same time develops, tests, and sharpens). It was Blake's genius to be—I impose an anti-positivist, or anti-pseudo-scientific, sense on the word 'psychology'—a great psychologist. The characters, then, in his attempts at Shakespearian epic, are separated aspects,

---

[4] Bentley, *Records*, p. 310. [5] John Beer, *Blake's Humanism*, Manchester, 1968.

or constituents, or potentialities of complete human nature, which is thought of as the whole inclusive essential Man. The difficulty besetting such an undertaking is that characters in dramatico-epic action and interaction must inevitably be imaginable as actors—that is, as full human persons. The consequence for Blake's long poems is that, while specialist scholars offer to guide us diagrammatically through their bewildering complexities, no diagram provides the help we need: the fissions, coalescences, doublings, overlappings, and psychologico-symbolic subtleties of changing interrelation wear down our powers of attention.

To make this criticism is in a way to pay Blake a compliment: he has a profound insight into human nature and *la condition humaine*, and is the master of an incomparably subtle psychological realism. Only the novel as represented by the concept one adduces with the names of Dickens, George Eliot, Tolstoy, Conrad, and Lawrence could have rendered such anti-Cartesian insight and psychological mastery in successful art, and to blame Blake for not having invented the subsequent 'modern novel' would be absurd. As it is, the effect to which he learnt from Shakespeare is a marvel of genius.

But it was not by the problem of 'Life and lives' alone that Blake was beaten in his major works. An irreconcilable foe to the 'positive culture', yet not accepting human defeat, he inevitably in that age, having to explain to himself the necessity of the creative battle he preached and practised, invoked the Christian tradition of the Fall. The τέλος in view, the goal and upshot he posited as the end that gave the battle its meaning, was the reversal of the Fall. In the variously presented action that makes the poems epic, it ensues on the culminating Apocalypse. But Blake can no more know, or imagine, what follows the reversal of the Fall than he can what preceded it. In essence as he posits it (and, for all his offers of a transcendentalizing ecstasy, he can do no more than posit), it is the restoration of the Eternal Man—who is also Woman, for in Eternity the sexes are abolished. It is in keeping with the Blakean habit of symbolism that Jerusalem, the Eternal Man, is a city too.

For us, of course, it isn't the supreme reality attained at last, the really real; it is a plunge into wordy and boring unreality. Human reality, the human condition to which art belongs, is inescapably a matter of individual human beings in their relations with one another, the only conceivable way in which Man could be 'there'. Whatever the promptings of religious or metaphysical thought may be, the creative agents of human insight and wisdom must resist them when they incite to the presentation of the unimaginable. That is what Lawrence meant when he said: 'Blake was one of those ghastly obscene knowers.' The immediately relevant point I have to make is that, in postulating a τέλος, a *terminus ad quem*, Blake was involving himself in a fundamental contradiction. In his insistence on a human creativity that means human responsibility he was repudiating all forms of determinism; to posit an ultimate end ('In my beginning is my end') that gives significance to the creative effort, being its final cause, is to gainsay the repudiation.

My emphasis is not on the adverse criticism, but on the magnificent, and (for us) very timely, rightness this leaves exposed and clear for recognition. The creative *nisus* is essentially heuristic; the *ahnung* that informs it is not to be identified with the apprehension of a τέλος or ultimate goal. The new knowledge and the new sense of the real to which it leads involve a new apprehension of possibility, creative impulsion, and goal. Blake's reaction against Newton and Locke represents the really momentous new development associated with the complex spiritual and cultural eruption that we call the Romantic Revolution— eruption of ideas, impulsions, and intransigently conscious human needs. His compellingly presented conception of an ultimate human responsibility that, while the reverse of hubristic, manifests itself in human self-reliance—bold, yet deferential towards the life whose source is not to be possessed (though we may cut ourselves off from it and perish)—recommends itself peculiarly to our needs at this crisis of human history.

The crisis to which I refer is, in one very important aspect, that which Marjorie Grene points to here, in the Introduction to *The Knower and the Known*:

> We have come, or are coming, at last to the end of this epoch, the epoch presided over by the concepts of Newtonian cosmology and Newtonian method. We are in the midst of a new philosophical revolution, a revolution in which, indeed, the new physics too has had due influence, but a revolution founded squarely on the disciplines concerned with life: on biology, psychology, sociology, history, even theology and art criticism. Seventeenth-century thinking had to free itself from the bonds of scholastic discipline, and we have had to free ourselves from the bonds of Newtonian abstraction, to dare, not only to manipulate abstractions, to calculate and predict and falsify, but to *understand*. The revolution before us is a revolution of life against dead nature, and of understanding against the calculi of logical machines.

I should add of course (and underline) to Marjorie Grene's list of disciplines the discipline of thought that belongs to intelligent literary study—philosophers are always weak in dealing with language. My own preoccupation is not focused for any intellectual realm or specialist discipline such as the word 'philosophy' suggests—though Marjorie Grene herself intimates that the revolution she has in mind must involve very much more than philosophy. We may study the essentially Blakean conception that is peculiarly relevant by focusing on Los as he figures in *Jerusalem*, and inquiring into the significance of his becoming, as he does, the central figure in that poem. Blake there, *almost* closing a firmly explicit grasp on the intuition that makes him so important to us, can represent Los, human creativity in the fallen human condition (for 'fallen' put 'rising'), as working creatively though unpossessed of any vision of an ultimate goal. But, as prophetic poet with Swedenborg, Boehme, and Milton behind him, he can't help feeling that he must himself aspire to a clarity and certitude of such vision. Yet the idea of possessing an achieved knowledge of ultimate solutions and ultimate goals is not for poets or artists, or for those among us who, figured by Los, know that their business is to get the conscious and full human responsibility that the crisis of the human world calls for awakened and vindicated.

I ought then in closing to be quite explicit about that conception of our responsibility which, given in Los, represents the essential insight that makes Blake so important to us now. For Blake, the enemy of Locke and Newton, might have inspired Marjorie Grene's account of our need, and brings a good deal more than endorsement to the wisdom of Michael Polanyi, the scientist–philosopher whose pupil Marjorie Grene was. Few educated persons will dispute the reasonableness of the assumption that there was once a time when there was, in the world of nature, no life. Life emerged, and no scientist or philosopher has begun to explain how, or by what causation—apart from the persistent offer to explain it away. Though we have to recognize that Darwin's life testifies to the existence of intelligence and purpose, his theory of evolution offered to dispense with the need for those words. Nevertheless Collingwood, a very intelligent and conscientious and well-informed witness, reported only (so to speak) the other day:

> This at any rate seems clear: that since modern science is now committed to a view of the physical universe as finite, certainly in space and probably in time, the activity which this same science identifies with matter cannot be a self-created or ultimately self-dependent activity. The world of nature or physical world as a whole, on any such view, must ultimately depend for its existence on something other than itself.[6]

That would seem to be closely related to the intuition, unmistakably and inevitably asking to be called 'religious' as the great writer conveys it, expressed in Blake's insistence that he does not belong to himself.

Essential or Blakean responsibility manifests itself in the full accepting recognition that the directing *ahnung* implicit in life and the *nisus* that has led to the achieving of mind and anticipatory apprehension and initiative are to be thought of as, in the world we know (Los's world), pre-eminently represented by humanity. They *are*, as Blake conceives it, human responsibility. There is all the difference between that and the cock-a-hoop euphoria of those who tell us that Man has conquered nature, and that there is now nothing that emancipated human purpose can't achieve—not excepting the creation of life. What human creativity *has* created, and continually re-creates in response to change, is the human world, and it entails of its very nature the recognition that (in Collingwood's words) it

---

[6] *The Idea of Nature*, Oxford, 1945, p. 155.

84

'must ultimately depend for its existence on something other than itself'. For, as Polanyi insists, true creativity, like perception, is never arbitrary, but always seeks the real—which it knows that it can never with complete certainty, still less exhaustively or finally, know.

I am very much aware that there is too much assertion in what I have contrived to say about Blake in an hour. But my aim itself was limiting. For I think that some such initial presentment of one's claim for Blake, and of the supporting critical argument, would be necessary, whether what was to follow proposed itself as a book, or as a series of student sessions with the volume of Blake in front of us. The thorough grounding, testing, and refining of critical judgement and conclusion in a scrutiny of the data, a process necessarily long-drawn-out and distractingly complex, would thus be made possible.

V

BLAKE'S FRAME OF LANGUAGE

Josephine Miles

How does a poet surprise his faithful readers? By what he faithfully says, what is therefore inescapably present in the Concordance of his work? In the Preface of the Blake *Concordance*,[1] the editor, David Erdman, writes, 'We may have expected to find *man*, *love*, *eternal*, and *earth* among Blake's most used words, but not *death* so near the top or *night* so far ahead of *day*. And among those used only once we may be struck to see how many were memorably effective in their single impacts.' By a single *regale* or a repeated *eternal* may our reading seem confirmed, yet by a host of *deaths* and *nights* called into question? As a matter of fact, it is most-used *eternal* that should be surprising, because there are very few three-syllable words in the major language of English poetry.[2] But that is a metrical story, well treated by Alicia Ostriker in *Vision and Verse in William Blake*. Can we say with surprise after reading Blake, 'I had not thought death had undone so many?' Whether the surprise is induced by a planned or unplanned bias of writing or of reading, it may lead deeper to questions about the whole nature of the poet's work.

A Concordance, in giving line-contexts for the substantial half of a poet's vocabulary, the other half being particles of connection or pronominal reference, gives not only the range of usage of each word but also the range of distribution and frequency, how many times, how widely, recurrent, in what specific texts. For most poets, especially for Blake, there appear to be a few words, perhaps fifty, so essential to expression that they make up in number of occurrences nearly a fifth of the whole text. At the other extreme, the six or seven thousand words used only once to ten times apiece amount to another fifth.

It is the tendency of critics to feel that a word used strongly once can be more powerful than a word used over and over so much that one takes it for granted. But it is also true that the most-repeated words have their significance in providing the underlying fabric, the persistent content of the poetry. My pre-concordance study of Blake's major language[3] based on the chief content-words in a thousand lines made up from the first two hundred lines of major poems from *Poetical*

---

[1] Cornell University Press, Ithaca, N.Y., 1966.
[2] See G. K. Zipf, *The Psycho-Biology of Language*, Houghton Mifflin Co., Boston, Mass., 1935.
[3] *Eras and Modes in English Poetry*, rev. ed., University of California Press, Berkeley and Los Angeles, 1964.

Sketches to *Jerusalem*, established a list much like that which the *Concordance* has revealed for the whole twenty thousand lines, making clear the homogeneity and consistency of Blake's usage. Some strengths are related to simple beginnings, the early pastorals, for example; others, to later technical increases, like *spectre*, and the power of *Jerusalem*. But in the main the strengths are in continuities.

Because the *Concordance* lists separately the plurals of nouns, parts of verbs, and comparisons of adjectives, its list of frequencies for each word needs to be reorganized in order to gain a picture of major content. Though the differences between plurals and singulars may be formally significant, for a general sense of reference we need to combine *hill* with *hills*, for example, or *man* with *men*, or *come* with *came*, or *love* with *loved*. So the list of major terms I give here shows more adjectives, more verbs with their sum of parts (except for participles, which I take as adjectival), and more nouns with strong plurals, because of the higher totals of combined forms. Further, the *Concordance* prints frequencies but not contexts for the pronouns and connectives which bulk the largest, and does not separate poetry from prose for them, so that the reader must pursue his own sense of structure in Blake's rich prepositional quality.

What is this major substance thus structured? It consists of thirty or so nouns, fifteen or so verbs, fifteen or so adjectives, a number of main adjectives unusually large among poets. The nouns are human or superhuman figures: *man*, *son*, *daughter*, *child*, then *God* and *gods*, and *Satan*, then *spectre* and *form*, in a setting of *earth* and *world* and *heaven*, in *rock*, *mountain*, *cloud*, *fire*, and *light*, in a time of *day*, *night*, *eternity*, with the bodily *forms* of *eye*, *tear*, *hand*, *foot*, *voice*, and the concepts and feelings of *death*, *love*, *life*, *joy*; these thirty chief nouns are modified by the dozen or so chief adjectives *all*, *no*, *every*, *one*, *none*, *eternal*, *dark*, *sweet*, *human*, *divine*, *bright*, *deep*, *golden*, *little*, in their dozen or so chief actions *see*, *stand*, *rise*, *know*, *come*, *go*, *love*, *let*, *say*, *hear*, *behold*. As a whole, one can generalize from the *Concordance* much as I did earlier, that Blake's most traditional materials provide words of scene and feeling and perceiving, moving away from such classical generalities as *nature*, *youth*, *fate*, *virtue*, *thought*, toward the nineteenth century's *little*, *child*, *daughter*, *death*, *earth*, *weep*, and Blake's special *eternal*, *sleep*, *cloud*, *form*.

His colours *black*, *golden*, *red* are ballad terms, his *eternal* and *divine* eighteenth century, his *voice* and *cloud* seventeenth-century Biblical, especially in the Miltonic line from Sylvester's and Spenser's observing *hear*, *look*, Crashaw's *black*, *dark*, *heaven*, *fire*, *night*, Vaughan's *cloud*, *death*, *sun*, *weep*, *sleep*. In combining the low language of satire with the high of prophecy, Blake followed the tradition of many eighteenth-century odes on superstition: scenes, anatomies, feelings, and the many specific spiders, webs, spectres, clouds, like those in the poems of Samuel Wesley as early as 1700.

Far higher than the most frequent referential *all*, *men*, *Los*, *see*, are the thousands of particles, *the*, and *of*, and a dozen others which even in their bulk should not be ignored, as Rostrevor Hamilton's *Tell-Tale Article* has shown[4] and as any thorough contrast of pronominal or prepositional uses could well show. My study of the connectives, in *Style and Proportion*,[5] suggests that Blake is a giant user of locational phrases in the tradition of Biblical prose, *of*, *in*, *to*, *with*, *at*, *on*, *from*, *by*, and then, only less than a standard group of relative *whats* and *whichs* and a few logical *and* and *buts*, of another dominant set of connectives, *around* and *round*, *upon*, *over*, *down*, *up*, *through*, *beneath*, *forth*, *out*, *among*, *away*, which suit his chief verbs of presence and perception and give him high position in the eighteenth-century poetics of place signified by Thomson's innovative *around* and *beneath* and Gray's *amidst*, in what can be called the Spenserian-Miltonic tradition. For poetry in English, Blake's is an extremist structure, heightening eighteenth-century locational terminology, as Donne heightened seventeenth-century logical terminology, intensifying the spatial as Donne intensified the temporal.

Where do the chief terms lead us? The *Poetical Sketches* begin with embodied seasons, their joy of limb and voice, their daughters, blossoms, songs; the sceptre and iron car of monster winter, his seat upon the cliffs. Evening's fair-haired star shines on wolf and lamb, morning light rises from the chambers of the east, her feet upon the hills. 'Chill death withdraws his hand', 'the prince of love', 'His face is fair as heav'n', 'innocent eyes', 'make weep the eyes of day', 'light doth seize my brain', 'the voice of Heaven I hear', 'that sweet village', 'more than mortal fire', 'on chrystal rocks', 'children cry for bread', 'The armies stand', 'The King is seen raging afar', 'The earth doth faint', 'round the circle of the world', 'have thy soft piteous eyes beheld'. Each of the *Poetical Sketches* sets its major terms in the embodiments of form in feeling and scene. So also the *Songs of Innocence and Experience*: 'On a cloud I saw a child', 'he wept with joy to hear', 'the Shepherd's sweet lot', 'The Sun does arise', 'Softest clothing, wooly, bright', 'there God does live'.

Throughout his work Blake establishes the major terms as central. Poem after poem they recur, *death*, *dark*, *daughters*, *children*, *mountains*, *man*, *fire*, *cloud*, in varying contexts. In *Tiriel*, 'But now his eyes were dark'ned and his wife fading in death.' And in *The Book of Thel*, 'The daughters of the Seraphim led round their sunny flocks . . . / "Why fade these children of the spring, born but to smile and fall?"' And in *The French Revolution*, 'The dead brood over Europe . . . / Sick the mountains, and all their vineyards weep . . .'. In *The Marriage of Heaven and Hell*: 'The just man rages in the wilds . . . / Rintrah roars and shakes his fires in the burden'd air: / Hungry clouds swag on the deep.'

In *America*, 'The shadowy Daughter of Urthona stood before red Orc, / When

[4] Oxford University Press, New York, 1950.   [5] Little, Brown and Co., Boston, Mass., 1967.

fourteen suns had faintly journey'd o'er his dark abode; . . .' In *Europe*, ' "Five windows light the cavern'd Man: thro' one he breathes the air; / "Thro' one hears music of the spheres; thro' one the eternal vine . . .".' *The [First] Book of Urizen*, 'Of the primeval Priest's assum'd power . . .'. *The Book of Ahania*, 'And his right hand burns red in its cloud . . .' In the *Song of Los*, the vast geography: 'Adam stood in the garden of Eden / And Noah on the mountains of Ararat; / They saw Urizen give his Laws to the Nations / By the hands of the children of Los.' In *The Four Zoas*, the song of wrath: 'The Song of the Aged Mother which shook the heavens with wrath, / Hearing the march of long resounding, strong heroic Verse / Marshall'd in order for the day of Intellectual Battle.' In *Milton*, 'To Justify the Ways of God to Men', the question, 'And did the Countenance Divine / Shine forth upon our clouded hills? . . .'. And 'Daughters of Beulah! Muses who inspire the Poet's Song . . .'. And in *Jerusalem*, the joining anatomy, theology, cosmology: 'Again he speaks in thunder and in fire! / Thunder of Thought, & flames of fierce desire: / Even from the depths of Hell his voice I hear / Within the unfathom'd caverns of my Ear. . . . / "Awake! awake O sleeper of the land of shadows . . .".'

These bardic beginnings, these sweeps of the strings, are not all of Blake; they are not the vital minutiae of Blake; but they establish the scope of his steady reference in his major language. In the light of these beginnings, the siftings of the *Concordance* are understandable, the grains of sand do contain the heavens they reveal. On the cosmic stage—but this is an alien term—in the cosmic landscape, loom the bodily forms of human passions, the druidic identities of earth, anatomy, and belief. All the eternal, divine, and human, dark, bright, and deep forms of Man, god, Satan, spectre, son, daughter, child, in hand, foot, head, voice, eye, tear, joy, over the earth and heaven, mountain, rock, in cloud and light, shadow and fire, come, go, rise, stand to see, behold, and hear, to know, love, and weep. They move in the *states* of which Blake speaks, of vision rather than of action, in Laocoönish coils caught and beheld.

In this great scene are the smaller shapes we treasure, babe, lamb, worm, flower, the London streets, the middle vocabulary in all its variety, between the uncommon once-words and the essential always-words, ever-forms. General forms have their vitality in particulars, as *Jerusalem* says: yet in Gothic, not Grecian, living forms; forms cannot be annihilated, and divine humanity is the only general and universal form. The little reside in the bosoms of larger, and time moves by days and nights in the forms of eons.

Within the spatial frame is there a basic structure of contraries—counter, opposed, diametrically different, incompatible? Blake wrote often of contraries. Did he set up a contrarious structure for his poetry in the opposing of major terms? The primary *death* and *night* which surprise Erdman at their highest level of usage equal to that of the major proper names Los, Albion, and Urizen, and of *man* himself, meet a countering *life* and *day* not much more than half as frequent. The next strongest *love* has positive support in *joy*, but no major counter *hate*, *sorrow*, *tear*, *fear* except at lower levels of frequency. *Man* and *God*, *man* and *child*, *God* and *Satan*, *son* and *daughter*, *earth* or *world* and *heaven*, *earth* and *fire*, are contrary in a different sense, in pairings asymmetrical. *Light* and *shadow*, *time* and *eternity* make fairer pairs. *Eye*, *head*, *foot* are anatomies not seeming opposed. The other major nouns, some of these most special to Blake, are *voice*, *form*, *cloud*, *spectre*, *power*, *self*, and in these we may see some contrast of *form* to *spectre*, *cloud* to *rock* and *mountain*. In all, the diameters seem to suggest places of reference, high and low, substantial and insubstantial, rather than contrasting feelings or persons, a vertical rather than a horizontal *agon*.

Action too is not toe to toe. *See* is primary, along with *behold*; *hearing* and *knowing* are supplementary. Actions of motion are *come*, *go*, and *stand*; *let* is important along with *say*. Otherwise, *love* and *weep* are major, not necessarily contrary. These are verbs of the paintings—being there, seeing, expressing attitudes.

The chief epithet *all*, Blake's most frequent referential term, is countered by *no* or by *one* at only minor levels—no contest in the logic! The chief descriptive *eternal* is supported by *divine*, perhaps then countered by *human*. *Sweet*, *cold*, *deep*, *little*, *golden*, receive little contrast, except for some *great* and *black*; what happens to Milton's major *high* in its line from *deep*? *Cold* has little *hot* or *warm*. The one clear pair is *dark–bright*, with *dark* consistently the stronger. A lesser *loud* and *silent* support the noun *voice* and verb *hear*; *good* is lesser also, though important in the prose; it sets up little *bad* in moral opposition.

Blake gives us clearly strong contrast in visible light and audible sound, in conditions of perceiving; otherwise, we must look not to objects and persons but to qualities and forces if we are to find the nature of his conflict at its major scale.

Qualities, adjectives, as in Wallace Stevens's third world of perception, carry the power upward, from Hell and Earth to Beulah and Heaven in a dynamic of spiral motion, not classical and not Hegelian, not Greek but Gothic, as Blake says, forging forms on earth to rise high into eternal forms. For the engraver they must be engravable, to be seen by vegetable eyes; they do not win over or lose to each other but ascend out of the struggle which is scarcely even a contest.

> All Human Forms identified, even Tree, Metal, Earth & Stone: all
> Human Forms identified, living, going forth & returning wearied
> Into the Planetary lives of Years, Months, Days & Hours; reposing,
> And then Awaking into his Bosom in the Life of Immortality.

> (J 99; K, p. 747.)

In her helpful 'Visionary Forms: Blake's Prophetic Art and the Pictorial

Tradition' (unpublished dissertation, University of California, Berkeley, 1966), Margaret Shook clarifies the linear direction of the poetry. Blake's 'bounding line' recovered the clear and the universal from hazy blurs of pre-Romanticism. His particularity is not object, but species, or clearly delineated human part like Vasari's 'feet, hands, hair, and beards' (*Lives of the Most Eminent Painters, Sculptors, and Architects*, 1550).[6]

> Nature & Art in this together Suit:
> What is Most Grand is always most Minute.
> Rubens thinks Tables, Chairs & Stools are Grand,
> But Rafael thinks A Head, a foot, a hand.
>
> (*A Pretty Epigram*, K, p. 547.)

> And this is the manner of the Sons of Albion in their strength:
> They take the Two Contraries which are call'd Qualities, with which
> Every Substance is clothed: they name them Good & Evil
> From them they make an Abstract, which is a Negation
> Not only of the Substance from which it is derived,
> A murderer of its own Body, but also a murderer
> Of every Divine Member: it is the Reasoning Power,
> An Abstract objecting power that Negatives every thing.
> This is the Spectre of Man, the Holy Reasoning Power,
> And in its Holiness is closed the Abomination of Desolation.
>
> (*J* 10; K, p. 629.)

Of the Roman soldiers in his sublime painting 'The Ancient Britons', now lost, Blake says in the *Descriptive Catalogue* that each shows 'a different character, and a different expression of fear, or revenge, or envy, or blank horror, or amazement, or devout wonder and unresisting awe' (K, p. 580). Fuseli[7] relates these types of energies in various Greek heroes to 'emanations of energy that re-unite in one splendid centre fixed in Achilles'. These types are thus not generalities; they are a sort of shared particularity of type, as the eighteenth century would see it. That is, as human minds would see it. 'Mental Things are alone Real; what is call'd Corporeal, Nobody Knows of its Dwelling Place: it is in Fallacy, & its Existence an Imposture. . . . Error is Created. Truth is Eternal. Error, or Creation, will be Burned up, & then, & not till Then, Truth or Eternity will appear' (*VLJ*, K, p. 617). It is here that Blake asserts his vision of the sun not as 'a round disk of fire' but as 'an Innumerable company of the Heavenly host' (K, p. 617).

---

[6] *A Documentary History of Art*, ed. Elizabeth Gilmore Holt, Doubleday & Co., Garden City, New York, 1958, ii. 27.

[7] *Lectures on Painting by the Royal Academicians*, ed. Ralph N. Wornum, Henry G. Bohn, London, 1848, p. 359.

Yet early and late he can think of nature formally if he thinks of every eternal form.

The great and golden rule of art, as well as of life, is this: That the more distinct, sharp, and wirey the bounding line, the more perfect the work of art; . . . What is it that builds a house and plants a garden, but the definite and determinate? What is it that distinguishes honesty from knavery, but the hard and wirey line of rectitude and certainty in the actions and intentions? Leave out this line, and you leave out life itself; all is chaos again, and the line of the almighty must be drawn out upon it before man or beast can exist.

(A Descriptive Catalogue, K, p. 585.)

Idealized type is allegorical image. 'Moderns wish to draw figures without lines, and with great and heavy shadows; are not shadows more unmeaning than lines, and more heavy? O who can doubt this!' (*A Descriptive Catalogue*, K, p. 577).

The hard and wiry line is a springing, not a balancing, line, and the dynamics is not so much dramatic or narrative as lyric, as both Fisch and Hartman have recently shown,[8] rising from shadow to substance in form, from earth to heaven, from fire's heat to fire's light as the dualism is burned away. So the perspective of the poems is from death and from night and from son and man, and from earth, these being Blake's major nouns, moving towards less common life, form, heaven, joy, day, light, eternity by way of the body and light of fire and the qualities dark, sweet, human toward qualities bright, eternal, divine.

> . . . These are the Sons of Los: These and Visions of Eternity,
> But we see only as it were the hem of their garments
> When with our vegetable eyes we view these wondrous Visions.

(Milton 26. 10–12; K, p. 512.)

Form is true Nature—

> Whatever can be Created can be Annihilated: Forms cannot:
> The Oak is cut down by the Ax, the Lamb falls by the Knife,
> But their Forms Eternal Exist For-ever.

(Milton 32. 36–8; K, p. 522.)

The Oak dies as well as the Lettuce, but Its Eternal Image & Individuality never dies, but renews by its seed; just so the Imaginative Image returns by the seed of Contemplative Thought . . . (*VLJ*, K, p. 605.)

With Fuseli's thought that 'In forms alone the idea of existence can be rendered

---

[8] *William Blake: Essays for S. Foster Damon*, Brown University Press, Providence, R.I., 1969. See also in this volume Robert F. Gleckner, 'Blake's Verbal Technique'.

permanent',[9] Blake would have fire and forge hammer out forms even of wrongs

> That he who will not defend Truth may be compell'd to defend
> A Lie: that he may be snared and caught and snared and taken:
> That Enthusiasm and Life may not cease . . .
>
> (*J* 9. 29–31; K, p. 628.)

'Now intreating Tears & Sighs. / O when will the Morning rise?' (*The Golden Net*, K, p. 424). The true vision is a lowly and night-time vision:

> God Appears & God is Light
> To those poor Souls who dwell in Night,
> But does a Human Form Display
> To those who Dwell in Realms of day.
>
> (*Auguries of Innocence*, K, p. 434.)

Thus the topography of the poetics beyond night:

> For above Time's troubled Fountains
> On the Great Atlantic Mountains,
> In my Golden House on high,
> There they Shine Eternally.
>
> (Fragment, K, p. 558.)

Thus the paradox and asymmetry:

> To be in a Passion you Good may do,
> But no Good if a Passion is in you.
>
> (*Auguries of Innocence*, K, p. 433.)

> I slept in the dark
> In the silent night
> I murmur'd my fears
> And I felt delight.
>
> In the morning I went
> As rosy as morn
> To seek for new Joy,
> But I met with scorn.
>
> (*The Wild Flower's Song*, K, pp. 170–1.)

[9] Quoted by Margaret Shook, 'Visionary Forms: Blake's Prophetic Art and the Pictorial Tradition', unpublished dissertation, University of California, Berkeley, 1966, p. 170.

And thus the rising of forms:

> There is a place where Contrarieties are equally True:
> This place is called Beulah. It is a pleasant lovely Shadow
> Where no dispute can come, . . .

(*Milton* 30. 1–3; K, p. 518.)

> Awake, Awake, Jerusalem! O lovely Emanation of Albion,
> Awake and overspread all Nations as in Ancient Time;
> For lo! the Night of Death is past and the Eternal Day
> Appears upon our Hills. Awake, Jerusalem, and come away!

(*J* 97; K, p. 744.)

When he says in *The Marriage of Heaven and Hell* that 'Without Contraries is no progression. Attraction and Repulsion, Reason and Energy, Love and Hate, are necessary to Human existence' (K, p. 149), and says that good passive reason is Heaven, evil active energy is Hell, one sees his teasing of progression.

What dialectics there are are limited by the shiftings of the contraries in man, in the circling of day and night. 'Active Evil is better than Passive Good', he says; it springs from body, from energy; its relation to good is asymmetrical, it is capable of good, as good is not of it; it can be regenerated into good (*Annotations to Lavater's 'Aphorisms on Man'*, K, p. 77). It can be forgiven, not avenged (*J* iii). Its vigour, in experience, leads innocence to wisdom, to states beyond the fluctuating and the changing.

Blake, as he wrote George Cumberland, desires that state of entities beyond dialectic, that state 'in which every man is King and Priest in his own house. God send it so on earth, as it is in heaven.' He needs physical anatomy, an eye, an arm, a hand; he needs physical geography, rock, cloud, and mountain; he needs cosmology, heaven, time, eternity, divinity; he needs forms with names and feelings and monumental actions providing presence, he needs the earthly energy of bounding lines, in order to make his pictures. He needs wrath, forge, and fire to regenerate the generated and vegetable forms into their states beyond time, change, and progression. Contraries are for him not so much dramatic as lyrical, not so much clashing as pushing onward, from innocence, not ignorance, into experience, and from experience to a higher state of innocence related to wisdom.

Even his ballad lines carry paradoxes, so that they will not settle into the sequences of narrative; narratives press heroes onward to transformations— Adam to Satan and on, son to father to son, by jolts of energy. *Form* and *fire*, with all their visual trains, dominate the scene as they move upward from night to day and earth to heaven, the heat of fire regenerating the forms, to the light of states of eternal mental reality; a painter's sublime world springing beyond pathos.

94

The frequencies of the *Concordance* do not belie or conceal or distort this painter's reality but rather allow its naming. Coming to recognize the persistences in Blake's vocabulary, his chief bodily and sensory terms, his highly adjectival and phrasal structures, his vertical scenes read from below, his firm edges and boundaries springing into states without bonds but strong in identity, we can answer the question why among chief *Concordance* terms *death* is so dominant and *night* so far ahead of *day*, and realize how the guiding terms of substance, of dark, of death, of earth, of experience, of Albion, provide the ground for the feet of human figures, the forge for the lighting and consuming fires, the flame that, over and over and over, around and around, again and again and again, only sometimes, but into eternity, breaks forth to become light.

What about the reader's surprise? If he is able to get beyond surprise and to see in the pattern of major terms revealed by the *Concordance* a pattern revealed also in the text he has read, is he willing to change surprise to wonder at the thoroughgoing forces of the poetry? Many critics today emphasize a kind of discrepancy in the relation of author to reader: either a usage unconscious for the author yet discerned by the reader, or unconsciousness in the reader yet guided to his purposes by the author. In the middle ground of major usage, in the major vocabulary and sound and syntax of the text, is ground for agreement conscious or unconscious. The steady-going assumptions find expression in major frequencies and find corroboration in repeated recognitions. In poetry especially what counts is not only what the reader is carried toward but what he is brought back to. Blake's reader is brought back to engraved forms, on earth, in night, that he may begin again.

VI

BLAKE'S SONGS OF SPRING

Michael J. Tolley

IT seems no accident that the lyric set last in Blake's canon should recall the one printed first, though the recollection is, perhaps characteristically, unobtrusive. The three stanzas at the end of Blake's address to the Christians in *Jerusalem* 77 do not at first seem like a song of spring, yet they incorporate diction and imagery reminiscent of 'To Spring', the poem at the head of *Poetical Sketches*, and they express essentially the same devout expectation. Other songs of spring in Blake share this expectant mood: they are songs celebrating spring's coming rather than spring's presence. For both the early and the later Blake this mood is fully appropriate, for spring to him is more than a natural season: it is a type of the paradisaical state to which we may be called in death and which we may apprehend even during our mortal life through the power of Imagination. These songs of spring, as we shall see, express man's state on the brink of eternity and so are peculiarly expressive of the poet who died 'Singing of the things he Saw in Heaven'.[1] However, while Blake's first and final spring songs sound this note of anticipation, some others are expressions of delight in spring itself as a present reality; less cheerfully, others express the fear that spring will pass or in some way be blighted, while a group of what we may more specifically call May songs expresses the trials of youthful love. Blake's vision of spring is rarely that of the mere observer of a phase in the natural cycle; indeed, he wishes to call men off from the merely natural view of spring and to help free them from this cycle. Spring, the season of new growth after winter, may, like morning after night, readily stand for the eternal state to succeed this mortal one; indeed, traditional usage sanctioned Blake's employment of these cyclic ideas, spring and morning, to intimate a post-cyclic state.[2] As well as sharing his vision of an imminent eternal spring, Blake also tries to induce his readers to see a present eternity in and through the mortal spring, not content with the perceptible beauty of the external natural form. In both cases, Blake often finds it helpful to load his own songs of spring with allusions to the songs of others, employing them as it were as

---

[1] George Richmond's account; see Bentley, *Records*, p. 347.

[2] In the Christian tradition, at least as early as Eusebius, commenting on Luke 21: 20–31. Thomson's *Winter* 373 ff. provides a relevant passage. But this hardly needs exemplifying.

counters by which false and true ideas of spring have been previously communicated.

The song at the end of *Jerusalem* 77 runs as follows:

> England! awake! awake! awake!
>   Jerusalem thy Sister calls!
> Why wilt thou sleep the sleep of death?
>   And close her from thy ancient walls.
>
> Thy hills & valleys felt her feet,
>   Gently upon their bosoms move:
> Thy gates beheld sweet Zions ways;
>   Then was a time of joy and love.
>
> And now the time returns again:
>   Our souls exult & Londons towers,
> Recieve the Lamb of God to dwell
>   In Englands green & pleasant bowers.[3]

It is the idea of 'feet' on England's 'hills' and 'valleys' that most particularly recalls 'To Spring' (the second stanza), though we are likely to think first of the famous poem in *Milton* 1, beginning

> And did those feet in ancient time.
> Walk upon Englands mountains green:
> And was the holy Lamb of God,
> On Englands pleasant pastures seen!

As Blake envisages Jerusalem as a city, not a woman, at the end of the *Milton* lyric, it is unlikely that 'those feet' in the first line are Jerusalem's: the later lyric offers a fuller and more fully humanized picture of the 'time of joy and love'. However, it is significant that Blake repeatedly calls attention to the 'feet' of his divine beings, a surprising emphasis perhaps to the well-shod modern reader. In 'To Spring' the speaker urges 'let thy holy feet visit our clime'; in *J* 79. 15–16, it is lamented that Albion's 'hills & his valleys no more / Recieve the feet of Jerusalem'; similar is *J* 24. 50: 'The foot-steps of the Lamb of God were there: but now no more.' There is a quite proper humility in this, for the earth is God's footstool,[4]

[3] Quotations of Blake's text throughout are from D. V. Erdman, ed., *The Poetry and Prose of William Blake*, Doubleday, New York, 1965. However, in this case Erdman, p. 231, misprints 'Receive' in line 11, which I correct. The mood and subject of 'Recieve' are difficult to establish. The comma after 'Londons towers' should perhaps be read as a full stop, though it may be a 'breathing' stop, like that at the end of line 5. 'Londons towers' may be the subject of 'Recieve' or (jointly with 'Our souls') of 'exult' (for the latter construction in Blake cf. for instance lines 6–7 of the song in *J* 27). However, both 'exult' and 'Recieve' may not be present indicative but the hymnal imperative. For 'Recieve' to be Jerusalem's imperative in apposition to the three 'awake's of line 1 is formally appropriate. The question would be important to someone setting the song as a hymn, as there is a strong pause after the second line of the first two stanzas.

[4] Matt. 5: 35 etc. Christians often speak of kneeling before the feet of God (cp. *GA* 2. 3) and honouring Christ's

but the main point of the image is, it seems, to recall the beautiful feet of Isaiah 52: 7–8 and Romans 10: 15, particularly Isaiah:

7 How beautiful upon the mountains are the feet of him that bringeth good tidings, that publisheth peace; that bringeth good tidings of good, that publisheth salvation; that saith unto Zion, Thy God reigneth!
8 Thy watchmen shall lift up the voice; with the voice together shall they sing: for they shall see eye to eye, when the LORD shall bring again Zion.[5]

Isaiah's watchmen give Blake a precedent for singing the kind of spring song that celebrates the time 'when the LORD shall bring again Zion' or Jerusalem, as he does most clearly in *J* 77. We cannot doubt that Blake was sensitive to the apocalyptic associations of the plea, 'Let thy holy feet visit our clime', even as early as 'To Spring'. His clearest allusion to the beautiful feet of the Bible is in the early prose-poem 'Samson', where he sings: 'O Truth, that shinest with propitious beams, turning our earthly night to heavenly day, from presence of the Almighty Father! thou visitest our darkling world with blessed feet, bringing good news of Sin and Death destroyed!'[6]

From the first, Blake's vision of an English spring is apocalyptic, that time when the holy feet again visit our clime. With the increased theological precision that marks his latest work, however, the vision is clarified and, in one important respect, altered. The modest bride, 'our love-sick land' of 'To Spring', becomes, more modestly, only the setting or stage for the married Lamb and his bride, Jerusalem:

> She walks upon our meadows green:
> The Lamb of God walks by her side:
> And every English Child is seen,
> Children of Jesus & his Bride,

—to quote from the long poem in *J* 27 that most fully explains this symbolism (lines 17–20). It becomes enough that the marriage of Jesus and his Bride take place and have place in *our* land (for 'Zions Hill' was once in 'every Nation of the Earth', *J* 27. 49–50). What has been lost is not personal engagement, for 'Our souls exult' in *J* 77, but the exclusive and intense feeling for spring that characterizes the early song: it is now simply 'the time' that returns again. In so far as 'the time' is localized, indeed, it has become daybreak, as the first three lines

feet is a form of worship in the episode from Luke 7 that Blake painted, of 'Mary Magdalene Washing the Feet of Christ'.

[5] Also relevant is Eph. 6: 15. Here and elsewhere I quote from A.V. (the Authorized Version).
[6] Blake refers to feet in a similar way elsewhere, though without such strong signs of Biblical influence. Cf. 'To Morning' 8; 'Fresh from the dewy hill' 7, 16; 'Imitation of Spencer' 22; 'Night' 12, *Ahania* 4. 71; *The Four Zoas* ix. 127. 32; 130. 2.

indicate, with their obvious reminiscence of the Bard's call in the 'Introduction' to *Songs of Experience*:

> England! awake! awake! awake!
> Jerusalem thy Sister calls!
> Why wilt thou sleep the sleep of death?

More properly, one finds, spring has not *become* daybreak, but the coming of spring and the coming of day have fused together into a single 'time'. This is more fully apparent in the near 'reprise' of the J 77 song in J 97. 1–4:

> Awake! Awake Jerusalem! O lovely Emanation of Albion
> Awake and overspread all Nations as in Ancient Time
> For lo! the Night of Death is past and the Eternal Day
> Appears upon our Hills: Awake Jerusalem, and come away.

In the last two lines, Blake is recalling the Song of Solomon 2: 8–13, where it is 'winter' that is past as the 'beloved' comes 'skipping upon the hills', inviting his love to arise 'and come away'.[7] The Song of Solomon is for Blake the classic account of a true vision of spring; it also employs daybreak imagery in close association with that of spring, as in 2: 17, for instance, with its call 'Until the day break, and the shadows flee away, turn, my beloved.' The two times, spring and morning, are partly fused together even in 'To Spring'. I shall have more to say about this particular fusion in discussing 'To Spring', but to illustrate the importance of appreciating such fusions in Blake's work, it may be helpful at this point to digress by considering the fusions in 'Introduction' to *Songs of Experience*, a poem with many affinities to the apocalyptic songs of spring.

In line with the Bard's claim to see 'Present, Past & Future', the 'Introduction' exhibits masterly control of time confusions that even go beyond those found by Northrop Frye in his valuable article, 'Blake's Introduction to Experience' (*Huntington Library Quarterly*, xxi (1957), 57–67). One of these confusions is of evening and morning. As the Holy Word walks in the evening dew (I use the present tense to make the present point), he calls the 'lapsed Soul' to 'Arise from out the dewy grass', which is now that of morning, for

> Night is worn,
> And the morn
> Rises from the slumberous mass.

Christ (the Holy Word) calls to Earth at the point of lapse, which is evening, but Earth receives the call at the point of rise or return, which is morning, 'the break

---

[7] Harold Bloom notes the reference, *Blake's Apocalypse*, Doubleday, New York, 1963, p. 431. Paul Miner in his 'Visions' article (see next note), p. 463, n. 8, gives references for the whole passage to Isa. 51: 9, 17; 52: 1; Gen. 9: 19; Song of Solomon 2: 11–12.

of day'. The confusion is thus legitimate: these double points of evening and morning are always *present* with us while 'fallen', yet the evening of lapse and the call to rise were also there in the *past*, according to Blake's reading of the Fall story (in which man cast himself out of the garden despite the words of forgiveness uttered when Christ walked 'in the cool of the day'); they also challenge our *future* experience: 'Why wilt thou turn away', while the promise of renewal will be held out to us continually. There is another important time fusion, bringing together historical events according to the principle of typological identity that Donne, for instance, employs in his 'Hymn to God My God, in My Sickness', the difference being that Donne makes the identity explicit, whereas Blake leaves it implicit and so obscure. In 'Introduction', there is an unmistakable allusion to Genesis 3: 8–9 in Blake's reference to the Holy Word walking among the ancient trees and calling the lapsed Soul. But Blake has no authority in Genesis or *Paradise Lost* for the Word's 'weeping' at this time. Accordingly, Frye has suggested in his article (op. cit., pp. 59 f.) a reference to the occasion in John 11: 35 when 'Jesus wept' before calling to the dead Lazarus. The reference is pertinent, though I think that another text should spring more immediately to mind. I am thinking of Matthew 26: 36–46 (to be taken with the parallel, Luke 22: 39–46), where Jesus 'began to be sorrowful and very heavy' in the *garden* of Gethsemane, in the *evening* (cf. Matthew 26: 20), among *trees* (the Mount of Olives is specified, Luke 22: 39), as he faced for himself the challenge put by the Bard in 'Introduction', struggling against lapse ('the spirit indeed is willing, but the flesh is weak', Matthew 26: 41). The struggle is described as such an intense 'agony' by Luke (22: 44) that 'his sweat was as it were great drops of blood falling down to the ground'—an 'evening dew' indeed! Further, Jesus is described as repeatedly calling to the sleeping disciples, who serve well for Blake's 'slumberous mass' in line 15 of 'Introduction'. After this allusion has been absorbed by Blake's reader, Earth's wilful blindness and deafness in her answer come as an unpleasant shock:

> Cold and hoar
> Weeping o'er
> I hear the Father of the ancient men.
>
> ('EARTH's Answer' 8–10.)

Earth should have heeded Romans 13: 11–12, a text that lies behind 'Introduction' as well as the song in *J* 77 and the first lines of *J* 97:

11 And that, knowing the time, that now it is high time to awake out of sleep: for now is our salvation nearer than when we believed.

12 The night is far spent, the day is at hand: let us therefore cast off the works of darkness, and let us put on the armour of light.

(Romans 13: 11–14 is, I presume, the text cited approvingly at the beginning of the prose part of *J* 77: 'We are told to abstain from fleshly desires that we may lose no time from the Work of the Lord.')

My succeeding discussion of 'To Spring' has two purposes, to deepen our understanding of Blake's characterization of Spring through a study of the Biblical references in the poem, which will lead up to the proposal of a further typological identity involving time-fusion as a convenient basis for this characterization; and to establish both the pervasiveness of literary allusions in the poem and the leading principle governing the selection of these allusions.

Paul Miner has demonstrated conclusively that the Song of Solomon is Blake's major source for 'To Spring'.[8] It is by no means the only literary source, however. 'To Spring' is an astonishing poem because almost every minute particular of its diction and imagery is pointedly derivative, yet it strikes one throughout as fresh and original, marking Blake's notable break away from the limited personifications of his eighteenth-century predecessors. It is thus admirably placed at the head of Blake's first volume of verse, 'the production of untutored youth' doubtless, in A. S. Mathew's phrase, but of no unlettered muse.

Basically 'To Spring' is a rhetorical address by a British speaker to the spirit of Spring, who has the form of the male lover in the Song of Solomon, appealing to him to come to the waiting island, pictured as the female beloved in the Song. It communicates the expectancy of the whole land as spring approaches. This personification of spring is surprising to the reader who does not immediately make the connection with the Song of Solomon, because of its thoroughgoing exoticism: Spring is an opulent Oriental prince—so opulent indeed, with his 'perfumed garments', 'pearls', and 'fair fingers', that modern readers have been known to mistake his sex at first glance. The poem has none of the conventional floral or avian imagery we associate with spring: what Spring will bring with him is seen purely as bodily adornment for his bride: Spring is described therefore not so much in terms of what he brings as of who he is: that he *as a person* will come is the desire expressed. Equally surprising, perhaps, is the intensity of feeling attributed to the waiting land ('longing eyes', 'love-sick land that mourns', 'languish'd head'), when it is coupled with no concern at the wintry conditions that Spring will supersede: the present and past are unimportant, as *external* conditions: the land's feeling of pain is caused entirely by her love for the absent Spring. There are no distractions in the poem: every feeling expressed is directed towards the awaited visitor. The poem begins 'O thou' and ends 'for thee'.

Blake's intense focus on the person of Spring has fused together several scattered descriptions of the lover in the Song of Solomon. A remarkably high proportion

[8] 'Visions in the Darksom Air: Aspects of Blake's Biblical Symbolism', *William Blake: Essays for S. Foster Damon*, ed. Alvin H. Rosenfeld, Brown University Press, Providence, R.I., 1969; see pp. 259 f. Bloom was the first to notice the general connection in print (op. cit., p. 15) but Miner goes much further in providing a remarkable list of certain and possible links between the two works.

of the words and images employed in 'To Spring' are found also in Canticles and almost all are found in the Bible. This striking evidence of common diction is only a crude index of indebtedness, yet it is worth considering.

Excluding the title, there are 129 words in 'To Spring', 92 of these being different words. Of these different words 53 are also found, in the same form, in the Song of Solomon (Authorized Version). A further 26 of these different words are also found, in the same form, elsewhere in A.V. Of the 13 different words remaining, 9 are special cases, being found in variant forms in the Bible. Of these special cases 4 are in the Song of Solomon, the outstanding example being 'love-sick', which is a contraction of 'sick of love' in the Song 2: 5, 5: 8.[9] Thus, we may say that 88 of the 92 words in 'To Spring' are also Biblical. In 'To Spring' 16 words are repeated and these are all Biblical, making a total of 125 of the 129 words in the poem as a whole that are Biblical words; of these words 98 are found in the Song of Solomon alone, one of the shortest Biblical books. The 4 non-Biblical words are unobtrusive, unlike some of those in the other three 'season' poems.[10]

These four non-Biblical words are 'choir' (which is quasi-religious), 'clime' (a Miltonic word), 'tresses', and 'Spring' itself. Blake's use of 'tresses' is a sign of his debt to Collins, whose 'Ode to Evening' may well have suggested the scheme of Blake's four short season lyrics.[11] 'Spring' is the most interesting non-Biblical word.

At first it seems paradoxical that Blake's poem should be so heavily Biblical, in view of the absence of the word 'spring' for the season in the Bible. However, the celebration of the end of winter in Canticles 2: 10–15 is tantamount to a song of spring, though the figs and grapes appear surprisingly early for one accustomed to English seasons. Put another way, it can be seen that the effects of spring in the Oriental poem come with more dramatic suddenness than they do in England. If Blake—so we may put the case—has gone out of his way to avoid describing the normal English connotations of spring and if, instead, he has concentrated on the exotic Hebrew connotations of spring, does this not mean that he is not invoking an English spring at all, but rather an apocalyptic spring that will change England

[9] The other three special cases in the Song of Solomon are 'o'er' for 'over' (Song 2: 11); 'morn' for 'morning' (Song 6: 10); 'dewy' from 'my head is filled with dew, and my locks with the drops of the night' (Song 5: 2). The other 5 special cases found basically elsewhere in the Bible are 'list'ning' for 'listen' (Is. 49: 1); 'eastern' for 'east' (frequent in A.V.); 'hails' for 'hail' (e.g. Matt. 26: 49); 'approach' (sb.) for the verb frequent in A.V.; 'languish'd' (adj.) for the verb in A.V. (the past participle 'languished' occurs in Lam. 2: 8).

[10] The non-Biblical words in 'To Summer' are as follows: curb, steeds, alley, limbs, fervid, car, mossy, draperies, bards, swains, sprightly, echoes, laurel, sultry (14 in all); those in 'To Autumn' number 7: autumn, tune, jolly, thrilling, pinions, roves, bleak; there are 6 or 7 in 'To Winter': car, yawning, direful, clings, strides, freezes (but 'frozen' is in A.V.), Hecla. The list excludes special cases like the 'obviously' non-Biblical 'ribbed' in 'To Winter' ('rib' itself occurs three times in A.V.).

[11] See 'Ode to Evening', lines 41–8. Collins is properly evoked by Blake in 'To Spring' as writing in the line of Milton, another unmistakably British poet. Blake's 'To the Evening Star' is also indebted to Collins. Cf. James D. McGowan, 'Rising Glories: A Study of William Blake's *Poetical sketches*', unpublished Ph.D. thesis, Rutgers, The State University, 1968, pp. 80–3.

with the suddenness of, say, the awakening at the end of *Jerusalem*? The more we consider the person of Blake's Spring, the more strongly do the poem's apocalyptic overtones assert themselves. It is, after all, common knowledge that the male lover in the Song of Solomon was usually interpreted in the eighteenth century as an allegorical personification of Christ courting his bride, the Church.[12] Blake would have embraced this interpretation warmly, not because he would have felt uneasy about reading an erotic pastoral poem in a sacred book on any other terms, but because it suited his ideals of love so well, and authorized them. The surprising thing, then, is not so much that we must identify the person addressed as 'thou, with dewy locks' with Christ, as that Blake should have been content to identify Christ as Spring, in a sequence of pastoral poems that may have been composed on a hint from Collins and that are, superficially considered, little better than unconventional lyrics, variations on a common theme. However, it does seem to me that there is a sound reasoning behind Blake's identification, beyond the associations of the Song of Solomon (where the lover announces spring and appears skipping on the hills like the morning sun). The culmination of the song of Zacharias, in Luke 1: 78–9, refers to the 'tender mercy of our God; whereby the dayspring from on high hath visited us, To give light to them that sit in darkness and in the shadow of death, to guide our feet into the way of peace'.[13] That Blake has Christ the 'dayspring' in mind is suggested partly by the verbal echo in 'And let thy holy feet visit our clime' (line 8), partly by the suggestion that Spring is to come from on high ('all our longing eyes are turned / Up to thy bright pavillions', lines 6–7) and partly by Blake's confusion of spring with day, morning, or sun imagery throughout his poem. Blake's second stanza is also partly reminiscent of Psalm 19: 1–6 in its parallel use of pathetic fallacy and, more particularly, in its use of imagery suggesting 'the bridegroom coming out of his chamber' (Blake's 'bright pavillions' avoiding the directness of A.V.'s 'tabernacle for the sun').[14]

Accepting that Blake's strategy of source-evocation is partly to identify Spring with Christ, the dayspring and bridegroom, we can see why it is necessary for

---

[12] In their introductions to Canticles, three commentators popular in the eighteenth century, Matthew Henry, Matthew Poole, and Thomas Scott, are all in agreement on this point, for instance. My emphasis is stronger than Robert F. Gleckner's, who caught the allusion, but thought that Blake only 'alludes lightly to Christ's coming', that Spring is 'perhaps Christ' ('Blake's Seasons', *S.E.L.* v (1965), 533–51, esp. 541–2). His 'perhaps' should be changed to 'certainly'.

[13] The connection of 'feet' with 'peace' recalls Blake's references to Isa. 52: 7–8 and Rom. 10: 15, mentioned above.

[14] Different connections between 'To Spring' and Psalm 19 have been made by Geoffrey H. Hartman in 'Blake and "The Progress of Poesy"', *William Blake: Essays for S. Foster Damon*, p. 57, and by Myrddin Jones in 'Blake's "To Spring": A Formative Source?', *N. & Q.* N.S. xvii (1970), 314 f. Hartman also makes comparisons with Collins and Milton. As well as Psalm 19, Psalm 65: 9–13 is part of the relevant Biblical background: on this cf. John Holloway, *Blake: The Lyric Poetry*, Edward Arnold, London, 1968, p. 16, who also refers to Psalm 114: 4.

him to present his Spring in almost exclusively Biblical terms. However, there is also a well-documented tradition of English sources for the poem: clear debts to Milton and Collins, possible debts to Akenside and Shakespeare, in addition to untraced or untraceable debts in the tradition of seasonal poetry that Blake so obviously inherited.[15] What is interesting about the strategy of the sources behind Spring's waiting bride, is that they are fully and almost exclusively Miltonic. Once we have granted the 'love-sick land' some essential qualities to establish her as Spring's Biblical partner, we find on turning to her non-Biblical attributes that her special characteristics are essentially located in Milton's verse, thus making her as fully English as she could well be—the daughter of England's greatest poet. The fineness of Blake's tribute to the elder poet is still more enhanced when we consider the wide range of Milton's work on which he has drawn.

The first reference to Milton that I note here influences action rather than character, however: this is Blake's reminiscence of *Paradise Lost*, v. 1–2:

> Now Morn her rosie steps in th'Eastern Clime
> Advancing, sowd the Earth with Orient Pearle,

—compare the invocation to Spring to 'let thy holy feet visit our *clime*. / Come o'er *the eastern hills*' and 'scatter thy *pearls* / Upon our love-sick *land*'. Blake's final stanza seems the most Miltonic. There the land's 'languish'd head' must, as F. W. Bateson has noticed, recall *Comus*, line 744, 'It withers on the stalk with languish't head' and/or *Samson Agonistes*, line 119, 'With languisht head un-propt'.[16] Further, the final image of the bride with her modest tresses bound up seems, as S. Foster Damon suggested, indebted to Milton's translation of 'The Fifth Ode of *Horace*, Lib. I', lines 1–5:

> What slender Youth bedew'd with liquid odours
> Courts thee on Roses in some pleasant Cave,
> > *Pyrrha* for whom bind'st thou
> > In wreaths thy golden Hair,
> Plain in thy neatness; . . .[17]

---

[15] Akenside's *The Pleasures of Imagination*, lines 312–19, is proposed as a stylistic rather than a thematic influence by M. R. Lowery, *Windows of the Morning*, Yale University Press, New Haven, Conn., 1940, pp. 156 f. In suggesting other debts, Lowery sometimes mistakes secondary for primary sources, as in a reference to Spenser's *Faerie Queene*, I. v. 2. 4–5, for the first two lines of 'To Spring'. Spenser and Blake were both influenced by the same Biblical source; Blake may have been aware of Spenser's lines but gives no clear sign of a debt to him. Cf. W. H. Stevenson, ed., *The Poems of William Blake*, text by David V. Erdman, Longmans, London, 1971, p. 4, for a possible debt to a conventional image familiar to us in *Hamlet* I. i. 166.

[16] F. W. Bateson, ed., *Selected Poems of William Blake*, Heinemann, London, 1957, p. 97.

[17] S. Foster Damon, *William Blake: His Philosophy and Symbols*, Boston, Mass., 1924, p. 253. For Blake as perhaps for Milton, the 'Youth bedew'd with liquid odours' is recognizably Solomon's lover; Pyrrha's golden hair may have suggested Blake's 'golden crown'. Some other suggested Miltonic references are more doubtful. Cf. Hartman, op. cit., p. 61, for a possible debt to *Lycidas* 163; Stevenson, loc. cit., for a possible reminiscence of *Paradise Lost* v. 653–4. For Blake's 'longing eyes', cf. Eve's 'longing eye' in *Paradise Lost* ix. 743, though the

It is perhaps needless to add that the diction used in 'To Spring' is even more Miltonic than it is Biblical: only two of Blake's words, 'garments' and 'love-sick', are not to be found in Milton's verse.

Before leaving *Poetical Sketches* to discuss, in chronological order, Blake's later songs of spring, it may be appropriate to consider briefly a few lyrics that may appear to be comprehended under my title, 'Blake's Songs of Spring'. These are poems of youthful love, one of which, beginning 'How sweet I roam'd', is set in May, and they may be grouped together as May songs, the others being 'Fresh from the dewy hill' and its companion 'When early morn walks forth'. These lyrics have some kinship with the folk-song broached by the Lawgiver in 'An Island in the Moon', beginning 'As I walkd forth one may morning'. In these songs, the season is only a setting for the human concern, the joys and torments of love, and is not itself the subject. Their natural successors are in some Songs of Experience and so ultimately they lead us to the tormented loves of Los and Enitharmon rather than to the fulfilled love of the Lamb and Jerusalem that is expressed characteristically in the songs of spring that are here my subject. Further, Blake seems to associate May (the only month of the year to be mentioned frequently in his poetry) with summer (as in line 2 of 'How sweet I roam'd') rather than with spring, to which it formally belongs in the modern calendar.

Of these songs, 'Fresh from the dewy hill' is particularly interesting, considered as an offshoot of 'To Spring', for it begins as if the speaker were Spring himself, with 'rising glories' beaming round his head, hastening with winged feet to meet his maiden 'o'er the dewy lawn'. While they are together, the setting is typically paradisaical:

> So when she speaks, the voice of Heaven I hear
> So when we walk, nothing impure comes near;
> Each field seems Eden, and each calm retreat;
> Each village seems the haunt of holy feet.
>
> (lines 13–16.)

These are 'times of innocence, and holy joy' (line 10), of Traherne-like rapture, but they do not last; the succeeding song betrays the voice of experience expressing the pangs of jealousy. In retrospect, then, the first song betrays infatuation rather than ideal love: each field and village only *seemed* Edenic. Thus, in beginning *Poetical Sketches* by invoking the real spirit of love, Blake has provided both the ideal condition to which his human lovers aspire and a standard of innocence against which their experience may be measured.

Less rapturous than 'Fresh from the dewy hill', breathing a spirit of quiet, yet

phrase is often found in other writers. Granted Blake's complimentary purpose in allusion, it is not absurd to propose even such doubtful reminiscences of Milton: they reinforce our sense of the deliberately Miltonic quality of Blake's phrasing.

deep affection, is the song beginning 'I love the jocund dance'. By itself, this beautiful lyric has no indisputable marks of spring about it, but it anticipates several of the *Songs of Innocence* and is largely reworked in 'The Ecchoing Green', one of the two songs of spring I shall next consider.

Unlike 'To Spring', the two songs of spring in *Songs of Innocence* are at once remarkable for their relative unallusiveness. David Erdman has suggested a general debt to Mrs. Barbauld for 'The Ecchoing Green'[18] and D. G. Gillham has observed that 'Blake takes the thread of the poem from *L'Allegro*, lines 91–9'[19] but the tally ends there, while E. D. Hirsch, Jr., has put forward three quite unconvincing possible Biblical sources for 'Spring'.[20] Most of the *Songs of Innocence* are similarly free from obtrusive allusions, particularly if one excludes from consideration the models, like Barbauld and Watts, that Blake is consciously superseding; only 'HOLY THURSDAY' seems richly allusive. This freedom contributes to their freshness, simplicity, and purity of tone so appropriate to the state of mind they express.

The idea of an 'Ecchoing Green' is surprising, considered naturalistically and compared with the echoing hills in 'Nurse's Song', for instance, and the sounds we hear in the poem are not so much echoes as responses, even in a competitive spirit as the birds sing louder while the bells ring; as the old folk almost determinedly laugh while they watch the merry children. The structure of the poem is exquisite, the three stanzas mirroring an echo pattern: youthful spring sounds in the first find an echo in the aged spectators of the second, while time causes both to die away in the third. The poem spans a single holiday and all human life.[21] It is customary for critics to point to the obvious differences between the playing children and the watching old folk but it is better to notice the way in which both are akin: young and old are both, in the state of Innocence, echoing or responsive beings. Just as the old folk of the second stanza are responsive spectators, finding echoes in their own life to enable them to share in the sports of the young, so that imaginatively they 'become as little children', so also the children of the first stanza are responsive listeners, attributing the merriness in their own hearts to the bells, birds, and even skies about them. The unselfconsciousness of the children is complete, so much so that the laughter and noise of their play is never mentioned

[18] David V. Erdman, *Blake: Prophet against Empire*, Princeton University Press, N.J., 1954, p. 114 n. (1959 ed., Doubleday, Garden City, N.Y., p. 124 n.).

[19] D. G. Gillham, *Blake's Contrary States*, Cambridge University Press, 1966, p. 23 n. Gillham regards 'The Ecchoing Green' as 'innocent counterpart' to 'LONDON' (pp. 22–7) and makes some sensible comparisons between the poems. From 'L'Allegro', it seems, come Blake's 'merry bells' that 'ring', the combination of young and old at play, and the suggestion of play 'Till the livelong daylight fail', but Milton's reference to dancing is not taken up. Blake's illustration to Milton, 'The Sunshine Holiday', is relevant, but see below on this.

[20] E. D. Hirsch, Jr., *Innocence and Experience: An Introduction to Blake*, Yale University Press, New Haven, Conn., 1964, p. 39. Hirsch strains to find apocalyptic overtones in the poem, a temptation he should have resisted, as it leads him into some absurdities.

[21] Cf. ibid. Hirsch's discussion of this poem is sensitive. He sees a reference to both old and young in the tired 'little ones' of the final stanza (p. 40).

by the singer, whom I take to be an older child, aware of his or her distance from 'the little ones' of the third stanza. This absence of sound is, of course, partly an effect of the 'seen/Green' rhyme but it is notable that the laughter and speech of the old folk are marked by the singer, who is so remarkably self-effacing as to speak only as one of a group—'our sports', 'our play'—thus extending our sense of the 'echoing' quality in the poem. Interestingly, too, while 'Old John' is seen by the singer as an individual, he soon merges into the group of 'old folk', whose memories of their past 'joys' are not individualized but collective ('When we all girls & boys'), memories, that is, of past mutual echoing or responsiveness. Further, the old folk remember themselves *as echoed*, as having been seen ('In our youth time were seen'), so that we have a pleasant receding image of old folk who in the past watched those 'girls & boys', remembering the time when they too were young, and so on. This echoing helps fix the suggestion of permanent recurrence in the poem's structure.

As, then, the subjects of the poem are echoing or responsive, the singer equally responsive, it would be a strange reader who did not respond appropriately by finding himself, too, to be an echoer (and so, in a sense, losing himself and sharing in the Innocent state that is evoked). The cause of all this lively responsiveness is the Sun—Spring (the two are not separate) of the first two lines, which could not be more appropriate. It is easy to draw analogies with the Son, Luke's 'dayspring', to whose continuous presence we should be echoing, but Blake is careful not to force the analogy, in contrast with his strategy in 'To Spring'. We are of course here, as in 'Spring', actual participants in the spring festival, not expectant waiters on the threshold of the new season, and so the imperative need is for pure enjoyment, not for definition through anticipation. Blake's use of the continuous present tense is important, giving the state he evokes a permanent or eternal quality. Because of it, we need not be gloomy about the last stanza. That a spring day ends is a fact of life, but there is no reason why another spring day should not follow, for 'The Sun does arise', whether we are young or old or have passed the 'little space' on earth.[22] In the state of Innocence, spring is perpetual, yet Blake respected the natural cycle: he knew the need we have of rest and so he supplied a Beulah for the inhabitants of his active eternal state, Eden. Acceptance of the need for rest is beautifully expressed in the third stanza and it has no sinister overtones for me. Further, it is, I think, a mistake to suppose that the old folk must be living in an inferior state to that of the children. Old John, after all, 'Does laugh away care'. Why should the old folk be seen as pathetic, just because of the realistic iteration

[22] 'The Little Black Boy', line 13. This poem, like the others in *Songs of Innocence* concerned with the fact of darkness in this world, 'The Chimney Sweeper' and 'Night', makes explicit a faith in life after death that has no formal place within the boundaries of the spring songs of Innocence. For a persuasively sombre reading of 'The Ecchoing Green', which my own tries partly to correct, the reader should consult Robert F. Gleckner, *The Piper and the Bard*, Wayne University Press, Detroit, Mich., 1959, pp. 91–4.

21, 22. 'The Ecchoing Green', from *Songs of Innocence and of Experience*, copy AA.
Relief etching finished in pen and water-colour.
Fitzwilliam Museum, Cambridge

23. 'The Sunshine Holiday', from Illustrations to Milton's *L'Allegro*.
Water-colour.
The Pierpont Morgan Library, New York

of their voices ('Such such were the joys') and their reliance on memory? Surely theirs is, if anything, a richer pleasure than that of the children, because more deeply resonant. One may also point to the equally realistic pathos of the little ones who 'No more can be merry' at the end of the day—one senses their bewilderment at their inability to sustain their joy.

In the illustrations that accompany 'The Ecchoing Green' an interesting feature is the unequivocal innocence of the sports depicted. In his great design, 'The Sunshine Holiday', a design for the same passage in Milton that evidently lies behind 'The Ecchoing Green' and its precursor in *Poetical Sketches*, 'I love the jocund dance', there are shown young men and women dancing round a maypole. Children would not be bothered by the presence of maypoles in songs of spring but adults very likely would detect in them such phallic symbolism as would distort their experience of the poem's text.[23] A delicate suggestion of sexual play may, of course, be seen in the image of the youth handing a bunch of grapes to an adolescent girl, though his extreme nonchalance may rather indicate a delight in his own gymnastic skill; but such a suggestion may perhaps best be read as one that does not exclude the invitation to love-play rather than as one that forcibly includes it. More intriguing, those ripe grapes on the gravity-defying vine are out of season and out of this world, to reinforce our impression that Blake is celebrating an eternal state of Innocence, not merely a Wordsworthian scene of youth and age. The grapes are there partly, perhaps, because of the 'tender grapes' in the Song of Solomon 2: 13, 15; 6: 11; 7: 12,[24] but mainly, I suspect, because the 'purple Grape' is a feature of the 'Eternal Spring' in Milton's Garden of Eden (*Paradise Lost* iv. 259, 268).

I do not propose to swamp 'Spring' with commentary: it is not, to me, a problematic poem. One can get a lot of harmless fun from chanting it; the pleasures of analysis are not comparable. Is the flute suddenly mute for any reason other than to provide a rhyme? Is the sudden apparent switch from imperative mood to

---

[23] Blake frequently uses sexual imagery in his designs but I personally disagree with those who follow Wicksteed in detecting organs of generation in 'The Blossom' or two kinds of womb in 'Infant Joy'. To see the flame-tree in 'The Blossom' as a phallic image is to obtrude thoughts of merely human sexuality, which the poem's text avoids, and so to narrow its meaning (usually so much as to turn it into a Song of Experience). This image rather expresses a universal vegetative force, a principle of joyful life and growth. The embracing cherubs in its upper 'branches' express innocent erotic pleasure without suggesting the perverse eroticism of Experience. I do not include 'The Blossom' amongst my 'Songs of Spring' partly because one has to stop somewhere, partly because it is more closely related to the group of Songs concerned with pity for another's sorrow.

[24] Further, in S. of S. 7: 8 the prince's daughter is told 'thy breasts shall be as clusters of the vine'. This erotic symbolism is recalled, presumably, in the manuscript draft continuation to 'INFANT SORROW': 'And I saw before me shine / Clusters of the wandring vine' (E, p. 720), which appear just before the speaker is cursed into marriage. These clusters are shown in the illustration to 'NURSES Song' in *Songs of Experience* where, however, the young boy shown is already under a sinister female domination, as indicated by her combing his hair (a clear reminiscence of the contemporary jocular metaphoric significance, usually applied to termagant wives). However, I repeat my point that the grapes in both designs for 'The Ecchoing Green' only remotely suggest eroticism, whereas they must be regarded as primarily erotic when encountered in 'NURSES Song'. The grapes in 'On Anothers Sorrow' are presumably quite non-erotic; those in 'The School Boy' almost so.

24, 25. 'Spring', from *Songs of Innocence and of Experience*, copy AA.
Relief etching finished in pen and water-colour.
Fitzwilliam Museum, Cambridge

present indicative more deeply motivated? I doubt it. Gleckner has a fine extended reading, though perhaps he puzzles too much over the identity of the poem's speaker.[25] I myself would identify him as the little boy of Blake's designs, who would be accustomed to confuse subject and object (compare my comments on the first stanza of 'The Ecchoing Green'), from a common nursery habit, and so would be closer to the child on the cloud in the 'Introduction' to *Innocence* than to Gleckner's Piper (though the Piper's imaginative participation in this confusion is, of course, what is 'really' going on). I take the poem as expressive of an earlier state of consciousness than that we find in 'The Lamb' (from an older boy, as the design suggests), one of participation in the purely sensual pleasure of springtime. There is a difficulty, however, in the designs, particularly in the forms of the four angels, set in different attitudes on leafy plants beside the text. The plants themselves have a suggestion of willow leaves with catkins, to my eye, rather than of green wheat, but either would be appropriate plants for spring and innocence.[26] The easiest way of reading these angels, I suggest, is to take them as representing the four seasons (otherwise it is difficult to account for the posture of the last figure, apparently out of key with the merriment in the song). The top figure on the first plate, the piper, suggests spring, season of innocent creativity; the lower figure on this plate, with wings outstretched, may suggest summer's youthful activity; the top figure on the second plate (who seems, from the facsimiles to hand, to be wingless) may less certainly represent autumn, a dancing leaf (coloured red in the Trianon Press facsimile of copy Z); while the lower figure, asleep or mourning (more likely), may represent winter, the time for sleep and the year's death. Hers would be the 'languish'd head' to be raised and crowned by the next coming of Spring.

Among other things, the *Songs of Experience* celebrate (if that is the right word) the premature blighting of spring. Winter has a place in the state of Innocence, as the natural close of the seasonal cycle, but in *Experience* winter comes out of season. This theme is adumbrated in 'The School Boy', which was set at first in *Songs of Innocence* but later transferred, in several copies, to *Songs of Experience*.[27] The speaker here is an Innocent struggling in the toils of Experience (school education) and appealing to his parents to rescue him from the fate to which they

---

[25] Op. cit., pp. 94–7. Gleckner finds that 'the "I'' includes the Piper of the song, both children, and both birds'. He emphasizes the lamb's identity with the Lamb of God and sees the Song as an announcement of Christ's coming, whereas I would tend to play down the reference to Christ, not because it is not there implicitly but because the poem's speaker is not making the reference explicit and is expressing a state of mind that comes before this awareness is achieved.

[26] Cp. the living willows in 'The Little Black Boy' (Pl. 2) and 'Nurse's Song' of *Innocence*. They are perhaps to be taken there as emblems of the divine pity (we have no clear guide from the Bible, as the willows there have various associations, good and bad). Cf. the beautiful willowesque tree in 'The Little Girl Lost' (Pl. 1). The dead willow branches of 'The Angel' and 'A POISON TREE' represent, in the first case, a refusal of pity; in the second, a hypocritical pretence of pity masking violent anger.

[27] Cf. Geoffrey Keynes and Edwin Wolf 2nd, *William Blake's Illuminated Books: A Census*, Grolier Club, New York, 1953, pp. 52, 55.

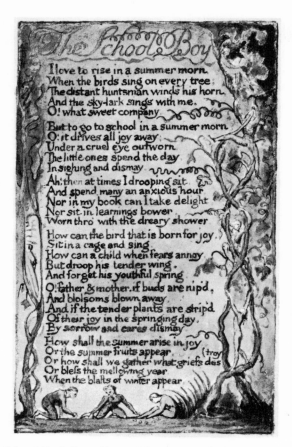

26. 'The School Boy', from *Songs of Innocence and of Experience*, copy AA.
Relief etching finished in pen and water-colour.
Fitzwilliam Museum, Cambridge

have committed him. Schematically, his song does not fit either group, strictly, but is intermediate between the alternatives of a return to Innocence (should the parents relent; cf. Blake's own situation in being permitted to stay away from school) or a confirmation in Experience (seen as inevitable should attendance at school be prolonged). 'The School Boy' is set appropriately in the season of summer rather than spring, to which the speaker looks back, as summer is the time of ripening towards fruition, hence the time for human education, for the drawing-out of our innate qualities. Learning is properly an enjoyable occupation 'in a summer morn', as we see by the boy at the top of the tree in the accompanying illustration, who takes delight in his book 'in learnings bower'. School, however, implies spending the day (i.e. wasting it) 'Under a cruel eye outworn' and the omnipresent fear of the birch. The schoolboy naturally expresses his fears, then, in terms of the premature blighting of 'his youthful spring':

> O! father & mother, if buds are nip'd,
> And blossoms blown away,
> And if the tender plants are strip'd
> Of their joy in the springing day,
> By sorrow and cares dismay,
>
> How shall the summer arise in joy
> Or the summer fruits appear
> Or how shall we gather what griefs destroy
> Or bless the mellowing year,
> When the blasts of winter appear.

We shall shortly find Ahania making a similar lament in *The Four Zoas*, but unlike Ahania's more gloomy fears, the schoolboy's find no reassuring, friendly answer. The illustration to 'The School Boy' is, however, affirmative, showing learning on a height to be climbed with pleasure, when one is not playing marbles with one's companions. It is pleasant to add that this poem reveals no book-learning at all, so far as I know, and so is a living proof of its assumption that 'summer fruits appear' when 'tender plants' are nurtured out of school.

All too frequently for our comfort, 'the blasts of winter appear' in *Songs of Experience*. Earth in 'EARTH's Answer' asks similar questions to those of the schoolboy, invoking spring as an ideal state by which to judge the freezing winter that binds her love. Ironically, if she only knew it, she herself is on the verge of a new spring, if she would heed the Bard's 'Introduction'. Instead of inveighing against her wintry god (Nobodaddy), Earth could be binding up her modest tresses in expectant hope of the Dayspring's joyful return. Similarly, though with a voice of 'honest indignation' untainted by selfish concern, the speaker of 'HOLY THURSDAY' in *Experience* denounces the 'eternal winter' that impoverishes the land and denies the values of the 'rich and fruitful' spring season (Holy Thursday falling usually in May). None the less, as the contrary song of *Innocence* shows, the charity children are, in their innocence, appropriately hymning praises in this spring season 'with radiance all their own'. This pair of songs, as others do, shows how tragically 'the Eye altering alters all'. In *Experience* 'The Ecchoing Green' is supplanted by 'The GARDEN of LOVE', with its 'tomb-stones where flowers should be'; the Nurse of 'NURSES Song' assumes that children are wasting their spring and their day 'in play', of all things (whereas she wasted her own by not playing); the rose is sickened by the invisible worm that flies in the night; the chimney sweeper is 'A little black thing among the snow' and the little vagabond complains that 'the Church is cold', though if it were warmed with 'some Ale / And a pleasant fire', he suggests, 'we'd be as happy as birds in the spring'.

Both *The Book of Thel* and *Visions of the Daughters of Albion* have thematic relevance to this study. *The Book of Thel* begins with the heroine's lament over spring's evanescence:

> O life of this our spring! why fades the lotus of the water?
> Why fade these children of the spring? born but to smile & fall.
>
> (1. 6–7.)

Her situation is thus, as she thinks herself equally evanescent, 'like transient day', comparable to that of the schoolboy in Blake's *Songs*. Both hover on the brink of Experience, but whereas the schoolboy questions an artificial social process that will bring spring to a premature end and spoil its summer promise, Thel questions the natural process itself. Despite reassurances from the creatures of the valley, Thel cannot see beyond the temporal illusion and fears that she will pass away only to become 'the food of worms'. In seasonal terms, Thel wishes to cling to spring and is unhealthily afraid of summer; in mortal terms, she clings to life, afraid of the change of state death will bring; in human terms, she wishes to remain in innocent virginity, having a phallic fear of the physical process of love that will alone bring her to motherhood, the state in which she will be most obviously of use. The devouring worm she fears, however, turns out to be only an infant, a 'helpless worm' whose 'little voice' cannot speak but only weep (i.e. whimper, I take it), with 'none to cherish' it 'with mothers smiles' (3. 30–4. 6). This infant worm, then, is presented in such a way as to appeal most to Thel's latent maternality. The Clod of Clay, hearing the Worm's voice, sets Thel the example, rising to breast-feed the infant ('and her life exhal'd / In milky fondness'). By a daring and subtle use of imagery, the phallic worm Thel fears as the means of dissolution into a new state is presented to her only in its most appealing form, as the end product, small and evidently harmless. Nevertheless, the Clod of Clay will not disguise the fact that even maternal caring will involve 'a little Death / In the Divine Image' (*J* 96. 27–8). It is this necessary self-giving from which Thel recoils in the end; her immediate answer to the Clod of Clay shows, however, a determined refusal to see any application of the Clay's action to herself. The feeding of the worm is not her responsibility but an external process, the work of an external God. She will not learn that 'God only Acts & Is, in existing beings or Men' but is still in the position of those who say 'Is not God alone the Prolific?' (*MHH* 16, from exactly the right context, a discussion of Prolific and Devourers). She insists still on regarding herself as 'without a use', being reassured by the consolatory thought that God is acting to help the unfortunate Worm. Thus, even before she enters the Clay's house, Thel is already stepping back into the state of irresponsible adolescence with which she was at first dissatisfied, the state of dependent Innocence on the verge of becoming fatally permanent and so appropriately named 'the vales of Har'. Her nightmare vision inside the grave (of her virgin state) only confirms her selfish timidity: the courtship process that must precede motherhood is a distortion of virgin fears. Summer, 'the youthful burning boy' (both infant and lover), is too overwhelmingly forceful for her timid soul: courtship is a state of Experience in which cosy dependence must be exchanged for naked vulnerability to frightening energies.[28]

Whereas the innocent schoolboy is betrayed from without, then, the virgin Thel is betrayed from within. She sees her approaching summer as a winter, a death, when she will become 'the food of worms'. Interestingly, she, like the waiting land in 'To Spring', looks forward at first to the coming of Christ, to usher in her new state of being, but she sees him purely as 'him that walketh in the garden in the evening time' (1. 14), one who announces a Fall (as in Genesis 3), she hopes gently, rather than as the Bridegroom she requires for progress to fulfilment. It is left to Oothoon to affirm the value of the phallic experience that Thel fears, though Oothoon too is tragically betrayed from without, for it takes two to mate in Innocence and her bridegroom is the God-tormented Theotormon (taught by the 'Father of Jealousy', *VDA* 7. 12–13):

> Does not the worm erect a pillar in the mouldering church yard?
> And a palace of eternity in the jaws of the hungry grave
> Over his porch these words are written. Take thy bliss O Man!
> And sweet shall be thy taste & sweet thy infant joys renew!
>
> (*VDA* 5. 41–6. 3.)[29]

[28] For the sake of bringing out this important strand of significance clearly, I simplify the story but do not, I hope, distort it. I have written more extensively on *Thel*, using a different line of approach, in 'The Book of Thel and *Night Thoughts*', *Bulletin of N.Y.P.L.* lxix (1965), 375–85.

[29] The previous lines, it may be noted, answer Thel's 'Motto'. I am partly indebted here to H. B. de Groot, 'The Ouroboros and the Romantic Poets', *English Studies*, l (1969), 553–64, esp. 557 f. This suggestive study is unfortunately marred by inaccurate observation, particularly in confusing worm and serpent.

Blake returns to these themes in *The Four Zoas* viii. There, Oothoon's assessment of the worm's place is questioned by Ahania in her gloomy address to the Caverns of the Grave that prompts Enion's major song of spring (pp. 108–10). These two great songs, Ahania's lament and Enion's assurance, are magnificent restatements of the two opposite views of death considered (perhaps more confusingly because with more local application) in the companion poems, *The Book of Thel* and *Visions of the Daughters of Albion*. Ahania's nightmare vision of 'how the horrors of Eternal Death take hold on Man' (108. 35) is far sicker than Thel's mainly sexual apprehension and easily surpasses in horror the individual *frissons* of the graveyard poets who formed some of Blake's lighter reading. Her reference, however, is mainly back to Oothoon's assertions and she begins by questioning some of Oothoon's boldest affirmations:

> Will you keep a flock of wolves & lead them will you take the wintry blast
> For a covering to your limbs or the summer pestilence for a tent to abide in
> Will you erect a lasting habitation in the mouldering Church yard
> Or a pillar & palace of Eternity in the jaws of the hungry grave.
>
> (108. 9–12.)[30]

To analyse Ahania's lament fully would take us too far afield, into the highly evolved imagery of the fallen Man, sleeping Albion, which draws particularly here on reminiscences of Job and of Jonah's fate in the belly of the whale. The questions with which she begins her cry recall those in Job 38–41 and it may be that the cry as a whole is a black parody of God's humiliating words to Man in the person of Job. The lion and horse figure in both texts, while Ahania's horrified image of the famished eagle seems to owe something to Job 39: 27–30. Her very first question, 'Will you keep a flock of wolves & lead them', recalls Isaiah 11: 6 particularly with its prophecy that 'a little child shall lead them', i.e. various animals including the wolf; Ahania seeks to deny such a fanciful hope.[31] The 'dark body of corruptible death' (p. 108. 21) recalls Romans 7: 24, one of seven such references in Blake. Paul asks 'who shall deliver me from the body of this death?' but Ahania lacks the imagination to postulate a deliverer. Miner notes the reference to Jonah 2: 3, 5 in lines 29–30 and we may add line 23 as a reference to Jonah 2: 6.[32] Stevenson relates 109. 4 to 1 Corinthians 15: 40–54, while Margoliouth notes that 109. 7–8 form a sick version of Judges 14: 8.[33]

---

[30] With the first lines, cp. *VDA* 7. 30–8. 8. It may be noted that whereas Oothoon particularizes: only the sea fowl covers itself with the 'wintry blast', only the wild snake with the 'pestilence', thus denying the principle of 'one law for both the lion and the ox' (*VDA* 4. 22); Ahania does not discriminate and so betrays an inferior, myopic vision.   [31] So Miner notes, op. cit., p. 268.

[32] Ibid., pp. 266, 468 n.-33. As well as verbal reminiscences, two designs also recall Jonah 2: *America* 13 and *Night Thoughts* ii, p. 41 (No. 74).

[33] Stevenson, op. cit., p. 425; H. M. Margoliouth, ed., *William Blake's Vala*, Oxford University Press, 1958, p. 179. Also noting this reference, Miner, op. cit., pp. 269 f., relates lines 9–11 (the horse becoming blind) to

Probably Ahania is so despairing because of two factors, her reliance on memory and her dependence on Urizen. She boasts of her memory in 108. 20: 'Listen to her whose memory beholds your ancient days.' However, unlike old John in 'The Ecchoing Green', she chooses to remember only the long-continued state of Fall, it seems; looking back offers her no consolation but probably handicaps her as 'in vain' she seeks for morning (108. 22). Dependence on Urizen in the Fallen state would naturally tend to continue a state of limited vision and, we are told, 'her Eyes are Toward Urizen'. As Ahania is Urizen's Emanation, this dependence is natural, but redemption must come from a higher source.

Enion has passed beyond Ahania's state of fear and despair, as she is actually in 'the Caverns of the Grave' that Ahania fears so much. Whereas she was once desolate like Ahania (who is pictured, with a reminiscence of Isaiah, as a 'land of briars & thorns'),[34] she now finds that 'hope drowns all' her torment, that the Earthworm's arrival is the signal for the approach of new life. At the utmost point of death, as at the darkest point of night or the coldest moment of winter, comes the seasonal change. Characteristically, Enion is reminded of the passing of winter in the Song of Solomon 2: 6–17 and of the bridegroom's arrival at midnight in Matthew 25: 6.[35] The reader may be reminded of two passages in which Enion's near relative Enitharmon misunderstands the Earthworm's significance. When Newton in *Europe* blows the last trump, Enitharmon underestimates his apocalyptic significance. Unaware that she has slept for eighteen hundred years, she continues to call up her children, saying:

> Arise Ethinthus! tho' the earth-worm call;
> Let him call in vain;
> Till the night of holy shadows
> And human solitude is past!   (13. 16–19.)

The night being already over, she is the victim of her own propaganda, not taking eschatological truth seriously. Enitharmon is as unready as the foolish virgins to meet the coming day, which rises cruelly for her.[36] Again, earlier in *The Four Zoas*, Enitharmon shows she has misunderstood the coming of Christ, in terms of the Earthworm's activity. What she says is valid, out of context, but in context

---

Zech. 12: 4 and (as he mentions to me in correspondence), 'the pale horse' of death in Rev. 6: 8 is necessarily recalled by line 9.

[34] Isa. 7: 24, as noted by Miner, op. cit., pp. 257, 462 n. 5. The phrase 'briers and thorns' occurs also at Isa. 5: 6; 7: 23, 25; 9: 18.

[35] Miner, op. cit., p. 259, refers this passage only to S. of S. 2: 11–12, but other verses are also involved. Damon was the first of several commentators to note the reference to Matt. 25: 6, op. cit., p. 390. The Earthworm's function, as Enion sees it, may be partly illumined by the design for *Night Thoughts* iii, p. 34 (No. 109), where Death is portrayed as serviceably unshackling the immortal spirit to free it for a higher life.

[36] Enitharmon in *Europe* also has affinities with the 'foolish woman' of Prov. 9: 13–18; the Fairy's song of plate iii describes the state of man under her bondage, alluding to Prov. 9: 17 to show the bait by which man has been caught.

she is twisting the significance of the Incarnation to suit her limitation of life to the natural cycle. She says (ii. 34. 80–2):

> For every thing that lives is holy for the source of life
> Descends to be a weeping babe
> For the Earthworm renews the moisture of the sandy plain,

meaning that the Incarnation demonstrates God's approval of merely mortal life and so ignoring the divine determination to redeem man from merely mortal life (becoming as we are, that we may be as he is). Thus she sees the Earthworm as the agent of merely earthly renewal, functioning in a closed seasonal cycle, whereas the Earthworm's real function is to consume the mortal body in order to release man to immortal life, as Enion in her song proves by experience. Enion is actually in the state of consummation, of being consumed by the Earthworm, to 'die a death / Of bitter hope'. Blake does not flinch from the anguish of her passing; he understands her attachment to her 'Spectre'—her mortal life with its cares and hopes which must now 'become invisible to those who still remain'. In presenting the paradox of the man gently fading away in his immortality, he draws on the assurance of Paul's famous analogy in 1 Corinthians 13: 8–12, for with 'improved knowledge' the former (in Paul 'childish') things are 'cast away'.

The second part of Enion's song becomes more properly a song of spring, as she tells Ahania 'what is done in the caverns of the grave'. Her vision expands beyond her personal consummation to an understanding of the apocalyptic expectancy in everything that lives and dies. As in the last plate of *The Book of Thel*, we understand that the caverns of the grave are the home of all mortal life, though the viewpoint has changed completely. We also find that the nature of the apocalyptic expectancy has changed from the relatively simple vision of 'To Spring', being now subsumed in Blake's Albion myth, with its obvious debt to the Osiris myth as recollected in Milton's *Areopagitica*.[37] Blake's beautiful image of the waiting seed is what stamps this most particularly as a spring song:

> The Lamb of God has rent the Veil of Mystery soon to return
> In Clouds & Fires around the rock & the Mysterious tree
> As the seed waits Eagerly watching for its flower & fruit
> Anxious its little soul looks out into the clear expanse
> To see if hungry winds are abroad with their invisible army
> So Man looks out in tree & herb & fish & bird & beast
> Collecting up the scatterd portions of his immortal body
> Into the Elemental forms of every thing that grows.
>
> (110. 1–8.)[38]

[37] The passage is important to Blake, not only for his Albion myth but, for instance, for the image of Orc scattering religion to the four winds in *America* 8. 5–6. It is in the paragraph that begins 'Truth indeed came once into the world' (1644 ed., p. 29).

[38] The apocalyptic references in the first two lines are to Matt. 27: 51; 24: 30; 2 Pet. 3: 7–13.

The seed-Man's principal cause of sorrow is the cyclical nature of mortality, from which he longs to free himself.

> He touches the remotest pole & in the Center weeps
> That Man should Labour & sorrow & learn & forget & return
> To the dark valley whence he came to begin his labours anew
> In pain he sighs in pain he labours in his universe.
>
> (110. 18–21.)[39]

Thus the final image of spring with which Enion leaves us is a poignant one:

> . . . whereever a grass grows
> Or a leaf buds   The Eternal Man is seen is heard   is felt
> And all his Sorrows till he reassumes his ancient bliss.
>
> (110. 26–8.)

A leaf budding is a sorrowful event seen in this changed perspective, because it is a leaf budding only to the cyclical mortal life, not to the eternal spring celebrated in *Songs of Innocence*. Even this assertion of renewal is, however, symbolic of the eternal renewal we should, being in the caverns of the grave, hourly expect.

This eternal renewal is celebrated at large in Night IX of *The Four Zoas*, which includes the lengthy spring song of the risen Vala. Luvah and Vala come to leave 'the shadows of Valas Garden' (126. 18 ff.), the natural universe (as I take it), and 'saw no more the terrible confusion of the wracking universe'. Reminding us of *The Book of Thel*, Luvah hovers invisible in bright clouds over Vala's head and thus, we are told, 'their ancient golden age renewd'. Recalling both Christ's classic resurrecting command to Lazarus (John 11: 43) and the Bard's plea in 'Introduction' to *Experience*, Luvah calls:

> Come forth O Vala from the grass & from the silent Dew
> Rise from the dews of death for the Eternal Man is Risen.
>
> (126. 31–2.)

This time there is no despairing 'Earth's Answer' to reject the appeal, for the Soul truly awakens. However, at first Vala can hardly believe that she is effectually awoken and so she repeats Thel's fears of transience:

> Then O thou fair one sit thee down for thou art as the grass
> Thou risest in the dew of morning & at night art folded up . . .
>
> (127. 14 ff.)

Being assured that 'Yon Sun shall wax old & decay but thou shalt ever flourish', Vala now finds in her bosom 'a new song' arising to her Lord, which is appropriately Biblical in mode, a psalm of rejoicing (128. 4–24). In this song are several

---

[39] The Biblical references in lines 19–20 are to Ps. 90: 10 and Job 1: 21. Miner gives the latter, op. cit., p. 464 n. 17); he included the former in an early draft of his paper.

Biblical reminiscences (particularly of the Song of Solomon, emphasizing its authenticity of inspiration), with some touches of Milton's Eden.[40] The Biblical quality of Vala's song is further emphasized by its varied parallelism, yet 'the voice of [her] rejoicing' is fully and freshly individual, a 'rapturous song' indeed, expressive both of firmer assurance and gladder excitement than could easily be paralleled in the Bible or in Milton. Particularly pleasing is her delight in sharing her enjoyment and her discovery of kinship both with her flocks and with the 'birds that sing & adorn the sky'. Hers is the mild authority of a child who commands others but to enable them to join in her own explorations of felicity.

The drawings on *FZ* pages 126 and 128 have a problematical relation to their text. Page 126 shows a small figure running with what looks like a shepherd's crook and it would be easy to identify this figure with Vala who 'walks yea runs' in line 34, except that the drawing looks more likely to represent a male than a female. However, it could be a female figure wearing the peculiar dress of the sleeping woman on p. 128 and it is hard to resist the temptation to identify both of these figures with Vala, who falls asleep in lines 24 ff. of p. 128. The woman's dress, with its turban-like hat, seems Oriental, and I would like to suggest provisionally that Blake is deliberately drawing Vala so that she may look like the bride in the Song of Solomon (rather than, for instance, a Marie Antoinette playing at shepherdesses)—a bride pretty obviously available for the pleasures of love. The tambourine-like instrument under her left hand may confidently be identified as the Biblical timbrel, which is characteristically a female instrument.[41] That she is not lying 'on the downy fleece / Of a curld Ram' is no barrier to the identification, as her sleeping accommodation is quickly changed in the poem to 'a downy bed' (lines 25–6, 33). One is on shakier ground in identifying the flautist above her as Luvah, her natural companion, as this figure also looks to be feminine. However, this seems to be a composite scene looking forward to later pages, where the treading of grapes (in which the figures at the left of this design are engaged) becomes an important motif (esp. p. 136), to the accompaniment of 'Timbrels & Violins' at one place (136. 28), though the flute has a place with other instruments at another (135. 33).[42]

There are several reminiscences of the Song of Solomon in the sequence (pp. 129–31) in which Tharmas and Enion, risen like children, join Vala in her

[40] For line 7, cf. S. of S. 2: 12–13; line 10, 5: 6; lines 11–12, 2: 8; lines 16–17, 6: 11; lines 19–20, 2: 3. For the hint, cf. Murray Roston, *Prophet and Poet*, Faber, London, 1965, p. 170. There are of course several other references to Canticles in the immediate context of the song of Vala, as well as elsewhere in the Night. She is in a garden authentically similar to that of Solomon's Song. Cf. note 43, below.

[41] Cf. Miriam the prophetess, Exod. 15: 20; Jephthah's daughter, Judg. 11: 34; the 'damsels playing with timbrels', Ps. 68: 25; Blake's *Job* illustrations, Plate 3.

[42] There seems no good reason to suppose that Blake's illustration serves for 137. 21, where 'Luvah & Vala slept on the floor o'erwearied', though this is a remote possibility.

pleasant garden.[43] Later, Enion is given another song of spring, which recapitulates themes in her earlier song and is more hopeful in mood (132. 18–24).

> O Dreams of Death the human form dissolving companied
> By beasts & worms & creeping things & darkness & despair
> The clouds fall off from my wet brow the dust from my cold limbs
> Into the Sea of Tharmas Soon renewd a Golden Moth
> I shall cast off my death clothes & Embrace Tharmas again
> For Lo the winter melted away upon the distant hills
> And all the black mould sings. . . .

The reminiscence of Song of Solomon 2: 11–12 is obvious and is almost the last in the Night.[44]

I close this study with a consideration of one of the finest of all these songs of spring in Blake, the double song celebrating birds and flowers in two strophes of eighteen lines each in *Milton* 31. This song is written to different purpose from the others, consonant with Blake's broader purpose in *Milton* to deny natural causes (which only seem) and affirm spiritual causes of natural effects (cf. *Milton* 26. 44–6). The song of spring in *Milton* 31 is one of several passages subserving this aim, for instance 24. 48–76; 25. 66–26. 12; 26. 31–27. 63; 28 and 29 *passim*, etc. Blake's campaign is conducted by means of three rhetorical persuasives. The crudest method is bald assertion: thus, for instance, 'Bowlahoola is the Stomach in every individual man' (24. 67) and our perceptions of flowers and birdsong are visions 'of the lamentation of Beulah over Ololon' (31. 45, 63). The second method is systematic humanization and spiritualization of natural objects, as they are described: thus, for instance, the 'sportive Root' and 'the wise Emmet' dance with other creatures 'round the Wine-presses of Luvah' (27. 11 ff.) and the 'awful Sun' looks on the Lark, who 'vibrates with the effluence Divine', with 'eyes of soft humility, & wonder love & awe' (31. 35–8). The third method is more daring, the writing of self-evidently better nature poetry than had been achieved by poets aware only of natural causes. This third method reveals to us again the poet compelled by his youthful genius to break away from the pastoral forms honoured by his contemporaries. However, the mature poet, while still wishing to invoke more authentic literary sources, no longer retreats from natural descriptions, instead choosing to challenge comparison with the greatest nature poet of the previous

---

[43] For 129. 34, cf. S. of S. 2: 14 (as Margoliouth notes, op. cit., p. 150): for 130. 5 (also 127. 33, 36), cf. 1: 8 (given by Miner, op. cit., p. 269); for 130. 32, cf. 6: 11; for 131. 1–3, cf. 2: 5, 5: 8, and 4: 16 (Miner, pp. 260 and 463 n. 12); for 131. 10–11, cf. 2: 11–12 (Miner, p. 463 n. 12).

[44] There is another reference to 2: 11, 17 when the sons and daughters of Luvah (and perhaps Luvah and Vala also, though this is confusing) are cast by the Eternal Man wailing into the world of shadows 'till winter is over & gone' (137. 28–31). The poem ends with a magnificent evocation of the new earth that follows the consummation. Though this is a good deal more than a song of spring, it incorporates spring images, as in 139. 1–3.

generation by occupying the same ground, singing of spring as a pageant of flowers and a chorus of birds.

Thomson's 'symphony of Spring', as he calls it (*Spring*, line 580), is written to celebrate 'a theme / Unknown to fame—the passion of the groves' (580–1). His thesis is ''Tis love creates their melody': the birds 'in courtship to their mates / Pour forth their little souls' (614, 619–20). Blake rather carefully witnesses the same effects, but he ascribes them to a different cause—though still the cause is love. I quote the relevant descriptive passage in Thomson (lines 590–613):[45]

>   . . . Up springs the lark,
> Shrill-voiced and loud, the messenger of morn:
> Ere yet the shadows fly, he mounted sings
> Amid the dawning clouds, and from their haunts
> Calls up the tuneful nations. Every copse
> Deep-tangled, tree irregular, and bush
> Bending with dewy moisture o'er the heads
> Of the coy quiristers that lodge within,
> Are prodigal of harmony. The thrush
> And wood-lark, o'er the kind-contending throng
> Superior heard, run through the sweetest length
> Of notes, when listening Philomela deigns
> To let them joy, and purposes, in thought
> Elate, to make her night excel their day.
> The blackbird whistles from the thorny brake,
> The mellow bullfinch answers from the grove;
> Nor are the linnets, o'er the flowering furze
> Poured out profusely, silent. Joined to these
> Innumerous songsters, in the freshening shade
> Of new-sprung leaves, their modulations mix
> Mellifluous. The jay, the rook, the daw,
> And each harsh pipe, discordant heard alone,
> Aid the full concert; while the stock-dove breathes
> A melancholy murmur through the whole.

Characteristically, Thomson makes an effort to arrange his choir in groups that mimic symphonic effects, using several orchestral metaphors, though he does not manage to suggest the form of an actual piece of music. Though less concerned with musical technique, Blake improves on Thomson by skilfully arranging his birds in a genuine musical pattern. Thomson's effects are detached though complex, Blake's follow a musical progression and we have a real sense of music worth hearing, for his birds are raptly attentive to each solo performer. Both

[45] Text, here and elsewhere, from J. Logie Robertson, ed., *The Complete Poetical Works of James Thomson*, Oxford University Press, London, 1908, reprinted 1961.

Thomson and Blake devote several early lines to the lark, leader of 'the Choir of Day', though Blake seems to take from Thomson only his word 'springs' and his reference to the lark's 'loud' song. However, Blake for his final image must have taken a hint from a later line in Thomson, line 630, which describes the courting birds who 'shiver every feather with desire': on Blake's Lark 'every feather / On throat & breast & wings vibrates with the effluence Divine'. Thomson's lark is conventional; Blake's description superlatively exciting with its splendid rhythm, daring onomatopoeia, and astonishing visual clarity. One is not surprised that 'All Nature listens silent to him' and he stops the Sun in his tracks: Blake's Lark is a vibrant miracle and must have a miraculous effect on his listeners. This, indeed, is the measure of the vast difference between Thomson and Blake. Thomson is confessedly striking out in a fresh course, yet he is rather plainly describing natural effects by means of natural causes; Blake is responding to natural beauty as to a miracle: his Lark 'vibrates with the effluence Divine'. All of Blake's birds of song partake of this miracle, they attend 'with admiration & love' and their choir is a loving sharing of divine inspiration, not a sexually motivated outpouring from 'coy quiristers'.[46]

Thomson's pageant of flowers is in *Spring* 529–55:

> Fair-handed Spring unbosoms every grace—
> Throws out the snow-drop and the crocus first,
> The daisy, primrose, violet darkly blue,
> And polyanthus of unnumbered dyes;
> The yellow wall-flower, stained with iron brown,
> And lavish stock, that scents the garden round:
> From the soft wing of vernal breezes shed,
> Anemones; auriculas, enriched
> With shining meal o'er all their velvet leaves;
> And full ranunculus of glowing red.
> Then comes the tulip-race, where beauty plays
> Her idle freaks: from family diffused
> To family, as flies the father-dust,
> The varied colours run; and, while they break
> On the charmed eye, the exulting florist marks
> With secret pride the wonders of his hand.
> No gradual bloom is wanting—from the bud
> First-born of Spring to Summer's musky tribes;
> Nor hyacinths, of purest virgin white,
> Low bent and blushing inward; nor jonquils,
> Of potent fragrance; nor narcissus fair,

---

[46] Thomson and Blake have in common the lark, nightingale (Philomela in Thomson), thrush, and linnet. Thomson has the bullfinch, Blake the goldfinch.

As o'er the fabled fountain hanging still;
Nor broad carnations, nor gay-spotted pinks;
Nor, showered from every bush, the damask-rose:
Infinite numbers, delicacies, smells,
With hues on hues expression cannot paint,
The breath of Nature, and her endless bloom.

Thomson's pageant is certainly attractive but Blake's shows up its defects. Although Thomson begins by ordering his pageant chronologically, with the earliest flowers first, after the discursive lines on the natural causes of variations in tulips (at which Blake may have secretly raged), he degenerates into mere catalogue. Blake speeds up the movement of his pageant by restricting himself to a single May morning, the time of richest spring flowering, dramatizing it as a synaesthetic dance with a brilliant climax as the Rose (last to be listed by Thomson) 'bursts her crimson curtaind bed / And comes forth in the majesty of beauty'; his following brief list does not seem a mere catalogue but a rich effloresc-ence, where 'Exuberance is Beauty', whose 'innumerable Dance' is more stimulat-ing to the Imagination than Thomson's vaguer 'Infinite numbers, delicacies, smells' with hues 'expression cannot paint'. Thomson's pageant, that is, becomes merely quantitative, whereas Blake's is individual and qualitative and is shaped 'in order sweet & lovely', not merely accumulated. There is a very striking dif-ference between Thomson's interest in the superficial aspects of his flowers, mainly their colours (shades from Newton's prism!) and Blake's immediate concern with the hidden causes of the wondrous achievements of his flowers, who are seen as lovely individuals rather than as objects with single striking aspects. The flowers are like his 'little winged fly, smaller than a grain of sand' in *Milton* 20. 27–40, whose interior gates to Eternity are not closed. The contrast between Blake's flowers (one should say, 'Flowers', because he dignifies them with a capital) pouring out their fragrance from their own infinite centre and Thomson's flowers, some of which seem to have their beauty added from the outside, could hardly be greater. Thomson's wall-flower is 'stained with iron brown' and his auriculas are 'enriched / With shining meal o'er all their velvet leaves', while his pinks are 'gay-spotted'. The reason for the difference is that Thomson is observing his flowers from the outside, with the eye of a still-life painter, whereas Blake is trying, with the help of his imagination, to share his Flowers' life. Thomson, that is, copies from nature; Blake copies from Imagination. It would be absurd not to admire the skill of the still-life painter (and Blake might well be prepared to admit that Thom-son's auriculas, like Spenser's allegory, are not free from Imagination despite the formal distinction); it would be equally foolish to miss the sharpness and integrity of Blake's appreciation of the external appearances of his Flowers, particularly that of the White-thorn, lovely May, who 'Opens her many lovely eyes: listening'.

Blake and Thomson have five flowers in common only, the wall-flower, jonquil, carnation, pink, and rose. However, Thomson mentions the wild thyme and the lily in the near context (lines 514, 495). It is typical of the poets that Thomson should delight in flowers with exotic names like polyanthus, auricula, and ranunculus and that Blake should prefer to name only familiar English flowers. (Similarly, in the list of birds, Thomson has 'Philomela' but Blake sticks to 'Nightingale'.)

It seems likely that, while wishing to improve on Thomson's natural description, Blake also wished to compliment the elder poet Milton on his sensitive humanization of spring flowers in *Lycidas*, lines 142–51. Milton is the subject of Blake's epic and it is beautifully appropriate that Beulah's lamentation over Ololon, Milton's Emanation, as she proceeds to follow Milton into Eternal Death, should be envisioned in a recollection of the flowers who mourned the death of Milton's friend:

> Bring the rathe Primrose that forsaken dies,
> The tufted Crow-toe, and pale Gessamine,
> The white Pink, and the Pansie freakt with jeat,
> The glowing Violet,
> The Musk-rose, and the well-attir'd Woodbine,
> With Cowslips wan that hang the pensive hed,
> And every flower that sad embroidery wears:
> Bid *Amaranthus* all his beauty shed,
> And Daffadillies fill their cups with tears,
> To strew the Laureat Herse where *Lycid* lies.[47]

Recognition of this allusion seems necessary to explain the vision as a 'lamentation', as it is only on a superficial view that Blake's flowers might seem to be weeping: they are actually embodiments of joy, but a 'Joy even to tears, which the Sun rising dries'. It is, none the less, exquisitely right that Blake should insist on calling these visions of joy visions 'of lamentation': the best lamentations, the best elegies—like *Lycidas* or *Adonais*—are most profoundly paeans of joy.

In context, the two visions of lamentation come as a distinct surprise. The preceding sequence exhibits increasingly anguished reactions to the revelation that Ololon's descent, as an *imitatio Christi*, a repetition of his self-sacrificial descent to redeem mankind, is the Second Coming. First 'All Beulah wept, for they saw the Lord coming in the Clouds' (31. 10). Next, 'all Nations wept in affliction Family by Family', and 'all the Living Creatures of the Four Elements, wail'd /

---

[47] I take the hint from Susan C. Fox, 'The Structure of a Moment: Parallelism in the Two Books of Blake's *Milton*', *Blake Studies*, ii. 1 (1969), 27, who says that Blake's dance of flowers is 'described in the language of the *Song of Songs* with recollections of *Lycidas*'. The first remark is an exaggeration. Text of *Lycidas* quoted from Helen Darbishire, ed., *The Poetical Works of John Milton*, Oxford University Press, London, 1958.

With bitter wailing' (31. 12, 17–18). These last are Marlowe's elements, warring within our breasts for regiment:

> These are the Gods of the Kingdoms of the Earth: in contrarious
> And cruel opposition: Element against Element, opposed in War
> Not Mental, as the Wars of Eternity, but a Corporeal Strife
> In Los's Halls continual labouring in the Furnaces of Golgonooza
> Orc howls on the Atlantic: Enitharmon trembles: All Beulah weeps. (31. 23–7.)

It is immediately after this vision of conflict that we are reminded of the Nightingale beginning the song of spring—a song which exhibits only a beautiful harmony and sympathy of feeling between natural creatures. The contrast between the state of Satan just evoked (cf. 31. 18) and the ideal life of spring creatures could not be greater or more reassuring—sounding 'comfortable notes' indeed![48]

Although Blake's two visions picture the ideal response of living creatures to the Second Coming of the Lord, they are definitely visions of this world, with its limitations, visions such as Blake describes in his letter to Trusler of 23 August 1799, no doubt. Although 'the nightingale has done lamenting' (to borrow a phrase from *Visions of the Daughters of Albion* 2. 24), the Lark's song must re-echo from the 'heavenly Shell' (*Milton* 31. 33)—an outer barrier—while the Biblical figures Og and Anak 'fiercely guard' the inner gates to Eternity at the heart of each Flower (31. 48–9).[49]

The human participation in this vision is only briefly mentioned in a phrase borrowed from the Song of Solomon: 'Men are sick with Love' (31. 62, cf. Canticles 2: 5; 5: 8). This love seems more generalized than the sexual love-sickness of Solomon's Song: it seems to be a response to the 'sweet & lovely' order of nature seen imaginatively, to the almost cloying richness of nature in the spring season rather than to the almost cloying richness of Solomon's prince. I feel, however, that in essence both are the correct responses to the same object of adoration, perhaps especially in view of Peter Alan Taylor's suggestion that Blake has taken up Milton's parallel between the lark and Christ in *Paradise Regained* ii. 279–83.[50] Certainly this would fit Enion's insight that

> . . . whereever a grass grows
> Or a leaf buds   The Eternal Man is seen is heard   is felt
> And all his Sorrows till he reassumes his ancient bliss.
>
> (*The Four Zoas* viii. 110. 26–8.)

---

[48] Cf. *Milton* 34. 1 and note the words of 'the Divine Voice' in Plate 33 (which follows directly the visions of Plate 31, as Plate 32 is a digression), which explain true marriage and the sexual purpose of Ololon's descent.

[49] For Og and Anak cf. Num. 13: 21 ff. and 21: 33–5. These strange guardians deserve separate study. From one point of view they are offensive 'blocking characters'; from another they are servants of the Divine Mercy, protecting fallen man from the too unbounded visions of Eternity. Milton associates them together (as the Bible does not) in *Samson Agonistes*, line 1080. For both visions, Miner suggests another Biblical reference (op. cit., p. 463 n. 8), comparing Canticles 2: 11–12, where after winter 'The flowers appear on the earth; the time of the singing of birds is come'.   [50] 'Providence and the Moment in Blake's *Milton*', *Blake Studies*, iv. 1 (Fall 1971), 54 f.

In the spring time, this ancient bliss is resumed and the whole creation fully humanized, as we see at the very end of *Jerusalem*. In the words of Romans 8:21–2, a very important text for Blake, this is so

21 Because the creature itself also shall be delivered from the bondage of corruption into the glorious liberty of the children of God.
22 For we know that the whole creation groaneth and travaileth in pain together until now.[51]

In his work, Blake makes many efforts to push man to the brink of Last Judgement, of recognizing every thing as it is, infinite, of entering into 'the glorious liberty of the children of God'. The return of the spring season provided him with a metaphor of great power and flexibility to suggest this state, the nearest we may come in this world to Eternity. At the end of *Milton* he leaves mortal man trembling on the verge not of spring, however, but of autumn: 'the Great Harvest & Vintage of the Nations'. Yet in a characteristic confusion of the seasons, he has the Lark and the Wild Thyme, the singer and the dancer of spring, announce the autumnal harvest (42. 29–30)—optimistic auguries.

[51] Cf. Margoliouth, op. cit., p. 151, in another connection. Blake makes several direct references to the text, e.g. in *J* 16. 25–6 (where the 'blue Mundane Shell' is also mentioned); 50. 5; 98. 42 ff.

VII

CHRIST'S BODY

Jean H. Hagstrum

IN 1798, in a moment of angry and radical protest, Blake affirmed his belief in the Bible and professed himself a Christian.[1] That belief appears virtually everywhere in his poetry, except perhaps in his first work, the unillustrated *Poetical Sketches*. In *Innocence* Christ is immanent in nature and appears as child, shepherd, lamb, and lion. In *Experience* and the Lambeth prophecies Jesus is implicitly present as a revolutionary hero, as Orcan energy, or as a phase of historical consciousness. In the 'terrific parts' of the later prophecies, properly called Christian, the historical Jesus and the mythical Christ are both prominent. And in many of the late personal lyrics and prose declarations Jesus is often at the centre of devotional attention. It is with the later work that this paper is primarily concerned.

Blake was that rarest of phenomena in English art, a Christian painter. Christian themes, remarkably scarce in English art even in its earlier period, abound in Blake, who was born in a century when in European art generally there was an absence of religious feeling.[2] Romantic painting did, to be sure, return to religious themes, but these were often 'transformed' into secular substitutes. The traditional Lamentation and the expiration of a saint, for example, reappeared in Romantic art as domestic and ostensibly secular deathbed scenes in which the deceased on his bed was surrounded by a mourning family—a theme present also in Blake.[3] The greatest of the Romantic painters, Goya, did paint Christ—but infrequently compared to Blake. Goya's Christ usually appears in flickering lights and shadows, his body or his face obscured, a mysterious force that generates its own kind of power but one that lacks a palpable physical presence.[4]

What Goya's Christ lacks Blake's possesses fully, a human body. And in this

---

[1] Annotations to Watson (1798), K, p. 387.

[2] See Ellis K. Waterhouse, *Painting in Britain 1530 to 1790*, Penguin Books, London, 1953, whose 192 plates contain not a single Christ; Eric Mercier, *English Art 1553–1625*, Clarendon Press, Oxford, 1962, whose 96 plates contain only one Christ; and Chap. VIII ('Le Renouveau de l'Art Religieux') in Marcel Brion, *Peinture Romantique*, Editions Albin Michel, Paris, 1967, esp. p. 231.

[3] See Robert Rosenblum, *Transformations in Late Eighteenth Century Art*, Princeton University Press, Princeton, N.J., 1967, pp. 28–9.

[4] See the dozen or so paintings that portray Christ in Pierre Gassier and Juliet Wilson, *Life and Complete Work of Francisco Goya*, Reynal & Co., New York, 1971.

respect it is the Englishman and not the Spaniard who is closer to the central Christian tradition. For, although the interpretations have varied enormously through the centuries, the language of the Bible proclaims loudly that Jesus possessed and possesses a body. It is called a 'temple', as is the body of his followers, for in his role as Redeemer he is also 'the Saviour of the body'. In his death he 'bare our sins in his body'. Sacramentally, his body is broken again and again in the Mass, and Christians are mystically regarded as the several members of his one body. There are in Pauline theology two bodies, the natural one, which is sown in corruption, and the spiritual or glorious body, which rises from the dead.[5]

The Biblical expressions of the preceding paragraph reappear often in Blake, sometimes in the kind of pious ejaculation characteristic of dissenting Christians through the centuries and sometimes in shockingly bold interpretations of orthodox doctrine. From the revised *Vala* until the last letters, Blake quotes, echoes, amplifies, and revises the resounding scriptural utterances about Jesus' body, while in his paintings, from the hundreds of illustrations of Young's *Night Thoughts* in the nineties to the last great Dante illustrations, the person of Christ is an unmistakable physical being. For our discussion of this important theme in word and design we may choose as an epigraph the following sentence, engraved on the *Laocoön* plate about 1820:

> The Eternal Body of Man is The Imagination, that is,
> God himself ⎫
> The Divine Body ⎭ [Yeshua] Jesus: we are his Members.
> (K, p. 776.)

This sentence, which runs like a border on the left-hand side of the plate, reveals metaphorically the circular motion that many of Blake's designs literally possess. It moves from man to imagination to God to Christ and back to man again. One can enter the sentence, as it were, at any point and come out with all elements present, each assimilated with the others. The nouns being all nominative, they remain unaffected by the simple copulative verb: God is Christ, Christ is Imagination, Imagination is Man. One may put these noble nouns in any other order one chooses—the important fact remains that all are equal and each ends up becoming the other. This process takes place without loss of identity, for each entity possesses a body, the pivotal and uniting concept in the declaration. Just as there are three bodies (Laocoön's and his two sons') on the plate[6] that bears this engraved sentence, so there are three bodies in the sentence: man's, Christ's, and God's. The *primus inter pares* is that of Christ, since it mediates between God and man. It is Jesus' body that redeems man and God alike, both man's art and man's mind. With equal justification it could be argued that man is the first among equals,

---

[5] For the Biblical passages quoted or alluded to in this paragraph, see John 2: 21, I Cor. 6: 19, Eph. 5: 21, I Peter 2: 24, Col. 1: 24, I Cor. 12: 12, 15: 44.

[6] For a reproduction see E, plate 3.

since it is his image that Christ assumes in revealing the essence of God. God says to Christ in the *Everlasting Gospel* (ll. 41–2):

> Thou art a Man, God is no more,
> Thine own Humanity learn to adore.   (K, p. 750.)

But then Blake, as if to upset either of the priorities just mentioned, gives bolder lettering to *Imagination* than to any other word in the sentence we have chosen as our epigraph, warning us that Jesus must also be viewed psychologically and artistically.

The Man Jesus: A Context for Blake

The central Christian paradox, that Jesus was at once very man and very God, has encouraged radically antithetical beliefs about his person during the Christian centuries. Blake, with unmistakable and reiterated force, emphasizes the human. He endows the historical Jesus with a 'vegetable' body like our own.

It would be difficult to exaggerate the disconcerting originality of Blake's portrayal of the physical humanity of 'the man Christ Jesus' (1 Tim. 2: 5). But his character of Christ does not stand alone. It is not unrelated to the revolutionary attempts of some of his English contemporaries to displace the divine figure enshrined in the churches. Paine was one of these, and Blake in that angry moment alluded to at the outset found it possible to see in Paine's work the inspiration of the Holy Ghost and to find him a truer Christian than his indignant and frightened episcopal adversary.[7] But Paine's 'Religion of Humanity'[8] is, in the last analysis, timid and imaginatively thin and did not command Blake's respect for long. While Paine saw in religion 'a law and a tye to all able minds', Blake found that the 'religion of Jesus was a perfect law of liberty'.[9] Although Paine grudgingly conceded that the story of Christ was 'the least hurtful part' of the Bible, Jesus remained essentially inaccessible to modern man—the 'Christian church [having] sprung out of the tail of heathen mythology'. Paine's Jesus was a 'virtuous and an amiable man', to be sure, an admirable preacher of benevolence; but he lacked the energy that animates Blake's portrayal. In Paine there was too much of the bland Shaftesbury or the smiling, cynical Voltaire to nourish for very long the mind of a man who loved the Bible and adored Christ.[10]

It is different with Joseph Priestley. His pages have been called 'uninspired and

---

[7] See Annotations to Watson *passim*, but esp. K, p. 396.

[8] This phrase Paine coined in *The Crisis* (vol. vii, 1778); it is quoted by Moncure Daniel Conway, ed., *The Writings of Thomas Paine*, G. P. Putnam's Sons, New York, 1899, iv. 6.

[9] Frederick Tatham's manuscript Life of Blake (c. 1832) in Bentley, *Records*, p. 531. The phrases quoted are not marked as direct quotations from either Paine or Blake; the language may therefore be Tatham's.

[10] The quotations from Paine in this paragraph come from Conway, *Writings*, iv. 25, 26, 423. For other comments on Jesus and the Bible, see pp. 32, 34, 39, 45, 165, 169, 293. For Paine the resurrection was the story of an apparition created by timid minds (p. 169), and he confesses to knowing Job and the Psalms poorly (p. 48).

uninspiring',[11] but his view of Christ was anything but arid. And Blake must have admired his courageous defiance of many establishments as he attempted to free the Church of the corruption of historical Christianity. There are of course differences between the two reformers, the chief being that Priestley, a Unitarian, stresses the superiority of God the Father while Blake's Christ regularly tends to replace the Father until he has been truly softened into a loving and forgiving Jehovah. But the similarities are more important than the differences, and one finds in the polemical learning and homiletical eloquence of Priestley much that was congenial to Blake. Priestley, regarded by his foes as a dangerous heretic, wanted desperately to live within the faith, professing himself a Christian both among the freethinkers of Paris and the ecclesiastics, Roman and Anglican, of his own country. He attacked the orthodox views of Jesus' divinity and came to disbelieve in his miraculous conception. He derided the view of Jesus as a 'super-angelic spirit or *the Arian logos*', as an off-spring of that '*Platonic nous*' that entered Christianity with the Gnostics and persisted among the theologians of the eighteenth century. Priestley wanted a man of flesh and blood, not a Jesus who was 'one of the *aeons*', a being so depersonalized that he 'ate and drank in a peculiar manner, not voiding excrements'. Priestley found the doctrine of the substitutionary atonement of Christ a 'gross misrepresentation of the character and moral government of God', a doctrine 'greatly disfiguring and depraving' the 'scheme of Christianity'. On the positive side, he, like Blake, placed Jesus well above that noblest of the ancients, Socrates; he accepted as necessary and crucial the belief in Jesus' Resurrection and the immortality of the human spirit—'a prospect which nothing but the gospel can give us'. He had faith that the kingdom of Christ would one day embrace all mankind and extend to the end of time. He found, even in a superstitious time like the Middle Ages, the salutary sweetness of individual piety and belief in a personal Christ. He believed that Jesus was blasphemed more by Christian corruption and the hideous cruelties of religion than by almost anything else. To the author of 'The Grey Monk' and the prose passages in *Jerusalem* all this must have seemed to restore saltness to preaching that had lost its savour. For Blake was also a confessed soldier of Christ, fighting corruptions in Christianity and cruelties in all religions and attempting to restore belief in '*the simple humanity of* Jesus', Priestley's obsessively recurring phrase.[12]

[11] Kathleen Raine, *Blake and Tradition*, Princeton University Press, Princeton, N.J., 1968, ii. 15.

[12] The quotations from Priestley in this paragraph are drawn from the following: *An History of Early Opinions concerning Jesus Christ*, 1786, i. 61, 179; iv. [1]; *The History of the Corruptions of Christianity* in *Theological and Miscellaneous Works of Priestley*, 1818, v. 92; *A General History of the Christian Church*, 1790, i. iv. For the ideas attributed to Priestley in this paragraph, see also ibid., i. 12 (on the resurrection and immortality); *The Doctrines of Heathen Philosophy*, 1804, dedication and p. v (on his profession of Christianity and on Socrates and Jesus); *General History*, i, p. xxii (on medieval Christianity); *Institutes of Natural and Revealed Religion*, in *Works*, ed. Joseph Rutt, 1817, ii. 84 (on depraved religions, including the burning of wicker-works filled with men); and *Autobiography*, ed. Jack Lindsay, Fairleigh Dickinson University Press, Teaneck, 1970, p. 111 (Priestley's profession of faith while in Paris).

A subtler and grander Christ than one could expect from the polemical prose of a dissenting preacher and chemist was Blake's heritage from that great Christian reformer, John Milton. How Blake softened and humanized the austere and sublime religion of Milton in the linear delicacies and the chromatic harmonies of his water-colour illustrations has been described elsewhere. But there was enough of the loving human Jesus in Milton's prose and poetry to warrant considering that poet an important source of stimulation for Blake's more insistently human Saviour. In *Paradise Lost* (i. 4) the first mention of Christ refers to him as the 'one greater Man', the new Adam who will regain the 'blissful Seat' (i. 5) lost at the Fall; but it is perhaps 'th'exalted man' of *Paradise Regained* (i. 36) who is Blake's nearest prototype. In response to this poem Blake created nine separate portrayals of Christ; in response to the much longer *Paradise Lost*, he created only five.[13] Milton's Christ in *Paradise Regained* is in 'youths full flowr' (i. 67), a man of 'deep thoughts' (i. 190), who 'into himself descended' (ii. 111). As a youth he had burned with heroic ambition to save his people from the Roman yoke, and, abjuring violence, he had tried to fight for equity and freedom with 'winning words' that would make 'perswasion do the work of fear' (i. 221–2)—a promise of Mental Fight and Intellectual Battle that Blake must have cherished. Blake, however, goes beyond even the Milton of *Paradise Regained* in humanizing the Son of God, whose central characteristic in the earlier poet remains filial piety and obedience. Blake's Christ seems to undergo a deeper sensual temptation than Milton's stoical, heroic God-man. In 'The Banquet Temptation' (Plate 27) Blake tempts Christ with much more than the 'pompous Delicacies' (ii. 390) of food and drink that the fasting Son of Man had rejected in Milton. Blake's Christ recoils, open-mouthed—as though both tempted and repelled in horror—at the women the artist has drawn—women who can best be described in the words of that 'dissolutest Spirit that fell', Belial: they are 'expert in amorous Arts', 'skill'd to retire, and in retiring draw / Hearts after them'. They are capable of 'draw[ing] out' the 'manliest . . . brest' with 'credulous desire' and 'voluptuous hope' (ii. 150, 161–7). That kind of temptation Belial had desired but Satan and Milton had rejected as unworthy of Christ and doomed to failure. But Milton's description of the rejected temptation stimulated Blake to confront Christ with the alluring and swelling curves of seductive women and so humanize the scene much beyond what Milton would have regarded as appropriate. For Blake's Christ, possessing

---

[13] I refer to the Huntington series; the illustrations in the Museum of Fine Arts, Boston, contain only four designs in which Christ appears. For a reproduction of all the *Paradise Regained* illustrations, see Joseph A. Wittreich, Jr., ed., *Calm of Mind: Tercentenary Essays . . . in Honor of John S. Diekhoff*, Case Western Reserve University Press, Cleveland and London, 1971, plates 1–12. For an interpretation, see Wittreich's article, 'William Blake: Illustrator–Interpreter of *Paradise Regained*', ibid., pp. 93–132. For an account of Blake's 'softening' of Milton's religion, referred to above, see Jean H. Hagstrum, *William Blake, Poet and Painter*, University of Chicago Press, Chicago, 1964, p. 126.

27. *The Banquet Temptation*, from Illustrations to Milton's *Paradise Regained*.
Water-colour.
Fitzwilliam Museum, Cambridge

a body whose flesh is apparent under the flimsy dress he wears, is tempted by female blandishments; but Milton's is at this point tempted only by food on a 'stately board' near which stands a chaste and orderly array of solemn youths, Diana's nymphs, and ladies fairer than 'Fairy Damsels' (ii. 350–61).

Thus Milton, for all the heroic humanity of his Christ, cannot be said to anticipate fully the extremely physical Christ of Blake's vision. Only Michelangelo can be said to have done that. Nowhere in the antecedent tradition is there a Christ closer to Blake's than his. In the Tondo Doni at the Uffizi, Florence, the child Jesus is a nude, dark-haired little Italian boy. The nude Christ-child in Bruges has chubby legs and thighs and unusually large testicles. Even in the late Crucifixions, a spiritual vision if there was one in art, where Christ is less corporeal than usual, a real physical presence is still communicated. In the *Pietà* of the Vatican the dead body is handsome, its flesh supple and yielding.

In his portrayals of the risen Christ Michelangelo also anticipates Blake, for the fiery glory of resurrection has not consumed the flesh or the form. In 'The Risen Christ', a statue in Santa Maria Sopra Minerva, Rome, the body is nude, the musculature is prominent but more delicate than that of Christ's body in the 'Last Judgment' on the Sistine walls, which is also emphatically human. The face of the statue is Grecian, though lightly bearded; the nose delicate, the eyes pensive, the hair soft and curly, the genitals unconcealed. One of the most remarkable of Michelangelo's achievements in linear art is his study, now in the British Museum (Plate 28), in which Christ rises effortlessly, almost soaringly, from the tomb in the kind of inspired levitation with which Blake often endows Redeemer and redeemed.[14] Both artists were led to show the power of line over matter by the thought of resurrection.

Blake's 'Vegetated' Christ

Blake's belief in the human body of Christ has its lighter and darker side. The example of Michelangelo leads naturally to the congenial aspect. In Blake's paintings the child Jesus, curly-headed, his male member visible, sleeps as the mother hushes the young Baptist. The boy in the house of the carpenter recalls the Poet of Innocence, holding in his hand, however, the compass and the rule, iconic signs of future ominous import that may foreshadow Experience.[15] The man Jesus appears to be especially close to poets, infants, mothers, and lovers. As the Good Samaritan in the Young illustrations, he ministers to a wounded traveller lying partially nude under a tree, a figure who of course stands for suffering Man but

[14] Department of Prints and Drawings, 1860–6–16–133. Reproductions of the other works by Michelangelo referred to appear as follows: Paolo D'Ancona and others, *Michelangelo*, Bramante, Milan, 1964, plate 1, illustrations 29, 41, 213; Ludwig Goldscheider, *Michelangelo*, Phaidon Press, London, plates 155–7, 229; Frederick Hartt, *Michelangelo Drawings*, Harvey N. Abrams, New York, n.d., illustrations 180–5, 350, 408–30.

[15] The paintings referred to so far in this paragraph are reproduced in Keynes, *Bible*, under the following titles: 'The Virgin Hushing the Young Baptist', plate 99 and 'Christ in the House of the Carpenter', plate 108.

28. Michelangelo: *The Resurrection of Christ* (detail). Black chalk.
British Museum, Department of Prints and Drawings

who also may recall the Poet. Even when bearing the scroll of judgement Christ is described by Blake as representing the 'Eternal Creation flowing from The Divine Humanity in Jesus' (K, p. 444). He stands in a cluster of grapes (that symbol of physical love), as lovers kiss and a mother nurses a child (Plate 29). He reclines at a table laden with vine and fruits, an 'omnipotently kind' Jesus who 'takes His Delights among the Sons of Men'. He, not God, creates Eve under a crescent moon and so institutes Beulah (Plate 30).[16]

A good summary emblem of Blake's human Christ of mild, gentle, and sexually fertile humanity is the Christ who baptizes. A reddish-haired Jesus attracts the gaze of a young Poet who looks fixedly at him. Beside the Poet are babes and children, mothers and old people, some of them nude or nearly so. Three or four couples are near or at the age of sexual awareness, into which Christ seems to be baptizing some of the young.[17]

Sexuality in Blake is seldom without a darker side, and Christ, who possesses a 'vegetable' body, cannot escape the terror and the tragedy of physical life. In the tempera of 1825, the Mother weeps, her halo is ominously spiked; behind her the night is dark, and the sky contains only pale golden stars. The child's eyes are red-rimmed at the bottom, and his whole colouring and mien suggest darkness. This holy pair does not reassure us; the picture is far from comforting.[18]

Now and then the gentle Jesus of Blake's paintings may seem to verge on sentimentality. But taken as a whole his portrait of the man Jesus is far from sentimental or simple, darkened as it is with ambiguity and conflict. In a watercolour, 'Christ taking Leave of his Mother', John shows the tender emotion, not Mary, whose tearless eyes stare and whose face wears an expression of harshness and distance.[19] In the concluding line of 'To Tirzah' Blake echoes Jesus' rejection of his mother, 'Woman, what have I to do with thee?' (John 2: 4 and K, p. 220). It is part of the unpleasant task of Los the Poet and his wife Enitharmon to 'draw' the Lamb of God 'into a mortal form' so that he 'may be devoted to destruction from his mother's womb'. By his 'Maternal Birth' he becomes the 'Evil-One', or Satan; he takes on the 'Satanic Body of Holiness' and as a 'Vegetated Christ' becomes a blasphemy.[20]

Jesus inherited his maternal humanity by the normal natural act, not by supernatural impregnation. He was conceived in adultery—a fact that Mary herself admitted and that Joseph did not deny but forgave (*J* 61). The body that thus originated in a secret act of sin was most certainly endowed with sexual appetite,

---

[16] Blake here illustrates *Paradise Lost*, viii. 452–90. The Young illustrations in this paragraph are the following, referred to by the number pencilled on the original in the British Museum: 68 (Night II, p. 35; the good Samaritan); 512 (Night IX, p. 94; Christ as the vine); 534 (Night IX, p. 116; Christ reclining at table).

[17] Keynes, *Bible*, plate III ('Christ Baptizing').　　　　[18] Frontispiece (in colour) to Keynes, *Bible*.

[19] Kerrison Preston, *The Blake Collection of W. Graham Robertson*, Faber & Faber, London, 1952, plate 14.

[20] *Four Zoas*, i. 293 (K, p. 272); *J* 90. 33–8 (K, pp. 736–7).

[94]

BUT wherefore more of Planets, or of Stars?
Æthereal Journies? and, discover'd there,
Ten thousand Worlds, Ten thousand Ways devout?
All *Nature* sending Incense to THE THRONE,
Except the bold LORENZOS of Our Sphere?
Opening the solemn Sources of my Soul,
Since I have pour'd, like feign'd ERIDANUS,
My flowing Numbers o'er the flaming Skies,
Nor see, of *Fancy*, or of *Fact*, what more
Invites the Muse ---- Here turn we, and review
Our past Nocturnal Landschape wide : ---- Then, say,
Say, then, LORENZO! with what Burst of Heart,
The Whole, at once, revolving in his Thought,
Must Man exclaim, adoring, and aghast?

" O what a Root! O what a Branch is Here?
" O what a Father! What a Family!
" Worlds! Systems! and Creations! ---- And Creations,
" In One agglomerated Cluster, hung,
" * Great VINE! on THEE : On THEE the Cluster hangs;
" The filial Cluster! infinitely spread

* *John* xv. 1.

29. Design for Young's *Night Thoughts*, No. 512. Water-colour.
British Museum, Department of Prints and Drawings

30. *Creation of Eve*, from Illustrations to Milton's *Paradise Lost*. Water-colour.
Museum of Fine Arts, Boston

and the bold and conventionally impious question of the *Everlasting Gospel* (sec. *e*. 1, K, p. 753), 'Was Jesus Chaste?', must, like all the other questions that introduce the several sections of that powerful and angry poem, be answered negatively. Jesus had assumed a body that felt 'the passions that with Sinners deal' (*i*. 14, K, p. 756). And Blake must surely have disagreed with those who 'say he never fell' (*i*. 15, K, p. 756). It is probable that the one who selected publicans and harlots (the Biblical *sinner* becomes *harlot* in Blake) for his company literally entered the Magdalen's 'dark Hell' and literally dwelled in her 'burning bosom' (*e*. 77, 78, K, p. 755). Even in so frank a poem as this Blake does not directly say that Jesus sympathized with Mary to the extent of sharing her physical passion; but it is consistent with his whole doctrine of incarnation and of the divine participation in the human that he should have entertained that notion. The 'shadowy Man' (the anti-Man Satan, a fiend of righteousness, the new Urizen) threatens Jesus with the 'festering Venoms bright' of venereal infection and with other diseases by means of which he 'binds' the 'Mental Powers' (*e*. 81–7, K, p. 755). (The last clause, incidentally, shows that Blake understood what a mischievous and poisonous deterrent to pleasure and to the sensual imagination the fear of illness could be. He also saw that sexual fears and hesitations inhibit *all* mental life.)

The veil of Blake's myth only barely conceals his entertainment of the notion that the vegetated body of Jesus knew passion or desire and that in his maternal humanity he may indeed have experienced the sufferings that often attend the indulgence of sexual appetite. He is said to have been born 'in the Robes of Luvah', the Zoa of physical passion. Disease forms a 'Body of Death around the Lamb / Of God to destroy Jerusalem & to devour the body of Albion'. And the clouds of Ololon 'folded' around Jesus' limbs 'as a Garment dipped in blood', the last being a phrase that invokes the passionate Zoa, Luvah.[21]

There is, therefore, much to put off on the Cross and in the tomb. In the magnificent water-colour that illustrates Michael's prophecy of the crucifixion in *Paradise Lost*, Book xii (Plate 31), the Orcan sexual serpent is nailed to the Cross along with the body of Christ, and at its foot lie dead the bodies of Urizen, or Death, and Vala-Rahab, fallen sexual nature, she too a 'Mother of the Body of Death' (*J* 62. 13, K, p. 696).

What may have reconciled Blake to so radically literal an interpretation of the physicality of Jesus as that we have been discussing is that he seems to have believed in the value of a spiritual *difficulté vaincue*. That is, the deeper the bog,

[21] *Four Zoas*, viii. 263 (K, p. 348); *J* 9. 9–10 (K, p. 628); *Milton* 42. 12 (K, p. 534). I recognize—and have studied in 'Babylon Revisited, or the Story of Luvah and Vala'—many other meanings of the mantle, or robe, of Luvah and the body of Vala, meanings that refer to the corrupt Church and the war-like State. But here I urge that the primary and literal meaning of physical passion be retained. See Joseph Wittreich and Stuart Curran, eds., *Blake's Sublime Allegory*, University of Wisconsin Press, Madison, 1972.

31. *Prophecy of the Crucifixion*, from Illustrations to Milton's *Paradise Lost*. Water-colour.
Museum of Fine Arts, Boston

the more heroic the rescue; the graver the sin, the more glorious the redemption; the greater the participation, the profounder the sympathy. Blake apparently craved an experienced rather than an innocent saviour. Forgiveness, always difficult, becomes truly sublime when it first understands and then pardons the guilt of sexual infidelity. Crime statistics keep showing that the sins of the flesh are among those most difficult to forgive. And so it is precisely at the point where mercy meets bodily sin that the spirit of Jesus is most fully revealed.

> O holy Generation, Image of regeneration!
> O point of mutual forgiveness between Enemies!
> Birthplace of the Lamb of God incomprehensible!
>
> (*J* 7. 65–7, K, p. 626.)

We have seen that Blake regarded the 'Birthplace of the Lamb of God' as an adulterous bed. That point alone is not significant. The redemptive fact is that the magnificent forgiveness offered Mary by Joseph released her from crippling fear, causing her to 'flow like a River of / Many Streams in the Arms of Joseph'. And her new joy seems somehow commensurate with the gravity of her fault: 'If I were Pure I should never / Have known Thee' (*J* 61).

Being born of Mary, Jesus came of a physical line that included that prostitutor of natural sexuality, Rahab (*J* 62). The result was that his natural body, capable of all the naturally innocent Beulah joys, also had its unpleasant clayey side. Blake dramatically makes the possession of a sexually sinful body a precondition of a glorious, sinless body—even for Christ. Blake certainly risked the censure implied in Paul's question, 'Shall we continue in sin, that grace may abound?' (Rom. 6: 1). The least calculating of men, Blake would scarcely have plotted in cold blood a sin–grace sequence. But sin was obviously deep in the human physical condition, and the death and resurrection of one whose body was compounded of clay did release an abundance of grace. So Blake sang a Hallelujah Chorus on the Fortunate Incarnation:

> He died as a Reprobate, he was Punish'd as a Transgressor.
> Glory! Glory! Glory! to the Holy Lamb of God!
>
> (*Milton* 13. 27–8, K, p. 494.)

The Resurrected Body

Since the death of Jesus purged away his mire and dross, the adoration of a physical Jesus is idolatrous cadaver-worship.

> He took on Sin in the Virgin's Womb,
> And put it off on the Cross & Tomb
> To be Worship'd by the Church of Rome.
>
> (*EG b.* 57–9, K, p. 749.)

A Resurrection is clearly necessary, and to Blake Jesus' acquisition of a new body was an especially precious belief. It supported his conviction that 'Mind & Imagination' were living realities that transcended 'Mortal & Perishing Nature' and constituted 'the divine bosom into which we shall all go after the death of the Vegetated body'. It is touching to read the last letters of the aged Blake as he is about to assume what he called 'our Eternal or Imaginative Bodies'. These bodies, constituting 'The Real Man' or the 'Imagination', can pre-date death and grow 'stronger & stronger as this Foolish Body decays'. And in that conviction Blake will follow his friend Flaxman into 'his Own Eternal House . . . Into the Mind, in which every one is King & Priest'. All these quintessentially Blakean phrases express a fervent personal faith, and there is testimony that Blake attained in his later years a kind of radiant sainthood.[22]

Blake's personal faith is serene, but it remains a faith and not a philosophy. Neither he nor the apostle Paul explains what a spiritual, eternal, or resurrected body is. But unlike Paul, Blake *portrayed* the risen Christ, and he may be said to have brought life and immortality to light in his art.

The primary fact about the resurrected Christ is that he still possesses a body. And that body remains in appearance very much what it was before the Crucifixion and Resurrection. Jesus is still blond, bearded, his cheeks red or pink, his demeanour tender and mild, his face and figure handsome, as the flowing garment he continues to wear follows the contours of his muscular body. He remains, except for a few scenes which are bathed in mysterious light, a clear and well-outlined human being, fully corporeal. One characteristic, already alluded to, seems to have become more prominent—that wonderful, gravity-defying lightness of movement, as Christ springs up, swirling with the clouds or flames, cutting a swath of human radiance as he rises (see Plate 32). His hands are now nail-pierced; his eyes are touched with wonder and suffering and sometimes appear bold and decisive. This figure is the harbinger of all the Resurrections Blake as a Christian poet of love and hope has sung about—of the earth that 'shall arise and seek', of the youth and the pale virgin who 'arise from their graves and aspire', of the nations and peoples, who, when the 'grave is burst', 'spring like redeemed captives. . . .'[23]

Michelangelo (Plate 28) may, as we have suggested, have taught Blake how to draw the movements of a resurrected body. But another artist, not hitherto

---

[22] Annotations to Reynolds (K, p. 475); *VLJ* (K, p. 605); *J* 77 (K, p. 717); letter to Cumberland, 12 Apr. 1827 (K, pp. 878–9).

[23] See Young illustrations (frontispiece to whole work (Plate 32): 127 (*Night* IV, p. 18); 121 (*Night* IV, p. 12); 'The Little Girl Lost' (K, p. 112); 'Ah! Sun-Flower' (K, p. 215); *America* 6. 2, 5 (K, p. 198). See also the following representations of the risen Christ: 'Christ Appearing to the Apostles' in Robert Essick's Finding List in *Blake Newsletter*, v (1971), 109; 'The Conversion of Saul' in C. H. Collins Baker, *Blake's Drawings and Paintings in the Huntington Library*, San Marino, 1957, plate 29.

32. Design for Young's
Night Thoughts, frontispiece.
Water-colour.
British Museum, Department of
Prints and Drawings

mentioned, may have created subtler examples of a physical–spiritual body streaming mildness and glory, a body that is spiritual without being vaporously unsubstantial and that is physical without being gross or earthbound. That artist is Fra Angelico, who, according to Samuel Palmer, provided Blake with an 'ideal home'—that is, with a resting place for his imagination. For, said Palmer, it was on this artist's memory that Blake, who 'fervently loved early art', dwelt 'with peculiar affection'.[24] If in Milton we see a Christ in whom the fullness of the Godhead bodily dwells—a being of power, justice, and righteous anger as well as mercy—in Fra Angelico we see a Christ full of grace and truth. As a child he is blond, fair, sweet, tender, sometimes extending his hand in blessing, sometimes instructing. The body that is taken from the Cross is still delicately handsome, the hair soft and tender, falling in long curls, the eyes clear even in death. In the *Noli me Tangere* at San Marco, Florence, the resurrected Christ remains blond and lightly bearded and the curly hair has been straightened. Lacking the curvaceous body beneath light clothing that Blake's Christs often have, Fra Angelico's here

[24] Bentley, *Records*, pp. 42 n. 1, 283.

possesses an almost translucent quality, an air of delicate and transcendental sadness. The body, though substantial, seems barely to touch the ground. In *The Entombment* now in Munich the dead body of Christ appears to be standing with very little help. Although it is in *rigor mortis*, the persisting life principle seems to be expressed by the fact that one man can lift it without strain.[25] Fra Angelico must have struck the poet–painter as one who had solved the problem of how to paint a resurrected body—of how to etherealize it without robbing it of substance.

Not all of Blake's Christs are individual beings whose physical humanity is paramount. Sometimes they are bathed in supernal light: Christ is born, is adored by the Magi, and prays on his bed as divine radiance lights the scenes.[26] Or Christ appears in allegory or emblem as the mediator between God and Man, as a personification of Mercy, or as a king who sits stiffly on a throne, attempting with one hand to put on the girdle of strength.[27] Or Christ may appear in 'Judgements' or 'Epitomes' along with almost hundreds of other bodies in comprehensive expressions of the whole truth about human destiny, large and complex works of art designed to express the 'Eternal Vision or Imagination of All that Exists'.[28]

These versions of the superhuman transcendental Christ, though relatively few in number, are important and require the attention of anyone who studies Blake's thought. But do they stand at the burning centre of the artist's vision of Christ? And are they as psychologically profound as the Christ whose resurrected body, however glorious, is still human?

Identification with the Glorious Body of Jesus

To 'internalize' an ideal—such is the modern way of describing the psychological process by which an admired person comes to fructify the inner life. Blake described it more poetically and humanly: the reader or spectator enters 'into these Images in his Imagination, approaching them on the Fiery Chariot of his Contemplative Thought' and then making a 'Friend & Companion of one of these images of wonder'. If we can do that, Blake says, then we too arise from our graves and 'meet the Lord in the Air'.[29] Blake's language is Biblical, and of course the process of identification with Christ has always been regarded by the Church as

---

[25] Germain Bazin, *Fra Angelico*, Hyperion Press, London, 1949, *passim* and esp. pp. 56, 78–9, 89–91, 116, 141; John Pope-Hennessy, *Fra Angelico*, Phaidon Press, London, 1952, plate 55 and *passim*.

[26] See Anthony Blunt, *The Art of William Blake*, Columbia University Press, New York, 1959, plate 35b and p. 67 (The Nativity); Keynes, *Bible*, plates 93 (Adoration), 105 (Child praying). Milton in the *Nativity Ode*, where Christ is referred to as 'That glowing Form, that Light unsufferable, / And that far-beaming blaze of Majesty' (stanza II), and some of Fra Angelico's paintings may have influenced Blake's portrayal of Christ in mysterious light. See the *Transfiguration* in Florence (Pope-Hennessy, plates 93–4) and *The Harrowing of Hell* in Wilhelm Hausenstein, *Fra Angelico*, Kurt Wolff, Munich, 1923, plate 23.

[27] Blunt, plate 34b (Mediator); Keynes, *Bible*, plates 27, 76.

[28] *VLJ* (K, p. 604). For a list of reproductions of 'Epitome of James Hervey's Meditations', see Essick's Finding List, item 112, and of the sketches and water-colours of 'The Last Judgment', Essick, item 191.

[29] *VLJ* (K, p. 611).

the essence of conversion. Blake engraved on one of the climactic plates (17) of his *Job*—that great story of the salvation of both God and Man—some ten verses from the Gospel of John, chapter 14: these verses present the ideal of union in love between God, Christ, and the believer—he in us and we in him. Blake had come to admire those Christians—Saint Teresa, Madame Guyon, Fénélon, and Wesley—who preached a gospel of pure love, pure because it was total and interior and ran counter to external formalities.[30]

There is considerable evidence that Blake renewed, perhaps more than once, his spiritual contact with Christ in moments of exalted and intense dedication.[31] Those moments are illuminated by the four designs we shall now study, ranging in time from the early 1790s to the last years of his life.

1. The Frontispiece to *Experience*

It does not seem to have been noticed that Christ appears on the frontispiece of the *Songs of Experience* (Plate 33). The halo in some copies has been ignored because we have not understood the baffling arrangement of the two figures. The design becomes clear if we see it as a version of the story of Saint Christopher bearing the child Jesus. That legend, extremely popular throughout the centuries, Blake could have encountered in many paintings, engravings, stained-glass windows, frescoes, and statues. Mrs. Jameson said in 1848 that figures of Saint Christopher were 'very common' on the walls of old English churches,[32] and the saint bearing the Christ-child was painted or engraved by Mantegna, Pollaiuolo, Altdorfer, Dürer, Van Eyck, and Rubens. One of the closest to Blake's frontispiece is the painting by Hans Memling that appears on one of the outside wings of a triptych (Plate 34).[33] The saint, who stands on a rock in a free-flowing mantle, is not the dark and grizzled giant often portrayed, but a more delicate man of Christ-like appearance.

As always, Blake adapts the legend to his own purposes. The shepherd advances from Innocence to the frontier of Experience, marked by the suggestion of water in the lower left-hand. The child is sometimes haloed but always winged—the divine joy of Innocence that has been revived in all of us by hearing the Piper's song and that must now be borne from Innocence into Experience by the Bard. The child

---

[30] Samuel Palmer said that Blake 'was fond of the works of Saint Theresa, and often quoted them with other writers on the interior life' (Bentley, *Records*, p. 41). See *J* 72. 51–2 (K, p. 712) and *Milton* 22. 54–62 (K, p. 506).

[31] See Jean H. Hagstrum, 'The Wrath of the Lamb: A Study of William Blake's Conversions' in F. W. Hilles and Harold Bloom, eds., *From Sensibility to Romanticism*, Oxford University Press, London, 1965, pp. 311–30.

[32] *Sacred and Legendary Art* (reprinted from ed. of 1896, AMS Press, New York, 1970), ii. 444.

[33] Memling's altarpiece bears the full title 'Virgin Enthroned with Saints, Angels and the Donor Sir John Donne of Kidwelly and his Family'. Now at the National Gallery, London, it was formerly in the Duke of Devonshire's collection at Chatsworth. Blake, who loved early Christian art, undoubtedly had seen Memling's originals and engravings. His friends, Charles and Elizabeth Aders, owned several Memlings, but apparently no Saint Christopher. See J. D. Passavant, *Kunstreise durch England und Belgien*, Frankfurt am Main, 1833, pp. 92–8 and Bentley, *Records*, p. 310 n. 1. I am not arguing a direct influence but saying that Blake knew the Christopher legend and found its expression in early (fifteenth-century) art congenial to his imagination.

33. *Songs of Experience*, frontispiece, copy E.
Relief etching with pen and water-colour.
Henry E. Huntington Library and Art Gallery

34. Hans Memling; *St. Christopher*,
from *The Virgin Enthroned with Saints*. Oil.
Reproduced by courtesy of the Trustees,
The National Gallery, London

does not straddle the shoulders, as in most representations of the Saint Christopher story, but sits on the head of his bearer: the artist who later portrayed Milton entering his foot may here be suggesting that Christ must be received intellectually, mentally. It is more likely, however, that Blake wants us to concentrate on the disturbed expression of the shepherd. It may express a deep and unconscious feeling that, although he is a 'Christopher' or 'Christ-bearer', he is not yet united with his ideal. Jesus is an external burden, not an inner vision.

2. Christ in the Illustrations to Young's *Night Thoughts*

In that large gallery of water-colours created to illustrate the once popular poem of Young, Christ appears again and again in impressive individual drawings and series of drawings that cannot here be studied in detail. He is often the visual counterpart of—one can even say the replacement of—God the Father. For when Young writes 'Dread Sire', or 'Father of all', Blake portrays Christ gathering the little children to himself; when Young writes of the 'Father fond . . . / Of Intellectual Beings', Blake draws a Christ blessing.[34] Christ in the Young series possesses all the human characteristics previously noted as belonging to his earthly ministry, and Blake is now in the 1790s affirming a cheerful cosmology—Christ transcends nature and will conquer death. Two aspects of this Christ throw light on the identification of the poet with his resurrected body. Christ has a special relation to the young Poet, from whom he receives a tribute of verse called 'A Miniature of Thee', or who appears in the guise of the Prodigal embraced not by a father but by Christ, or who reaches out toward the healing hand extended by Christ. The designs portray Christ and the Poet yearning to come together.[35]

But from some of the profoundest portrayals of Christ in the Young illustrations the Poet is absent. Four of these in a series show Christ attaining the resurrected or spiritual condition that will make the deepest unity possible.[36] In the first Christ stands on a cliff being tempted by a staring, youngish, beardless, blond, round-mouthed Satan, his hair flaming, a creature rude as well as nude. This Satan is a demon that Blake feared, a lawless and merciless power who creates State Religion and many other ills, an enemy who must be subdued. In the next Christ appears with another fearful enemy, Urizen as Death, kneeling abjectly before the 'bright Preacher of Life' (*J* 77. 21, K, p. 718) who is 'Stronger' than his enemy. In the next, to which we shall return, Christ, in a partial radiance, is emerging from the darkness that surrounds him. And finally the resurrected Jesus appears fully human as he reveals himself to the doubting apostle, Thomas.

The penultimate in this series of four (Plate 35) portrays a Christ who assumes

---

[34] 513 (Night IX, p. 95), 527 (Night IX, p. 109), 528 (Night IX, p. 110).

[35] 148 (Night IV, p. 39), 485 (Night IX, p. 67); 513 (Night IX, p. 95); 531 (Night IX, p. 113); and possibly also 518 (Night IX, p. 100) and 529 (Night IX, p. 111).

[36] 261 and 263 (Night VI, pp. 40, 42); 264 (an illustration with no text); 265 (a title-page illustration).

35. Design for Young's *Night Thoughts*, No. 264. Water-colour.
British Museum, Department of Prints and Drawings

the cruciform position and displays hands that are nail-pierced. The eyes, sad and upward-looking, show the marks of suffering, and the entire countenance is that of one who has known terror. Deep night still surrounds the figure and subdues his radiance. Though transfiguration is not complete, it is being achieved. This Christ is portrayed between the Cross and the tomb; the physical, sexual body is being put off and the resurrected body is being put on. The lower body remains obscured, while the head is irradiated, the hair flaming to each side. The moment is one of psychological tension. On its successful issue depends the salvation—the mental health—of the poet, for it is with the emergent Christ that he will henceforth be identified.

3. Christ in *The Four Zoas*

Christian imagery appears to enter this manuscript in a rush of revision, as Blake moves from *Experience*, where Christ is only implicitly present, to the Christian prophecies, where he stands at the apex of the myth. The Christ with whom we are most concerned here (Plate 36) appears in a cluster of three[37] within the manuscript, all of them portraying the risen body. A magnificent Christ in an engraving for the Young series which is here inserted into the manuscript is even more powerful in its rising motion than it was in the water-colour original (see Plate 32), where the beard and the radiance are less pronounced and the eyes less bright and piercing. (It appears that the humanity of the rising Christ is more strikingly affirmed in the engraving than in the water-colour.) On the next page, also an engraving imported into the manuscript from the Young series, the risen Christ stands in flames, the nails still in his hands and feet, his eyes mild but troubled as he looks down into a fiery abyss. Finally, at the culmination of Night VIII, an original pencil and crayon sketch (Plate 36) is a new inspiration, a profound and moving rendition of the resurrected body. Like Raphael's God,[38] the risen Christ pushes away the clouds. Lightly bearded as Blake's Christ nearly always is, his genitals are obscured by lines and shadows. Does Blake wish to say that the days of the Babylonian sexual captivity are over for Christ and can also be over for man? The eyes bear a more unmistakable message: calm now, they seem to have known turmoil; and if they reveal mercy, it is a mercy that has followed suffering. Distinctly a Christ, this figure may look like Milton, Los, the risen Albion, Blake, or any 'Christ-like man'[39] without being the less Christ for that. This masterpiece of few and energetic lines portrays a merciful hero, something quite new to history, available to all as an inner and also an outward-flowing energy.

---

[37] pp. 114, 115, and 116 in the manuscript of *Vala or the Four Zoas*. See the facsimile ed. by G. E. Bentley, Jr. (Clarendon Press, Oxford, 1963). For the Christian revisions of *Vala*, see ibid., pp. 174 ff.

[38] See Hagstrum, *Blake Poet and Painter*, plates 20–4 and p. 43.   [39] Bentley, *Vala*, p. 122.

36. Illustration to *The Four Zoas*, Night VIII, MS. page 116. Pencil drawing and crayon.
British Museum, Department of Manuscripts

4. The Christ of the *Paradiso*

In Canto XIV of the *Paradiso* Dante sees both Beatrice and Christ, each enveloped in a light so dazzling that the poet must in the end abandon speech and listen to music. The poet learns that the disembodied spirits he now beholds long for the new bodies and the redeemed organs of sense with which they will be endowed at the general resurrection. For the present the vision can only be a general illumination, an ever-changing play of light and shadow. Christ also appears in a fountain of light, in which the radiance assumes the form of the Cross. In rendering Dante's vision in an unfinished wash drawing Blake recalls the Cross and retains the light. His Christ stands in a blazing sun, his hair aflame and his arms extended in the cruciform position (Plate 37). But here, as always in Blake, light is only a garment, and the living form is a body. In Dante the spirits look to the future for their glorious bodies. Blake's Jesus already possesses his, and it is the fully human and totally recognizable body that we have come to know. Christ wears a light garment that conceals the genitals but does not cover the navel or obscure his pronounced musculature. The hair is curly, the beard short; and the eyes, like those of the Christs in the Young illustrations and *The Four Zoas*, are eyes that have suffered and known love.

How shall we explain the exaltation and intensity of this drawing, whose every line is instinct with energy? In portraying Christ, Blake had not always achieved so consummate a union of mildness and strength, of mercy and force. Here the vision is personal; and magnetic lines of identification seem to arise from the Poet at the bottom to his master at the top, for the linear sweep of this design is upward. The garb of Christ near his neck recalls—even reduplicates—the simple dress of the Piper of Innocence. Christ in apotheosis remains what he has always been—the shepherd, the sweet singer of the new Israel, the shoot from the stem of Jesse, a David *redivivus*. But now the intensity is such that one can think only of a consummated spiritual union between the Poet and Christ, that union which the Saint Christopher—Bard of Experience had not yet achieved and for which the youths of the Young designs yearned. To return to one of the equations of our epigraph, the Imagination *is* Yeshua, Jesus.

We should not be surprised by the audacity of this identification. Union with Christ is the consummation of the Christian dream, and Blake has prepared us for it. A series of other identifications move toward this climax. In a poetical epistle to Butts in 1802 Blake describes an encounter with Los, who flamed in his path as a real sun. The great Zoa of the Poetic Imagination, said Blake, burned with 'the bows of *my* Mind & the Arrows of Thought'.[40] That experience is recalled at least

---

[40] K, p. 818. Emphasis added. Albert S. Roe in his *Blake's Illustrations to the Divine Comedy*, Princeton University Press, Princeton, N.J., 1953, rightly believes that this epistolary poem is parallel to Dante's vision of Christ (which he reproduces as his plate 90); he also finds J 4. 1–5 (K, p. 622) and plate 76 (the Crucifixion) to be parallels (p. 176).

37. *Dante Adoring Christ*, from Illustrations to Dante's *Paradiso*.
Pencil with pen and water-colour.
National Gallery of Victoria, Melbourne

twice in *Milton*. On one plate Los steps from the sun just behind Blake, who is putting on his sandal and who looks back at the fiery man behind him (Plate 38). The language on plate 22 interprets the scene; Los, says Blake,

> kissed me and wish'd me health,
> And I became One Man with him arising in my strength.
> . . . Los had enter'd into my soul:
> . . . I arose in fury & strength.   (22. 12–14, K, p. 505.)

Blake's union with Los is only an earnest of the even greater union with Christ, whose 'Divine Appearance *was* the likeness & similitude of Los'.[41] When in the moment of great artistic and prophetic inspiration Blake says that he became 'One Man' with Los, he is virtually saying that he became Christ, who is often called One Man, the authenticator and supporter of all artistic form, the breath and finer spirit of all prophecy.

We are now at the glowing core of Blake's vision, and we must be careful to be precise. Blake's sense of identification with Christ is profound, and he must surely have felt that he had in vision attained that 'Eden' in which Jesus lives 'in us, and we in him . . . in perfect harmony', since he hopes that his reader will with him become 'wholly One in Jesus our Lord'.[42] But however intense the identification, individuality is never lost. It would be ironic if the Christ who preserved the 'Eternal Individuality' of the sleeping Albion should allow it to be weakened when the Eternal Man awakens to vision (*J* 48. 1–4, K, p. 677). But of course Blakean identification always keeps identity intact. In the portrayal of Dante's vision (Plate 37) the Poet stands before Christ open-armed and receptive but as a distinct and separate identity. It is so also when Adam stands before the crucified Christ (Plate 31) or when Albion contemplates his Lord on the cross (*J* 76).

Thus of Blake's climactic portrayal of Christ we may use the term *identification* but not *absorption*, which tends to blur outline and lineament. Union, yes; fusion, no. Christian oneness, yes; mystical, Neoplatonic, Oriental, Gnostic unity, no. From that kind of vagueness and insubstantiality Blake was preserved by his conception of the body of Christ. A body may be attracted to another body, but it is also the nature of a body to resist absorption and to keep some kind of distance.

It was surely his unwavering commitment to a bodily Christ that underlay his conception of essential artistic form as human and bodily. We do well, therefore, not to confuse his idea with that of the Romantic naturalists, for whom form is organic as a plant or a vegetable is organic. Blake's form is organic, to be sure, but as a man is organic. And Blake's larger forms are conceived of as purely human reduplication and extension. The lineaments in Blake's forms 'tend and seek with love & sympathy' the 'Divine Humanity'. When individual forms are fruitful and

---

[41] *J* 96. 7 (K, p. 743). Emphasis added.   [42] *J* 38 [34]. 20–1 (K, p. 665) and *J* 3 (K, p. 621).

38. *Milton*, copy A, plate 21. Relief etching with water-colour.
British Museum, Department of Prints and Drawings

multiply, they constitute a family, One Family, which is another name for Christ—
a family united in love and benevolence, joy and sorrow, as brothers, sisters, sons,
fathers, and friends are united in a human community.[43]

Blake's belief in the one family of man united in benevolence and brotherhood
may suggest Shaftesbury and the Latitudinarian divines of the eighteenth century.
But for Blake these thinkers must have seemed to produce only 'Swell'd &
bloated General Forms', a phrase that not unjustly characterizes the mental forms
and the prose style of the third Earl, whose hymn to nature celebrates a being who
is 'boundless, unsearchable, impenetrable'. Pope, who in the *Essay on Man* never
once mentions Christ, says that God 'loves from whole to part but man loves from
self to whole',

> As the small pebble stirs the peaceful lake.

Blake must have found Pope's spreading circles only another example of deadly
abstraction. Closer in time to Blake, Rousseau may have been for a time attractive; but Blake came to believe that the confessor knew of no way to cast out sin
and that the writer who began by calling everyone good by nature ended a friend-
less creature haunted by evil men. Blake early proclaimed himself of another
school, in which particularity and Christianity were united. Lavater wrote that
'mankind differs as much in essence as they do in form, limbs, and senses—and
only so, and not more'. To that sentence Blake responded: 'This is true Christian
philosophy far above all abstraction.' Describing the 'Beauty proper for sublime
art' (that is, the 'idea of intellectual Beauty'), Blake said it consisted of 'lineaments,
or forms and features that are capable of being the receptacles of intellect'. If these
words had been written by someone else, Blake would surely have exclaimed in
the margin, 'A golden sentence. This is our Lord.'[44]

[43] For the passages quoted in this paragraph and for the conception of form as manly and familial, the crucial
passages are J 38 [34]. 10–28 (K, pp. 664–5) and J 43 [38]. 19–24 (K, p. 672).

[44] For the quotations and allusions in this paragraph, see J 43 [38]. 19 (K, p. 672); Apostrophe to Nature
from Shaftesbury, *The Moralists*; *Essay on Man* iv. 361–6; J 52 (K, p. 682); Annotations to Lavater (K, pp. 65,
66, 76); A Descriptive Catalogue (K, pp. 579–80).

VIII

THE CHAPEL OF GOLD

G. Wilson Knight

I OFFER an interpretation of Blake's poem 'I saw a chapel all of gold', with the especial purpose of indicating what I mean, and have always since my earliest publications meant, by the 'interpretation' of poetry. Here is the poem:

> I saw a chapel all of gold
> That none did dare to enter in,
> And many weeping stood without,
> Weeping, mourning, worshipping.
>
> I saw a serpent rise between
> The white pillars of the door,
> And he forc'd & forc'd & forc'd,
> Down the golden hinges tore.
>
> And along the pavement sweet,
> Set with pearls & rubies bright,
> All his slimy length he drew,
> Till upon the altar white
>
> Vomiting his poison out
> On the bread & on the wine.
> So I turn'd into a sty
> And laid me down among the swine.[1]

To start with, we have a chapel: the poem is to be about religion. Though sexual implications occur, there is no sexual partner: the chapel is a chapel, and not a woman. 'Gold' in poetry has the obvious connotations. The religion indicated is one of an unusual and superlative kind.

But no one *dare* enter the chapel: it strikes fear. This is usual in all higher visions, as in Coleridge's *Kubla Khan*:

> And all should cry, Beware! Beware!
> His flashing eyes, his floating hair!

[1] In Blake's Manuscript Notebook there is an earlier, and weaker, variant to line 8: 'Till he broke the pearly door'. Text and punctuation follow K, p. 163.

The Chapel of Gold

> Weave a circle round him thrice,
> And close your eyes with holy dread,
> For he on honey-dew hath fed,
> And drunk the milk of Paradise.

Any attempt to state too uncomprisingly some aspect of the Golden Chapel arouses fear. To offer an example from my own experience: I find that what I call the 'seraphic' intuition among poets of quality, that is, vision inspired by male youth, is likely to be greeted by either opposition or silence.

Meanwhile religious people are outside the chapel, weeping and worshipping. They represent the Christian Church as Nietzsche was to see it in *Thus Spake Zarathustra*, saying (ii. 4): 'They must sing better songs ere I learn belief in their Saviour . . . Whom doth this mummery of sorrow convert?' Christianity is, or has become, febrile, given over to the negations of crucifixion and grief. It is a religion of self-abasement and worship rather than one of virility and life. It is, as it were, castrated; the sexual powers have not been incorporated. The Chapel of Gold corresponds to the higher state of being, wherein sexual instinct is contained, defined throughout *Thus Spake Zarathustra*.[2]

And now, the Serpent. What is it? Having regard to its frequent use as a phallic symbol, I read it in that light. This will only be legitimate if the symbolic use is well known and has authority from tradition; otherwise interpretation should flower inevitably from the surface statement; as with the Golden Chapel. I cannot see the Serpent as referring to the priesthood. S. Foster Damon, in *A Blake Dictionary*, 1965, lists a number of different correspondences to the Serpent in Blake, and though the priesthood is one of them, examples are more in the nature of comparison than identification. The context at least makes the meaning clear: this scarcely allows us to assume the correspondence when the context does not. Foster Damon himself reads our present poem as describing sexual activity: '"I saw a chapel all of gold" is based on the thesis that a forced and unwanted act of sex (the Serpent) is a pollution of the sacrament of real love' (p. 366). Without wholly committing ourselves to that statement, we can say that the authority for a sexual reading of some sort is strong, and that the subsequent manipulation is such that no reasonable doubt is left.

The Serpent rises between white pillars. 'Rise' suggests sexual erection, with the pillars as legs; but there is also a contrast between 'white' as purity and the Serpent, though no necessary contrast as yet between the Serpent and the gold. The Serpent is enough at home with the gold to be able to break in. The insistent and not-to-be-denied power of sexuality is indicated by the reiteration of 'forc'd';

---

[2] My interpretation of *Thus Spake Zarathustra* was set out in *Christ and Nietzsche*, 1948. Some points of it are given in *The Golden Labyrinth*, 1962, pp. 293–7; and others appear in *The Malahat Review*, xxiv (Victoria, B.C., Oct. 1972).

its strength is such as to be able to tear down the 'golden hinges'. In this success there is honour, though there may also be desecration. What Nietzsche would call the 'lion' in man (*Thus Spake Zarathustra* i. 1) is sufficient to force an entry. We are now inside.

There follows an interesting juxtaposition. The pavement is called 'sweet', and is inlaid with 'pearls & rubies'. Rich stones are throughout poetry used as correlatives to spiritual worth. The Serpent is, in contrast, 'slimy'. Slime suggests a blend of water and materiality. Now either we can see the Serpent's entry as an insult to the spiritualities, driven home by the use of 'sweet', or we may suppose that we are at a moment when we accept the slime as worthy to be among them. Though 'length' suits a real Serpent, 'slimy' does not, and presumably comes in through sexual associations.

The 'altar white' stands for religious purity, in the conventional sense, with anti-sexual intimations, whereas 'gold' has, or might be supposed to have, sexuality within it. We are not now so sure about that. That the colour 'white' holds ambivalent associations, pleasant and unpleasant, is well argued by Herman Melville in his chapter 'The Whiteness of the Whale', in *Moby Dick*. So we have a white altar, bread, and wine: we seem to be within orthodox, traditional, religion after all, with all its negations and prohibitions. The Nietzschean gospel appears to be forgotten.

I once observed that whereas the three Synoptic Gospels, in their account of the Last Supper, record the partaking of bread and wine, the Gospel of John *instead* records the love-association of Christ with the Beloved Disciple, who lay in his 'bosom'. These are significant alternatives, of food and love; and love is surely the higher. The Chapel of Gold was, we had thought, like that, beyond the biological; but it is now a chapel of white altar, bread, and wine; of Crosstianity rather than, in the best, golden, sense, Christianity.[3]

The Serpent vomits his poison. 'Vomited' suggests, negatively, food; and it is natural enough that the Serpent should attack the bread and wine with a nega- tion. That there is, however, something wrong is clear in that, though a serpent might well eject, though scarcely 'vomit', poison, sexual ejaculation, which I take to be also implied, expels a life-force. The symbol jars us, though the wrongness is germane to the poem's content, which turns on the ethical ambivalence of sexual activation. We have now been persuaded to see sexuality as ugly and dangerous; above all, as desecrating. After ejaculation, there is likely to be a psychological change, and on certain occasions a revulsion: that happens here. The experiencer is utterly abased and thinks himself only worthy to lie among the 'swine'. It is important to recognize that the Serpent, the 'he' of the poem, represents the sexual side of the experiencer, and that the 'I' is the experiencer himself.

[3] For my views on this more 'golden' Christianity, see *The Christian Renaissance*, 1933; enlarged 1962.

The poem expresses the failure of sexuality to enjoy the Chapel of Gold. Sexuality, and perhaps it alone, can force entry; but it remains somehow inadequate. Perhaps, for a perfect sublimation, sexual activation should have been withheld. John Cowper Powys can perhaps help us. A passage from *Maiden Castle* (vi. p. 240: repr. p. 252) runs:

Don't you see what force there is in sterile love? Why, my dear boy, it's the strongest force there is! Rampant desire unfulfilled—why, there's nothing it can't do. Stir up sex *till it would put out the sun* and then keep it sterile! That's the trick. That's the grand trick of all spiritual life.

And yet, 'sterile' begs a question: does it imply lack of sexual activity or simply lack of intercourse? May functioning be allowed in private? There is here no love partner; the Chapel is not the body of a mate, or the worshippers outside it would have been meaningless.[4] The poem expresses a *solitary*, but sexually motivated, experience; and how far should it go? Man's total, and therefore sexual, self, should somehow achieve success, if we are not to remain among the weepers and worshippers. Perhaps the Serpent was too hasty. In *Thus Spake Zarathustra* (i. 1) we read: 'To create new values—even the Lion is not able to do this: but to create for himself freedom for new creation, for this the Lion's strength is sufficient.' The Serpent (= Lion) was able to force entry, but the rest must be done by Nietzsche's 'Child', signifying 'innocence'. Perhaps to come near to a high visionary experience, and yet fail to master it, may leave one in a plight unknown to the less adventurous.

We need not regard the poem as a final statement. It reports a single experience, to be so read, as a recognizable handling of the problem, and only valid within limits. Even so, it is 'a poem of terrible power, and terrible beauty' (J. Middleton Murry, *William Blake*, 1933, p. 125).

Such is my interpretation. I have followed every curve of the poem, and have tried to remain true to it. Where paradox is involved, I have allowed it to stand, as paradox. I have kept as true to the surface as possible, and only applied to the symbols arbitrary meanings where they are reasonably certain. I have not let my own views interfere; I have not made the poem say what I wanted it to say. I should myself want it to say something rather different.

Apart from calling on literary analogies to clarify my own statements, I have relied entirely on the poem itself, and as itself. There may be snakes and temples in Ovid and Virgil (as discussed by Walter Pache and Ursula Salacki, 'Blake and Ovid', *Blake Studies*, vol. iv, no. 1, pp. 89–92), but that is nothing to my purpose, which is concerned solely and wholly with Blake's poem and not with 'sources'. And

[4] The poem might conceivably refer to the desecration, through physical union, of a homosexual idealism, which would suit 'none did dare to enter in'; but there is no explicit evidence of that. I cannot see the chapel as a woman: what would there be to be afraid of there?

so with any other supposed influences; they may be there, and from a certain standpoint interesting and even important, though their relevance, except as analogies, is hazardous. If, as Kathleen Raine suggests (*Blake and Tradition*, 1969, I, 195–9), there is a relation to Apuleius' handling of the Eros and Psyche myth, that is, peripherally, interesting. I have often (e.g. *The Starlit Dome*, 1941, pp. 302–4; *Christ and Nietzsche*, 1948, pp. 136–8) argued that the myth treats of such solitary engagements as we are here discussing. But all this does little to advance what I call 'interpretation'. Nor have I brought in Blake as a person, his supposed views, and intentions, or his life, though biographical comment may be legitimately used *after* interpretation of the poetry, if one is concerned with a man's total artistic and human importance; as, for example, with Byron and T. E. Lawrence. I would not feel at all put out if Blake were here saying that he meant something else, since poets, as Plato stated in the *Apology*, regularly misunderstand their own poems.

Above all, I have made no judgements as to the merits of the poem. Such judgements belong to the highly subjective pursuit of 'literary criticism', which is only too often based on an inadequate understanding. Interpretation must come first, and it usually leaves little room for any criticism but the reader's own: it will be for him to formulate his critical response. I assume that the poem in question has already been accepted and ratified by the imagination as a consistent whole: there is no obligation on us to treat with such respect a poem not so ratified.

My interpretation may, of course, be wrong, but it is of a kind whose errors, if there, can be pointed out and opposed.

To meet a possible objection. If I were to be accused of pulling the poem to pieces, I answer that whereas false interpretations do exactly that, attending to details without regard to the whole, my own has been concerned not with pulling it to pieces but with putting it together again. It is already in pieces; our minds react irrelevantly, remember parts only, and think about them inconsequentially. Where a right interpretation is not forthcoming, wrong ones will appear. But I do not claim, and never have claimed, that interpretation does more than assist the poem to say what it wants to say. It simply aims to remove the barrier between the reader's intellect and imagination. The poem's further significance may, indeed, be uninterpretable, though the full meaning will be more, and not less, than what interpretation, provisionally, offers. Poetry remains magical. Though the sad content of an elegy may remain sad under interpretation, the poem itself, made so largely of aesthetic imponderables, gives joy. So does the poem we have been discussing. It recounts what appears to be a disaster, but the total effect is one of completion and satisfaction.

IX

READING THE ILLUMINATIONS OF BLAKE'S *MARRIAGE OF HEAVEN AND HELL*

David V. Erdman
with Tom Dargan and Marlene Deverell-Van Meter

Two years ago we began, in a seminar, an attempt to describe and to suggest interpretations of all the large and small illustrations or illuminations in Blake's famous early work in 'Illuminated Printing', *The Marriage of Heaven and Hell* (1790–2). Interpretations of the symbolism of the larger pictures abound, but there are few precise descriptions of their particulars.[1] And recently, even as the complexity and harmony of Blake's illuminations have become recognized and their relations to the text better understood—as alternate or contrapuntal or free-flying symbolic statements—critics have hesitated to attend to the ground level of Blake's composite art, to the pictures' directly illustrative function as graphic transpositions of metaphoric language and as thematic clues and emblems. As for the small but often clearly 'readable' marginal and interlinear hieroglyphs, presumably always of at least subliminal effect, when we have quoted Samuel Palmer's impression of 'spectral pigmies rolling, flying, leaping among the letters'

---

[1] Except for an odd comment here and there in Blake studies, reported below in these notes, the only substantial attempts to describe as well as interpret the illuminations of the *Marriage* have been those of Samuel Palmer, in a letter of 27 June 1862 to Anne Gilchrist, used in the Gilchrist *Life* (i. 86–8 in the 1863 ed.; pp. 75–7 in Ruthven Todd's 1954 ed. with misreadings corrected); of Sir Geoffrey Keynes in his *Bibliography*, 1921, revised in the Keynes–Wolf *Census*, 1953, and again in the Blake Trust facsimile of 1960; of S. Foster Damon in *William Blake: His Philosophy and Symbols*, 1924, pp. 327–8; of Max Plowman in a note in his facsimile ed. of 1927, pp. 13–16; and of H. M. Margoliouth in *William Blake*, 1951, pp. 76–7. The Damon and Plowman notes are conveniently brought together in Clark Emery's cheap facsimile ed., 1963, pp. 100–2.

In a special category are the titles for twelve of the designs reported in the *Census* (p. 36) as pencilled on a fly-leaf of the Cumberland–Beckford copy (A), a leaf now missing; for these appear authentic on the level on which Blake and Cumberland could understand each other, to judge from the similar titles in Cumberland's autograph in his copy of *Europe*. They start off, like the titles for *The Gates of Paradise*, with the four elements. See below.

A number of contemporary scholars are engaged in studies of the illuminated works, and the present essay has benefited greatly from the critical suggestions of John E. Grant and Irene H. Chayes and Irene Tayler, of W. J. T. Mitchell, Robert Essick, Stuart Curran, and many others; also from consulting Essick's thesis, 'The Art of William Blake's Early Illuminated Books', San Diego, 1969, and the theses of Everett C. Frost, 'The Prophet Armed: William Blake's *Marriage of Heaven and Hell*', University of Iowa, 1971, and Anne Tidaback Kostelanetz [Mellor], 'The Human Form Divine in the Poetry and Art of William Blake', Columbia University, 1967. Stony Brook graduate students Jerry S. Blake, Ronnie Brucker, Barry Fruchter, Donald K. Moore, Sally Sevcik, and Bob Waxler have also been helpful.

(1862) and Northrop Frye's dismissal of the small designs as sometimes 'a rather irritating form of punctuation' (1951) we have exhausted the commentary: there was none in the years between and has been almost none since.[2]

There have been some brave assaults upon the riddling account of the Printing House of Hell, in Plate 15, but no published unriddlings of the related pictures. The confidence with which we now present a reading of the entire *Marriage* as a printed and illuminated account of Blake's 'method' of transmitting knowledge through print and illumination must spring from the thoroughness with which we have read and have come to believe we understand Blake's leaping fairies and elves. While pointing our way through the text, they show us the uses of line and surface, text and illumination, etching in copper and colour-printing on paper; in the process they both exemplify and suggest the manifold marriages of contraries that open and display the infinite hidden in 'apparent surfaces' (to quote Plates 15 and 14). Yet some readers of a draft of the present essay have been troubled by our focusing so strongly on the surface particulars, wishing some resurrection of the infinite without these little deaths.

Having no wish to be deadly, either by clinging desperately to the surface of the abyss or by attempting to express all the levels of meaning to be read in every particular, we have tried to point out every bird, beast, tree, rock, orb, and human form we see and to do so in terms meaningful on many symbolic levels, even while we focus on meanings that suit our immediate purpose: to observe the function of flames and outspread wings as modes of and metaphors for creations in space, i.e. pictures for 'displaying the infinite', and the function of spiralling vines and vipers as modes and metaphors for melodic and verbal progressions in time, i.e. lines of text running toward the eternal. One of Blake's graphic signatures is a bird singing, with closed wings, on a looping but leafless tendril.[3]

We have examined the nine known copies of the *Marriage* originally etched, printed, and coloured by Blake, but we attend to their variants in colour and shape only when pertinent to emblematic detail.[4] Our first problem, especially with some

---

[2] Palmer, as cited in Todd, p. 77; he also appreciated 'the ripe bloom of quiet corners; the living light and bursts of flame, the spires and tongues of fire, vibrating with the full prism'. Frye, in 'Poetry and Design in William Blake', *Journal of Aesthetics and Art Criticism*, x (1951), 35–42, was surveying the whole canon, in which he found the *Marriage* one of the 'less successful pictorially' and read three of the marginal decorations on Plate 11 as following the text too 'closely and obviously'.

For published examples of current discussion of the less obvious particulars see Mitchell and Grant in *Blake's Visionary Forms Dramatic*, ed. Erdman and Grant, 1970, pp. 63–5, 98, and 182–6 (with a much closer look at Plate 11). (Hereafter abbreviated *VFD*.)

[3] See Blake's first illustration for Gray's 'Ode for Music' and the engraved 27th design for Young's *Night Thoughts*.

[4] Copy A printed in golden brown (Harvard College Library) (William Muir facsimile, 1885); copy B printed in greens and browns (Bodleian Library); copy C printed in green (Pierpont Morgan Library) (reproduced in black and white in June K. Singer's *The Unholy Bible*, New York, 1970; frontispiece not from C but from the facsimile of D with the colours wrong); copy D printed in blue-green (Lessing J. Rosenwald Collection) (Blake Trust facsimile, London, 1960); copy E printed in shades of brown (collection of Sir Geoffrey Keynes); copy F

of the small hieroglyphs and with some details in the larger pictures, has been to make out what may have been on Blake's copper plate but failed to print clearly or was obscured by opaque colouring; our second, to discern whether the changes made by added colour were iconic. Some details are obscure in all copies, one at least (in Plate 2) intentionally enigmatic, but collation has resolved most of these difficulties, especially the comparison of unpainted or lightly colour-washed pages with painted or colour-printed ones. To work with copies A and G, C and F, H and I, side by side in their respective libraries, has been to see many things clearly. Our final problem, to communicate these visions to persons not sitting with us at a table of facsimiles and photographs, may in part be solved by our singling out the difficult particulars for illustration. For these figures we have drawn upon copies C, E, and I—and at times upon the Hotten facsimile of 1868, which reproduces very well and is quite faithful to its original (copy F) and other copies in all the instances for which we employ it, with the notable exception of Plate 11.[5]

The differences of colours, shapes, emphases, and hence ranges of tone and spirit which we cannot discuss fully here may be indicated briefly by a survey of the different treatments of Plate 1, the combined frontispiece and title-page upon which Blake lavished greater attention than on most of the other plates.[6] In copies A to F the shapes of trees at the top, flames at the left, and clouds (rising into rocks or earth) at the right are fairly identical and represent what was on the etched copper, though in A the colouring of the subsurface area somewhat obscures the tier of rocks. In copy D the second point of flame from the top blends into a root from the trees above. In E and F some of the flames are thickened above and below the embracing human devil. In G three of the flames attach to three roots, implying some continuity of fire into sap. In H and I the flames on one side and the cloud-rocks on the other have been extended into the page centre—in I the rocks all turned to clouds, in H overwhelmed by the flames and rising as smoke. The trees are unchanged in most copies, but the two pairs of trees at the left are colour-printed into two single trees in E and F; the three short stumps at the right are

printed in grey and olive-green (collection of Mrs. Landon K. Thorne) (Camden Hotten facsimile, 1868); copy G printed in red-brown (Harvard College Library); copy H printed in red (Fitzwilliam Museum); copy I printed in brick-red (Fitzwilliam Museum) (Dent facsimile, 1927; Micro-Methods colour film, with greens shifted to blues). For a fuller account see *Census*, pp. 36–9. I have also examined the fragments of four and three plates listed as K and L, but the latter not recently.

[5] In the illustrations herewith the Camden Hotten facsimile is indicated by a superscript 'f'. The facial expressions and sometimes the outlines of the larger pictures are badly managed in this facsimile, varying from copy to copy, but the small details seem to have been reproduced from retraced photographs, without serious distortion. See also note 40 below.

[6] There is a frontispiece in copy B, a proof in black with pale green wash of 'Our End is Come . . . June 5 1793' (described in the *Census* as 'the second state'—actually the first—of the plate known as 'The Three Accusers'). But copy B seems a miscellaneous collection of proof pages (some very badly printed) with a few fine exceptions, Plates 11, 13, 19; it lacks pagination and was not necessarily assembled by Blake himself.

made a bit taller in F and are painted in I into three or four fat trunks rising beside and partly replacing the original single tall tree backed by a stump. In E the trees are shown as black and charred as well as blasted—and the colour-printing gives large hips to the strolling figure at the left, perhaps to match the female devil in the flames: in this copy all humans, above or below the surface, are pink and almost naked (though the second stroller still seems clothed) and pink shadows are upon all the lettering, with a darker colour for 'Marriage of' and for the birds, as on the outlines of the embracing devil and angel. In D there are varieties of body colour. In copies where the grass is attended to (in EFGI) it is green.[7]

The sky behind the trees is more or less clear in all copies, with various bands of sky blue (with other light colours in G and H) in all except E. The lower sky area is uncoloured in B and E, grey in C and F. In D it is pale blue with pink near the flames and a tongue of pink running up above ground at the left; in G pale pink near the flames and pale blue under the leafing tree. In I it has patches almost as blue as the upper sky. The colouring of this lower area in A and H, however, hardly suggests sky at all. Deep purples and blue (night sky if you will) in A make the whole underground space a dark foil for the triangle of strawberry-red and pink flames (not extended beyond the etched shapes) which is matched almost symmetrically by the triangular shelf of clouds, in the golden brown of the printing. The pale brown world above ground seems ignored rather than threatened by the flames or the embracing light-haired angel and devil. The painting of H gives an opposite impression: the angel is backed by one yellow cloud, above which the upper tiers are burnt into blue and golden smoke; the flames, filled with dramatically rising human forms painted round, lick at the roots and seem already to have consumed the stumps in their diagonally upward path. At the far left a surge of gold from the flames is repeated above the surface, almost forming a duplicate trunk of gold alongside the darker trees.

In four copies, BEFI, the colouring of the right side blends the rock and cloud areas into a single mass (browns except I, which adds a blue-black wash). In the other five copies the cloud-rocks and the cushiony clouds are contrasted: sharply in A and G (purple and golden brown, indigo and yellow green), less emphatically in C and D (grey-green or red-brown against green-edged white) and in H (dark smoke above yellow cloud). Always at the dramatic centre are the horizontally cloud-borne angel (the symbolism indicates) and the flame-borne diagonally rising devil—both naked human forms, not as dissimilar as the graphic and textual polarities might imply—embracing to marry the horizontals and diagonals of the whole page. In copy I their heads share a gold-plate halo, in A a background of deep blue. But more about them in a moment.

---

[7] Hereafter we will say simply that the grass is green, when it is so in all copies where that detail has been coloured. It seems needless to add that it is not green in uncoloured copies printed in colours other than green.

39. *The Marriage of Heaven and Hell*, copy C, Plate 1, title-page.
Relief etching with water-colour.
The Pierpont Morgan Library, New York

It must be evident that to interpret these varying emphases extensively or even to describe them for each ensuing page would be to capsize the present undertaking. In the main body of our comment, consisting of explicatory description page by page of all the pictorial particulars, we must attend primarily to the meanings which shed light on our task. Reference will be made to particular copies when there are iconic variants or when the details under discussion are not clear in other copies. For simple reference we have resorted to using copy letters superscript.[8]

Plate 1. Title-page

Two couples, the first strolling, the second kneeling and reclining on England's green earth, are framed and separated by arching trees stripped of most of their branches or blasted by storms or decay. Above the strollers two small (or distant) birds are seen under an enclosing branch, the liveliest held out by the two paired but leafless trees (two single trees [EF]). At the right a half-fallen tree leaning against a larger upright tree backed by a broken trunk extends the only living bough, green with leaves [EG], over a kneeling musician serenading (with lyre perhaps, not pipe for the shape is oval) a woman who lies on her left side with her legs drawn up, pillowing her head against the living trunk. In D she wears yellow stockings the colour of the centre of the fire below.[9] Above this musical couple a distant falcon or eagle, perhaps,[10] and five smaller birds rise toward open sky, one finding the gap between branches. This configuration of birds, suggesting the five senses escorted by the imagination, is frequent in Blake; here it recurs in Plates 17 and 27, where it heralds the words 'every thing that lives is Holy'.[11]

The word 'MARRIAGE' inscribed in swash capitals characterized by several round loops lies across broken or breaking branches and ends between the leaves and birds; its final loop runs into or points toward a circled scroll with slightly

[8] Thus: green[EG], blue[H]. We have not reported all detail colouring, let alone the full colouring of plates; yet we risk implying a colour symbolism by reporting as much as we do. Flames and prominent birds are usually painted red, but when the birds are painted bright blue against red ink, as in copy G, there is no reason to infer a symbolic change.

[9] Samuel Palmer, examining copy H, saw 'scant & baleful trees; little else than stem and spray'; the couple reclining and kneeling seemed a corpse with one bending over it (Todd, p. 75). Damon (p. 327) saw 'tiny human figures' walking and lamenting in the 'forests of error'; to Martin K. Nurmi, *Blake's Marriage of Heaven and Hell: A Critical Study*, 1957, p. 58, the surface level appears to be 'the "paths of ease" which the "Argument" tells us the just man was forced to leave'. Emery (p. 100) sees two humans walking 'with dignity and no lamentation, and one (naked), drinking or holding a child near a cow or a rock (or a shepherd playing his Pan-pipes near his sheep)'.

[10] A large bird is sometimes plainly a bird of paradise, with long split tail, sometimes an eagle, sometimes, I think, a lapwing (see next plate). When indistinct, as here, we are entitled to see the bird given most prominence in the work, in the *Marriage* an eagle (shown close up on Plate 15). Yet in a musical context we may imagine a lark.

[11] See illustrations 17. 10c, d–h and 27. 20a–f—i.e. Plate 27, line 20 (count including headings and carried-over lines), details a to f.

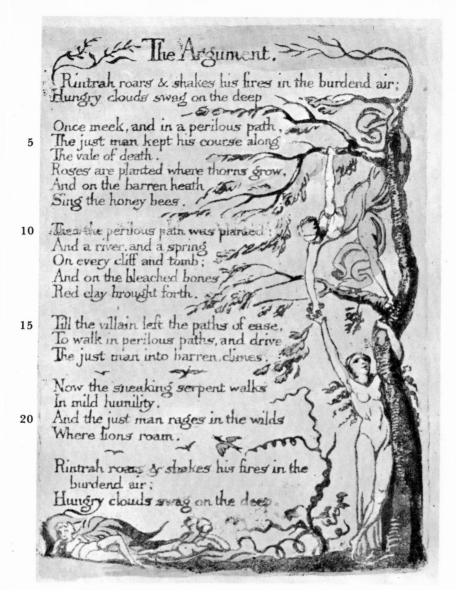

The Argument.

Rintrah roars & shakes his fires in the burdend air;
Hungry clouds swag on the deep

Once meek, and in a perilous path,
5   The just man kept his course along
The vale of death.
Roses are planted where thorns grow,
And on the barren heath
Sing the honey bees.

10   Then the perilous path was planted:
And a river, and a spring
On every cliff and tomb;
And on the bleached bones
Red clay brought forth.

15   Till the villain left the paths of ease,
To walk in perilous paths, and drive
The just man into barren climes.

Now the sneaking serpent walks
In mild humility.
20   And the just man rages in the wilds
Where lions roam.

Rintrah roars & shakes his fires in the
burdend air;
Hungry clouds swag on the deep.

40. *The Marriage of Heaven and Hell*, copy C, Plate 2, 'The Argument'.
Relief etching with water-colour.
The Pierpont Morgan Library, New York

thickened tip[EFHI] suggesting an ear of grain atop the bare branches of the living tree. (On Plate 10 the scroll is being read; on 27 it presents the 'Chorus'. Here, just below, it helps to join 'HEAVEN' and 'HELL', both deadly block-letter words by themselves.)

Below the apparent surface of turf is an abyss or another sky, teeming with naked children and couples, who dance, embrace, soar, in the warmth of flames that leap toward the word 'and' (which loops around itself and tapers off, evidently emitting a bird in the air above it). Of the children, three dance singly, two hold hands as though skating, and three soar in formation. Of the four couples of soaring adults, the most closely embracing have a child in tow. (See the contrast on Plate 4.) On the side of the abyss opposite the hell-mouth flames, the tiers that seem earth or rock from an earthly perspective are clouds in the heaven of Hell, and resting on an unmistakable cloud ledge at the bottom, over a black abyss indeed, is an angel who turns to embrace a devil, each looking the other squarely in the eye—though to call them angel and devil (when there is a halo, they share it) or to inquire into their sexes (not strictly pertinent to angels or devils) or to make much of the angel's being darker in copy H and having a brown body in D (yet a left arm and a face as pink and white as the embracing devil's) may be to fall into an error like those corrected on Plate 4—or to accept the ironies of the text itself. As Mitchell has said, every aspect of the composition of this page is deployed to present a vision of contraries that wins our sympathy for the devil's wisdom, and we are given much of it in the ensuing text. But we shall not see this marriage again, in human form at least.[12] It represents the end and culmination of the work, a picture to be remembered when we read, on the last page before the 'Song of Liberty', of 'the Angel who stretched out his arms' (Plate 24) and when we join in the 'Chorus' at the end of the 'Song'.[13]

Plate 2. The Argument

On the green surface of the earth, now at page bottom, we see reclining a single girl or boy, chin in hand, backed by a large leaf, and a naked couple making neither music nor love—to compare these to the couples on the surface in Plate 1. Here 'the deep' with its fires and clouds appears only in the text, in the refrain that begins and ends the page and hangs heavy over these humans. Above the refrain

[12] We see an important marriage of serpent and eagle in Plate 15. And we do see a tiny man and woman (always skirted) miming the relations of body and soul and holding hands from time to time (3. 9ab; 3. 13cd; 4. 9de; 9. 29ab; 19. 26ab). W. J. T. Mitchell (*VFD*, p. 65) offers a valuable analysis of 'the whole kinesis of the composition' of the title-page; in pp. 63–4 he and John E. Grant debate the proposition that the embracing figures illustrate the text of Plate 24 (with some confusion of copies, citing copy D as F and I as H).

[13] Plate 1 is called 'The Union of the Elements' in the Cumberland—Beckford list of titles (*Census*, p. 36). Plates 2–5 are entitled 'Earth', 'Fire', 'Water', 'Air'. George Cumberland is probably the author of these titles though our authority for them, a transcript made by William Muir, makes no attribution.

five birds fly, surround the stanza in which 'the just man rages', and perhaps function as sparks of hope like the birds and humans on the title-page. (The refrain is retraced in red ink in H, the four inside stanzas in blue.) Here there is no sixth bird, but two of the five are larger than the others, and the one taking the lead, crying out and seeming to spring forth from a five-looped tendril on a tough but thwarted grape-vine, looks like a lapwing.[14] The vine, appearing to seek some grip on this stanza, is kept apart from its natural support, a parental elm tree (in emblem tradition, anyway, and this is not oak or fruit-tree or birch or willow, to consider Blake's repertoire). Clasping the tree instead is a tall girl (with hair spiralling on both sides of the tree) naked down to her midriff[ABC], in a full gown (topless[DEF]) in later copies. Someone in the tree hands her something we are not allowed to see, while her legs are crossed as are Gwendolen's in *Jerusalem* 81 when Gwendolen clutches an invisible 'falshood' [*sic*] in her left hand. In unretouched copies[ABI] the gift or theft looks almost like grapes or birds' heads poking out of a nest; in C retouching in green makes the suggestion of grapes stronger—but green grapes; in E and H like nothing distinct. In G the details are painted in green as other leaf clusters on the tree, to show them as leaves on the branch that descends behind the touching hands, and the fingers are drawn as touching the palm with nothing in them (unless a secret message behind the thumb). A similar effect is differently achieved in D.[15] Blake's art was obviously used here to conceal or hint, not to make manifest.

The hander down, with bared breast[ABC] and a garment extending in gravity-defying scrolls, has often been taken as a boy but has as prominent breasts as the girl below, bared[ABC] or bulging her clothing.[16] In D and E the dark dull reds of the upper flames of the title-page are repeated as red sky behind the cross-legged girl,

[14] Blake cared for the lapwing, advising it to head from the perilous heath to harvest fields. This bird has a lapwing crest, light feathers[F] on the forward part of the wings (inexact but as may appear), and a more swallow-like tail than it should be (but the lapwing's toes can protrude to that effect). Blake repeats the two-colour effect in the rather larger bird in 'The Shepherd', adding a bird-of-paradise tail. This bird is often the most prominently coloured object on Plate 2: bright blue[AG], yellow[D], red[CEI], or red and grey[F]. The more distant bird above is blue[EG]. The two birds beside the lapwing are red[F]. Red, the colour of flames and grapes and blood, is obviously the imagination's colour; blue replaces it in A and G for contrast to the brown inks. The lapwing's cry is popularly described as a high-pitched 'weep'.

[15] In D the small branch above the lower girl's head is darkened, as is the potential thumb of the upper girl; the hand, turned to the right, cannot be holding the green leaves (as they must be, coloured like the lower leaves on the branch) that appear on the left. In E the upper hand is touched with dark blue, but no object emerges. In F some patches of leaves are reddish-brown, i.e. dying, including some (around green ones) on the small branch, the leaf cluster at the top near 'path', and the mysterious object—again letting the sceptical see only leaves on the branch behind the hands but encouraging others to speculate. (Camden Hotten, in at least one copy of his 1868 facsimile—in the New York Public Library—guessed at ripe grapes, painting the object red and enlarging the small branch at right into a large red cluster of grapes by way of explanation; on another copy, in the Morgan Library, the same branch is unenlarged and green.)

[16] Palmer saw the upper figure as a man, Damon as 'A youth in the Tree of Life' handing 'to a girl the grapes of ecstasy'. Margoliouth, p. 76, more cautiously observed: '. . . an energetic figure in a tree strains down to clasp the hand of, or perhaps to hand a fruit to (but the tree is no apple-tree) another less enterprising figure standing on the ground.'

whose dress is the yellow[D] or white[E] of the central flames; the upper figure is green against blue sky; indeed in copies up to G Blake keeps the upper girl green, brown[E], or blue[G], giving the more fiery red[F] or pink[CG] dresses to the lower (switching in H to blue and green, in I to pink and blue). If we take the title-page as the beginning of a picture story, apart from its obvious function as a prospect of the whole work, we may see these imperfectly relating humans as a step in some direction from the musical couple above ground in the title-page, or as some cloaked, above-ground version of the embrace of naked angel and devil in the flames and clouds. But perhaps in the work's broader context of the correction of errors about Good and Evil we are meant to be shown the 'Argument' and its illumination as a poser, an enigma enigmatically illustrated, an apparent surface. The fires shaken by tyrannous Rintrah supply regenerative warmth for the just man; the illusion of 'the religious' that a serpent's gift turned woman's love to sin is confronted by the devil's account that trouble comes when joys are stolen in secret. By this reading, the two humans here are not up to any good but the title-page embrace has shown how they could be. The bright bird flying back that way asks them to start over.[17]

The topmost branch of the tree is barren (except in D and E), but a leafy sprig grows near 'Rintrah' on the left. In H blue water is added in the foreground.

Plate 3

As the 'new heaven' (line 1) palls, 'Eternal Hell' (2) is reviving and is being welcomed by five naked humans with outstretched arms: at top a female comfortable in strong flames (cf. the title-page devil); at bottom, illustrating what can be the quick consequences of energy's flames sweeping through (for example) one of the women on page 2, we see a new birth, the infant awake at first breath and both mother (a) and child (b) looking up with open arms; then male and female contraries embracing—a girl (d), still in space, but kissing a boy (c) as he flies:[18] except for crossed legs (cf. Plate 2) the girl is like the woman in flames at the top of the page; the running boy, except for the direction of his running, is like the young man with outstretched arms running in flames in Plate 3 of *The Book of*

---

[17] John E. Grant in a note on 'Regeneration in *The Marriage of Heaven and Hell*' in *William Blake: Essays for S. Foster Damon*, ed. A. H. Rosenfeld, 1969, pp. 366–7, argues that, from the textual clue in Plate 3, 'Now is . . . the return of Adam into Paradise', we are to see a boy in the tree 'reversing the primal transgression' by handing the girl a joy (such as grapes or a nest of linnets), 'though the position of the woman indicates that all is not yet well . . .'.

Grant points to the boy handing grapes to a girl, from a grape vine, in 'The Ecchoing Green', and, in a later design for Gray's Eton ode, a boy handing to a girl a nest of three peeping linnets from a tree. The analogues may help us guess but imposed no rule on Blake.

[18] These details are illustrated below, p. 175: see 3. 13a–d. In copy G the girl's legs, crossed right over left, are redrawn to cross left over right—perhaps a matter of indifference, since Blake was simply retouching lines that printed badly.

Urizen. Note the optical illusion of married perspectives of time and space: the legs insist that she is still, he is running, but the heads, arms, torsos that they are embracing. Again, but in a manner contrasting with Plate 2, a paradoxical emblem illuminates the paradoxical text, of marriage without restraint.[19]

Turning now to the small interlinear figures (see detail illustrations below, pages 175 ff.) we see a reader's welcomer with red[E] body above 'a new' in the first line (3. 1a)—fresh from the title-page of *The Book of Thel*—who mimics the flame-girt welcomer in the top picture and is followed by a red[E] plume or leaf (b), swirling banners (c, d), and, below the line, a rising bird and more banners. Above 'Adam into Paradise' is another forward-pointing and flying human (3. 6a), a male to match the female of 1a. After the statement that Contraries are necessary a man and woman (3. 9ab) clasp hands on an ogee curve of beauty (see Hogarth).

As for the indications that this page develops themes of the title-page, the flames that were on the left side are now at the top, and the beds of cloud that were on the right side now support the whole lower scene and are aglow. We are in the abyss and find it no desert.[20]

Plate 4

Flanking 'The voice of the Devil' are three cloaked angelic trumpeters (formerly emblems of Biblical prophecy and the poetic muse) who announce the Devil's corrigenda list. Under the trumpets are a fanfare of banner-unfurling tendrils and leaves which we may understand to be living notations of the trumpeting voice. We may also recognize in the first tendril the pattern of the corkscrew grape-vine in Plate 2 and at the end of the row a rising bird or insect repeating the flight direction of the phoenix there. After the word 'Errors' soar a woman and child, free (not quite touching hands).

After error No. 1 (that Body and Soul are two) a flying figure (4. 6a) leaves a figure seated on a leaf (b)—presumably the Soul leaving the Body, which then becomes vegetable. Correction No. 1 (down the page) ends in a thrusting branch (4. 16a) and then a vignette of Soul (b), above clouds, turning back toward Body (c), who leaves his vegetable wrapping (d)[21] to spring toward Soul. After error No. 2 (treating Energy as evil and bodily, Reason as good and 'alone from the Soul') five active, varied figures (the senses of course) sporting (4. 9a–e) are

[19] Palmer saw the two figures 'rushing away'; Keynes's note in the facsimile has them also 'rush energetically away' yet accounts for the crossed ankles by allowing one to rush by 'floating on air with feet together'.

[20] In copy A the flames around the woman at top begin at her foot and end at her wrist and are enclosed by dark grey clouds at both ends, with the effect of balancing Plate 14.

In G, and somewhat in other copies, the flames fill the area. (Everett C. Frost, op. cit., pp. 201–2, sees the flames emanating 'principally from', and her attention 'riveted on', her thighs.) In A there is some blue sky behind the lower clouds; in several copies there is a triangle of dark shadow under 'Evil is Hell'.

[21] We shall come to see this as a cliff edge: cf. 7. 5f and 7. 11b.

followed by three huddled stone-like reasoners (f–h), perhaps seen as monkeys, on a vegetated flat greensward. After error No. 3 (that God will torment us for following our energies) a heel-flinging animal (4. 11a) is being watched by two unattended children (b, c) while another child (d) is directed by an adult (e) to consider the patient grazing ox (f). Surrounding correct answers 2 and 3 (hailing energy as life and delight and reason as its outward circumference) a man (4. 16f) is led by a small animal on a leash (e)—i.e. is following his energies—and a child (g) is groped toward by a blindfolded or bearded adult (h) followed by what may be a shadow or ghost (i)—or perhaps the whole scene is set off by bracket-like trees (d, i). At the left end of the next line (17) an adult walks with a cane. Between answers 2 and 3 we see a procession of six figures (4. 19a–f) moving forward on their own but exhorted by Reason (h) following them; then a bracket-like leaf (i);[22] then two horses (j) drawing a man in a chariot or cart (k)—the profile and foreleg of the far horse being too lightly indicated in some copies. We may take this as Energy drawing Reason in the immediate context. The rider's hand holds invisible reins.

In the large picture at bottom a naked couple lunge toward each other, he backed by flames, she by a rayed sun; both running or standing on the deep (ocean waves, variously white-capped). They are scarcely heading for the embrace of Plate 1 but appear to be kept apart by her clutching of the infant (whose out-stretched limbs now suggest not joy but fear) and by a chain on his right ankle[23]— i.e. by the false, jealous separation of Soul and Body. In unretouched copies (such as B) the woman and man have facing profiles, eyes open, and the child, face turned toward right arm, appears to be regarding the man. In copy H child and mother look solemnly at him; his eyes are open. In F we see only the back of the child's head. In G a face turned toward the sun is drawn on the top of the head, with nose in air. In I the child is drawn with shut eyes and mouth open round for cry-ing; the woman looks at the man, but he has eyes shut or looking down.

Plate 5

Phaëton-like, down hurtle a naked sword, a naked man, a saddle cloth and broken chariot wheel,[24] and a horse with wildly curling mane and tail, falling headlong into flames. Falling with them, or lighting them, is an orb, pinkish or bright red or, in I, painted yellow and black with a larger orb added at the far left, red and

[22] In copy I the left line of the bracket is given two arms and made into another exhorting man; detail g may be a tree stump, or a podium.

[23] No chain or manacle [ABC], a manacle perhaps [D], both [EFGHI]; both in the colour-printed drawing *The Good and Evil Angels*, in which the figures are no longer male and female and both stand in air above surf and shore, not over water. When Blake added the chain, was he making a thematic link to the eagle in Plate 15? He would have known that an eagle thus straining at a chain is an emblem of Ambition.

[24] Spokes are visible in most copies; when omitted [DF] there is the effect of a saddle.

flaming. The red orb may be the sun, or Mars (cf. *America* 5. 1–5); the added burning orb, as sun, would leave the smaller orb, yellow with black crescent, to serve as moon (new, with old in arms). Yet Blake's original etching of the orb has the crescent ring; it can stand for an occulted sun.[25] Presumably the picture is adaptable to both parties' histories of the fall (see text). Yet we have just seen what may be Reason charioted (4. 19jk), and in Plate 11 we will find the sword the symbol of reason-worship. In terms of Plate 4 the fall illustrates error No. 3; Reason must have forgotten to let the horses do the pulling; a sword is not a bridle. But the horse's fall, despite his energetic mane, implies that Energy accepted restraint. Between them they have let the sun fall, connoting the universal ruin which warriors, chariots, and horses share in Plate 26, verse 15.

The first interlinear figure, in line 3 (5. 3a) is 'weak enough' (2); next, lying flat in a desert he has become a 'shadow' (5. 5a)—coloured as green as the grass[CEFI]. Under 'Paradise Lost' a reclining figure (5. 7a) is being instructed by a man (c) with compasses (b), his back to a wavy serpent (d) headed away from them. In front of the next line (8) someone walks away with arm out like a blinded man (no energy to lead him?). Under 'calld the Devil or Satan' is a flying red[EF] serpent with bat wings (5. 10a)—a conflation, as we shall see, of the eagle and viper (in present terms, Soul and Body); hence a tiny emblem of the marriage we must not forget when we see in line 12 a red or green and black serpent alone, wingless but spiralling rapidly along on a strip of green[D] with red[EF] tongue active.[26] (We saw the same energy in isolation in the corkscrew tendrils of grape-vine in Plate 2, the human who stood between vine and tree in danger of being a paradise-loser there.) The passive figures in this page (3a, 5a, 7a) repeat the languor we noticed on Plates 2 and 3.

The twig and leaf in the lower left margin are green in copy I; there is grass at the bottom of the page[GI]. In copy H the paragraphs of text are coloured respectively red, golden, blue, blue on red, blue, pale golden, bluish.[27]

Plate 6

Underneath the Devil's charge that Reason as false Messiah 'formed a heaven of what he stole from the Abyss' (1–2) a fleeing figure (6. 2b) seems to be handing something—we remember the obscure transaction of Plate 2—to someone who reaches for it (c). Both almost kneel; the first runs like Cain fleeing in *Milton* 15.

---

[25] In G a shadow spot is added over the crescent. On images of solar eclipse in the *Night Thoughts* designs and in *Jerusalem*, cf. *VFD*, pp. 330, 397.

[26] In G the serpents are touched with dark blue spots, against the red-brown ink. The lone serpent may be an emblem of Milton's earth-bound interpretation of Satan.

[27] Palmer noted the resemblance to 'the catastrophe of Phaeton, save that there is but one horse'. The Cumberland title, 'Air', may imply a relation to the 'Air' emblem in *Gates of Paradise*, the worried reasoner in clouds, though visually there is a closer resemblance to 'Fire', Satan with spear and shield. Essick (p. 144) sees 'a descent of free vision into contraction encompassing both falls'.

E3:1 _As a new heaven is begun, and it is now thir-_
        a   b   c   d

E3:6 _Adam into Paradise_
       a

f3:9 _rgy, Love and_ / _stence._
       a b

E3:13

f4:6 _a Body & a Soul._
       a   b

f4:9 _the Soul._
      a   b c d   e   f g h

f4:11 _3. That God will torment Man in Eternity for following his Energies._
       a bc de   f

f4:16 _age_ _2. Energy is the only life and is from the Body_
       a   b   c d e f g h   i

f4:19 _and Reason is the bound or outward circumference of Energy._
       a bc def g h i   j   k

41. _The Marriage of Heaven and Hell_ (details)

The green vegetation around them puts forth two leaves (a) behind the first figure and a bumpy serpentine flourish (d) behind the second.

The deletion of the word 'Devil' in the centre of line 6 is covered by a flame[D] or a red and gold blot[I]. A figure of Christ risen (6. 7a) illustrates '. . . after Christs death, he became Jehovah', subtly combining the trailing gown of the benevolent Jesus (as in 'The Little Boy Found') with a suggestion of a serpent tail (as in 5. 10a or in the split garment of the girl in the tree in Plate 2). Around the title 'A Memorable Fancy' appear joyous flames like those of the title-page (without threatening points as in Plate 5) and three merry figures giving themselves to 'the enjoyments of Genius', one (6. 14a) walking on fire (as on water: cf. Plate 4), one (c) giving his head to the flames (his hands not defensively downward as Phaëton's in Plate 5: warring angels see as fall what is enjoyment to genius), one (b) dancing above the word 'walking'—all three defying Nebuchadnezzar, so to speak.[28]

At page bottom Blake diagrams the etching process that he must 'come home' to (line 22) if he is to communicate the wisdom his genius or imagination has been collecting among the fires. Here we must study the text and illuminations of the bottom of Plate 6 and the top of Plate 7:

> When I came home, on the abyss of the five senses, where a flat sided steep frowns over the present world, I saw a mighty Devil folded in black clouds, hovering on the sides of the rock, with corroding fires he wrote the following sentence now percieved by the minds of men, & read by them on earth.

> > How do you know but ev'ry Bird that cuts the airy way,
> > Is an immense world of delight, clos'd by your senses five?

To reduce the infinite vision of his imaginative 'walking' to illuminated printing, to words and pictures that can be read, he must return home to his workshop from what the senses can only record as an abyss. (In the fourth Memorable Fancy on Plates 17 to 20 Blake pictures himself, as devil, hanging by the roots of a tree over a deep in which Leviathan appears: 20. 19a). With corroding acid he must cut words and pictures in the sensory surface of this abyss (the mirror-like surface of the copper, looking *through* which we can see immense worlds of delight). From the perspective of 'the present world' the copper plate looks like a flat steep frowning or swagging overhead. The devil Blake sees in its clouds is himself at work on the printing surface or 'sides of the rock'—which he pictures as Dover cliff, the edge of dry land.

On Plate 6 we see, darting from black[D] clouds (6. 26d), a streak of lightning (c) (the etching acid or engraving tool) cutting into the side of a cliff (a) the letters

---

[28] As did the three whom he threw into the fiery furnace (cf. Dan. 3: 25), not a far-fetched allusion, since Nebuchadnezzar is given the climactic role in Plate 24 (of impatient ox). Their being joined in the flames by a fourth 'like the Son of God' gives the comparison spiritual validity here.

E5:3

unwilling.

a

E5:5

degrees becomes passive
sire.

a

E5:7

a   b c   d

E5:10

Devil or Satan
th

a

f6:2

ah fell. & formed a heaven of what he stole from the
Abyss

a   b   c   d

E6:7

in flaming fire
Jehovah.
the Son, a

a

E6:14

of the Devils party without knowing it
6 A Memorable Fancy.
As I was walking among the fires of hell, de.

a   b   c

f6:26

clouds, hovering on the sides of the rock, with cor-
ro-

a

b   c

d

42. *The Marriage of Heaven and Hell* (details)

'HOW' (b)—the first word of the verse on Plate 7 beginning 'How do you know . . .', identifying birds as 'airy' engravers: cf. the eagle in Plate 15. That word 'How' is Blake's own secret stolen from the abyss to build a heaven; we must look again at the youth in the tree of Plate 2 and his scroll garment that hints a devil-poet.[29]

Plate 7

The preliminary loops before 'How' suggest that it is the serpent who draws the line or does the lettering, his tongue the lightning of the diagram on Plate 6. The bird cutting the airy way opens up the spaces of the plate, perhaps with colour washes, sunbursts, and Illumination generally. In the 'Proverbs of Hell' that follow, some of the pictograms continue the imagery of ploughing the surface and opening immensity: by now we have some new thoughts about that surface above the fires and clouds of the title-page. Before the 'Proverbs' title a stooping figure, tree-enclosed (7. 5a), studiously pokes the ground with a small stick or dibble ('In seed time learn', the first proverb begins), presumably learning while seeding the surface. After the title (with a happy banner on 'Hell') in a green valley beside a rising cliff, for we are now inside the copper rock, in more senses than one, we see a speaking serpent (b) and a gowned upright figure (d) with hands out-stretched over two hand-raising children (c, e): parent and children, teacher and pupils sharing in the communication of the serpent's messages of delight ('in harvest teach, in winter enjoy').[30] The serpent, now rising at an angle that marries horizontal and vertical, symbolizes the line of text; the bird 'that cuts the airy way' (represented minimally by a free curve below 'cuts') symbolizes the illumina-tion of mental space rising infinitely above the line, 'an immense world of delight'.

In the words of the second and sixth proverbs a homely version of the sun-chariot, closer to the small figure of 4. 18a than to Phaëton, appears in the work-ing 'cart and plow'. For a personal illustration we might have been shown William Blake ploughing the furrows of his etched lines (a level of meaning he sometimes travels); instead we are shown a runner (7. 11a), like the second dancer in flames (6. 14a), cutting the air with his right hand, in a green valley: the poet ploughing a furrow in the copperplate; ourselves running as we read his line of text. The ground and cliff edge (b) repeat the edge of 7. 5f; we are *in* the etched rock. His running in the narrative line is matched at page bottom by a robe-trailing trumpeter (7. 26b) in clouds (a), apocalyptic spatial illumination that transcends linear time. (Cf. the body and soul figures of Plate 4.) The line that

[29] There are some strokes that show us the cliff and some obscuring lines on the 'H' that keep Blake's secret unless we inquire closely. Keynes wondered if the letters are 'WAOW' or 'WHOW'. In copy G, with which Blake took great pains, he redrew this diagram over grey paint, repeating the cloud and lightning lines exactly but quite deliberately fracturing the 'H' and not completing the 'O'. (The facsimile reproduced here is very accurate for copy A as well as for F.)

[30] In copy F the red of the serpent is repeated in the children and in the woman's arms.

loops and curves above 'you' at the end of proverb 18 diagrams the 'sublime act' of that proverb.

In copy I the line below 'wise' (7. 26c) loops into a serpent head facing the trumpeter, in D a flying wingless snake; in I there is a suggestion of a recumbent figure below the trumpeter being awakened.

If we look through any copy given colour washes, we may notice that all the text of the Proverbs of Hell, in Plates 7 to 10, appears to be inscribed on white clouds—an effect eschewed in the preceding and following plates, though resumed in the 'Song of Liberty', Plates 25–7, and sometimes present in the Argument page and less distinctly in some of the pages after 17; the blue wash in Plate 22 is used rather to suggest water.

Plate 8

Acorns among oak leaves[31] and a serpentine grape tendril and leaf adorn the running head 'Proverbs of Hell', and the margin hints at immense joys: ripe grapes (red or purple), 'the bounty of God', tendril and leaf, birds more individualized than usually: the four in the margin may be identified at a hazard as a lapwing (8. 12a), a gull or dove (b), a bird of paradise (with long split tail) the colour of the grapes (c), and a swallow (d). A fifth bird, also the colour of the grapes, an eagle with open beak (cf. Plate 15), is busy in the next line (8. 15a) illustrating figures in the text: lion, man, woman, sheep (b, c, d, efg). The man and woman are at work, presumably making clothes of skins. Above 'watch the roots' a foolish man is watching an empty-handed tree with neither roots nor fruits (8. 19a, b).[32] Wiser watchers are marked by a cluster of acorns at the left (8. 23a) and a branch of hazelnuts after 'fruits' (b).

A landscape–seascape illustrates the cistern–fountain idea (23) and the proverb 'One thought, fills immensity' (24). Down a rocky cliff (8. 23i) a tall force of water (j) falls into the ocean (drops filling immensity) which carries a boat (g) and ships (d, e, h) near and distant (one going over the horizon).[33] Ocean and cliff repeat the shape of the valley and rock in Plate 7 (5f and 11b). The stream of thought fills the valley (prepared copper surface), carries the vessels, nourishes a green palm tree on the cliff edge (i) (a coconut visible in the top[c]), and innumerable birds (the largest grape-coloured again) which flow out to fill the air beyond—and overflows into text and illumination conveying (to read on) 'an image of truth'.

---

[31] The acorns in this line are often turned to leaves in the colouring[DGI].

[32] Or, as Everett Frost suggests (p. 220) the adjacent proverb, 'What is now proved was once, only imagin'd', may be intended: the watching figure, a boy, imagines while the dead tree proves.

[33] The waterfall stands out clearly in most copies, with an extra ledge and fall near the base in E and F; in D it is hidden by paint, in I obscure (and Blake seems to be turning the cliff into a bending tree-trunk, using the small trees as branches). I take the second ship (e) to be in full sail, viewed endwise; it might, however, be a distant two-storey lighthouse. In G the red birds are, as usual, blue; the grapes purple; waves are added to the ocean.

In the next images, a snake coiled to strike (8. 26a) and a stag (b) lunging toward it, after 'speak your mind, and a base man will avoid you', Blake draws on the tradition that stags and serpents are natural enemies.[34] Grape leaves at the bottom, with the eagle's submitting 'to learn of the crow', may hint at the fable of fox and crow.

Plate 9

The repeated title is flanked by sinuous scrolls (9. 1b, c, e), a boy at left (a) who directs us to read, 'The fox provides for himself', and someone (d) above 'God provides for the lion' who may be a lazy reader in a hammock.[35] The proverbs otherwise are allowed to proceed without aid. We may read them with active cunning like the fox's, or receptively, like lions. Blake's confidence that we are reading properly is indicated at the bottom of the page, where a dancing and pointing couple assist the catchword in directing us onward. These figures (9. 29a, b), having represented body and soul separately on Plates 3, 4, and 7, here fly forward together, dressed somewhat like the strolling couple on the title-page.

Plate 10

After the wish of the crow that 'every thing was black' and of the owl 'that every thing was white', the body and soul figures pose together (10. 8a, b)—body, darker, over soul—in a moment of embrace like that of boy and girl in Plate 3, and then apart (c, d). Below 'murder an infant' a vegetable infant (10. 14a; compare 25. 15a, where the infant is invisible but textually present) is approached by a man holding out a rope or scarf (b) for strangling; behind him a human infant (soul) soars upward (c). And dancing beside 'barren', to show how life is 'where man is', are body (d) and soul (e) together again, with two birds, possibly lapwing (f) and gull (g).

The vine under 'the sea to a fish' (4) may be a kind of seaweed; the leaf bearing the cocoon infant (14a) may be its contrary. For the rest of the vegetation on this page seems to be organized by contraries. Obviously so (10: 16a, b), around the climactic words 'Enough! or Too much!', which are flanked by angular ivy beside 'Enough!' and a wide grape leaf beside 'much'—a broad leaf of illumination growing at the apocalyptic end of a serpentine linear tendril, its four loops contrasting with the four sharp ivy leaves. (Our choice here is further cued by the grape leaf hung below 'Truth'.) Slyly so, around the title at the top of the page, with grape

---

[34] There is an emblem tradition in which a stag at bay represents Christ; neither here nor in Plate 26 does it seem applicable. It is the serpent, here, not the stag, that receives the accent of red colouring [F].

[35] The figure (d) is difficult to make out as a human form, and in all its printings Blake never tried to mend it; in G he painted it green with the adjacent vegetation.

How do you know but ev'ry Bird that cuts the airy way,
Is an immense world of delight, clos'd by your senses five?

Proverbs of Hell.

f7:5   a   b   c d e f

ot, breeds pestilence.
plow.
loves water.

f7:11   a   b

knavery.   wise

f7:26   a   b   c

E8:12   a b c d

the fell of the lion. woman the fleece of

E8:15   a   b   c   d   e f g

rod.
the roots

f8:19   a b

the fruits.
The cistern contains; the fountain overflows
One thought, fills immensity.

f and C8:23   a   b   c d e f   g h i j

Always be ready to speak your mind, and a base man
will avoid you.

f8:26   a   b

43. *The Marriage of Heaven and Hell* (details)

and chestnut leaves at the right and elm leaves at the left, the latter from the tree of the Argument page, from which only imagination can conjure fruit. In the large picture below the text, of an instructing Devil (c) who is reaching the end of his scroll of proverbs[36] (a scroll that parallels the looping vine), his right wing, almost occulted by his head, points to 'Enough!' and his left wing, free and expansive, to 'Too much', while enclosing vegetation dramatizes the contrast: a trap-like jaw of vegetation (a), the *Dionaea muscipula* or catchfly shown in Erasmus Darwin's *Loves of the Plants* (1789), beside the slow learner on the Devil's right and a large wing-shaped leaf beside the quick apprentice devil on his left—Blake himself, perhaps, who shares concern about the progress of the stiff angel who is at least attending to the text (to be converted as promised on the title-page but not until Plate 24).[37] The viper-like tendril rising from the wing-like leaf (10. 17e) reverses the relationship of tendril and leaf just above; both (repeated in 11. 1f, h) prepare us for the eagle and serpent emblem of Plate 15. The leaf's shape also suggests how close leaves and wings can be to flames.

The scene vaguely parodies the orthodox picture of God on Judgement Day flanked by recording angels. Compare, in Blake's *Vision of the Last Judgment*, Jesus seated on the throne or Judgement Seat 'with the Word of Divine Revelation on his knees'. The cushioned Seat is visible, but, knowing that he must become as we are if we are to embrace the flame, the active Devil is on his knees, with his wings open: compare the eagle's on Plate 15. In some copies added ground beyond the grass on which the Devil kneels (earth-brown[EF] or black[D]) suggests a brink or a cliff edge; in some[HI] a stream fills this area, with white foam[I]—the acid eating the copper? Plowman sees it as 'inky'.[38] Is this the shore of the sea of Time and Space, the brink of the abyss, where thinking and writing and illuminating are done? In I there are clouds on either side, as in Plates 15 and 20. In G red, yellow, and blue flames, as in Plate 1, swirl in this gulf and up the margin to lick at the leaf of Truth and rise toward the flying birds.

[36] The scroll is being rolled up at page right; the pupil on that side has presumably read ahead and wants to learn the final proverb being transcribed by the other pupil before the text gets to him. In copy I the idea is changed—or Blake in 1825 is inattentive to the idea of the unrolling; a matching roll is painted on to the scroll at the left end.

[37] The Devil, naked, is variously flesh coloured, or blue[I]; the copyists beside him are dressed in contrasting colours (except in B and H), but the contrasts are not for characterization, since each in turn is allowed colours ranging from grey or tan to purple or red. Here is the tally: A (tan/purple), B (no colours), CD (blue/yellow), E (scarlet/tan), F (brown/blue-brown), G (grey/red and blue), H (both blue-grey), I (purple/orange). Characterization *is* given by the Venus' flytrap beside the one and the vegetable wing and viper beside the other.

[38] Plowman, p. 19. Ink would be for the recording angels, whom Palmer saw as taking down the accusations of 'an accusing demon with bat-like wings' pointing 'fiercely to a . . . great parchment scroll . . .'. Keynes sees 'Satan . . . dictating to two seated women'. But one avid recorder of the proverbs of Hell, according to the text, is the author himself—whom for simplicity we call Blake. We take him to be the quick reader on the right (the Devil's left), since his profile is very like the Devil's—whose resemblance to Blake has often been noted. Yet the ambiguity of the clothing permits us to see both figures as female (though lacking the full breasts of the two in the Argument page). Note the evidently crossed legs.

Proverbs of Hell

The fox provides for himself, but God provides for the lion.

E9:1   a   b   c   d   e

not!
not!

f9:29   a   b

f10:8   a   b   c   d

desires

E10:14   a   b   c   d e   f   g

not be believd .   Enough! or Too much

E10:16   a   b

I10:17   a   b   c   d   e

44. *The Marriage of Heaven and Hell* (details)

I11:1

f11:1   a   b c d e f g   h   i

enlarged & numerous senses could percieve.

E11:5   a   b   c d   f   g

thus began Priesthood.

E11:11   a

E11:14   a bcd ef   g   h

that All deities reside
in the human breast.

E11:16   a   b

45. *The Marriage of Heaven and Hell* (details)

Plate 11

The large picture illustrates the poets' animating 'sensible objects with Gods or Geniuses' (1–2). At the left we see the green[AC] human form (11. 1a) of a sharp-petalled daisy or sunflower with arms outspread (cf. the small figures in Plates 6, 7, 9, 10) rising from the green earth. In copy D an orange disc on the left horizon matches this spirit in colour and enforces a sun-god identification. (The Cumberland title for the page is 'The Dawn'.) Next we seem to see an old stump (b) with bearded face (surely an oak)—yet curiously splintered at the top or extended in thin sprays[EFGHI], and too green for a tree trunk, even blue toward the top[FGI]; perhaps a plant of some sort. Further right two groping hands (c, d) on two slender arms reach up from the ground. And then a large open plant or flower (green[AC] and yellow[DH]; blue[EFGI]), the top 'wing' of which bears the same viper-like tendrils (f, g) we saw on the roughly similar wing of vegetation in Plate 10, extends a rather different lower wing, undulating like flames or waves, to form a bracket of shelter in which a mother and infant, geniuses of flower and bud, face each other with gestures of embrace, not clutching; in G the woman's hand holds a bright red flower against the baby's skin, in I they share a patch of gold under the curve of the leaf like the halo in the title-page. In copies G and I the whole scene is inside a dark cavern, reddish green[G] or oak brown and double arched[I]—or we are looking outward from our mind's cave. (For illustration of the varieties of detail, we use here both copy I and the 1868 facsimile, f, though the latter is inaccurate in an important detail; see note 41.)

This is what our senses perceive, an island or world of green, in the un-elaborated copies[AC], with even the sun a flower clothed in green and the nursing mother green or in green (with one pink leg showing[A]) or in pink with yellow hair[C]. In D the green surface is extended to the left horizon, though the right sky is filling with a storm-dark blue and the figures now are naked, the sun-god orange, the woman red-skinned. But there are latencies we have failed to perceive. A sort of water-line across the child's thigh and the woman's hips at the level of her extended arm, etched on the copper, suggests that Blake meant to represent the lower half of the scene as under water, hence the undulations of the lower part of the huge blue[EFGI] plant or lily blossom. His broadest hints appear in copy F (see facsimile here). There the lily is given the shape of an octopus, with a round head and a large eye where a lower tendril (i) used to be, and the right leg of the mother is crossed over instead of under her left leg and revealed as a mermaid's tail! (The facsimile-maker carries the hint too far and changes her left leg as well.) Comparing other copies, we can see that it was there all along, crossing under the left (human) leg and emerging as swirls that could be disguised as a skirt or as green grass. In copy I Blake paints in a section of her right thigh (a garter conceals the joinery) to let us see that her right leg crosses *under* her left (which now tapers without a foot) to emerge as a dolphin-like tail, though viewers with unenlarged senses will be thrown off by a heavy suggestion of pink dress, rainbow coloured where it enters the water. Two-tailed mermaids were often exhibited in England among heraldic devices and in printer's ornaments. Blake's innovation was to 'percieve' a genius with one human leg and one fish tail, also a flower half cactus and half waterlily, and a stump bursting into a fountain (we can see his idea that waterspouts rise like this demonstrated in his engraving of Fuseli's *Tornado*).[39]

In this plate Blake prepares us to 'animate' the objects we perceive, as gods of the earth and of the sea, and to understand that both grow 'in the Human Brain' (to borrow terms from 'The Human Abstract'). He had the mermaid suggestion ready in his basic etching, and in his text the idea of gods or geniuses of woods and rivers, mountains and lakes (paired with cities and nations as though to imply that water is the more inclusive element). In the picture as first presented[ABCD] we are invited to 'study the genius' or 'mental deity' of an oak-centred green little island and be gently led to perceive its wider relation to the sea around it. Perhaps only when he was engraving Fuseli's design for *Tornado* for the 1795 edition of *The Botanic Garden* did Blake conceive of the stump as waterspout. In colour-printed copies E and F he began to release the tree-god's hair in upward, watery spoutings that turn and fall, in F, like fountain spray. In copy E he established a new water line, below the woman's foot, which the water faintly mirrors, and he added light oblong patches to show something reflected, or floating, on the surface below the infant. In F he restored the original water-line just above the merwoman's finny leg and just below the eye of the octopus and the beard of the tree-god, now perceivable as a Neptune. In the background he painted an undulating horizon in dark blue that can be taken for rolling waves or distant hills; in the foreground the brown and reddish brown earth can all seem under water, as also the sand-coloured ground from which the sun-god now rises, naked as a swimmer[EFGI]. In H he rounded off the island with blue water at both sides, keeping the sand and vegetation yellow and green, with green grass behind the sun spirit—yet adding gold on the blue horizon at left and touching the merwoman's dolphin leg with blue.

Finally, in the late, cave-enclosed copies we are led to see either the two worlds distinct (in G), with water in the foreground running under the left wall of the cave (the water-line returned to the level of E), or (in I) the worlds of earth and sea married: the foreground green, for both grass and water (but a bluish rather than a yellowish green); the lily's upper and lower wings both dark blue, like

[39] Blake's engraving, dated 1 Aug. 1795, is reproduced in Ruthven Todd, *William Blake the artist*, 1971, p. 42. Fuseli imagines the human form of 'Tornado' with bearded human–lion face (surmounted by a nightmare-faced serpent); Blake in Plate 11 paints the bearded old man's face directly on the base of the spout or trunk; cf. the very similar Plate 17 in *Milton*.

waves breaking from the dark blue sea at the right; the tree/waterspout, shaded from green to blue, gushing up out of sight above the roof of our cave;[40] the element from which the sun-god emerges, mingled green and blue, with a sort of shelf at his side that seemed in the etching to be a mere sketch for grass but easily reads as a breaking wave. In both these copies we are invited to look upon the whole range of 'sensible objects' as neither simply of earth nor of water before our minds begin abstracting. Perhaps the Cumberland title for Plate 1, 'The Marriage of the Elements', was truly inspired if not authorial. In Blake's own hand we have the inscription for this picture (Plate 11) in his 'Small Book of Designs': 'Death & Hell team [sic] with life'.[41]

As we enter the text an ancient poet or blue-robed Druid (11. 1) stands hospitably beside 'The ancient Poets'. And a hieroglyphic animating of words as birds occurs in each space between lines in the first paragraph—ten birds in all, including a large one (11. 5g) after 'percieve' painted golden[D], red[H], blue[FG], or blue and white[I].[42] The second paragraph begins with a human standing in a curve of engraving. Banners on many letters, often serpentine, keep up the animation until 'thus began Priesthood' leads to a cut-serpent abortion (11. 11a)—or, un-animated, a mere green tendril and leaf.

After priests have 'pronounced that the Gods had ordered such things', a dark stick figure (11. 14a), a priest or animated stump, is directing four or five devotees, two or three kneeling (b, c, d) and two huddling (e, f), to worship a headless warrior with sword (g), an abstraction of the corporeal half of the falling sword and man in Plate 5. In copy D the two kneeling figures are clothed in the orange colour of the sun and sun-god at top left: a reminder of how the poets' animation of the sun has been 'abstracted' into power-worship. Beyond the sword-bearer is a patch (h) of ocean waves (or cloud-cliff, as in Plate 1?).

At page bottom (11. 16) is illustrated the illusion that deity is a bearded man in a cloud (b) whose outstretched finger creates man (a). Our thin modern Adam,

[40] Robert Essick's perception of 'a stream or waterfall cascading from the sky' (p. 149) can be supported by this copy (I) but no other. His suggestion, however, that Thomas Taylor's translation of Porphyry's ninth hymn of Orpheus, 'To Nature', and Taylor's interpretation of it in 1792 are pertinent to Blake's picture would not depend on the direction of flow. According to Porphyry, Queen Nature steadily whirls the world, and its parts keep flowing 'Like swift descending streams'; according to Taylor this flow represents the continual influx of God into nature. 'Priestcraft!' might be Blake's comment, though.

[41] As with the central enigma of Plate 2, careful attention to Blake's handling of the details should dispel any notion that he was incapable of plain depiction, or just careless. If we wonder whether he gave the woman one leg for land and one for sea to make her an emblem of universal Nature, or to assist an apprentice prophet to see the human form of one elementary vision or another, as he chose, or to see both—we can be helped by Camden Hotten, the facsimile maker of 1868. Just as he pushed Blake's hint for Plate 2 into a big fat bunch of grapes, he turned the picture of two kinds of legs into a traditional, rattletrap mermaid, human above the water and fish or dolphin below. The consequent banality speaks for itself.

[42] The two birds under 'senses' (11. 5de) are very small; the two above 'enlarged &' (ab) are odd and larger but leave the largest size for the red or blue bird (g), often the most prominent object on the page. The flying serpent (c) and serpentine banner (f) tie the birds together, while assisting with the concepts 'numerous' and 'percieve'.

limp as the 'weak' governed figures of Plates 2 and 5, drifts away from the cloudy God he has abstracted; he has plainly forgotten where 'All deities reside' (15).[43] Compare the contrary illumination of the bottom of Plate 6, with lightning from the clouds creating words with its tongue.[44]

Plate 12

The serpent line runs right into the title, and two naked humans (12. 1b, e) and two birds (c, d) come running and flying to see and hear. These and the few other animal and human figures on this page and the next may seem little more than elegant printer's indicators. Yet the grape leaf (a) beginning the first paragraph and the open-mouthed serpent (blue-black[G], red[H], or green[EF]), beginning the next are introducing prophets; in contrast the figures surrounding the words 'cause of imposition' are a bird flying downward (12. 6a), perverted inspiration, and a headless contrary to the serpent, a mazy worm (b). Above 'perception' in the eighth line a small bird flying upward reminds us of the large bird flying the same direction beside 'percieve' in 11. 5g. Birds flying upward can open the airy way to infinite delight (in *Jerusalem* Blake likes to use birds over the word 'salvation'); downward they may act as beasts of prey, like Theotormon's eagle (in *Visions of the Daughters of Albion* 5 and *America* 11). The important statement 'All poets . . . thing' is set off by soul and body figures flying respectively left (12. 14a) and right (18a), flanked by serpentine scrolls. Firmly identifying the import of these scrolls is the elaboration of rising and descending strokes in the word 'prophecying' in the bottom line (27a). (In copy E the bottom scroll is doubled in length; for its human extension see 13. 25a.)

Plate 13

In line 1 two infants signal the word 'be', and when the word recurs its rising stroke is given a looping banner. Emphatic underlining is given to 'fervently' and 'patheticly', but a very wormy downward squiggle descends from 'we' alongside

[43] John Grant (*VFD*, pp. 182 n., 183 n.) calls attention to the headless warrior (11. 14g) and develops the interpretation of 11. 16b as 'the deity as a human artifact'.

Palmer saw at bottom 'an awful, ancient man [who] rushes *at* you as it were, out of the page'. Plowman, though annotating copy I, saw (p. 13) the woman simply as the Earth, i.e. as identical in figure to 'the Matron Clay in *The Book of Thel*', nourishing 'the babe of Inspiration within the cave of the mind' and the same babe, at page bottom, 'fleeing in terror from the aged tyrant . . .'.

The contrast between the loving mother and child at one pole of the picture and the separating man and bearded god at the other brings to mind Rowlandson's sarcastic etching of 1784, *The Historian Animating the Mind of a Young Painter*. The word 'animating' is put to different, indeed opposite, use here. But Rowlandson's contrast between a loving mother and child, the artist's rejected subject, and a bewigged old historian, the focus of his rapt attention, suggests not simply an influence but a residual theme: the proper study of the artist.

[44] In copy G the plates that follow (12–15) were rearranged in the sequence 15, 14, 12, 13, confirmed by Blake's inscription of page numbers within ruled borders. Graphically the effect is to hurry from little Adam separated from his God-image in the abyss to the stout eagle and serpent collaborating in it; textually to step from the history of poets and priests to the printing house.

A Memorable Fancy.
The Prophets Isaiah and Ezekiel dined with

f12:1   a   b   c   d   e

the cause of imposition

f12:6   a   b

a firm perswasion that a
?

f12:14   a

f12:18   a   b

ries, and prophecying

f12:27   a

Grecian.

f13:19   a

present ease or gratification?

f13:25   a

finite
For man has closed himself up, till he sees

f14:19   a   b

A Memorable Fancy

I15:1   a   b

46. *The Marriage of Heaven and Hell* (details)

'cursed in his name . . .'. At the paragraph's end the cloaked soul figure (yellow in blue sky^F or red with blue cloak^I) directs our attention onward. After 'Diogenes the Grecian' (19) two horizontally twining grasses with spikes at their right ends support a caterpillar (a) on their first curve. At page bottom, in the curve of a long banner, Ezekiel lies on his right side (13. 25a; cf. 20–1), the banner perhaps taking the pun in 'lay so *long*'. The prophet's evident comfort, in the picture, seems to belie his spoken denial of 'present ease' in the line under which it hangs. But his hammock is painted dark against sulphur sky in copy G.

Plate 14

In variously coloured flames which, like those in Plate 4, burn in reverse direction to the flames of the title-page and Plate 3, a woman with streaming hair and a black or purple blindfold (except in G and I) hovers above a naked greyish male body on green grass^{GHI}. In G and I her face is made visible, shouting^I—implying, in the iconography of *Jerusalem*, a vision of the soul as that portion of man that wakes him from sleeping as body. Max Plowman (p. 13) saw 'the resuscitation of the body by the soul' here, with the consequence on Plate 15: 'the eagle of genius . . . bearing in its talons the unaspiring serpent [of] the purely instinctive life'.[45]

In the centre, chestnut leaves and burs follow 'sensual enjoyment', and another leaf hangs from 'body' (compare the hanging lily in 'The Lily'). Near the bottom a naked prancing chestnut^D horse (14. 19a) against pink sky^F suggests the 'infinite' prospect when 'the doors of perception' are open. (We saw an energetic but falling horse on Plate 5; this one is on his feet and going fast; we shall see still more energetic displays on Plate 27.)

Plate 15

Here the subject of the text is Blake's printing, allegorically described: each metal plate, cut and burnt into by tool and acid fire, is a 'cave', each process the cave goes through is a 'chamber' in his printing house.[46] But the result of the process, the surface of the paper printed and coloured, which we also call a 'plate', is a 'cave' too; the student enters it to find the immense palaces the poet–artist has

---

[45] The Cumberland copy title for the picture is 'The Body of Hector', an allusion to the battle that lost Troy with symbolic implications perhaps analogous to those of the *America* title-page. Closer is Blake's pencil drawing (related to an early Notebook sketch) of a woman hovering over a man whose lyre and tambourine, silent beside him, imply that it is the artistic life that must be awakened. (Keynes, ed., *Drawings of William Blake*, 1970, No. 40.) Note that it is most probably a lyre that the serenader holds in Plate 1. On the other hand the inscription for this picture in the 'Small Book of Designs', 'a Flaming Sword Revolving every way', links the flames in the picture directly to the text's 'flaming sword', the guardian cherub's weapon that keeps body and soul from consummation.

[46] See my note, 'The Cave in the Chambers', *William Blake: Essays for S. Foster Damon*, ed. Rosenfeld, pp. 410–13.

built for his delight. (Perhaps one of the things Thel shrinks from doing is the making a friend and a companion of Blake's 'images of wonder'.)

Body (a) on the left of the title and soul (b) on the right are threaded together by the line that writes 'Fancy' (15. 1), and after the words about transmitting knowledge there is a continuous worm–serpent–tendril of curves and loops, ending ironically in a Shandean delete sign (15. 4a).

In the first chamber the 'Dragon-Man clearing away the rubbish from a caves mouth' is depicted as a burin or graver given head, arm, and legs (15. 5a). The sprig of small leaves that fills out line 6 may hint that we are preparing the printed leaves of a book: note the detached and attached leaves at 1a and 2a. All we are shown of the 'adorning' process in the second chamber are a standing and a reclining human figure (15. 10b, c) with a book lying between them; they are preceded by a viper-shaped scroll (a); the second figure (c) may be melting into the ground. In chamber three, leaf-topped curves after 'immense cliffs' (14) mark the cliff-edge, of which we saw two examples in Plate 7, i.e. the edge of the cavity in the copperplate. We are not shown the furnace of the fourth chamber. In the fifth, following 'expanse' (18) is a feathery scroll. Following the words about books in libraries (sixth chamber), a viper line and an oak leaf are combined (15. 21d) to suggest ink and paper, the leaf of a tree being an easy hieroglyph for the leaf of a book.

Below, a distant long-winged bird flies leftward (b) above the large emblem of serpent (a) and eagle (c)—not fighting each other, as in the Homeric omen, but collaborating to produce linear text and infinite illumination. In some copies[EFGI] their being inside the cave or trough of the copper plate is indicated by the addition of cloud-rock sides and floor. The snake's tongue 'cuts into' the rock just as the lightning does on Plate 6. The eagle's wings, beak, and eye are opened wide (a double ring around the eye in G). According to the text (11–14) the eagle with wings of air (i.e. brushes drawing pictures on the copper and brushes adding colours to the expanse of paper) causes 'the inside of the cave to be infinite' and builds 'palaces in the immense cliffs', i.e. these Illuminated Writings. We see why the Devil of Plate 10 has wings as well as serpentine scroll. And we see why the tendrils of the isolated vine on Plate 2 turn down, while the similarly looping tail of the serpent here turns up (as the eagle's head) then forward and up (as the viper's body in 7. 5b). Vine and leafing tree, divided, could bear no blossom or fruit; serpent and bird, married, like body and soul, poet and artist, craftsman and genius, can together transmit 'knowledge' and cause the inside of our cave to be infinite.[47] The intentional relation to the cave framing the visionary work of ancient poets in Plate 11 is made manifest by Blake's adding cave outlines to these

---

[47] In the language of Alchemy, 'an eagle bearing a serpent in its claws [is a] symbol of the union of sulphur and mercury, matter and spirit'. (Désirée Hirst, *Hidden Riches*, 1964, p. 135.)

plates (11 and 15) at the same time, i.e. in copies G and I (the outlines in copies E and F, on Plate 15, being very tentative and experimental). The space shown is the abyss of the title-page and Plates 4 and 20; the eagle or some bird of similar feather representing enlarged perception we have seen flying upward in Plates 1, 2 (the distant bird), 8 (12d—and in 15a the eagle in this same pose), and 11 (5g) and will soon see in 17 (10c) and in the final 'Chorus' (27). The serpent is to appear as Leviathan in Plate 20. Small emblems of a winged serpent are 5. 10a and 19. 26d; the small cognate emblem of snaky twig and oak leaf seen here (15. 21d) and in 10. 16b is repeated in Plate 20, where William Blake takes the place of the leaf: there poet is to root as eagle is to snake.[48]

Plate 16

In the large top picture we see what happens if the collaborators separate, if cunning priests impose their errors of abstraction: our senses sit in prison not palaces. The prison scene is a variant of *Gates of Paradise* 12, where the motto referring to priestly vengeance identifies the imprisoned five humans as Ugolino and his kindred.[49] There Blake shows the family as lean, exhausted, and presumably on the verge of their notorious approach to self-devouring (a son's offering his body to his father); here, in copies A to C at least, the gaoling is the main point, the gigantic human potential walled in and darkening. Here the 'Giants' who form this world of 'sensible objects' (Plate 11) 'seem to live in it in chains'—though no manacles are shown: any gaoling that is a consequence of imposed vision is alterable to free flying, as the numerable and innumerable birds on other pages keep reminding us.

The five bodies are giants grouped in one rank and clutched together like the fingers of a closed hand, only one head erect and its eyes blank[ABC]. (The *Gates* emblem shows five humans spread about the cell like so many individual studies in isolation.) Their garments are variously coloured, each differently and forming different bouquets in different copies—not from changes in a colour code but as symbolic of variety.

In the early copies there are lighter surfaces at the left indicating windows, perhaps in a door. In D a brown wash almost hides these surfaces, and in E to H the background is painted solid and dark. In D Ugolino is given eyes, glancing to the right; in E, F, and H his eyes stare directly forth. Then suddenly in copies G and H we are shown Ugolino's incredibly long arms, always there (visible in A to C though hidden in E and F), stretched around the two bodies beside him. And in G an astounding piece of theatricality occurs. We follow his eyes to the right

---

[48] 'In the copy I saw', wrote Palmer to Anne Gilchrist, ' "printing-house" are the only black letters. They are very black. It has a droll and good effect.' (*The Life and Letters of Samuel Palmer*, 1892, p. 245.) The description fits copy H.   [49] The Cumberland title is simply 'Ugolino'.

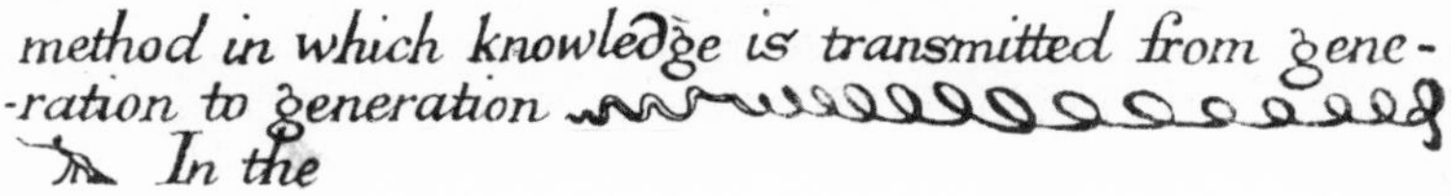

method in which knowledge is transmitted from gene-
-ration to generation ⌇⌇⌇⌇⌇⌇⌇⌇⌇⌇
In the

f15:4   a

f15:5 a

others adorning it

f15:10 a   b c

were arranged in libraries.

I15:21   a   b   c   d

fic would cease to be Prolific

E16:12   a

E16:15   a

E16:18 a   b   c   d

E17:6   a b c   d

Energies. *A Memorable Fancy*

E17:10   a b   c   d e f g h

47. *The Marriage of Heaven and Hell* (details)

and below his open left hand we see a bloody red lump gleaming on the floor, plainly some flesh he has tried eating! Copy I remits this horror, but guilty eyes still peer sideways. The youth at his right now shows his face (shown also in H); the youth at his left opens an eye; the background is lighted and we see the window again.[50]

At the end of the paragraph a small light figure sitting on a long line (16. 12a) illustrates the proper soul–body relationship: arms outstretched as wings, body balanced in a trough of line. At the next break a little flower (16. 15a) shows how to fill the immense (its left leaves splashed with gold, its right purple[I]). At the next, the light soul and dark body (16 : 18a, b) separated and backed by vegetation (gold leaves on the branch behind body[I]) but reaching toward each other, diagram the reference to 'existing beings'—and to what follows, 'two classes of men'.

Plate 17

A pine tree with three branches holds the top right margin; in illustration of Christ's opposites, sheep and goats, Peace and Sword, we see a horizontal sheep (17. 6a) and an upright goat (b), a walking horizontal horse (c) and a leaping horse (d: repeated from 14. 19a)—reminding us that the 'Sword' of Christ is for intellectual not corporeal war, the horse (cf. the giants) loosed from the dens imposed by 'weak and tame minds' (16. 5). These horses—of prophetic instruction, as we come to realize by Plate 27—are visions released from the caves of copper and paper. Above 'A Memorable Fancy' a red[EF] or orange[DH] or blue[G] or green and red[I] phoenix (our eagle of Plate 15) flies (17. 10c) from a drooping tree (b) (the phoenix's mythical resting-place after burning) toward a reed-bordered watery area, probably the abyss of the vision that follows, over which our familiar five birds are circling (d–h), the central bird perhaps a reappearance of the phoenix. Looking quite the other way stands a traveller (a) with short staff, his back to the tree: there is just nothing in sight.[51] Considering the parable of the text, is this the angel Reason, looking out upon nothing, contrasted to the red diabolic 'young man' who sees with imagination and senses?

During the frightened angel's speech and vision that begin the Memorable Fancy, no living emblems can fly; there are only some crevices (or roots) in front of the second paragraph, and suggestions of rebellious viper shapes in 'So' and upward from 'twisted' (28–9).

[50] Yet it is hard not to see the red on his fingers as blood. In the 1827 tempera panel of 'Ugolino with his Sons and Grandsons in Prison' in Sir Geoffrey Keynes's collection (reproduced in his edition of *The Letters*, 1968, Plate 12) Blake returns to the *Gates of Paradise* design, adding sympathetic hovering angels to emphasize the closeness of available hope and help, which none of the wretched family quite seems to see.

[51] The traveller's staff or cane is visible in A and E, partly so in C and H, but lost in the printing of other copies. In I there is a pool beside the willow, perhaps implying an oasis, in G a large blue area, in D and F a green plain.

Plate 18

The vision of the angel imposes barrenness on the lettering, except for an occasional floral flourish on 'deep', 'vast', 'deep', and 'sea', all wilting downward. But the approach of the spiritual leviathan is marked in some copies, by a touch of green or a marginal check-mark, or, in copy H, by the picking out in blue-black ink of the word 'Leviathan'. (In copy D the colouring at top and bottom shades from blue to yellow to white and pink as though in anticipation of the angel of Plate 23 who 'became almost blue but mastering himself . . . grew yellow, & at last white pink & smiling'.)

Plate 19

The angel and his dark vision having departed, the soul-and-body figures (19. 9a, b) flying parallel escape horizontally through clouds (c) toward, or as, two rising birds (d, e), the first one red[F]. After the angel's asking 'how I escaped?' a curlicue (19. 12b) of communication points, again, to two birds (c, d); then a human form (a) comes running with 'I answered'.

Finally, when 'I . . . leap'd into the void', soul and body (19. 26a, b) hold hands in free space, beside a gull (c) and a marvellous eagle-winged viper or serpent-tailed bird (d), red and black (or yellow or green) or in a red band of sky—compacting into a small hieroglyph the eagle–snake emblem of Plate 15 (and cf. Plate 5).

Plate 20

The fantasy that Blake imposes on the angel[52] is barren of adornment also, only concluding with three figures (20. 14a, b, c) for 'monkeys, baboons, & all of that species' (1).[53] At bottom in a 'twisted root of an oak tree' hanging over the deep (20. 19a) is Blake, as described at the Fancy's beginning, 'sitting in the twisted root' (17. 30). (Since both the angel and Blake sit there, the picture can be of either; but since it is a prophetic position, like Ezekiel's in Plates 13 and 23, from the reader's point of view the sitting figure must be Blake. Actually, at the right margin, sketched in a bend of the oak root as it grows down from Aristotle's 'works', is what appears in some copies (cf. C) to be another figure, the angel.)

In the large picture, the leviathan, showing three bodily loops above the tide, is churning the deep with 'all the fury of a spiritual existence' (19. 1). As a Biblical, apocalyptic version of our prophetic viper working in the cave with corrosive fires, Leviathan directs his bright red tongue straight upward, in a position

---

[52] The Cumberland title for the page is 'A Dream'.
[53] Or monkeys with their tails eaten off? (Everett C. Frost's suggestion: see text of Plate 20 just above.)

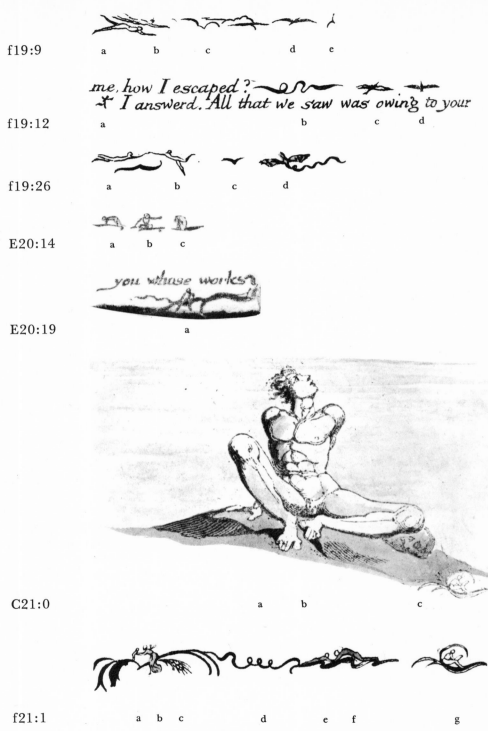

f19:9   a   b   c   d   e

me, how I escaped? ~
I answerd. All that we saw was owing to your

f19:12   a   b   c   d

f19:26   a   b   c   d

E20:14   a   b   c

you whose works

E20:19   a

C21:0   a   b   c

f21:1   a   b   c   d   e   f   g

48. *The Marriage of Heaven and Hell* (details)

deliberately reminiscent of the eagle's beak in Plate 15. He is variously multi-coloured as described (18. 26–32). White foam indicates the fury of his movement (cf. the acid bath of Plate 10). A dawning of rose and gold (variously shaded, more like a dull red cloud in D) spreads from the left horizon. In G and I clouds have been added to the sides, as in Plate 15.[54]

Plate 21

This breath-of-air picture brings the relief promised when Blake escaped the dark fantasy to sit 'on a pleasant bank' (19. 5). The text and its merry, diabolical flourishes triumph over Swedenborg's works, defined in Plate 3 as the mere clothes left behind in Christ's sepulchre. His human head pointed upward like the serpent head of Leviathan on Plate 20 and the head of the eagle on Plate 15, his mouth open in utterance [ABCH], this naked human phoenix sits on the green turf over 'the bones of the dead' (cf. Proverb 2, Plate 7), his knee on the skull of dead thought, his right hand on a leaf of paper (21. 0a, clearly visible in copies A to D and H but painted over in the rest, Blake perhaps not wishing to seem to trivialize, as our attention to such things may seem to do: the skull must stand for more than the copper cave; the paper is simply a part of the green earth). This is an emblem of the human form of the illumination of this page, of resurrection from 'works' that are 'only Analytics' (20. 18–19). Blake uses this picture in *America* 6 with a poetic text of a Declaration of Independence; later he develops it into an emblem of 'the regenerated man' to illustrate Blair's *Grave*. In copy A the man looks through a bright gap in blue clouds above his head; in D a yellow and red sunrise is added at his left; in G and H bands of colour ray out from a sun behind him; in I to a similar effect is added a curtain of arched clouds melting in the rising light. (In most copies the man's penis is shown, in H full genitals.) In copy D the man is backed by two overlapping pyramids; in E and F by a shadowy single pyramid. A man standing naked before pyramids is a traditional emblem for wise silence (there is a visual similarity in Wynne's Emblem 2; *Choice Emblems*, 1772); possibly Blake is suggesting the wisdom of quiet prophecy or vision (in D and E the lips are closed) as against 'the Contents or Index of . . . publish'd books' (6–7); in *America* the thematic contrast is between freedom and imperial slavery.[55]

[54] John Beer can see Leviathan both as 'symbolizing the coils of Reason in the Sea of Time and Space' (*Blake's Visionary Universe*, New York, 1969, p. 272) and as 'the serpent of energy . . . reduced to analytic coils' there (p. 372).

[55] 'This design symbolizes, in a different way, the idea shown in the little engraving, in *The Gates of Paradise*, of the winged child (regenerated man) bursting from the mundane egg (the grave) into the regenerated world of the imagination.' (Raymond Lister, *William Blake*, New York, 1968, p. 45.) The Cumberland title is 'Satan addressing the Sun', a reference to *Paradise Lost*, iv. 32 ff. that would, applied prophetically to fallen man, mark his recollection of his former and potential glory.

Another dimension is apparent if we consider the sheet of paper at the left and the skull (presumably related

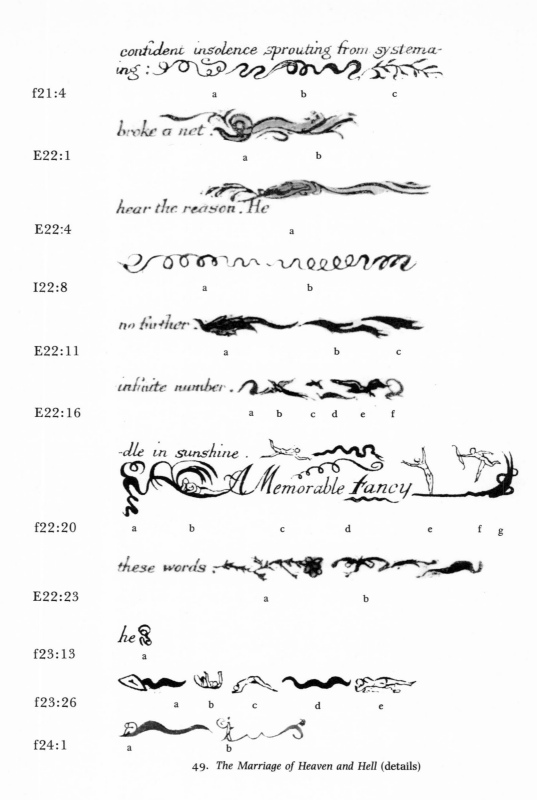

confident insolence sprouting from systema-

ing :

f21:4   a   b   c

broke a net .

E22:1   a   b

hear the reason . He

E22:4   a

I22:8   a   b

no further .

E22:11   a   b   c

infinite number .

E22:16   a   b   c   d   e   f

-dle in sunshine .

A Memorable fancy

f22:20   a   b   c   d   e   f   g

these words .

E22:23   a   b

he

f23:13   a

f23:26   a   b   c   d   e

f24:1   a   b

49. *The Marriage of Heaven and Hell* (details)

Education is the theme of the ornamental leaf and tendril lines that precede the text. An infant (21. 1a) is taken in hand by an intellectual nurse (b) (her psyche wings relate her to the woman welcoming the babe from its material mother in 'Infant Joy') who sits on the line properly (as the soul in Plate 16); the fruitfulness of this act is indicated by a ripe ear of grain (c). Some years later (count the curves and loops in (d)) a child (e) and nurse (f) (with red skirt[E]) study something on the ground; then the independent schoolboy (g) reads in a leafy cave, free of school (like the reader in the treetop in 'The School-Boy'). The picture line reads as progress towards the naked humanity of the large picture and counter to the wisdom of 'Angels' (1–2). Yet the rollicking brushwork applied to the mocking characterization of Swedenborg is not wholly unsympathetic to his 'confident insolence' (3). The squiggles following the colon after 'systematic reasoning' (21. 4a–c) are unconnected, but the third bears leaves. And there are leaves after 'publish'd books'—two very fat, two very thin, the former shaped[1] into legless chicken and duck.

Plate 22

In line 1, after 'ever broke a net', a large fish (22. 1a) twists wildly in a long net, its broken end held by a fisherman (b) who sits on a sloping bank at the right. (The details did not print clearly, and in some copies the whole scene appears a mere embellishment; in D the fisherman is made into a pink fish, perhaps.) After 'falshoods' an arm-pointing figure on a leafing branch (22. 4a) wrapped in a scroll garment or lying on a scroll couch, or both (cf. the figure in 'Introduction', *Songs of Experience*), directs us to 'hear the reason'. In line 8 Swedenborg's inability to converse with devils gives us a broken or discontinuous diagram (22. 8a, b) of the transmission of knowledge (contrast 15. 4a and note the reversal of looping here). His 'superficial' writings are marked by plain flat green leaves (22. 11a, b, c); the 'infinite number' of delights obtainable from Dante or Shakespeare is suggested by a widely various band: a fish (22. 16a), a long-tailed bird of paradise (b), a distant falcon perhaps (c), a green slug (d), a swan perhaps with feet trailing (e), and an ampersand (f). His candle-holding futility is represented by a man vainly trying to reach the tail of the viper of true delineation (22. 20c, d).

The next 'Memorable Fancy' contains the dramatic centre of *The Marriage*, a true conversion of doubting angel to prophetic devil (on Plate 24); so the title is vibrant with diabolic lines—above and below 'Fancy', jestingly vertical at the

to a buried skeleton) at the right as transformations of the contrast in George Wither's first emblem between life-giving 'knowledge', exemplified by a man at the left with his hand on a book (under a flourishing tree), and death-bound corporeal possessions, exemplified by a skeleton at the right sitting near a heaped table under a barren tree. *A Collection of Emblemes*, Plate 1, Book I, 2nd edn. 1635. (This emblem is cited by Elaine Mozer Kauvar, 'Blake's Botanical Imagery', dissertation, Northwestern University, 1971, pp. 13–14, for its contrast of living and dead vegetation.)

left (a), where the audience (b), that schoolboy of Plate 21, now lying on his right side like Ezekiel, is ready to read *this* book, i.e. to watch the action directly ('Once I saw'); coiling up the cliff edge (g) at the right. The conversion will occur when the attentive angel stretches out his arms to embrace the fire (24. 3). In dumb show here the figure stretching out his arms (e) is receiving an arrow (invisible), presumably of intellectual affection, from a naked leaping archer (f). (Compare Blake's being shot by Milton's star in *Milton* and the cupid shooting a woman in the genitals in page 19 of *The Four Zoas*.)

Between the announcement that 'the Devil uttered . . . words' (23–4) and the words themselves are a thorny wild rose (22. 23a) and a flying red worm (b), diabolic contraries, and two leaf banners. At page bottom a thick flourish that can be made to look like a salamander^D swims leftward.

Plate 23

The characterization of angelic rhetoric after line 5 seems consistent with 21. 4a. When the devil speaks of Jesus, a very plain pictogram of man with halo accompanies the pronoun 'he' (23. 13a), huddled, perhaps simply to fit the cramped space.

At page bottom, under 'Jesus was all virtue, and acted from impulse', float two curious squiggles and three dead or resting bodies. The first squiggle (23. 26a) has a triangular shield for a head, with perhaps a Greek or a Hebrew letter approximated in its centre—an emblem of triune God? The third human (e), lying on his left side, may be Ezekiel again. The second figure (b) is a human (or a dog^D) upside down; the next (c) is a diver. Perhaps this scene and Plate 20 are meant to suggest that (as in *Jerusalem* 93) everyone must enter the *aqua fortis* to be transformed.

Plate 24

At the end of the devil's persuasive argument we see the angel before and after conversion: first a figure huddled in doubt (24. 1a), face buried, Theotormon-like, on a vegetable curve, then a light figure (b) walking on waves, wind filling his scarf. We are then told of the angel's conversion to arise as Elijah and see a faintly sketched soaring figure after his name (24. 4l). Then a whole line is filled with a seminar (f–j) of five prophets ('we often read the Bible together') bracketed by four books (k) (two flat, two leaning against them) and some larger fascicles (c, d), prints perhaps—or fodder.[56] A shadowy figure (a), clearly meant to be so, is seen from behind, at the left; he has angel wings and dangling legs but no head;

---

[56] The object (e) behind the back of the first prophet is unmistakably the left profile of a horse's head and raised front leg, though not well printed in D. A horse of instruction, preparing for duty in Plate 27? Objects c, d may be related to the horse. Bundles of hay?

he seems to be holding out a dripping head toward the seminar. (Compare the headless warrior of 11. 14g.) This may well be the angel before consuming, i.e. mental decollation. At the other end of the group is a dividing tendril (l), the leftward prong of which is like the corkscrew tendrils of the Argument page except that it slants up instead of down. The other prong opens out in large flourishes, and the rest of the paragraph burgeons with foliage and loops and banners culminating in a wonderfully Shandean doodle after 'whether they will or no' (24. 10a). After 'if they behave well' runs an immediate customer (24. 8a)— or rather, perhaps, the prophet reaching out toward what may be a tiny helpless (armless) customer (b), or a hitching post. All these supra-serpentine coilings on this page depart widely from the viper lines of simple transmission; life is richer when 'One Law' is no more.

In the finis picture, of the oppressor (King Nebuchadnezzar) with spiked crown retreating and reverting in terror on all fours, we see the face of the bearded god which in 11. 1b was simply the ancient poets' animation of a tree or vegetable or waterspout. Graphically the face is now returning to the tree stump; but there are two great trunks behind the red-skinned[DEF] king, in elephantine embrace, with the suggestion of another pair behind, at right. In *The Marriage* we first saw such twining trunks, less gigantic, in the top compartment of the title-page.[57] (In I the nose and right eye of the face of an ox lurk in the triangular shadow above Nebuchadnezzar's waistline.)

A Song of Liberty

That a 'Marriage' which culminates in a gathering of prophets to 'read the Bible together' should end with a 'Song' printed in biblically numbered verses ought to be attractive if not surprising. And we should be ready for the primacy now given the word. There are no more large, separate pictures; instead, the lettering is given more space and fills the space more liberally. (Vertically the spacing is no wider than in Plates 21 to 24—five lines to the inch, i.e. 14 point measure—nor are the letters taller, except for some ornamental capitals; but they are broader and the spaces between words are ampler. And the climactic typography of the Song is more dramatic than the almost imperceptible rise in the second part of Plate 24, from 14 point to 16 point.)[58] But the small pictures are also ampler, matching the lettering in scale, and free to dilate with the lettering

---

[57] Nebuchadnezzar lacks a crown in the Notebook sketch (p. 44) and in the 1795 colour print, but it is restored to his 'Visionary Head' in 1819. The Cumberland title is 'The Arbitrary Power', a proper Enlightenment epithet.

[58] The typographical variations in Plates 2 to 24 may be described as functional and unpatterned. The only pages in 16 point (p. 3, the opening, and pp. 11–13) are from the earlier portion of the text marked by conventional *g*'s—to which belong also the Argument page (which begins in 11 and expands to 12 point with the second stanza) and pp. 6, 21–4, all 14 point. The newer pages (with unconventional *g*'s), which include the three pages of the Song, are all within the 12 to 14 point range.

& he was consumed and arose as Elijah.

Note. This Angel, who is now become a Devil, is

f24:4   a   b   c d e f   g h   i j   k   l

behave well.

E24:8   a   b

Hell: which the world

or no.

E24:10   a

hands she took the

ing;

mountains of light

f25:15   a   b

jealousy among the flaming hair.

f25:24   a   b   c

hurl'd the new born wonder thro' the starry

night.

11. The fire, the fire, is falling!

f26:2   a   b   c   d

f26:8   a   b   c

gloomy king.

f26:23   a   b   c d   e

in his eastern

f27:3   a   b

50. *The Marriage of Heaven and Hell* (details)

in the final 'Chorus'—where the interlinear horses enlarge with the letters of that word to 54 point! The effect is a sort of levelling *up*, but even the large, standing horse, who looks up like the eagle, seems to be reading and pointing out the words above his eyes.

Nevertheless, if there are no more pictures unmarried to text, there is no text free of pictures. True, they are only allowed what space there happens to be at the ends of the verses. But the poetry itself has absorbed and now gives particular delineation to the images of fire and falling and rising that were first presented in the large pictures of the Marriage.[59] That the Song is integral to the Marriage was not always recognized, and Max Plowman's assertion (p. 16) that it 'sums up the whole matter' of the Marriage 'in a highly abstruse symbolic poem' was helpful, as were his brief notes (p. 24) suggesting comparison of the picture of child-bearing on Plate 3 to verse 1, 'The Eternal Female groand', the picture of child-clutching on Plate 4 to verse 7, and the picture on Plate 5 to the falling fire of verse 11. Yet it is necessary both to take note of the transmutation that pictures undergo when they enter verses—and to consider how absent (or very abstrusely transmuted) some of the major images of the Marriage seem to be.

Plate 5 can be found everywhere, applied to contradictory visions, as the Devil warned. Reason's interpretation of the falling sun, sword, and unhorsed champion of Plate 5 as 'Desire . . . cast out' (5. 14–15) is spelt out in verses 10, 11, and 13 as the act and vision of a jealous starry king. (References to France's dungeon and to Spain and Rome make the allusion almost as political as the concluding lines of *America*.) The contrary interpretation of falling weapon, warrior, shield (red orb), chariot, and horse as the fall of a jealous king with hosts like the falling angels led by Satan is enumerated in verses 15 to 17. And a third, prophetic interpretation that turns Plate 5 upside down but is implicit in 'the Devils account . . . that the Messiah . . . formed a heaven of what he stole from the Abyss' (5. 15–6. 2), is expressed in verses 12, 14 perhaps, and 19–20, where the symbolism of fires and clouds reorients the images of the title-page or forms a heaven of what can be appropriated from the title-page and Plate 5 together. In this reversed vision the occulted sun, falling or hurled down 'into the western sea' (verse 13) reappears (verses 19–20) as a sun at dawn rising out of 'his eastern cloud' with the liberated horses of Eternity. What the pictured horses find it best to do, however, is purely to celebrate their looseness—and their ability to read the holy word.

As for the birds who have the role of circling the last word of the poem, 'Holy', they take no part at all in the text—except in the ironic epithet 'jealous wings', for jealousy of course lacks the imagination, the wings, to fly except downward. The

---

[59] If Keynes is right in dating 'A Song of Liberty' after the *Marriage*, argues Essick (p. 163)—and the evidence of the unconventional *g*'s confirms this—'the pictorial vision antedates the abstract concepts or allegory presented in writing . . . a process which is the reverse of allegory . . .'.

fashion in which this symbolism 'sums up the whole matter' is abstruse indeed. Finally, as for the eagle's collaborator the serpent, neither he nor the leviathan nor the small viper of the printing house is residual in a single word of the Song. We are driven to recognize that the whole purpose of the printing house and its processes has been so fully achieved in the Song itself as to need no further mention. The text has been loosed 'from the dens of night', an image (as also 'Urthona's dens' in verse 16) that does not ask to be analysed into relations to the caves and caverns of etching and printing.

Likewise there are no devils or angels in the Song or its illuminations. As for the naked and clothed couples and occasional single females, strolling, reclining, embracing, conniving, dancing together, or bathing in flames—the ones who presumably are to be freed from 'pale religious letchery' in the Chorus—the transmutations are almost evaporation. Except for the groaning Eternal Female, both described and shown recognizing an infant in a green flame in 25. 15a, the men have all the starry and fiery parts—Nebuchadnezzar, for example, whose portrait on Plate 24 unfolds marvellously into verse 18, in which the fallen 'gloomy king' still dreaming that he leads 'hosts' and 'promulgates . . . commands' must glance 'his beamy eyelids over the deep in dark dismay' as the new son rises. Nevertheless, if both these considerations are allowed for, the Plowman summation can be sustained.

Plate 25

Graphic motifs do carry over, graphically. The familiar emblems of tendril and leaf establish their importance at once in the adornment of 'Liberty' with a looping tendril such as grew from 'Fancy'—and the connecting of 'Song' and 'Eternal' with loops that recall those in the title-page after 'MARRIAGE' and around 'and'. Grape leaves, lacking since the Proverbs of Hell, propitiously return, qualifying the groan 'heard over all the Earth' (1) and putting small banners on the vine lifting 'keys' beside rising red birds. The red-gowned 'Female' (25. 15b) taking the green flames (a) in 'her trembling hands' looks like a variant of our earlier Soul figure; her accepting the new infant before it is visible in human form seems a variant of the angel's embracing the flame.

Three birds, bringing the total to five, and some drifting vegetation mock the 'jealous wings' of verse 9; the large red[DF] bird near the wild red rose on a vine running up from 'deep' suggests the rose vine as a variant of the eagle—serpent emblem. In the last line a knot (25. 24a) is tied (overgrown with a leaf[EI]) in the graphic line below 'jealousy'; the line is divided in three under 'among' (b) and spread wide under 'flaming' (c).

Plate 26

The threatening stag (26. 2a), who represented 'a base man' in 8. 26b when threatening a serpent, may represent the jealous king; his antagonist, the 'new born wonder' or falling 'fire', appears as a red[D] human form (c). Between them is a bush or bent tree (b) with branches that repeat the menace of the stag's raised hooves. Metamorphosed into a bush or tree (painted as tawny[D] as the stag) he can threaten the human wonder only statically. (Compare the similarly horizontal human tree in *Milton* 19 that menaces the approaching new-born bard.) The 'starry night' (1–2) is drawn (d) in a shape perhaps related to the cloudy cliffs of the title-page.

After Blake's advice to the Londoner as Jew and African, two sitting figures like those in the street bonfires of *Songs of Experience*, one (a) preparing something, the other (b) blanketed, beside a tree stump (c) (beyond which a long whip attaches to the word 'shot') may be studying to become prophets, i.e. to 'look up'; compare the seminar of Plate 24. After verse 14 a strip of bare earth is all that is left when the ocean 'roaring fled away'. The falling of king and warriors in verse 15 is shown as blades of seeding grass bent horizontal; the consequence in verse 16 is pictured as a flying back of soul toward green[D] body, their hands outstretched to touch (reversing the abstracting process of 11. 16a, b). The scene of verse 17 is enacted by four counsellors or warriors, in two pairs (26. 23 ab, cd), hailed by their 'gloomy king' (e) with a long train and an outstretched arm.

Plate 27

At the end of the third line we see (27. 3b) 'the son of fire in his eastern cloud' (4–5), image of the boy running in Plate 3, now with left foot forward but no girl on the cloud behind him. The figure (a) with arm and right leg stretched toward him is either the king giving chase with spear in hand, falling backward as he runs, or, more likely, a shepherd-priest with crozier or crook, fallen on one knee 'in dark dismay'. Spurning the curses, the son of fire is 'loosing the eternal horses', and we see two (27.6 ab) resting in a golden meadow (the first facing us, with its head against the tail of the second) and two others approaching at a gallop, one (c) carrying a man, the other (d) riderless. (In copy D the horses are brown, except the first, which is pink; in E and F all red-brown.) All may be enjoying liberty in different ways; compare the horse with rider to the swan carrying Paul Revere in *America* 11.

At the 'Chorus' we see two horses rearing and riderless, the second learning to stand on two feet (27. 13c) with head up like the eagle's in Plate 15, the leviathan's in Plate 20, and the resurrected man's in Plate 21. Bird feather and serpent-tendril intertwine around the word, with a flying bird above (b), something like the loop and bird around the marrying word 'and' in Plate 1. A warning banner is attached to the last false note, 'call' (19). In the final picture the bright phoenix, our eagle, with five attendant birds, springs up from the fiery meaning of 'Every thing that lives is Holy'.[60] In copy H the final line is picked out in red, the word 'Raven' in the first line of the Chorus in blue. Raven and eagle have attained similar prophetic roles[61] now that 'Empire is no more!'

With its final upward look the bird directs our understanding to the human form 'in his eastern cloud' of the bright sun which our Imagination must steal from the abyss whither the dying sun plunges in Plate 5. When we look up, as so stoutly directed throughout the book, our enlarged countenances will accept the falling fire as the rising sun; will recognize in the 'fiery boy' the babe born in Plate 3, the infant reaching toward or crying for the western sun in Plate 4, the naked man turning from shadowy bones and grass toward the sunrise in Plate 21; an incarnation of the fires and wings that sweep the book from title-page to chorus with the incendiary doctrines of liberated desire and active imagination. What it all has to do with Urthona's dens may be left to the Bible of Hell in William Blake's subsequent illuminations.

---

[60] The final bird is painted yellow[D], pink[E], red (with the horses)[F], backed by a blue wash (with the other birds)[G], blue and green[HI]. The colouring of the Song is otherwise relatively restrained in most copies. The only colour in A is a blue wash around the horse at left of 'Chorus'; in B some retouching and colouring of letters in the title 'A Song of Liberty'; in C grey wash on the two Chorus horses. In E there is pink on nearly all the flying or soaring figures in Plate 25 and on the two figures and crescent in 27. 3, and the final bird; brown on the horses. F has red in Plates 25 and 27 on the woman, the birds (on only two in Plate 27), and the horses, and blue washes behind the horses in verse 19, the Chorus, and the lower birds.

Copy D is rather fully washed and painted; on Plate 27 there are blue, pale orange, and pale red washes, pink and brown paint on the horses, golden paint on the meadow grass (line 6), on the cut flower around 'Chorus', and on the final bird and the ribbon on 'Holy'. G has various blue, pink, and yellow washes, green leaves here and there, blue in 25. 10, and the blue in 27 as described. Of H it must at least be reported that the final line is in red, the word 'Raven' in blue. I has washes of blue and pink and patches of gold, with a yellow wash beginning at the left of Plate 26 and growing very strong in the top section of 27. The birds are given blue edges to seem white, most other figures unpainted. Some of the vegetation is darkened; on 27 the horses' meadow is deep green, and the 'Chorus' flower, and three of the lower birds and the ribbon on 'Holy'.

[61] Kauvar, 'Blake's Botanical Imagery', p. 49, points out that alchemically ravens or crows denote putrefaction, imparting life.

A NOTE ON BLAKE'S USE OF GOLD LEAF: in copy I patches of gold leaf are distributed rather liberally in Plates 1 to 14 and 16 to 19, at which point Blake's supply seems to have given out, though there is a slight glint on the serpent in Plate 20. Faint smudges of gold in Plates 23 and 27 seem to have been transferred by thumb from remaining dust or from earlier pages; it would be unwise to argue a symbolic intent from the disappearance of gold leaf at this point. To single out only the simply definable effects: in Plate 1 the gold supplies a halo for the embracing devil and angel, in Plate 2 a patch of light on the grass, in Plate 3 a centre of fire and bright bands outlining the woman in the flames, half shaping a halo over her forehead. Gold encircles the sun in Plate 4, adds tips to the flames in Plate 5, emphasis to fires and lightning in Plate 6, bands of light beside the contrasting plants in Plate 10. In Plate 11 it gives a halo to mother and infant, shines in patches above her thigh and at her feet, and makes a heap (of rainbow gold?) on the blue plant behind the child. In Plate 14 it glows around the legs of the naked man and forms a large mound at his feet. In Plate 18 gold is used between lines, in 19 in a streak of blue at the top. After the glint in Plate 20 there are only faint smudges on Plates 23 and 27, giving golden emphasis to the sleeping horse, the name of the Raven, and the final 'Holy'.

f27:6   a b   c   d

f27:13   a   b   c

but acts not!
For every thing that lives is Holy

f27:20   a b c   d   e f

51. *The Marriage of Heaven and Hell* (details)

X

BLAKE'S FIGURES OF DESPAIR
MAN IN HIS SPECTRE'S POWER

Janet Warner

CERTAIN images in the designs of William Blake occur often enough for us to assume that they hold for him a symbolic meaning, and are components of a language of art based on the human form.[1] One of these recurring images is a hunched figure with drawn-up knees, viewed from the front, as in *Jerusalem*, Plate 41 [37] (Plate 52). This figure and its related form, the bent-over, kneeling figure, as in *America* 16 and *Job* 6 (Plates 53 and 54) are recognized by most readers to be Blake's primary visual symbols for mankind in the state of Despair. Two other images are important to this complex: the head-clutching, falling figure as in *Urizen* 6 (Plate 55) and the prostrate adult figure, with arms close to its side, exemplified by Job in *Job* 6.[2] An exploration of Blake's use of these four forms and their variations may help to reinforce our understanding of Blake's subtle perceptions of one of mankind's most devastating emotions.

Although we may think of Blake as a supremely energetic and cheerful man, that he wrestled with despair many times in his life is evident to the reader of his works and letters. It is very moving to read the simple entry in his Notebook: 'Tuesday, Jan^ry 20, 1807, between Two and Seven in the Evening—Despair.'[3] Despair is one of the names given to the Spectre in *Jerusalem*, and it is this connection between the concept of the Spectre and the concept of Despair in Blake's work which I hope this study will illuminate.

Blake's meaning for both has many facets, yet the destructive aspects of the

---

[1] Northrop Frye suggested that Blake seemed 'to be striving for an "alphabet of forms"' in *Job* in *Fearful Symmetry*, 1962, p. 417. For a further application of this idea, including some preliminary comments on the visual images discussed in this essay, see my 'Blake's Use of Gesture', *Blake's Visionary Forms Dramatic*, 1970, ed. David V. Erdman and John E. Grant, 1970.

[2] Some indication of the frequency of these repeated images in Blake's designs can be demonstrated by the following list, which is by no means exhaustive:

1. Huddled, front view: *Jerusalem* 41, 51; *America* Frontispiece, 1; *Vala*, page 5; *Gates of Paradise* 4, 16; *Urizen passim*; *Job* 12; *VDA* Frontispiece, 4, 8; *Hecate*; *Dante* 3; *Night Thoughts*, *passim*.

2. Bent-over, side view: *America* 16; *Europe* 5; *Vala* viib, page 96; *Job* 6 and *passim*; *Night Thoughts* 19, 28, and frequently.

3. Falling: *VLJ*; *America* 5; *Urizen* 6; *Spiritual Form of Nelson Guiding Leviathan*; *Job* 16.

4. Prostrate: *Job* 6, 11; *Jerusalem* 33, 63, 94; *Lazar House*; *Vala* viia, page 78.

[3] K, p. 440.

power of reason which is essentially the Spectre is one of the basic components of Despair:

> This is the Spectre of Man: the Holy Reasoning Power
> And in its Holiness is closed the Abomination of Desolation.
>
> (J 10. 15–16, K, p. 629.)

Not only 'Desolation', but the traditional medieval suicidal implications of Despair are expressed by the Spectre's speech in *Jerusalem*, Chapter I:

> O that I could cease to be! Despair! I am Despair,
> Created to be the great example of horror & agony; also my
> Prayer is vain. I called for compassion: compassion mock'd;
> Mercy and pity threw the grave stone over me, & with lead
> And iron bound it over me forever. Life lives on my
> Consuming, & the Almighty hath made me his Contrary
> To be all evil, all reversed & for ever dead: knowing
> And seeing life, yet living not; how can I then behold
> And not tremble? how can I be beheld & not abhorr'd?
>
> (J 10. 51–9, K, p. 630.)

This passage is a reflection of medieval theological ideas of Despair—*wanhope*, despair of the mercy of God—found most clearly expressed in Chaucer's Parson's account of *Accidie*, or Sloth: 'Now comth wanhope, that is despair of the mercy of God, that comth somtyme of to muche outrageous sorwe, and somtyme of to muche drede, ymaginynge that he hath doon so muche synne that it wol nat availlen hym. . . .' The attributes which Blake gives to the Spectres of the Zoas in *Jerusalem* appear to be closely based on the description of *Accidie* in *The Parson's Tale*, which makes a man 'hevy, thoghtful, and wraw'. Doubt, 'cooldnesse', 'sompnolence', 'ydelnesse', and sorrow which 'werketh to the deeth of the soule and the body also' are all succinctly described by Blake as the behaviour of the Zoas when they turn against Albion and become Spectres:

> They saw their Wheels rising up poisonous against Albion:
> Urizen cold & scientific, Luvah pitying & weeping,
> Tharmas indolent & sullen, Urthona doubting & despairing,
> Victims to one another & dreadfully plotting against each other
> To prevent Albion walking about in the Four Complexions.
>
> (J 43 [38]. 1–5, K, p. 671.)

This passage is reiterated with further emphasis on *Accidie* or 'deadly stupor':

> And the Four Zoas are Urizen & Luvah & Tharmas & Urthona
> In opposition deadly, and their Wheels in poisonous
> And deadly stupor turn'd against each other, loud & fierce,

52. *Jerusalem*, plate 41 [37] (detail), copy I. Relief etching.
Lessing J. Rosenwald Collection, The Library of Congress

Over the hills, the vales, the cities, rage the red flames fierce;
The Heavens melted from north to south; and Urizen who sat
Above all heavens in thunders wrap'd, emerg'd his leprous head
From out his holy shrine, his tears in deluge piteous
Falling into the deep sublime; flag'd with grey-brow'd snows

Naked came I out of my mothers womb, & Naked shall I return thither
The Lord gave & the Lord hath taken away. Blessed be the Name of the Lord

And smote Job with sore Boils
from the sole of his foot to the crown of his head

W Blake inv & sc

London, as Act directs Published March 8: 1825 by William Blake N°3 Fountain Court Strand

Blake's Figures of Despair: Man in his Spectre's Power

> Entering into the Reasoning Power, forsaking Imagination
> They became Spectres, & their Human Bodies were reposed
> In Beulah by the Daughters of Beulah with tears and lamentations.
>
> (*J* 74. 4–9, K, p. 714.)

Thus *Accidie* or *Accidia*, the deadly sin which is Despair,[4] is part of what happens to Albion, and may indeed be the 'deadly Sleep' that the Four-fold Man has fallen into. This is certainly suggested by the design of *Jerusalem* 41 [37] (which has been called Humanity Asleep)[5] in which Blake explicitly tells us by the words on the scroll that the form represents Man in his Spectre's power:

> Each Man is in his Spectre's power
> Until the arrival of that hour
> When his Humanity awake
> And cast his Spectre into the Lake.

Clearly, before the full implications of this design can be realized, it is necessary to explore further what the 'power' of the Spectre implies.[6]

Blake would have been well acquainted with the concept of Despair as it was treated not only in Chaucer but other literature and art from medieval times to his own. It was a subject which 'profoundly affected the Medieval imagination, the sin against the Holy Ghost, the sin of sins, in that it tempted to self-destruction and thereby shut off every hope of repentance and salvation'.[7] Dante, whose work Blake was illustrating at the time of his death, had made Despair, the Abandonment of Hope, 'the very condition of entrance into Hell'.[8] Blake translated Dante's inscription ('lasciate ogni speranza, voi ch'entrate') literally as 'Leave every hope you who in enter' when he pencilled it in over the Gate in his drawing, 'The Inscription Over The Gate'.[9] Personifications of Despair and the other cardinal sins were common in Middle English poets such as Lydgate, Langland, and Gower, and the tradition flourished in English fifteenth-century literature (Dunbar, Hawes), eventually crowned by Spenser's *Faerie Queene* with its descrip-

---

[4] In this paper, I use the terms 'deadly sins' and 'cardinal sins' interchangeably, as is usual in modern terminology, to refer to Pride, Wrath, Envy, Avarice, Sloth, Gluttony, and Lust. (This is the Gregorian list which Dante, Chaucer, and most important medieval writers used, i.e. *superbia, ira, invidia, avaritia, acedia, gula, luxuria*). St. Thomas Aquinas called these sins *cardinal*, meaning chief or capital, but not *deadly* or mortal. They were final causes which gave rise to other sins but these seven were not the only sins in his ethic, nor, as Bloomfield points out, 'did their commission, if unconfessed, inevitably lead to damnation'. However, by the fifteenth and sixteenth centuries the concepts of capital and deadly sins had merged. See Morton W. Bloomfield, *The Seven Deadly Sins*, 1952.

For an account of the concept of Accidia up to 1500 see Siegfried Wenzel, *The Sin of Sloth*, 1967.

[5] Geoffrey Keynes, *Drawings of William Blake*, 1970, Plate 55.

[6] Damon has written 'The Spectre is ruthless in getting its way, and cares nothing for the Individual it obsesses: it will drive him into unhappiness, disaster, and even suicide.' *A Blake Dictionary*, 1971, p. 381.

[7] F. I. Carpenter, 'Spenser's Cave of Despair', *MLN* xii (1897), 129–37.

[8] Ibid.

[9] Reproduced in Martin Butlin's *A Catalogue of the Work of William Blake in the Tate Gallery*, 1971, Plate 57.

tion of the Cave of Despair and the procession of the Sins.[10] Blake attempted something in this tradition in his rather obscure fragment, 'Then She Bore Pale Desire'. Richard Burton, whose *Anatomy of Melancholy* was the culmination of a series of English writings on Melancholy, devoted the last six subsections to a discussion of the sin of Despair. However, it was the figures of Despair as personified in Spenser and Bunyan which stimulated Blake's imagination, as I will later indicate, and his designs for Milton's *L'Allegro* and *Il Penseroso* show him well aware of the tradition as it was adapted by that poet. There is an interesting similarity in Blake's designs, 'Milton Led by Melancholy' and 'The Wood of the Self-Murderers: the Harpies and the Suicides' (Dante design).[11] In both, a poet is about to be led into a wood where unhappy spirits animate the trees, the experience being part of a process which leads to the ultimate regeneration of the poet. Melancholy is of course allied to Despair (there are several 'Despair figures' in Blake's Milton designs), and the implication that sorrow may be turned to the good of man, that it is not an end in itself, is a message that Blake shares with Milton and projects in both design and poetry.

The relation between the concepts of Melancholy and Despair, and the iconographic tradition behind them, is of course extremely complex, and has been traced in the monumental study by Klibansky, Saxl, and Panofsky, *Saturn and Melancholy*. They have demonstrated that by the late Middle Ages, the notions of Melancholy and Accidia were equated, and that by Milton's time, Melancholy had indeed become an intellectual force or tutelary spirit. The Miltonic Penseroso 'combined all the aspects of the melancholic: the ecstatic and the contemplative, the silent and Saturnine no less than the musical and Apollonian, the gloomy prophet and the idyllic lover of nature, and welded their manifoldness into a unified picture, mild on the whole rather than menacing'.[12] Blake seems to have understood *Il Penseroso* in much this way, for his representation of Milton in 'Milton and His Mossy Cell' follows an iconographic tradition for figures of Melancholia, that is, a seated, pensive figure, often viewed from the front.[13] Blake would have known this tradition from Michelangelo, Cesare Ripa's *Iconologia*, and Dürer's *Melencolia I* and it is this tradition to which I believe all his hunched Despair figures are related.[14] Blake shows Milton seated in a cave or 'cell', surrounded by various spirits of nature, flowers, and stars, with his arms outstretched

---

[10] This background is documented in detail by Bloomfield, *The Seven Deadly Sins*.

[11] The design for *L'Allegro* and *Il Penseroso* may be found in Adrian Van Sinderen, *Blake, The Mystic Genius*, 1949, and in *Blake Newsletter*, xvi (Spring 1971). The Dante design is in Butlin, Plate 61.

[12] Klibansky, Saxl, Panofsky, *Saturn and Melancholy*, 1964, p. 236.

[13] Cf. Ripa's 'Malinconia' in ibid., p. 405.

[14] For Blake's familiarity with these artists, see Jean H. Hagstrum, *William Blake, Poet and Painter*, 1964. Blake's hunched Despair figures are frontal, like the Ripa reproduced in Klibansky or Jesse of the Sistine Ceiling, as distinguished from the semi-profiled figure of Dürer's *Melencolia I*. They differ from the tradition in that they have an exaggerated slump or huddle.

in a gesture of creativity, this variation indicating the possible regenerative aspect of Melancholy.[15] Blake's involvement with the concepts of Melancholy and Despair as they were treated by eighteenth-century writers who further refined and extended these notions is of course evident in his illustrations to Gray's poetry, and especially in his more than 500 designs for Young's *Night Thoughts*. In the *Night Thoughts* designs, the hunched figure is consistently used to represent Despair or deep sorrow.[16]

In his own poetry, Blake came to associate Despair with a reasoning power cut off from Imagination (*J* 74. 10–13) and 'Desolation', much as Saint Thomas Aquinas had defined Accidia as *tristitia de spirituali bono*, the sorrow about, or the aversion man feels against, his spiritual good[17] (taking the spiritual good, in Blake's terms, to be Imagination), or as Spenser had demonstrated by the apparently reasonable argument for suicide that Despair put to the Redcrosse knight (*Faerie Queene*, Canto IX). Thus for Blake, the Spectre is both the 'Reasoning Power in Man' and the Despair which such reasoning brings about.[18]

Now the source of Accidia as well as all the other deadly sins is Pride. The false Pride of mankind which both Swift and Pope rail against comes under attack from Blake, too, who early uses the same weapons of satire and parody (as in 'An Island in the Moon' and *The Marriage of Heaven and Hell*), but with the added advantage of being able to use his graver to produce other dimensions of social comment. Like Swift and Pope, Blake's work intensifies in tone as his vision encompasses man's enormous vanity and selfishness, which he calls the Self-hood, the very basic difference being that Blake saw that the Selfhood was 'worship'd as God by the Mighty Ones of the Earth' (*J* 33. 17). The Selfhood is the Spectre that Blake's Milton recognizes as Satan and himself ('I in my Selfhood am that Satan: I am that Evil One! He is my Spectre!').[19] The Spectres of the Zoas possess this pride also:

> The Four Zoas rush around on all sides in dire ruin:
> Furious in pride of Selfhood the terrible Spectres of Albion
> Rear their dark Rocks among the Stars of God, stupendous
> Works! (*J* 58. 48–50, K, p. 690.)

This Satanic activity and Milton's explicit reference recalls the words of the Spectre's 'Despair' speech quoted previously, 'the Almighty hath made me his Contrary / To be all evil!' We should therefore expect to find designs in which the

---

[15] See also John E. Grant, 'Blake's Designs for *L'Allegro* and *Il Penseroso*', *Blake Newsletter*, xvi (1971), 134.

[16] Good examples are evident in the unpublished designs to Nights v and vii.

[17] Wenzel, *The Sin of Sloth*, p. 48.

[18] In reference to Blake's own personal experience, Morton Paley has explored the connection between the Spectre and a despairing man in 'Cowper As Blake's Spectre', *Eighteenth Century Studies*, i (1968).

[19] *Milton* 14. Note that Blake uses the same design form for Satan in the water-colour, *Satan in His Original Glory*, and for Milton in plate 13.

Spectre is drawn as Satan (the traditional archetype of Pride) in conjunction with huddled, falling, and prostrate Despair forms, and this is indeed the case, as in *Job* 6 and the design *Satan Calling Up His Legions*, to name only two.[20]

There is a relation, then, between the Spectre, Despair and Pride in Blake's work which bears examining, for to reveal the paradoxes of these concepts appears to be the purpose of much of his poetry and painting. Thus in *MHH*, 'Milton is of the Devil's party without knowing it', 'The pride of the peacock is the glory of God', and a whole dualistic world view is called in question. The Spectre Selfhood must be 'put off & annihilated alway' (*Milton* 40. 36) but in the process a humanizing creative energy is released, as Blake describes in the struggles of Milton and Los.

In Blake's art, it is always necessary to distinguish between representations of man in the power of the Spectre, and thus in the state of Despair, and representations of the Spectre itself. Blake appears careful to make these distinctions both visually and verbally. The individuals taken over by Spectres are blameless:

> . . . Iniquity must be imputed only
> To the State they are enter'd into, that they may be delivered
> Satan is the State of Death & not a Human Existence . . .
> Learn therefore . . . to distinguish the Eternal Human
> . . . from those States or worlds in which the Spirit travels.

> (*J* 49. 65–79, K, p. 680.)

The visual images for the Spectre include recognizable Satanic figures, beasts, bat-winged hovering forms, and serpent–dragon forms—designs which it is outside the scope of this essay to discuss in detail. However, it is significant that Blake's roster of Spectre images follows to a surprising extent the traditional iconographic representation of Pride when it is symbolized by animals in literature or art. The list, compiled by Bloomfield, includes: the lion, peacock, eagle, horse, bull, elephant, unicorn, cuckoo, basilisk, dromedary, ram, and leviathan.[21]

The links between the state of Despair, the Spectres, and the deadly sins of Accidia and Pride which I have been tracing can be extended to include the rest of the cardinal sins: Envy, Lust, Gluttony, Avarice, and Wrath. Traditionally they are all aspects of Despair,[22] and reflected in the Spectre's behaviour. As I have indicated, Blake appears well aware of religious tradition regarding the Seven Deadly Sins, which in his poetry are sometimes called spiritual diseases:[23] 'The

---

[20] *Satan Calling Up His Legions* is reproduced in Figgis, *The Paintings of William Blake*, Plate 9, and Keynes, *Writings of Blake*, 1925, vol. iii. The figure of Nelson in *The Spiritual Form of Nelson Guiding Leviathan* is demonic as Morton Paley has discussed in his excellent Chapter Seven in *Energy and The Imagination*, 1970, and Despair forms are found surrounding Nelson in this picture. See Paley, Plate 3.

[21] Bloomfield, *The Seven Deadly Sins*, Appendix I.

[22] 'Moreover, Acedia is one of the capital sins . . . producing other, even quite distinct, sins.' *New Catholic Encyclopedia*, vol. i.

[23] Damon, *Dictionary*, p. 104.

Seven diseases of the soul settled around Albion' (*J* 19. 26). The sins are the creation of Satan in *Milton* (9. 20) and are thus linked to the Spectre Selfhood much as theology links them to Pride. Basically the sins to Blake are products of frustrated desire and are not in themselves evil. In *The Book of Los* he writes of a time when

> . . . none impure were deem'd:
> Not Eyeless Covet,
> Nor thin-lip'd Envy,
> Nor Bristled Wrath,
> Nor Curled Wantonness;
>
> But Covet was poured full,
> Envy fed with fat of lambs,
> Wrath with lions gore,
> Wantonness lull'd to sleep
> With the virgin's lute
> Or sated with her love.
>
> (K, p. 256.)

Blake had connected Despair with frustrated desire in *There Is No Natural Religion*: 'If any could desire what he is incapable of possessing, despair must be his eternal lot.' (Plate 6, 2nd series, K, p. 97.) Under the category of frustrated desire it is possible to place Envy, Lust, Gluttony, and Avarice and to see them all embodied in this speech of the Spectre of Urthona:

> Thou knowest that the Spectre is in Every Man insane, brutish,
> Deform'd, that I am thus a ravening devouring lust continually
> Craving & devouring . . .
>
> (*Four Zoas*, viia. 304–6, K, p. 327.)

It would be possible to demonstrate at much greater length that each of the fallen Zoas (with their Emanations) experience most of the sins at one time or another. The example of Tharmas will serve as an indication.

The Spectre of Tharmas appears early in *The Four Zoas* as a golden-winged human form, '. . . rapturous in fury / Glorying in his own eyes / Exalted in terrific Pride' (K, p. 267). This Wrath and Pride are followed by Lust for his Emanation ('burning anguish', K, p. 269). Enion herself experiences Envy ('jealous fear') of Enitharmon and commits murder (K, p. 278). Eventually Tharmas becomes the very embodiment of Accidia, a death-wish personified:

> . . . give me death
> For death to me is better far than life death my desire
> That I in vain in various paths have sought but still I live.
>
> (*Four Zoas*, vi. 57–59, K, p. 313.)

Along these lines, Tharmas is described as 'indolent and sullen' in *Jerusalem*, as previously quoted. However, in his fallen aspect as the Covering Cherub, Tharmas also suggests the sins of Avarice and Gluttony from the repeated references to his covering of 'precious stones' and his 'devouring Stomach' (J 89, K. pp. 734–6). Tharmas is also the personification of the senses of touch and taste,[24] the 'Angel of the Tongue', and when by his fall he becomes '. . . the Vegetated Tongue, even the Devouring Tongue . . . the False Tongue' (J 14, K. p. 634) it is Wrath which dominates his utterances. Thus, in the fall of Tharmas, the 'Parent Power', all the sins are suggested.[25]

Recalling that for Blake frustrated desire is the basis of the cardinal sins, a resulting Wrath is a psychologically valid result, and incidentally a reaction which an artist can depict vividly in a visual medium. When the Zoas divided originally they divided in rage (J 74. 1, K. p. 714), which is the keynote sounded by the first line of *Vala*. Fury creates the fallen world, and the sins assume living form in Chapter iii of *The Book of Urizen*:

> Rage, fury, intense indignation
> In cataracts of fire, blood & gall
> In whirlwinds of sulphurous smoke,
> And enormous forms of energy,
> All the seven deadly sins of the soul
> In living creations appear'd
> In the flames of eternal fury.
>
> (K, p. 225.)

It is significant that the visual images which dominate *The Book of Urizen* are the falling and huddled images of Despair figures.

It will not have escaped the close observer of Blake's designs that some of the variations of the hunched and falling figures, particularly those in *Urizen* (e.g. Plate 16 or Plate 22) emanate a powerful energy which seems the contrary of Accidia. Wrath, however, is the daughter-sin of Despair which can be redemptive, becoming the force of revolution, Orc, and the angry prophet Rintrah. *America*, the first poem in which Orc plays a dominant role, begins and ends with figures of Despair, the Frontispiece (Plate 56) and Plate 16 (Plate 53), underlining for the reader the paradoxical connections between the 'contraries' of energy and despair which can imply 'progression'.[26] I have written elsewhere that most of Blake's

---

[24] Frye, op. cit., 281.

[25] Although the implications of this brief catalogue cannot be explored here, it does indicate that Blake was adapting into his own myth a tradition whose psychological validity has been thoroughly explored by the Middle Ages and the Renaissance.

[26] Discussions of the Frontispiece figure can be found in Erdman, ed., *Blake's Visionary Forms Dramatic*, pp. 99 and 194 f.

55. *The Book of Urizen*, plate 7 [plate 6 in other copies].
Relief etching with water-colour.
Lessing J. Rosenwald Collection, The Library of Congress

recurring images can have a redemptive as well as a demonic interpretation. In the case of Despair figures, however, I am of the opinion that their truly redemptive form is actually a contrasting 'energy' figure: for example, an upward-soaring rather than a falling figure, a dancing or striding figure rather than a huddled or prostrate one. Energy figures have their demonic meanings (e.g. Satan in *Job* 6 is a demonic Albion of *Albion Rose*) but I have not found a Despair form used to suggest a regenerated state. At their best they connote sleep, which in itself suggests a fallen state.

At this point it is necessary to recall that in *There Is No Natural Religion*, immediately after stating in Plate VI that Despair must be the eternal lot of the man who desires what he is incapable of possessing, Blake asserts: 'The desire of Man being Infinite the possession is Infinite & himself Infinite' (vii, K, p. 97). By this juxtaposition we know that the state of Despair means the opposite of 'Infinite'—that is, the closed-up world of boundaries and ratios—Urizen's world, the world of fallen Nature.

The repeated circular huddled representations of Los and Urizen in *The Book of Urizen* suggest that the form is emblematic for the material world.[27] Thus the Despair form and the Spectre come together again in the fallen Urizen: 'The Spectre is the Reasoning Power in Man, & when separated / From Imagination and closing itself as in steel in a Ratio / Of the Things of Memory, It thence frames Laws & Moralities / To destroy Imagination. . . .' (*J* 74. 10–14, K, p. 714.) Blake's representation of the worm-Mother, Tirzah, in *Gates of Paradise* 16 also indicates that fallen nature is a meaning we should attach to the huddled pose.

Here the text of the poem *To Tirzah* becomes important, for the binding of the senses in 'mortal clay' is a tyranny both physical and mental which Blake often indicates by using chains and manacles in his illustrations. In a world produced by self-enclosure, Despair becomes a gaoler. Blake has graphically illustrated both the gaoler dangling keys and his huddled victim in one of his illustrations to Bunyan's *Pilgrim's Progress*, Christian and Hopeful in Doubting Castle (Plate 57). Bunyan's gaoler Giant Despair is represented as a Satanic Spectre-form—indeed he is a kind of rear-view version of Satan in *Job* 6. (This design should be compared to *Europe* 13, which includes the same gaoler with keys disappearing up the cell stairs, and a hunched Despair figure.) The giant appears again in Plate 25 of the Bunyan illustrations, this time with a club. Bunyan's description of the Giant Despair is brief: 'He had a cap of steel upon his head, a breast-plate of fire girded to him, and he came out in iron shoes, with a great club in his hand.' Blake omits the cap and armour in the illustrations, but seems to have had

---

[27] See also R. E. Simmons 'Urizen: The Symmetry of Fear', ibid., p. 152.

56. *America*, frontispiece, copy E. Relief etching.
Lessing J. Rosenwald Collection, The Library of Congress

57. *Christian and Hopeful in Doubting Castle*, from Illustrations to Bunyan's *Pilgrim's Progress*. Water-colour. Copyright The Frick Collection, New York

Bunyan's passage in mind when he described the Spectre of Urthona as an iron man:

> A spectre Vast appear'd, whose feet and legs with iron scaled . . .
> Round his loins a girdle glow'd with many colour'd fires,
> In his hand a knotted Club . . .
> Black scales of iron arm the dread visage; iron spikes instead
> Of hair shoot from his orbed skull . . .
>
> *(Four Zoas*, vi, 297–308, K, p. 319.)

This passage amplifies the 'naming' of the Spectre as Despair which we have seen in *Jerusalem* 10, and the Bunyan designs, executed late in Blake's life, indicate how consistent he was in both his use of visual images, and his care in distinguishing visually between the Spectre and the man in the Spectre's power.

With the iconography of Melancholy also in mind, Blake may have been further stimulated to create the hunched-over figure as a symbol of Despair by Spenser's stanzas describing 'That cursed wight . . . A man of hell, that calls himself Despaire . . .' in Book I of *The Faerie Queene*:

> That darkesome cave they enter, where they find
> That cursed man, low sitting on the ground,
> Musing full sadly in his sullein mind:
> His griesie lockes, long growen and unbound,
> Disordred hong about his shoulders round,
> And hid his face; through which his hollow eyne
> Lookt deadly dull, and stared as astound . . .
>
> (Canto ix, xxxv.)

Two more designs using the hunched figure, each with connotations of Hell, are the Dante design, 'The Mission of Virgil'[28] and Blake's colour print, *Hecate*. Another Dante design repeats the form with similar connotations: it is the Urizenic winged Angel in 'Dante and Virgil Approaching the Angel who Guards the Entrance of Purgatory'.[29] All these forms make an interesting comparison to the winged hunched figure in the frontispiece to *America*, and a related sketch in the Vala manuscript of the winged Spectre of Tharmas (p. 5), for they are all guardians of some kind of portal: Hell, the Underworld, Purgatory for the first group, and Generation for the last two which have associations with the Covering Cherub or 'Eternal Death'.[30]

Up to this point, I have been referring mainly to hunched, front-view figures, which if examined more closely could be seen to range from the rather noble

---

[28] A. Roe, *Blake's Illustrations to the Divine Comedy*, 1953, Plate 3.
[29] Reproduced in Martin Butlin's *A Catalogue of the Work of William Blake in the Tate Gallery*, Plate 72.
[30] 'The Spectre of Tharmas is Eternal Death' (*Four Zoas*, i, 106, K, p. 267) and so is Orc (*America* 2. 17, K, p. 196).

representation of Albion in *Jerusalem* 41 [37] to the grotesques of *Urizen*. Blake's variations are always subtle—a head bowed or unbowed, a gesture of arm or hand, knees open or ankles crossed—and yet they are always important clues to meaning, underlining the anger or frustration or malevolence or simply the passivity which is part of the spiritual condition. In this respect, the bent-over kneeling figure, which is often a woman, has a slightly different Despair meaning. It is a somewhat more grief-stricken figure, which can never express wrath, for example, but radiates fear or worshipful subjection (Plates 53 and 54). Blake suggests the meaning for this form in a passage in *The Four Zoas* where Albion and Vala worship the Urizenic shadow of Albion:

> Man fell upon his face prostrate before the watry shadow . . .
> And Vala trembled & cover'd her face, & her locks were spread on the pavement.
>
> (Four Zoas, iii. 54–6, K, p. 293.)

The prostrated image of Mother Nature on the final plate of *America* (Plate 53) seems to be an embodiment of these words, and becomes in its context in the poem a kind of emblematic form of subjection to a tyranny, the Urizenic cycle of nature. These lines, of course, come from a passage which, as Damon has demonstrated, is repeated in *Jerusalem* (29. 33–83) and is closely connected with the story of *Job*, for in it Albion accepts his Shadow as God, rejects his emotional life, and is smitten by Luvah with boils:[31]

> And Luvah strove to gain dominion over mighty Albion:
> They strove together above the Body where Vala was inclos'd
> And the dark Body of Albion left prostrate upon the crystal pavement,
> Cover'd with boils from head to foot, the terrible smitings of Luvah.
>
> (Four Zoas, iii. 79–82, K, p. 294.)

The relation between this passage and the design of *Job* 6 is important, for it demonstrates how a picture which Blake expressed first in words could remain in his imagination for several years, to take concrete form in a design. Not only the picture, but the very elements of the design, the individual figures, are given visual expression in forms which he consistently used throughout his life with symbolic meanings. Blake's *Job* designs are effectively a guide-book to his symbolic forms. Each of the Despair figures are found in the *Job* series—a natural enough expectation, given that Job's experience is intimately connected with that state. Two of the four forms are found in *Job* 6, the third figure being Satan, whose relation to the Spectre and Despair I have already mentioned.

Job's affliction with disease is in Blake's term, an affliction with sin, 'The Seven diseases of the soul' (*J* 19. 26). *Job* 6 (Plate 54), therefore, is the picture of a man

---

[31] S. Foster Damon, *Blake's Job*, 1966, p. 3.

being sickened with spiritual diseases by his Spectre, resulting in the despair of his emanation. The figures are all so intimately connected—Job's feet touch her knees and Satan stands on Job's body—that they are obviously all aspects of Job's psyche: this is man in his spectre's power with a vengeance. Job's prostrate form here and in plate 11, where he is also menaced by Spectres, is a symbol of Despair also. Comparable images are the prostrate figures in the colour print, *The Lazar House*, and the top design of *Jerusalem* 94. Some qualification is necessary here, however, for the gesture of Job's hands in both cases indicates a kind of protest (it is like the gesture of the huddled despair figure in *Europe* 13) and the other figures in the designs mentioned are contorted. These details help us to see Blake's distinctions—I have discussed elsewhere the prostrate *cruciform* figure which has slightly different connotations of lost divinity[32]—and when, for example, we find a prostrate figure making no gesture at all, on a bier, menaced by a bat-winged spectre, as in *Jerusalem* 37 [33], we can assume a nadir has been reached. I believe there are subtle differences between Blake's use of a corpse form like *Jerusalem* 37, a prostrate cruciform figure, like Adam in *Elohim Creating Adam*, and a prostrate 'moving' or gesturing figure like Job. In the latter, the connotations of illness and suffering are uppermost, while with the corpse the associations of spiritual death are dominant; with the cruciform figure, the capacity for regeneration is emphasized. With Blake's designs, the observer of minute particulars is always rewarded.

Finally, as many scholars have noticed, a consistent gesture used by Blake with Despair figures is head-clutching. The early design which accompanies Plate 6 of *There Is No Natural Religion*, whose words define Despair as frustrated desire, shows a seated figure clutching his head. This gesture is used often in *Urizen*, and frequently with falling figures. Blake described such falling figures as 'attitudes of Despair and Horror' (*Description of a Vision of the Last Judgment* (K, p. 443)). Of the same figures he has also written that they are, 'attitudes of contention representing various States of Misery, which alas, every one on Earth is liable to enter into, & against which we should all watch' (*VLJ*, K, p. 608).[33]

The frequency with which the serpent is drawn wound about or associated with these falling figures emphasizes the relation of the idea of the Fall into mortality or Generation, and Despair. The serpent is a spectre form analogous to Satan, and Blake's words, 'Man is born a Spectre or Satan' (*J* 52, K, p. 682) is another way of saying we are all in our spectre's power in the fallen world. The form of Albion in *Jerusalem* 41 tells us the same thing, as I have tried to indicate, and one other detail also gives us the same message: the words on the scroll saying 'Each Man Is In His Spectre's Power . . .' are in reversed script, or mirror

---

[32] Warner in Erdman, ed., *Blake's Visionary Forms Dramatic*, pp. 174–95.
[33] The source for these figures may be Michelangelo's *Last Judgment*. See Hagstrum, op. cit., p. 40.

writing. The reflecting agent thus becomes the reader: we are all mirror-images of Albion.

But, of course, to concentrate on figures of Despair is not really being fair to Blake, for his whole message concerns the awakening of Albion, the way the Spectre must be made to work for man in the fallen world, and embraced as a brother. Even the 'diseases' of the Seven Deadly Sins are curable by fortitude and forgiveness, and would presumably return to their eternal state of spiritual energy.[34] This awakening is described in Blake's letter to Thomas Butts (22 Nov. 1802) in terms of emerging into light from darkness. (Significantly, in Blake's poetry, the adjective which most often collocates with the word 'Despair' is the word 'dark'.)

And now let me finish with assuring you that, Tho' I have been very unhappy, I am so no longer. I am again Emerged into the light of day; I still & shall to Eternity Embrace Christianity and Adore him who is the Express image of God; but I have travel'd thro' Perils & Darkness not unlike a Champion. I have Conquer'd, and shall still Go on Conquering. Nothing can withstand the fury of my Course among the Stars of God & in the Abysses of the Accuser. My Enthusiasm is still what it was, only Enlarged and confirm'd.

(K, pp. 815–16.)

At this point we realize that the spiritual form of such a man is no longer huddled in self-enclosure or prostrated by emotions, but standing upright, like the figure of Albion in his dialogue with Christ (*J* 76), ready to embrace all the world.

[34] Damon, *Dictionary*, p. 105.

XI

THE TITLE-PAGE OF
THE BOOK OF URIZEN

Morris Eaves

AROUND the time of the 1793 Prospectus that Blake addressed 'To the Public' as an advertisement for the works that he had spent the previous five years creating in his new medium, he was naturally thinking more than ever not about his art only, but also about the art of his countrymen in his century. He compacted much of that thinking into a single etched plate, the title-page of *The Book of Urizen* (Plate 58), which is Blake's report on the state of the arts—which is the state of the nation—in 1794.

The principal object of the satire is Law. The appropriate text is from *The Marriage of Heaven and Hell*: 'One Law for the Lion & Ox is Oppression' (E, p. 43). One way of looking at the title-page design is as a study of the effect of law on art. The vertical aspect of the design is almost equally divided between the top spaces and the bottom; the script of the title is the focus of the top, the bearded patriarch of the bottom. The spaces are equally divided but unequally filled; the lower part of the design is far denser. The unusual balance of forces is dictated by Newton's Law of Gravity, which earthward drags lion, ox, and man alike. Newton's Law tugs so strongly at the design that nothing but the stone tablets of the Law can stand upright. One who wishes to be most comfortable in such a universe will lie prone on a dead level, like a corpse, a posture suggested by the vertical tablets behind the patriarch, which are not only tablets of the Law, but also tombstones. The horizontal tablets on which the patriarch is writing with one hand and etching with the other are also sepulchral, and they may be seen in several ways: as two separate and more or less square tablets, as a single long tablet extending from left to right, or perhaps as two long tablets extending from the patriarch in the foreground to the upright tablets in the background.

The force of the Law has tugged the trees into earthbound arches, and the arches are deathly, like everything else in the design. We might say that the trees have been brought into line, as they have in more ways than one, for in their arrangement Blake seems to have used the 'laws' of perspective to suggest a corridor of arched, dead trees endlessly receding. It has been said that the effort to

58. *The [First] Book of Urizen*, title-page, copy G. Relief etching with water-colour.
Lessing J. Rosenwald Collection, The Library of Congress

transfer the third dimension to the pages of books helped to exhaust the medieval illuminated book,[1] and the use of Newtonian space may be unusual for Blake,[2] but it is apt in a design whose subject is the effect of Laws of the Universe on art.

Urizen, who has sunk to the bottom of the design like a stone, is depicted as a man unable to stand erect in a universe of his own creating. His flesh weighed down by the heaviness of his thought, inward drawn he squats. If we enlarge the scope of our vision, he becomes the fleshy pistil of a huge stone flower with petals of geometric shape. The roots that start out to the left and right belong as much to the flowering monument of Urizen, book, and tablets as to the arching trees; all are tightly rooted to earth. In fact, both the Urizenic flower and the arching trees are made parts of a single organism by the vertical aspect of the design, which is a stack of convex curves. The lowermost curve is the implied dome formed by the roots. The other curves are implied by the outline of Urizen's beard and head, the outline of his body and the right and left edges of the book on which he squats, the standing stones, and finally the succession of tree arches. Thus the vertical aspect of the design is marked by its unity under the Law.

The horizontal aspect, on the other hand, is strictly divided into left and right halves by the implied line down the centre of the page. But then, this aspect has the symmetry of an ink-blot, or, more to the point, of a printed book, as the open book at the bottom of the page suggests. Thus the strict division is a division of sameness. Blake emphasized this aspect of the design when, upon its inclusion in a 'Small Book of Designs' apart from the rest of *The Book of Urizen*, he gave it a caption: 'Which is the Way / The Right or the Left' (E, p. 662). Diversified monotony, a confusion that Blake thought necessary to Newtonian science, is the Urizenic reflection in the mirror of the natural world of various unity, which is one of Blake's own artistic principles. One Law—the wisdom of experimental science—reduces all phenomena to some common unit that makes them 'inter-measurable'. The result is uniformity in fragments—atoms, for instance. In 1827, the year he died, Blake stated his opinion to George Cumberland:

I know too well that a great majority of Englishmen are fond of The Indefinite which they Measure by Newton's Doctrine of the Fluxions of an Atom, A Thing that does not Exist. These are Politicians & think that Republican Art is Inimical to their Atom. For a Line or Lineament is not formed by Chance: a Line is a Line in its Minutest Subdivisions:

[1] See David Diringer, *The Illuminated Book: Its History and Production*, Faber, London, 1958, p. 25; also David Bland, *The Illustration of Books*, Pantheon Books, New York, 1952, p. 242.
[2] See Nikolaus Pevsner, 'Blake and the Flaming Line', ch. 5 of *The Englishness of English Art*, Praeger, New York, 1956, pp. 117–46; ch. 4 of Robert Rosenblum, 'The International Style of 1800: A Study in Linear Abstraction', Diss. New York University, Institute of Fine Arts, 1956; and Rosenblum's *Transformations in Late Eighteenth Century Art*, Princeton University Press, Princeton, N.J., 1967, pp. 154–9, 189–91. W. J. T. Mitchell, in 'Poetic and Pictorial Imagination in Blake's *The Book of Urizen*', *Eighteenth-Century Studies*, iii (Fall 1969), p. 104, speaks of Blake's 'systematic refusal to employ the techniques of three-dimensional illusionism which had been perfected in Western art since the Renaissance'.

Strait or Crooked It is Itself & Not Intermeasurable with or by any Thing Else. Such is Job, but since the French Revolution Englishmen are all Intermeasurable One by Another, Certainly a happy state of Agreement to which I for One do not Agree. God keep me from the Divinity of Yes & No too, The Yea Nay Creeping Jesus, from supposing Up & Down to be the same Thing as all Experimentalists must suppose.[3]

Those preliminary remarks help us to understand the squatting patriarch, whose activities are the central enigma of the design. He is sitting on a book with his legs pulled under him and crossed, his right foot showing through his long beard. His arms are extended sideways along horizontal stone tablets, and each hand grips some kind of writing instrument. From these few facts we move into another order of doubt to ask what Urizen is doing. He may be writing with one hand and engraving with the other.[4] But since there is no sign of handwritten or engraved script on either tablet, and no sign of life or motion in either arm (both arms rest on the tablets), Urizen may have sat down only intending to write. Pascal may be applied to my purpose here: 'Reason acts slowly and with so many views upon so many principles which always must be present, that at any time it may fall asleep or get lost, for want of having all its principles present.'[5] Urizen's eyes are closed. His book may have put him to sleep, or into a hypnotic trance. He may be blind, or he may be dead. At any rate inaction, not action, blind or otherwise, is the over-all effect of the design, from its rigid symmetry without contraries, to its dead vegetation, Urizen's closed eyes, and the lifeless pull of gravitational forces that order the design as a magnet orders iron shavings.

Urizen is depicted as a composite of reader, writer, and etcher. The only person who reads and writes at the same time is a scribe. A scribe is a professional copyist. As a satire on Law in eighteenth-century writing and engraving, then, the design is directed first against imitation. Urizen copies his Law from a book, that is, from authority, from the ancients, no doubt, since they have the most authority, and most obviously from the Hebrew ancients, since the Tables of the Law are the most oppressive symbols of ancient authority, though also possibly from the Greek and Roman ancients, since their authority in artistic matters superseded that of the Bible in the Enlightenment minds of Pope and Joshua Reynolds.[6] He might just as easily be shown copying nature, since, as Pope declared, nature and the ancients are the same. Before Urizen dropped off to

---

[3] *The Letters of William Blake*, ed. Geoffrey Keynes, 2nd ed., Harvard University Press, Cambridge, Mass., 1968, p. 162. All subsequent references to this edition appear in the text, with the abbreviated title 'Letters' followed by the page number.

[4] This is Mitchell's suggestion, op. cit., p. 84. He also suggests that Urizen is holding a 'burin'; but the instrument in the squatting patriarch's left hand bears no resemblance at all to a burin. It is probably an etching needle, though it might also be a 'pencil', i.e. the kind of paintbrush used for fine work.

[5] Quoted in Marshall McLuhan, *The Gutenberg Galaxy: The Making of Typographic Man*, 1962; rpt. New American Library, New York, 1969, p. 295.

[6] There may be the suggestion of an aleph near the end of Urizen's beard at the viewer's left.

sleep, he was obeying the first rule of the copyist, which is to pay attention to what has been written rather than what is being written.

But Urizen as a copyist does not even possess the virtue of being what we would call a transparent medium. Instead, from one book he makes two stone tablets, one written and one engraved. Acts of division, translation, and rigidification are characteristic of the reasoning intellect. The disposition of Urizen's limbs emphasizes the division of one into two: he needs one foot to keep his place in the book, but two hands to write down what he finds. His foot, which acts as book-mark for his mind, also reveals the pedestrian nature of his intellect, whose operations are limited to the linear and the step-by-step only. These, however, are the operations of literacy itself, the mental movements necessary to get a reader through a book. The act of reading a printed page embodies all that Blake despises in schooling. The pupil, whose drudgery is the subject of 'The School-Boy' in *Songs of Experience*, is imprisoned in the modes of conventional literacy. When a child beginning to read moves his eyes with his place-marker across the line and down the page of print, he scans the lineaments of Urizen word by word and line by printed line. The lineaments of Urizen are the modes of conventional literacy, and the lineaments are complete when the education is complete, by which time the student has become what he beheld.[7]

It is here worth noting of the title-page design that if Urizen's book contains true Vision he will miss it, not because his eyes are closed, but because he will be sitting on it. His posture is the product of his intellect. It tells him to accept the pages passively one word and one line at a time, left to right, top to bottom, first page to second to third, a method well suited to copying, less well to illumination.

A discussion of the squatting patriarch must eventually include a discussion of the apparatus of death that surrounds him. Urizen and his environment are of a piece, and for two reasons: a man becomes what he beholds, and 'As a man is, So he Sees' ('Letters', p. 30).[8] These principles operate jointly to fuse subject and object in a cycle of perception that gives the power of creation to the taker. Thus either man makes his environment or it makes him. Urizen has clearly not taken control of his environment; he has been put to sleep, entranced, or blinded by it. Nature has made him over in her image, which is the image of Natural Law. The first of Nature's laws is the inevitability and finality of death, of which the title-page design is an elaborate study.

As it pertains to the health of eighteenth-century art, the apparatus of death in the design shows both a hopeful and a less hopeful side. The sides are condemnation and remedy, a familiar pair in satire, which Blake displays in a

[7] 'Terrified at the Shapes / Enslavd humanity put on he became what he beheld' (*The Four Zoas* 53. 23–4, E, p. 329). This is Blake's first use of an idea that he used many times.

[8] Cf. 'A fool sees not the same tree that a wise man sees' (*MHH* 7, E, p. 35) and 'As the Eye—Such the Object' (Annotations to *The Works of Sir Joshua Reynolds*, E, p. 634).

corresponding pair of paradoxical Christian symbols, the grave and the cross. He has ingeniously incorporated the grave into the cross and made the cross emerge from the configuration of book, stones, and Urizen, who is ignobly crucified, crouching on the ground. His arms are nailed to the arms of the cross by quill and etching needle, though the force of gravity and the sleep of reason would be sufficient to fasten him.

The remedial side of Blake's meaning is beyond the range of this essay, though the remedy seems to grow out of the condemnation. If we take as evidence the amalgamated cross and tomb on the title-page of *Urizen*, the English arts of writing and engraving were crucified, dead, and buried in 1794. The design also shows that the crucified arts crucify; Urizen is his own victim. 'He became what he beheld' should be his epitaph. Whatever he is writing and engraving on the arms of his cross indeed is his epitaph, since his cross is also his tomb.

XII

BLAKE, COLERIDGE, AND WORDSWORTH SOME CROSS-CURRENTS AND PARALLELS 1789–1805

John Beer

THAT Blake's major works should be read in the context of English Romanticism has been increasingly recognized in the twentieth century. Although the date of his birth still causes him to figure in some bibliographies as an eighteenth-century poet, and although *Poetical Sketches* looks back to Akenside, Collins, and Gray, the early prophetic books fall naturally with the early work of Wordsworth and Coleridge. It is instructive, for example, to read Coleridge's *Religious Musings* (1794–6) alongside Blake's *America* (1793), *Europe* (1794), and *The Song of Los* (1795) as attempts to offer a visionary and prophetic account of contemporary events.

The prophesying involved is of a particular sort, of course. None of the poets of the time foresaw the full implications of current events, such as the subsequent alienation of the English working class.[1] They were more urgently concerned to find an immediate and dominating pattern by which international events could be interpreted. In view of the cataclysmic implications for European civilization of the American and French revolutions it is not surprising if the pattern for which they reached out was an apocalyptic one; nor (in view of the place held by orthodox religion) if the apocalypse was imaged in Biblical terms. In 1794 Joseph Priestley published his *The Present State of Europe Compared with Ancient Prophecies*, in which he interpreted the French Revolution as the beginning of the events, prophesied in Revelation, which were to follow the opening in heaven of the fifth seal, and to be followed by the beginning of the Millennium.[2] Coleridge's poem, following the same pattern, announces the downfall of religious Mystery ('She that worked whoredom with the Daemon Power') and prefigures a millennium in which Newton, Hartley, and Priestley will appear in their true glory.[3] Blake,

---

[1] This theme, implicit in E. P. Thompson's *The Making of the English Working-Class*, 1962, has been developed in an essay, 'Disenchantment or Default? A Lay Sermon' in *Power and Consciousness*, ed. C. C. O'Brien and W. D. Vanech, 1969, pp. 149–81.

[2] See H. W. Piper, *The Active Universe*, 1962, pp. 49–50 (from which this account is taken), for a fuller discussion of the relationship between Priestley's work and *Religious Musings*.

[3] Coleridge, *Poetical Works*, ed. E. H. Coleridge, Oxford, i. 108–25, especially lines 276–376.

in the same year, creates a more sardonic apocalypse. In *Europe* Newton, seen here as an angel of reason, has already blown the Last Trump, so that man is now in an apocalyptic world. Without some major renewal, the most likely prospect is a 'strife of blood', where (according to a subsequent poem) the bodies of mankind will be given to the whorish grave in a final riot of lustful destruction.[4]

Contemporary political events are not my main theme here, however. The attempt to read them in apocalyptic terms was necessarily a short-lived venture, for once the Biblical parallels were established little more could be said. The events of the Terror made it hard to contemplate direct revolutionary action with complacency, while the general support for the declaration of war against France in 1793 emphasized the magnitude of the task confronting any who wished to change the course of events in England by peaceful persuasion. In such a situation it seemed more profitable to draw back from public events and turn one's attention to the human nature that was participating in them. The task was the more inviting in view of various ideas, thrown up by recent English and continental writers, which seemed to offer materials for a more optimistic view of human progress.

In this respect London, along with some major provincial centres, was then a stimulating place. Gradually the effects of the war between England and France would be felt in a growing stranglehold upon freedom of expression; but for a time the political ferment abroad had assisted the excitation of a milieu in which speculations of all kinds (many of which had already been current in the previous decade) could gain a sympathetic hearing. Blake, who was living in London throughout the decade, was, I shall argue, one of the first to respond—but also responded more slowly; Coleridge and Wordsworth, as younger men, made a swifter and more immediate response, particularly during their brief sojourns in the capital. The aim here will be less to demonstrate direct influences either way (despite the existence of a number of channels along which such influences could easily have flowed) than to draw attention to certain parallel themes and preoccupations in the work of all three poets, whose varying responses to the common speculative atmosphere often set off one another illuminatingly.

Coleridge and Wordsworth (who had not at this time met) visited London in swift succession during the winter and spring of 1794–5. For Coleridge, in particular, London had a familiar face: he had already spent nine years there, when the life of the streets on 'whole-day-leaves' must have provided a welcome—if limited—relief from the privations and discipline of Christ's Hospital.[5] Already new ideas had been abroad: the Swedenborgians were teaching that everything in

---

[4] *Europe*, Plates 13–15; *The Song of Los* 7. 24–40. See also my *Blake's Humanism*, 1968, pp. 132, 138.

[5] In his essay 'Christ's Hospital Five and Thirty Years Ago', drawn (according to Coleridge, *Letters*, ed. Griggs, v. 127) largely from Coleridge's own recollections, Lamb speaks of noses pressed to print-sellers' windows and of the cold and boredom that would sometimes set in (*Essays of Elia: Works*, ed. Lucas, 1903, ii. 13–14).

nature, rightly understood, corresponded to an inner spiritual reality in man, while the animal magnetists, introducing the phenomena of hypnotism for the first time to an eager public, were enjoying a runaway success.[6] Just as the American Revolution was opening new political horizons, so scientific discoveries, such as that of oxygen, were opening new intellectual ones, suggesting that man's understanding of himself might yet be transformed. In such a setting, dismissal of optimistic thinkers as 'visionaries' could begin to sound hollow. Perhaps, after all, such visionaries were the true and original realists.

There are many signs that Coleridge had been absorbed by such ideas during his schooldays and that he remained haunted for the rest of his life by the liberated imaginative life which they had offered. His return to London in 1794, on the other hand, was undertaken in a more sober frame of mind. His experiences as a dragoon had been chastening; and if he was now committed to the 'visionary scheme' of Pantisocracy, it was a scheme that had been conceived in conjunction with the serious and upright Southey, as providing the only practical means for achieving a just society.

The establishment of Pantisocracy also involved a continuous engagement with the ideas voiced in Godwin's *Political Justice*. It must, indeed, have been hard to escape the influence of the book at this time. Contemporary records describe Godwin's universal fame after its publication in 1793, his book being 'everywhere the theme of popular conversation and praise', while Hazlitt later recalled Godwin 'blazing as a sun in the firmament of reputation'.[7] His implied doctrine that an improved environment must necessarily lead to an improved society, which was welcome to those whose enthusiasm for the Revolution had been disturbed by its violence, was one of the very foundations of the pantisocratic scheme. Although Coleridge seems to have been disenchanted when he actually met Godwin (probably in December 1794) he had by that time written a complimentary sonnet to him and had evidently been for some time under the spell of his ideas.[8]

For those who were simply concerned to establish new standards of honesty, sincerity, and justice in public life, Godwin's book was a welcome ally. Examined more closely, on the other hand, it might carry less overwhelming conviction, since the necessitarianism which was one of its chief doctrines needed to be expounded psychologically if one were to explain how, without free will, the mind could still be expected to move towards perfection. A single sentence of Coleridge's

---

[6] See my *Coleridge the Visionary*, 1959, pp. 56–8, 51, and refs.

[7] See D. Fleisher, *William Godwin, a Study in Liberalism*, 1951, pp. 24–5, and refs.

[8] For a good discussion of Coleridge's relations with Godwin see *The Watchman* (ed. Patton, *Collected Coleridge* ii. 197 n.). Although Coleridge wrote to Godwin that he composed the sonnet before reading his work, he claimed in Oct. 1794 to have read *Political Justice* 'with the greatest attention' just after making a point concerning the psychological implications of ethical action (*Letters* i. 115). Cf. *Letters* (ed. Griggs) i. 138–9, 141; and letter to Thelwall, 13 May 1796: 'I was once and only once in Company with Godwin . . . he talked futile sophisms in jejune language' (ibid., p. 215).

at this time suggests that he had not only pondered Godwin's chapters on this question but had made them the spring-board for a speculation of his own. On 11 December he wrote to Southey,[9] 'I am a compleat Necessitarian—and understand the subject as well almost as Hartley himself—but I go farther than Hartley and believe the corporeality of *thought*—namely, that it is motion—.'

As it stands it is a riddling statement, offered without further explanation, but it testifies to the extent of Godwin's influence at that moment that he should commit himself so completely to necessitarianism. And the latter part of his statement seems to fall into place as soon as one reads the following passage in *Political Justice*:[10]

It is far from certain that the phenomenon of motion can any where exist where there is not thought. Motion may be distributed into four classes, the simpler motions which result from what are called the essential properties of matter and the laws of impulse; the more complex ones which cannot be accounted for by the assumption of these laws, such as gravitation, elasticity, electricity and magnetism; and the motions of the vegetable and animal systems. Each of these seems further than that which preceded it from being able to be accounted for by any thing we understand of the nature of matter.

(Godwin then moves into a discussion of dreams, where, he argues, the life of the mind is not as free as it might seem.)

The paragraph, thrown off rather casually by Godwin in the course of trying to explain the ways in which, whatever we may think to the contrary, our mental processes are subject to necessity, seems to have started a train of speculations in Coleridge's mind. If all motion involves thought, may it not be that all thought, in turn, *is* physical motion? What has evidently given depth to the idea for him, however, is Godwin's discussions both of mental activity and of the different *kinds* of physical motion, for these prompt the speculation that there may also be different kinds of thought, corresponding to the kinds of motion associated respectively with gravitation, electricity, magnetism, vegetable growth and animal energy. The idea that the life of the mind might consist of more than one 'motion' was one that would occupy Coleridge for many years.

There was much more at this time to stimulate speculation concerning the mind and the nature of its powers. H. W. Piper has drawn attention to the speculations of French *philosophes* on the theme of the 'active universe', suggesting the existence of certain inner powers working in matter and corresponding to equivalent powers in human beings.[11] The publication of the first volume of Erasmus Darwin's *Zoönomia*, in 1794, brought more grist to the mill. Early in his volume Darwin dwelt, like Godwin, on the different kinds of motion: gravitational,

[9] *Letters* i. 137.   [10] Godwin, *Political Justice*, 1796, i. 339.
[11] H. W. Piper, *The Active Universe*, 1962, esp. ch. i.

chemical, and those of 'all the motions of the animal and vegetable world'.[12] It is the last two of these that dominate his own discussions in his volume; and his discussion of vegetable and animal motions seems to have suggested another important idea to Coleridge. A passage in *The Friend* refers almost certainly to his first reading of *Zoönomia*:[13]

So long back as the first appearance of Dr Darwin's Phytonomia, the writer, then in earliest manhood, presumed to hazard the opinion, that the physiological botanists were hunting in a false direction; and sought for analogy where they should have looked for antithesis. He saw, or thought he saw, that the harmony between the vegetable and animal world, was not a harmony of resemblance, but of contrast; and their relation to each other that of corresponding opposites. They seemed to him (whose mind had been formed by observation, unaided, but at the same time unenthralled, by partial experiment) as two streams from the same fountain indeed, but flowing the one due west, and the other direct east; and that consequently, the resemblance would be as the proximity, greatest in the first and rudimental products of vegetable and animal organisation. Whereas, according to the received notion, the highest and most perfect vegetable, and the lowest and rudest animal forms, ought to have seemed the links of the two systems, which is contrary to fact. Since that time, the same idea has dawned in the minds of philosophers capable of demonstrating its objective truth by induction of facts in an unbroken series of correspondences in nature. From these men, or from minds enkindled by their labours, we hope hereafter to receive it, or rather the yet higher idea to which it refers us, matured into *laws* of organic nature; and thence to have one other splendid proof, that with the knowledge of LAW alone dwell Power and Prophecy, decisive Experiment, and, lastly, a scientific method, that dissipating with its earliest rays the gnomes of hypothesis and the mists of theory may, within a single generation, open out on the philosophic Seer discoveries that had baffled the gigantic, but blind and guide-less industry of ages.

The idea that vegetable and animal worlds should be seen not as two successive steps in a hierarchy but as contrasting opposites springing from a single fountain, was another which was to work in Coleridge's mind for years afterwards, play-ing an important part in, for example, *The Theory of Life*. Its presence may be traced in the contrast between rooted vegetable forms and animal energies in some of the poems—the old oak stump of the hermit as compared with the play of the water-snakes in *The Ancient Mariner*, or the serpent under the old tree of Bracy's dream in *Christabel*, or the ancient forests (enfolding sunny spots of greenery) and sinuous rills in *Kubla Khan*. Among his later papers there is a long note concerning the contrast between plant life and insect life which shows how the

---

[12] E. Darwin, *Zoönomia*, 1794–6, i. 5–6.

[13] *The Friend*, ed. B. Rooke, *Collected Coleridge* iv (i). 469–70. Although Coleridge runs together the names of *Zoönomia* (1794–6) and *Phytologia* (1800), I agree with the editor that he is more likely to mean the former. He would hardly have referred to 1800 as 'earliest manhood'.

idea could ramify in his mind as a way of interpreting the dialectic between yearn-ing and desire in human beings;[14] in more general terms this habitual way of thinking leads to a particular resonance whenever Coleridge speaks of the vegetable creation, which by its undestructive use of energy is always for him less ambiguously beautiful than the animal.

A very similar contrast seems to have been at work in Blake's mind during these years. From the time when he composed 'Tiriel', with its symbolism of the aged tyrant wandering far from the etiolated innocence of Har and Heva, the traditional tree and serpent of paradise being transformed, by human failure, into the futile garden of Har and the final deathly serpent form of Tiriel, he seems to have been haunted by the contrast between the 'innocence' of human vegetative life and the 'experience' induced by its encounters with energy.[15]

The same play of opposites, which may be traced through the illustrations to the Prophetic Books, is particularly bold in the productions of 1793–4, where the triple counterpointing of flamy, serpentine, and vegetable forms already to be found in *Songs of Innocence* is more vividly developed.[16] It is as if Blake had moved during these years from a rather despairing contemplation of the contrast between vegetating innocence and tyrannical energy to a vision of possible conjunction between the two states; this he sets forth in vivid designs where serpentine forms, flames, and foliage are sometimes seen in contrast, sometimes run together by his organic wit. (In the last plate of *America*, for example, close examination of the design at the foot (see Plate 63) shows, corresponding symmetrically to the snake emerging to the right, a flower's head emerging to the left, of which the lower features match the snake's head, tongue, and lower jaw.)

While the distinction is present in Blake's imagery from *Tiriel* onwards, it is not articulated explicitly until later in the decade. Only in *Vala or The Four Zoas* and later works do we find the use of terms such as 'vegetated' and 'vegetating'. In these later contexts the usages suggest a continuing criticism of those human beings who are content to live and perceive without calling on their own inward energies. The praise of energy which runs through *The Marriage of Heaven and Hell* is not now so openly voiced, perhaps, but its exercise is still seen as a key to the life of the imagination, underlying the assertion, for example, in *Jerusalem*: 'I know of no other Christianity and of no other Gospel than the liberty both of body & mind to exercise the Divine Arts of Imagination, Imagination, the real & eternal World of which this Vegetable Universe is but a faint shadow.' It is equally implicit in his famous declaration that true vision must involve something more than making the eye a mirror to the spatial forms of nature: 'I question not my

---

[14] *Inquiring Spirit*, ed. K. Coburn, 1951, pp. 223–5.

[15] See my *Blake's Visionary Universe*, 1969, pp. 60–7 (and cf. 336–42) for an extended interpretation.

[16] Both *Innocence* and *Thel* are dated 1789. Plate 6 of the latter, which has a serpent of 'organized energy' at its foot is tentatively dated 1791. (See *The Book of Thel*, ed. N. Bogen, Providence, R.I., 1971, p. 3 and n.).

Corporeal or Vegetative Eye any more than I would Question a Window concerning a Sight. I look thro' it & not with it.'[17]

An important point of distinction between Coleridge and Blake emerges. Both Blake and Coleridge were evidently impressed by the relationships between the powers of vegetation and those of animal energy, as forming a central dialectic, operative in all forms of life, but laid their stresses differently. For Coleridge, it would seem, the idea of the innocent vegetable, its perfumes awakened by the playing breeze (as in the beanfield of 'The Eolian Harp') remained the ideal form to which all others should aspire; for him the ideal of the human spirit was to grow up in its true organic form, opening itself to the sun and breeze of divine impulse. Flowers and blossoms play an important part in the imagery of his poetry, therefore, and the intervention of demonic energy (as in *Christabel*) is seen as presenting a crucial and even threatening challenge to the growing human being.

For Blake, by contrast, simple 'vegetating' is always a dangerous process. It is through the exercise of all his faculties that man thrives; and human failure consists in a refusal to cultivate such energies. From the time when Har and Heva grow old and foolish in their enclosed garden to the time when the ageing Job finds his world of innocence threatened by the incursions of energy and is forced to learn the universe anew, Blake inveighs persistently against all philosophies and world-views which contrive to survey the world of life simply as a world of vegetable forms, taking little or no account of its inherent energies. His own approach is persistently one of self-energizing. Where Coleridge's artist waits patiently for the revival within himself of the 'symphony and song' that will attend the creative process, Blake would argue that it is in the individual's task to make his own symphony and song—and so induce the creative process more directly. Thus he can affirm in his annotations to Lavater (*c.* 1788) that whereas 'the omission of act in self & the hindering of act in another' is vice, 'all Act is Virtue'; and in his prologue to *Jerusalem*, many years later, still invite the reader to 'love me for this energetic exertion of my talent'.[18]

To this stress on energy we need only add Blake's belief in a relationship between vegetative form and imaginative form ('The Oak dies as well as the Lettuce, but its Eternal Image & Individuality never dies, but renews by its seed')[19] to see how closely the vegetable/animal contrast underpins the imagination/energy dialectic in this thought.

As I have pointed out, Coleridge's elaboration of the distinction between vegetable and animal processes would seem, by his own account, to owe a good deal to his reading of Darwin. Blake also may have read the book, which was

[17] *J* 77; *VLJ*, K, p. 617.   [18] K, pp. 88, 621.
[19] K, p. 605.

published by his friend Joseph Johnson, but there is no direct evidence that he did so, and the underlying distinction involved would seem to have been working in his mind for some years before. Morton Paley has shown in detail how the concepts of imagination and energy were both at work in European thought in the eighteenth century, and John Armstrong has discussed the long tradition which looks to the *contrast* between the tree and serpent of paradise for an alternative and allegorical version of the Fall, based on failures of self-realization rather than upon a single, original act of disobedience.[20] The idea of human growth as a dialectical process is, of course, one that may also be traced in Blake's acknowledged masters, Paracelsus and Boehme.[21] It remains a curious phenomenon, nevertheless, that in the years 1793-5, while Blake was etching *America, Europe,* and *Songs of Experience,* with their new and positive visual images of organized energy, Coleridge was drawn to the idea of energized organism which he celebrates in 'The Eolian Harp'. It is as if during those years a variety of sources offered up the idea of a dialectic between vegetable form and animal energy which hovered in the air long enough for both Blake and Coleridge to seize and appropriate it to their respective concerns.

How were such ideas propagated? It is possible, of course, that there existed in London some organized group of people (a Theosophical Society, for example) in which a number of these issues were discussed, and which served to stimulate the speculations of individuals, but if so, no record of their proceedings has come to light. It is safer to assume that the spread of such notions was informal, based on chance groupings and accidental discussions. That a speculative atmosphere of the kind existed is suggested further by a small book published in January 1795, with the bold title, *A Dissertation on the Universe.* The author, Richard Saumarez, was a surgeon of some distinction, who later assisted Coleridge's appointment as a lecturer, and to two of whose books Coleridge in turn paid a handsome public tribute.[22] The main purpose of his little book was to prove the immateriality of the soul, drawing on both scientific and traditional sources. The case as presented was based on an assertion of the immateriality of memory, which he argued ingeniously from the common scientific assertion that the matter of the body changed completely every seven years. If this was so, he maintained, it followed that the memory of events which took place more than seven years ago could not have been held in any material form: if it had been it would have disappeared with the dissolution of that matter. And if an immaterial memory, why not an immaterial soul? In urging the latter he adduced Thomas Taylor's translations of Plato, with their evidence of the belief in ancient times, as providing strong

[20] M. D. Paley, *Energy and the Imagination,* Oxford, 1970, esp. chs. i and viii; J. Armstrong, *The Paradise Myth,* 1969.
[21] See *MHH,* Plates 21-2.
[22] *Biographia Literaria,* ed. J. Shawcross, Oxford, 1907, i. 103 n.

additional authority.[23] Such running together of ancient tradition with observations taken from contemporary science—a method later taken up by Shelley—would seem to be one distinctive feature of speculation during these years.

That Coleridge meditated on the relationship between vegetable forms and animal energies (a relationship which is also implicit in certain writings of the Neoplatonists) some time between the publication of Darwin's first volume and the following summer, when he wrote 'The Eolian Harp', would seem clear. The most natural time for his speculations, moreover, would have been during the winter in London, when they might well have formed a part of the 'metaphysics and poetry' which he discussed with Lamb over Welsh-rabbits, egg-hot, and Oronooko in the small room at the Salutation and Cat.[24] From this congenial atmosphere he was drawn away in mid January by Southey, who urged a return to Bristol and Sara Fricker.

When Wordsworth arrived in London a month later he no doubt picked up some echoes of Coleridge's visit, since he was mixing in much the same circles. On 27 February he drank tea at Frend's amid a company which included Godwin, Holcroft, and Dyer—to the last of whom Coleridge was writing at this time—and during the spring and summer he saw a good deal of Godwin.[25] His current concerns were different from Coleridge's, however. Having been involved in the French Revolution to the point of intimacy with the Girondist leaders, yet also having been repelled by the concomitant violence, he was still in search of a role for himself. The Church, which might once have offered a niche, was no longer a possible source of income which his conscience would allow him to consider; yet he was still faced with the task of making an honest living in a society where professional life involved not merely conformity to certain attitudes but to various forms and elegances of speech which must have sounded hollow in the ears of one who had been present where the foundations of Western society were shaking.

In these circumstances it was not surprising that he too should have been attracted for a time to Godwin—who figured (thinly disguised) in a contemporary novel where he appeared first as the antagonist of a 'man of fashion'.[26] To many young men Godwin was the epitome of the man of integrity, penetrating and demonstrating the shams and injustices that permeated English society. And indeed Wordsworth would seem to have been temporarily swept up in the current enthusiasm—at least if we may believe Hazlitt's story that he once told a young

[23] R. Saumarez, *A Dissertation on the Universe*, 1795, pp. 11–16. According to the author, his book was published in January of that year.

[24] See Lamb, *Letters*, ed. E. V. Lucas, i. 17, 29–30, 33.

[25] M. L. Reed, *Wordsworth: A Chronology of the Early Years 1770–99*, Cambridge, Mass., 1967, pp. 164 ff.; Coleridge, *Letters*, ed. Griggs, i. 151–3.

[26] Mary Hays, *Emma Courtney*, 1796, pp. 36–7, 61 (cf. Frieda Knight, *University Rebel*, 1971, p. 203).

student at the Temple to throw away his books of chemistry and read Godwin on necessity.[27]

Yet he, like Coleridge, became disenchanted. By 1796 he was writing disparagingly about the second edition of *Political Justice*,[28] 'I expect to find the work much improved. I cannot say that I have been encouraged in this hope by the perusal of the second preface, which is all I have yet looked into. Such a barbarous piece of writing I have not often seen.' The fact that he did not renew the acquaintance in later years seems to speak for itself. Yet what was it that he felt needed improvement in the work? E. P. Thompson has recently suggested that it was not so much Godwin as the Godwinians that he distrusted, and more particularly, perhaps, Basil Montagu, with whom he shared chambers at this time.[29] It may even be that Hazlitt's anecdote in his essay, concerning the young man who agreed to go into chambers with another on a basis of equality, only to discover that he was expected to fetch water from the pump and clean the other's shoes, refers to Wordsworth and Montagu. It must also be observed that Wordsworth in 1795, no longer a young man fresh from university but one who had seen certain aspects of human nature brutally exposed in France, might well find Godwin a man over-confident in his rationalism.

An implicit critique of Godwinianism is to be traced in *The Prelude*. H. W. Garrod pointed out many years ago that the last two lines of the adverse description of the dominating state of mind among young men at this time who wished to

> Build social freedom on its only basis,
> The freedom of the individual mind,
> Which, to the blind restraint of general laws
> Superior, magisterially adopts
> One guide, the light of circumstances, flash'd
> Upon an independent intellect

had also been used to describe the opportunism of the villain in *The Borderers*.[30]

Although, as Godwin's supporters have pointed out, this is not a version of Godwinianism that he himself would have accepted, it is a development of one of his own principles: 'The true dignity of human reason is, as much as we are able to go beyond them (i.e. general rules), to have our faculties in act upon every occasion that occurs, and to conduct ourselves accordingly.'[31] In isolating and developing it in this way, Wordsworth was drawing attention to a contradiction inherent in Godwin's work: that although it favoured 'disinterestedness',

---

[27] Hazlitt, 'William Godwin', in *The Spirit of the Age* (*Works*, ed. Howe, xi. 17; cited Reed, op. cit., p. 163).
[28] Wordsworth, *Letters 1787–1805*, 2nd ed., 1967, p. 170.   [29] In an unpublished lecture.
[30] *Prelude*, 1805, x. 824–9; cf. *The Borderers*, lines 1493–6, *Poetical Works*, ed. de Selincourt, Oxford, i. 187. H. W. Garrod, *Wordsworth*, 1923, pp. 89–90.
[31] Godwin, *Political Justice*, 2nd ed., 1796, i. 347 (quoted E. Legouis, *The Early Life of William Wordsworth*, 1897, p. 263). Godwin, it must be noted, guards himself immediately against such an interpretation.

the attitude of mind which it encouraged might as logically lead to a dangerous egotism.

Much has been written on the question of Wordsworth's relationship to Godwin, ranging from the claims for a direct and important influence to the assertion that all Wordsworth's apparent Godwinianisms could have been picked up from other sources.[32] Wordsworth must certainly have read *Political Justice* shortly after its appearance in 1793; we know that he took part in discussions in Godwin's circle during 1795; and he received the much revised second edition of 1796. He was thus thinking about Godwin's doctrines over several years, sometimes in consultation with Godwin himself. Any features of Godwinianism which appeared in his poetry, therefore, had been thoroughly examined and absorbed. But how much was he directly influenced? The question is perhaps clarified a little if we think in terms not of influence but of interaction. Although scholars have asked whether Godwin influenced Wordsworth, there has been little or no mention of Wordsworth's possible influence on Godwin; yet it is quite likely that criticisms by Wordsworth and his friends prompted the alterations which Godwin made in his second edition—particularly his attempts to give more of a rationale to the 'disinterestedness' which he had called for in his first. Now he would try to relate it to human faculties in general.

It is even possible that we have some oblique reference to Wordsworth in the course of Godwin's long discussion of benevolence and its nature. In one of the most interesting sections Godwin describes the types of man whom he sees about him in his civilization; first the unthinking peasant, then the unthinking man of pleasure, then the more welcome picture of the 'man of taste':[33]

. . . like the mere man of fortune in comparison with the peasant, he acquires new senses, and a new range of enjoyment. The beauties of nature are all his own. He admires the overhanging cliff, the wide-extended prospect, the vast expanse of the ocean, the foliage of the woods, the sloping lawn and the waving grass. He knows the pleasures of solitude, when man holds commerce alone with the tranquil solemnity of nature. He has traced the structure of the universe, the substances which compose the globe we inhabit and are the materials of human industry and the laws which hold the planets in their course amidst the trackless fields of space. He studies and has experienced the pleasures which result from conscious perspicacity and discovered truth. He enters with a true relish into the sublime and pathetic. He partakes in all the grandeur and enthusiasm of poetry. He is perhaps himself a poet.

Whether or not this is an attempt on Godwin's part to place the type of attitude

---

[32] For a good account of the earlier discussions see F. L. Priestley's introduction to his edition of *Political Justice*, Toronto, 1946, iii. 102–3. His position now needs to be modified in the light of Godwin's diaries, which make it clear that he and Wordsworth were in constant communication in 1795 (see M. L. Reed, *Wordsworth Chronology*, pp. 163–6; L. F. Chard, II, *Dissenting Republican*, The Hague, 1972, ch. vi).
[33] Godwin, op. cit., i. 446.

which he encountered in young men like Wordsworth, it is certainly an accurate delineation of the stereotype which Wordsworth was measuring himself against and gradually breaking. For Godwin that attitude represented a welcome but inadequate step towards his own ideal, voiced immediately afterwards:

> Study is cold, if it be not enlivened with the idea of the happiness to arise to mankind from the cultivation and improvement of sciences. The sublime and pathetic are barren, unless it be the sublime of virtue and the pathos of true sympathy. The pleasures of the mere man of taste and refinement 'play round the head, but come not to the heart'.

Godwin later claimed that it was he who had persuaded Wordsworth to abandon a self-regarding philosophy in favour of one based on altruism; Wordsworth himself looked back at late 1795 as the time when he shook off his habit of letting his eye dominate his heart—and made no mention of Godwin. It may be that the discussions between the two men resulted in a recognition by both of an important shortcoming in the first edition of *Political Justice*: that while it urged an immediate sincerity of response to events, it afforded no guarantee that sincere responses would necessarily be benevolent. Some further insight into human nature was needed—which Godwin tried to give in his second edition in his long discussion of benevolence.

If this is so, it could be that the course of events was rather more complicated than at first appears: the following theory may be proposed, which at least has the virtue that it accounts both for Wordsworth's initial enthusiasm and for all the various subsequent claims and statements we have examined. We might suppose that Wordsworth, having found himself totally persuaded at first by Godwin's arguments concerning necessity, came to see, particularly during his long walk across Salisbury Plain in 1793, when he was led to compare 'what we know or guess of . . . remote times with certain aspects of modern society, and with calamities, principally those consequent upon war, to which, more than other classes of men, the poor are subject',[34] that the same principle of necessity could be used to support a very pessimistic view of history, whereby the small existing proportion of disinterestedness among individuals was likely to remain constant, while the lives of most of the population would continue to be dominated by large impersonal forces. With these reflections he arrived at Tintern Abbey for the first time and found in the beauty of its landscape a source of immense delight for himself—yet also discovered that this could not be communicated directly to other men, such as the 'rover' whom he met in that country, and who later became the model for Peter Bell.

Still in the frame of mind induced by these experiences, we might further suppose, Wordsworth met Godwin in London and voiced his doubts about the

---

[34] Preface to 'Guilt and Sorrow': *Poetical Works*, ed. de Selincourt, 1940, i. 94–5.

implications of necessitarian doctrine. Godwin, in reply, asserted his belief in the power of the human heart to be moved towards courses of benevolence. Wordsworth accepted the argument, but not as it stood; instead, he felt that it was necessary to look more closely at the forces which influenced the workings of the human heart—and so found it a logical next step to retire to Racedown with Dorothy and embark on a period of seclusion in which he could meditate further. Godwin, meanwhile, seeing the force of some of the arguments against his system, found it necessary to include (in a wide-ranging revision) a rewriting and expansion of his chapters on self-love and benevolence. So such a reconstruction might conclude.

Blake, meanwhile, was playing little or no part in such Godwinian debates. According to Gilchrist he knew Godwin but 'got on ill with him and liked him worse'.[35] And his lack of interest in the issues that were being discussed may perhaps be due to the fact that (as with the vegetation/animal distinction) he had already anticipated the trend—and indeed Wordsworth's response—before Godwin. Many years before, we are told, he had become *persona non grata* in Mrs. Mathew's circle for his 'unbending deportment',[36] after which he seems to have moved out of fashionable literary circles in favour of the pursuit of a rugged honesty and individualism. By 1793, when he published the prefatory stanzas to *The Marriage of Heaven and Hell*, he was asserting that whereas the honest man could once have made his home in the wilderness, the hypocrites were beginning to take over there as well.[37]

Instead of moving with current fashions, then, Blake seems simply to have made the acquaintance of a few individuals—particularly of some who were associated with Joseph Johnson the publisher. Johnson's list included some of the most adventurous authors of the day, including[38] Price, Priestley, Holcroft, Tom Paine, Fuseli, Godwin himself, and Mary Wollstonecraft (whose ideas may have played a part in *Visions of the Daughters of Albion* and other similar writings).

Of this circle, Blake was most drawn to Fuseli, a man who, like himself, had pursued his independent way through the artistic scene of the late eighteenth century without succumbing to the pressures of fashion and who had vehement opinions on many topics, including that of 'genius'. Like Blake, he never settled down to a firm and unalterable style but experimented continually.

Fuseli's influence on the younger painter is discernible in choice of subjects—his fondness for depicting particular scenes from great artists such as Shakespeare, Milton, and Dante being directly echoed by Blake—and in certain common ideas. Blake knew, and annotated Fuseli's translations of Lavater's *Aphorisms* (1788), the preface to which promised shortly a similar book, by the translator

[35] Bentley, *Records*, pp. 40–1 (cf. D. V. Erdman, '"Blake" Entries in Godwin's Diary', *N & Q* cxcviii (1953), 354–6).   [36] Bentley, *Records*, p. 457, from J. T. Smith, *Nollekens and his Times*, 1828.
[37] 'The Argument': K, pp. 148–9.
[38] Bentley, *Records*, pp. 40–1, citing Gilchrist.

himself. In the event publication did not take place, since the proofs were damaged in a fire and Fuseli did not have the patience to undertake a revision, but the work appeared after his death and could easily have been seen by Blake, either in manuscript or in the ill-fated proofs, at the earlier date. Writing of the different ways in which various artists handle their subjects, Fuseli writes:[39] 'The fiery sets his subject in a blaze, and mounts its vapours; the melancholy cleaves the rock, or gropes through thorns for his; the sanguine deluges all, and seizes none; the phlegmatic sucks one, and drops off with repletion.' Three of the four figures here bear a curious resemblance to three in the group of four plates in Blake's *The Gates of Paradise* showing man in relation to the elements (man, that is, before he 'breaks the shell', only to release himself into the equally unsatisfactory world of pure energy and desire).[40] Blake's figure of 'Fire' is seen, like Fuseli's, mounting on the vapours of a blaze; his 'Earth' tries to cleave the rock as he struggles upwards; his 'Water' sits surrounded by the excess of an ocean. The fact that Fuseli is dealing with the humours, while Blake is dealing with the elements, marks one essential difference, of course; and there is no readily discernible parallel between Fuseli's phlegmatic man and Blake's 'Air' figure; but the threefold parallel suggests that the imagery and scheme of Fuseli's aphorism may have influenced Blake's visual imagination when he came to portray man's condition under the natural law. One of the dominant themes of the collection, moreover, the praise of genius and the lashing of mediocrity, foreshadows the vehement assertions of *The Marriage of Heaven and Hell*.

Little direct evidence concerning the relationship between Fuseli and Blake during these years has survived, unfortunately, but the indirect evidence suggests a continuous and important interplay of ideas between the two men. Fuseli's remark that Blake was 'damned good to steal from' has sometimes been taken as evidence that the borrowings were all on his side, but a dispassionate look at the surviving works suggests that the traffic of images and ideas was a two-way affair.[41] Blake's swift reference, 'And when Flaxman went to Italy, Fuseli was given to me for a season'[42] indicates not only an important date (Flaxman went to Italy in 1787) but also one of the main alternating patterns of his artistic development. Where Flaxman encouraged the more imaginative side of his art, Fuseli was a more energetic influence (who, according to Stodhard, misled Blake into extravagance).[43] By contrast with the quietist Flaxman Fuseli was honest and vehement, delighting particularly in the portrayal of active

[39] J. Knowles, *Life and Works of Henry Fuseli*, 1831, iii. 64.

[40] See my *Blake's Humanism*, 1968, pp. 231–43; and K, pp. 762–4.

[41] A. Gilchrist, *Life of Blake*, 1863, ch. vii. For some convincing instances of Fuseli's originality see E. C. Mason, *The Mind of Henry Fuseli*, 1951, pp. 41–57. Cf. also A. Federmann, *Johann Heinrich Füssli*, Zurich 1927, pp. 60–2.

[42] Letter to Flaxman, 12 Sept. 1800. K, p. 799.

[43] Bentley, *Records*, p. 58, citing Farington's *Diary* for Jan. 1797. Fuseli is not named but is fairly obviously the person meant.

human figures. In his designs sardonic portrayal of the forceful and the grotesque mingles with suggestions of a more gentle sensibility.

Blake's respect for Fuseli ('The only Man that e'er I knew / Who did not make me almost spew')[44] remains constant throughout his career. Even the insistence of Fuseli and Johnson that he should devote more of his time to commercial engraving, which would have left him with less time for his own original designs, did not provoke him to outright hostility. The only hint of reservation is to be found in a letter of November 1802, where he discerns as a possible threat: 'And Butts shall give what Fuseli gave, / A dark black Rock & a gloomy cave.'[45]

The precariousness of Blake's confidence, here expressed dramatically, is an observable phenomenon throughout the intervening years, and corresponds to a pattern of behaviour to be traced in other creative artists of the time. On the one hand, it seems, the general intellectual atmosphere was stimulating an expansiveness of speculation and encouraging the growth of new and more optimistic ways of looking at man and the universe; on the other, the rigid social patterns inherited from the past threatened the security of those who might be so stimulated, causing them to contract again in defensiveness. Those who were exploring new ways of thought might find themselves a prey not only to their own self-questionings but to public attack as Jacobins or infidels. Faced with this undermining of their personal security and with evidences of intractable conservatism in the society around them, where the mob could turn its fury on men as enlightened as Priestley, it was hard to resist the suspicion that their optimistic vision might be no more than a temporary illusion. And in order to keep it alive at all it became natural to look outside the immediate issues of the time and to ask whether there were not, in history or elsewhere, evidences of any human tradition to correspond with these more generous impulses.

For Wordsworth, the search was less difficult. He believed that he had experienced, with the Dalesmen among whom he spent his childhood and early youth, an independence of mind and a generosity of heart superior to anything which he had later discovered in large cities. These qualities might perhaps be directly attributable to a life in independent isolation and close to the direct influences of nature. If so, the main hope for the amelioration of mankind lay in their being willing to return to the same resources. He, at least, would do so and try to promulgate through his poetry the lessons he learned there.

For Blake and Coleridge, on the other hand, bereft of so immediate a resource, it was natural to look further back and inquire whether among the traditions of ancient mythologies and foreign religions there might not lurk the rudiments of some tradition that was now largely submerged—a tradition which, paying more

---

[44] Notebook epigram: K, p. 551.
[45] Letter to Butts, 22 Nov. 1802. K, p. 817.

respect to the innate genius of mankind, saw evil as the result not of some primitive act of disobedience but of the misuse of human faculties.

I have written elsewhere of this side to their activities.[46] In the case of Coleridge, I have argued, it involved him in an inquiry concerning the traditions of sun-temples and serpent-cults, of illuminated geniuses and haunted sons of Cain, which found its most important expression in the poem *Kubla Khan* but also exercised a strong influence on the symbolic structure of *The Ancient Mariner* and *Christabel*, as well as reappearing from time to time in his later imagery. For Blake, on the other hand, the interest would seem to have played its part in a larger enterprise, his attempt to construct a complete mythical epic poem using elements from earlier myths to create a great psychological drama, in which the godlike participants are seen to correspond to the various energies of mankind.

There is no need to go over that ground again here, except to call attention once again to the remarkable and central potency which seems to have been exercised by Egyptian mythology at this time. Several reasons may be suggested. The tradition of Isis, Osiris, and Typhon, with the destructive heat-demon Typhon and yearning light-goddess Isis enacting a fruitless struggle as Isis tries vainly to re-create the Osiris who would reconcile both principles, bears a curious resemblance to one of the central principles of Swedenborgianism, where heat and light are seen as separated elements of the lost, true sun. The favourite Egyptian hiero-glyphic of sun, serpent, and wings could easily be aligned with this myth, which is, moreover, linked to one of the most powerful of traditional images: that of the ambiguous Nile, sometimes flooding its delta with dangerously destructive force before being swallowed up in a deathly sea, but also a necessary power of fertility, tracing its springs far back to Abyssinia, seat of a lost mountain-paradise. These two traditions, which could work together with curious power as emblems of the workings of human genius, had a further contemporary relevance, moreover, since it was only recently that the actual Nile-springs had been discovered by the explorer James Bruce, who published a memorable account of his travels in 1790.

The power of these myths to haunt the imagination is shown not only by Coleridge's use of the heat/light dialectic as a motif of moral argument over the years but by Blake's later use of images such as the moon-ark, or the sun, serpent, and wings in his illuminations for *Jerusalem*.[47] At the same time, each poet used the ideas and images involved in a slightly different way; and in discussing these differences it will be useful to turn to one of Blake's overt treatments of Egyptian myth, for as it happens this is also one of the very few early instances where we can be sure that Coleridge and Wordsworth came across Blake's work. In the first edition of Erasmus Darwin's *Botanic Garden* (1791), there appeared an

---

[46] In *Coleridge the Visionary*, 1959, and *Blake's Visionary Universe*, 1969.
[47] See *Coleridge the Visionary*, pp. 97–8; *Blake's Visionary Universe*, p. 372, and Figs. 23, 35–7.

engraving by Blake (Plate 61), based upon a design by Fuseli, entitled *Fertilization of Egypt*.[48] It is a strange design, and I know no exhaustive discussion of its elements. In Fuseli's original wash drawing (Plate 59) a dog-headed priest lifts up his hands to a giant star above. Clouds float around him, while a strong figure and wings are dimly discernible beyond. In Blake's wash drawing (Plate 60), various details are added, including pyramids; when he comes to engrave from the drawing he adds a sistrum—perhaps to suggest the noise associated with ancient ritual.

Although this strange design has been described more than once,[49] the only detailed discussion of its significance is that by A. S. Roe, whose article, 'The Thunder of Egypt', contains an extensive and valuable survey both of Blake's many references to Egypt and of various related elements.[50] Roe comes to the conclusion that since in Blake's later work Egypt is an analogue of the fallen world, *Fertilization of Egypt* is best interpreted as the first major statement of this theme. On this reading, the dog-headed priest is to be viewed, in the context of Enion's lament, 'I have chosen the serpent for a counsellor, & the dog for a schoolmaster to my children',[51] as a figure who has lost all contact with the Divine Humanity. 'His obeisance is to be construed not as an act of tribute to the life-giving waters of the Nile and to the star which signified the commencement of its annual rise, but as homage to Urizen, the God of the Fallen World.' Roe also argues that Fuseli had little or nothing to do with the significance he is suggesting, and that he may even not have executed the original drawing[52]—though this is hard to believe in view of the specific ascription, 'Fuseli del.', on the finished plate.

Roe's interpretation does not altogether square with the form of the design, in which it will be observed that the gestures of the dog-priest are directed not towards the hovering god in the Nile-cloud, but at the giant star above him. If the priest is forced to acknowledge the power of the storm-god (whom he has no doubt been invoking) his attention is, it would seem, more powerfully caught by the star. I should like to suggest an alternative account of this design, involving, in turn, the assumption that Fuseli had some part to play in the evolution of ideas as well as of imagery. Roe discusses the Egyptian lore to be found in Bryant's *Analysis of Ancient Mythology* (1774–6), but he is basically concerned to read back Blake's later attitudes into the earlier engraving; if we turn our attention in the opposite direction, on the other hand, it may be argued that Blake and Fuseli had

[48] Erasmus Darwin, *The Botanic Garden*, 1791, facing p. 127, illustrating the lines (on the Monsoon), 'High o'er his head the beams of *Sirius* glow / And, Dog of Nile, *Anubis* barks below' (iii. 129–34).

[49] See e.g. Keynes, 'Blake and the Wedgwoods', *Blake Studies*, p. 59; Blunt, pp. 41–2.

[50] In *William Blake: Essays for S. Foster Damon*, ed. A. H. Rosenfeld, Providence, R.I., 1968, pp. 158–95.

[51] *Vala or the Four Zoas*, ii. 389–90, K, p. 290. See also note 56 below on the possible related significance of these two emblems; but note also the version in *VDA*: '. . . wilt thou take the ape / For thy councellor, or the dog for a schoolmaster to thy children?' (K, p. 192), which suggests that serpent and dog were less closely linked in Blake's mind at the earlier date.

[52] Op. cit., p. 444 n. 9.

Sketched by Fuseli for Blake to engrave from

59. Henry Fuseli:
Fertilization of Egypt.
Wash drawing.
British Museum,
Department of
Prints and Drawings

60. *Fertilization of Egypt.*
Wash drawing.
British Museum,
Department of Prints and Drawings

61. *Fertilization of Egypt.*
Engraving after Fuseli for Erasmus Darwin, *The Botanic Garden* (1791).
Cambridge University Library

been for a time discussing the significance of Egyptian mythology and that the evolution of this design, at least, reflects their discussion. In this connection it may be significant that when Fuseli came to defend Blake's designs for *The Grave* some years later, a piece of Egyptian symbolism came readily to his mind. Commenting on the decline of traditional imagery, he wrote, 'The Serpent with its Tail in its Mouth, from a Type of Eternity, is become an Infant's Bauble.'[53]

At the earlier period, Egyptian mythology had been a more current concern. The sense of mystery surrounding the ancient civilization there and in Abyssinia, reflected not only in Bryant, but in Athanasius Kircher, Stukeley, and other writers, had been given a new topicality by the explorations of James Bruce, mentioned above. I have already drawn attention to some of the symbolic motifs involved; the design here is concerned with a different strand. The central figure of the dog-priest looking up at the star (which dominates Fuseli's wash drawing) evokes the curious relationship between Anubis, the dog-headed god of Egyptian myth, and Sirius, the 'dog-star'. Blake's wash drawing and engraving involve further comment on Egyptian civilization. His importation of pyramids (also to be found in the illustrations for *Tiriel* and in many of the later Biblical illustrations) represents a comment on the mindless geometric constructions of the Egyptians at their most tyrannical, while the hovering God in the cloud (based, as Blunt has shown, on motifs such as the Jupiter Pluvius of the Romans)[54] represents a God of law who at once presides over a flood which is sometimes inordinately destructive[55] and hovers to prevent any vision of the hidden paradise or access to the Nile-springs. The confrontation between dog-headed priest and aged cloud-god may be seen as imaging the perpetual confrontation between visionless human energy (especially sexual lust)[56] and the barriers of law which are reared

---

[53] Prospectus to *The Grave*, Nov. 1805 (Bentley, *Records*, p. 170). Was Fuseli, perhaps, recalling earlier discussions with Blake, in the course of which they had discussed the problem of referring to ancient emblems of the sublime which had now lost their force?

[54] Blunt, p. 41 (citing an engraving in Montfaucon's *L'Antiquité expliquée*) and Plate 25c.

[55] Cf. the Nile-imagery in *The Book of Ahania*, where Urizen's 'dire Contemplations / Rush'd down like floods from his mountains, In torrents of mud settling thick, / With Eggs of unnatural production' (K, p. 250). The idea that the sun could cause eggs to spawn from the Nile-mud was a traditional one (cf. *Antony and Cleopatra* II. vii. 26–7).

[56] Although the dog is one of the emblems in Blake's work which (like that of the mill) seems to be conceived both in socially realistic and in psychological terms, there is a persistent suggestion of sexual energy—and more particularly of sexual deprivation—running through the various usages. While the 'dog at the wintry door' which appears in three of his works (K, pp. 186, 235, 290) suggests primarily social deprivation, it is not the most obvious image for that; a beggar would be more apposite. Sexual implication gains in cumulative force as one looks in turn at Oothoon's mention of the village dog barking at the rising sun as she yearns for her lover (K, p. 190); the depiction of 'the serpent and the wolvish dog—two terrors in the Northern Mythology' as a final illustration to 'The Descent of Odin' in Gray's *Poems* (if the serpent here represents the residual energy of wisdom, the dog the residual energy of sexual love, this in turn throws light on the significance of Enion's taking the serpent as counsellor and the dog as a schoolmaster to her children (*Vala* ii. 390 (K, p. 290)); and the illustration 'The Dog' to Hayley's *Ballads* (where the geometric stylization of the crocodile-jaws into which the dog is falling suggests that, like the Leviathan of *MHH*, Plate 20, the crocodile represents analytic force at its most destructive, devouring a more animated energy). Since Leutha is Blake's most explicit protagonist of sexual desire

against it. A year or two later Blake uses the same sort of confrontation, with a new twist, on the title-page to *Visions of the Daughters of Albion* (Plate 62), where he shows a figure of female sexual delight rising like Aphrodite from the sea to be confronted by a similar ageing law-god, now more readily identifiable as Urizen. Here, the confrontation is more obviously one between exuberant energy and a restraining law.

In *Fertilization of Egypt*, by contrast, the tone is more sombre. The most striking feature of Fuseli's original sketch is the priest with his back turned; the suggestion that he is being portrayed sardonically is strongly reinforced by the fact that on both the occasions when Fuseli depicted similar figures on a large scale elsewhere in his work, they were figures of violence: on one occasion an executioner, on another Hephaestus among a group securing Prometheus on Mount Caucasus.[57] Although Blake is sometimes sharply satirical in his visual art, this particular sort of grotesqueness seems to lie beyond the range of attitudes that he normally expresses or would wish to express.

The one sign of hope in Fuseli's original wash drawing, on the other hand, the appearance, above the priest-god, of the giant star, is, by contrast, very like the giant stars of imagination to be found in Blake's later illustrations, and may be thought of as representing the latter's own peculiar contribution to the discussion. The curious and paradoxical relationship between dog-priest and Dog-star in Egyptian mythology is here, we may argue, being reinterpreted in terms of the dialectic between energy and the imagination. Sexual energy, in its purest form, is destructive, needing to be restrained by the law; yet when enlightened by the human imagination it may become a key to lost paradise; the theme is perennial with Blake. So while Anubis, lifting his hands to the star, may seem a ludicrous figure, he is yet figuring the elements of a truth which is always being lost by human beings in their cults of shame and restraint. And it is this dialectic which Blake continues to render in his following works.

It is hardly likely that either Coleridge or Wordsworth, coming across Blake's illustration to Darwin's poem, saw the full point of what was being presented

---

attention should also be drawn to the transformation of the Isle of Dogs into the Isle of Leutha's Dogs in *Jerusalem* (31. 15–16: cf. the Dogs of Leutha in *J* 83. 82); there is also an implicit shorthand use of the dog-image in the song of the Daughters of Jerusalem ('O it was lost for ever, and we found it not; it came / And wept at our wintry Door') immediately before their description of residual sexuality ('Gwendolen / Is become a Clod of Clay! Merlin is a Worm of the Valley': *J* 56. 26–8); while a starved dog accompanies a beggar, who is leaning on a crutch in the form of a phallic hammer (cf. *J*, Plate 6) in Plate 5 of the *Job* illustrations (see especially the Butts water-colour version).

[57] *An Executioner, c.* 1780–9: F. Antal, *Fuseli Studies*, 1956, Plate 15a; *Hephaestus, Bia and Crato securing Prometheus on Mount Caucasus, c.* 1810: *A Collection of Drawings by Henry Fuseli, R.A.,* ed. P. Tomory, Auckland, N.Z., 1967, Plate 24. A. S. Roe points out (op. cit., pp. 444–5 n. 10) that a minute figure of the same type stands on Bottom's hand in Fuseli's painting *Titania and Bottom*, painted for Boydell's Shakespeare Gallery in 1789 and certainly well known to Blake, and that the same pose is used in Blake's water-colour from Revelation, *The Red Dragon and the Woman Clothed with the Sun.*

62. *Visions of the Daughters of Albion*, title-page (detail), copy P.
Relief etching finished in pen and water-colour.
Fitzwilliam Museum, Cambridge

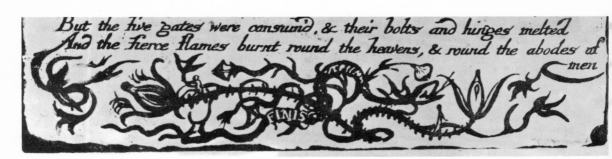

63. *America*, plate 18 (detail), copy P.
Relief etching with water-colour.
Fitzwilliam Museum, Cambridge

there;[58] and indeed the use made by Blake and Coleridge of the runs of imagery mentioned earlier differs in important respects. Where Coleridge seems to see the wings of the Egyptian hieroglyphic purely as wings of eagle-strength, of the invincible power of human love, Blake uses them more ambiguously, sometimes in that same sense, but often turned against man, to represent (as in *Fertilization of Egypt*) the powerful barriers created by law against the realization of man's vision. Where Coleridge dwelt more on the idea of the lost Abyssinian paradise, therefore, with its possible enshrining of a lost secret wisdom, Blake was more pre-occupied by the tyrannies of Egypt, in which he could find an analogue for the commercial tyrannies of eighteenth-century Europe. Yet the note of concealed hope remains, to be repeated when he mentions the cults of Osiris, Isis, and Orus in *Milton* some years later:[59]

> Osiris, Isis, Orus in Egypt, dark their Tabernacles on Nile
> Floating with solemn songs & on the Lakes of Egypt nightly
> With pomp even till morning break & Osiris appear in the sky . . .

Here, it seems, the dark rites of Egypt are seen as (like Anubis) shadowing forth a brighter reality: the appearance of Osiris in the form of the sun at sunrise will dispel the dark rites of the night, to replace them by humanized vision.

It would be good to know more about the collaboration between Fuseli and Blake. In another design of his which Blake engraved for Darwin, *Tornado* (Plate 64),[60] the wings and serpentine form (which follow Darwin's detail fairly closely but may also be based on Egyptian mythology)[61] are prophetic of later developments in Blake's visual art, where the serpent-coils around a figure are a permanent image for the ambiguity of energy and its relation to the human 'selfhood'. Again one is left asking how much the symbolism of the designs was discussed between the two artists.

We may seem by now to have moved a long way from Wordsworth, who was less given to the investigation of mythologies. His eye for the actual was more readily drawn to the immediate scene before him. In the case of Bruce's *Travels*, for example, his imagination was likely to be seized less by the ancient traditions and mysteries surrounding the Nile-springs than by the actual sight which greeted Bruce when he completed his quest. After many wanderings and evasions (for the local inhabitants were by no means anxious for their secret to be discovered)

[58] For unsympathetic comments on Fuseli by both poets see E. C. Mason, *The Mind of Henry Fuseli*, 1951, p. 40.
[59] *Milton* 37. 27–9.
[60] Erasmus Darwin, *The Botanic Garden*, 3rd ed., 1795, facing p. 168. For bibliographical discussion of this and the preceding plate, see Ruthven Todd, 'Two Blake Prints and Two Fuseli Drawings', *Blake Newsletter*, v (1972), 176–7.
[61] It is just possible that Fuseli and/or Blake had in mind the destructive Egyptian deity Typhon, who is linked etymologically to the phenomenon of the Typhoon (cf. *Coleridge the Visionary*, p. 241 and A. S. Roe, op. cit., p. 172); if so, the two plates for Darwin's books are linked further.

64. *Tornado*. Engraving after Henry Fuseli for Erasmus Darwin,
The Botanic Garden (1795).
Kerrison Preston Blake Library, Westminster Public Library

Bruce finally (and then only by peremptory demand) succeeded in persuading his guide to show him the place he was looking for. What greeted him was a scene of truly Wordsworthian 'natural piety':[62] 'I after this came to the island of green turf, which was in the form of an altar, apparently the work of art, and I stood in rapture over the principal fountain which rises in the middle of it.' To the author of the Preface to *The Excursion* the moral significance of this was no doubt clear: what men are searching for when they look for a lost paradise will eventually be found, if found at all, in the simplest manifestations and graces of nature. Nevertheless he was not likely to be altogether unmoved by Bruce's descriptions of such phenomena as a powerful fountain which sometimes forced itself out from a mountain with great violence. As J. L. Lowes pointed out, such passages, along with others in Bartram's *Travels*, contributed to the imagery of the 'mighty fountain' in *Kubla Khan*.[63] And if one goes on to maintain (as I should wish to) that Coleridge's interest in fountains was not simply a matter of delight in vivid images but reflected his own interest in the operations of genius, sometimes powerfully destructive, sometimes peaceful and self-delighting, one is led to ask whether Wordsworth did not share something of this interest.

Certainly he used imagery of the Nile—and was using it before he met Coleridge. His *Descriptive Sketches* of 1793 concluded with the prayer that those who were fighting for freedom should triumph, so that liberty might flow like a great flood:[64]

> Give them, beneath their breast while Gladness springs,
> To brood the Nations o'er with Nile-like wings.

The image was not original, even there: as de Selincourt notes, it echoed Gray's 'Education and Government':[65] '. . . where Nile . . . broods o'er Egypt with his watry wings.' Gray's image already suggests some acquaintance with Egyptian hieroglyphics; Wordsworth's was perhaps reinforced by acquaintance with Darwin's poem and the Blake/Fuseli engraving. But did he then go on, under Coleridge's influence, to interpret the work of the Nile psychologically, linking the imagery of Abyssinian springs and Nile fountains to the workings of the imagination?

This sort of speculation did not come easily to Wordsworth, yet it seems that he was not wholly unmoved, either. Although he makes little use of Nile-imagery in his writings, two of his references in *The Prelude* appear in contexts of consequence.

---

[62] J. Bruce, *Travels to Discover the Source of the Nile*, 1790, iii. 597, 619–20 (quoted J. L. Lowes, *The Road to Xanadu*, 1927, p. 371).

[63] W. Bartram, *Travels through North and South Carolina*, etc., 1792, pp. 163, 237–8 (Lowes, op. cit., pp. 367–9).

[64] *Poetical Works*, ed. de Selincourt, i. 88.

[65] Gray, 'The Alliance of Education and Government', ii. 10. 1–3 (*Poems*, ed. H. W. Starr and J. R. Hendrickson, Oxford, 1966, p. 97).

The first is in the great passage on the power of imagination where he argues that this power (operating like a flash of lightning in the midst of a cloudy storm) blinds the sense with 'a flash that has revealed / The invisible world' and in that moment reawakens our own innate sense of greatness, reminding us that[66]

> . . . whether we be young or old
> Our destiny, our nature, and our home
> Is with infinitude, and only there.

This perception is absolute, superseding with effortless power the aspirations and strivings which normally exercise the soul: and at this point the Nile-image (elaborated further in the 1850 version)[67] comes in to reinforce the climax:[68]

> The mind beneath such banners militant
> Thinks not of spoils or trophies, nor of aught
> That may attest its prowess, blest in thoughts
> That are their own perfection and reward,
> Strong in itself, and in the access of joy
> Which hides it like the overflowing Nile.

The experience which embodied this visitation in the Alps had not been one of unmixed pleasure; what Wordsworth seems in fact to be suggesting is that such experiences rarely are: his phrase 'the burden of mystery' comes readily to mind. On the other hand, bearing that burden may sometimes bring an unlooked-for reward: after the labours of the Simplon Pass, Wordsworth and his companion enjoyed days of peace and pleasure by Locarno and Como. And it is here that the

---

[66] *The Prelude*, 1805, vi. 537–9.

[67]
> Strong in herself and in beatitude
> That hides her, like the mighty flood of Nile
> Poured from his fount of Abyssinian clouds
> To fertilise the whole Egyptian plain.   (Ibid. 609.)

It will be observed that this version is closer to the details of the Blake/Fuseli design—as if Wordsworth had originally been recalling the imagery in more general terms but later felt that the whole passage would be better drawn together by a specific reference to the Abyssinian clouds, which provide a link between the original flash of the imagination in the clouds and the sense of overflowing power in the Nile-image. But (unless there is some further source common to both) it is hard to see how this imagery could have established itself in Wordsworth's mind in the first place as symbolic of creative inspiration without the Blake/Fuseli design, which, by incorporating the features of the Nile-god, and so recalling the cloudy God of inspiration on the mountain-top in the Bible (cf. Exod. 24, Mark 9) would seem to have set the train of imagery in motion. The possibility that Coleridge acted as an intellectual accessory here can by no means be ruled out, of course—indeed, the sense of sombre joy which informs the passage becomes more readily comprehensible if Wordsworth is thought of as assuming an attitude which mediates between the sardonic tone of the Blake/Fuseli design and Coleridge's tendency to interpret the imagery involved in terms of radiant inspiration (cf. *Coleridge the Visionary*, pp. 256–61).

Geoffrey Hartman, in an important discussion of the passage as marking a central apocalyptic moment in Wordsworth (*Wordsworth's Poetry, 1787–1814*, New Haven, Conn., 1964, pp. 39–48), remarks that the concluding Nile simile 'suggests not only a divorce from but also (proleptically) a return to nature on the part of the soul'. In the context of the present discussion, however, it would seem that the simile is itself drawing strongly on previous imaginative experience, Abyssinia and Egypt here being essentially countries of Wordsworth's mind.

[68] *The Prelude* vi. 543–8.

image of the Abyssinian paradise which was missing earlier enters the poem; Como is addressed as[69]

> . . . a treasure by the earth
> Kept to itself, a darling bosom'd up
> In Abyssinian privacy . . .

For Wordsworth, it would seem, the Abyssinian mountain-paradise is not (as with Coleridge) a place of absolute and radiant inspiration, but a place of repose which one is likely to reach only after the labours of struggling with a dark sublime. Abyssinia (with its 'Mountains of the Moon') is, in fact, a region like Blake's 'Beulah':[70]

> But to
> The Sons of Eden the moony habitations of Beulah
> Are from Great Eternity a mild & pleasant Rest.

The sublime that Wordsworth rests from, however, is conceived in darker terms than Blake's.

After 1800 the varying personalities of Blake on the one hand and Wordsworth and Coleridge on the other led them into divergent paths. The impulse to the sublime continued, however, as an enweaving factor in the development of all three. Each man was increasingly preoccupied with the prospect of producing some great and lasting work, each conceived that work in psychological terms. Blake's *Vala*, its participants corresponding to certain human energies, Wordsworth's attempt in *The Prelude* to describe and interpret the experience of an individual before any future prescription for mankind is undertaken, Coleridge's psychological and metaphysical work ('to which I hope to dedicate in silence the prime of my life')[71] are all conceived on the grand scale; all, equally, reflect in their various ways a common engagement with the achievement of Milton[72] and all are undertaken in isolation, whether it is the shared isolation of Wordsworth and Coleridge in the Lake District or the more absolute isolation of Blake.

There are still occasional hints of mutual influences, nevertheless. We know that four of Blake's lyrics were copied into one of Wordsworth's commonplace books between February and August 1807;[73] there is also the teasing possibility of a single, important influence several years earlier. Writing to Coleridge on 16 April 1802 Wordsworth inserted the following brief postscript: 'I have sent Thels Book, tell me something about it.'[74] The editor comments that this is probably

[69] Ibid. 590–2.
[70] *Milton* 30. 12–14.
[71] Letter to Josiah Wedgwood, 21 May 1799, *Letters*, ed. Griggs, ii. 519.
[72] Cf. *Blake's Humanism*, 1968, pp. 142 ff.
[73] See Paul F. Betz, 'Wordsworth's First Acquaintance with Blake's Poetry', *Blake Newsletter*, iii (1970), 84–9.
[74] *Letters 1787–1805*, 2nd ed., ed. C. Sheaver, 1967, p. 349. Copies of *The Book of Thel* were of course rare;

a reference to John Thelwall's *Poems written chiefly in Retirement*, published the previous year; but it would seem equally possible that Blake's *Book of Thel* is the work in question. In that case one possibility (among several) would be that Coleridge borrowed a copy from a friend in London, brought it back with him (leaving it perhaps with the Hutchinsons for Wordsworth to pick up), and then asked Wordsworth to return it for him.

The possibility that the Wordsworths had a copy of *The Book of Thel* in their house during April 1802 deserves serious consideration in view of the character of Wordsworth's writing at that time. The sense of natural phenomena 'speaking' directly to the human consciousness and of nature as invested with innocent radiance was then unusually intense. In the same letter that contained the postscript Wordsworth included both his famous poem on the glow-worm, which might have been prompted by the speech of the Worm in Blake's poem, and 'The cock is crowing . . .'—a poem endowed with a strong sense of the visionary elements in nature, and their contribution to the human sense of joy. It may also be significant that Dorothy's emotions at this time oscillate between a simple and imaginative delight in nature and a sense of melancholy very like that of Blake's heroine. 'The sunshine, the green fields, and the fair sky made me sadder', she wrote on 21 April; 'even the little happy sporting lambs seemed but sorrowful to me.'[75] Though not quite identical to Thel's language, this is surprisingly close; it is possible that Dorothy's depression at the thought of her brother's forthcoming marriage had found an echo in Thel's sense of uselessness in the Vale of Har.

If there were direct cross-currents of this sort at the time they would seem to have been on a small scale. Later, as Sir Geoffrey Keynes has described in a classic article,[76] Blake was drawn into the network of literary and artistic relationships which flourished for a time in Regency London. He criticized Wordsworth and was criticized by Coleridge; later still Blake and Coleridge met and discoursed like 'congenial beings from another sphere'.[77] But the characters of all three were by then fully formed, and less likely than in the closing decade of the previous century to respond to seminal influences.

The sort of investigation I have concerned myself with here is necessarily reliant on something less tangible than records of meetings and written criticisms: often it is a matter of discovering, from scattered pieces of evidence, parallels and near-convergences, varying responses to common themes and, occasionally, possibilities of more direct influence, perhaps via mutual acquaint-

on the other hand, Wordsworth's 'Tell me something about it' would suit a riddling text better than the more straightforward poetry of Thelwall.

[75] *Journals of Dorothy Wordsworth*, ed. E. de Selincourt, i. 135.
[76] Geoffrey Keynes, 'William Blake with Charles Lamb and his Circle', *Blake Studies*, pp. 74–89.
[77] *London University Magazine*, ii (1830), 318.

ances. If such an approach is necessarily concerned more with process than with product, it must also be acknowledged that there are certain periods in the history of art when the study of process can be particularly rewarding—as when, after the French Revolution, it was found possible to interpret the present struggles of the human spirit to realize its aspirations by reference to past traditions supposedly enshrined in ancient myths and symbols, and to new possibilities opened out by contemporary science. If new and bewildering situations could not be immediately organized, poets could still aim for an art in which a direct and honest response to current events and issues was given depth and stability by the invocation of traditions from the past and by glimpses of possible future patterns. Another of Fuseli's aphorisms puts the point succinctly:[78] 'Invention, strictly speaking, being confined to *one* moment, he invents best who in that moment combines the traces of the past, the energy of the present, and a glimpse of the future.'

The situation in England at the end of the eighteenth century provided unique occasions and materials for that sort of enterprise; the reader who takes his bearings accordingly is likely to be rewarded by a more satisfying interpretation of certain key texts and designs.

[78] J. Knowles, *Life and Works of Henry Fuseli*, 1831, iii. 82.

XIII

WILLIAM BLAKE, THE PRINCE OF THE HEBREWS, AND THE WOMAN CLOTHED WITH THE SUN[1]

Morton D. Paley

THE millenarian spirit, compounded of elements of Old and New Testament eschatology, the apocalypses of the Jewish and Christian Apocrypha, and the Sibylline Oracles, has continuously stirred the Western imagination. Though officially driven underground and frequently persecuted in the Middle Ages, its adherents emerged time and again to launch revolutions and even crusades: to try to turn their own cities into the New Jerusalem, as in revolutionary Münster, or to try to capture the real Jerusalem so that the eschatological drama of the Last Days could be enacted there.[2] The characteristic tenets of millenarian belief have been described by Norman Cohn as relating to salvation, which is pictured as 'collective', 'terrestrial', 'imminent', 'total', and 'miraculous'.[3] William Blake would have given his own unique meaning to some of these terms, but it scarcely needs to be demonstrated that his works are deeply imbued with the idea of the Millennium, rendered most extensively in Night IX of *The Four Zoas* and an important theme in virtually all his major works. Of the medieval proponents of the idea, perhaps those closest to Blake in spirit are Joachim of Fiore, who taught the coming of a third age or Age of the Spirit in which there would be perfect freedom without the Law, and the Amaurians, who held that 'each one of them was Christ and Holy Spirit'; the latter provided the basis for the doctrine of the Free Spirit, which in turn reached England in the seventeenth century through the sect known as the Ranters.[4] Millenarianism did not stop in the seventeenth century, however. It is interesting to compare Blake's treatment of the millennial theme with those of Joachim, the Free Spirit, and the Ranters; but it is at least as

---

[1] This essay was written while the author was a Fellow of the John Simon Guggenheim Foundation, to which grateful acknowledgement is made.

[2] See Norman Cohn, *The Pursuit of the Millennium*, rev. ed., Temple Smith, London, 1970.

[3] Ibid., p. 13. On millennial thought, see also Ernest Lee Tuveson, *Millennium and Utopia*, University of California Press, Berkeley and Los Angeles, 1949.

[4] See Cohn, op. cit., pp. 148–86, 287–330. A. L. Morton has suggested that the Ranters and other seventeenth-century antinomians influenced Blake (*The Everlasting Gospel*, Lawrence & Wishart, London, 1958).

interesting to consider Blake in relation to the millenarian movements of his own time, the chief of these being those of Richard Brothers and Joanna Southcott.

1

Richard Brothers[5] (1757–1824) was a half-pay officer who had foregone his allowance from the Navy rather than take the oath of loyalty required. In 1792 he began to prophesy against the impending war against France, addressing letters to the King, Pitt, and other ministers. On 12 May he tried to address Parliament 'To inform them', he says, 'that the war just going to be commenced by Prussia and Austria against France, was the very war alluded to by St. John, in the nineteenth chapter of Revelation, which God called a war against himself'; and 'To inform them of the approaching fall of Monarchy in Europe'.[6] In 1794 he published *A Revealed Knowledge of the Prophecies and Times*, denouncing the war now begun and predicting the return of the Jews to Jerusalem. This was shortly followed by a second instalment, subtitled 'Particularly of the Present time, the Present War, and the Prophecy Now Fulfilling'. Here Brothers described the league against France as 'many men fighting against the Spirit of God' (p. 7), beseeched George III not to prosecute the war, and predicted the destruction of England by 'Colonial conquest . . . which will break the Empire in pieces' (p. 18). On 4 March 1795 he was arrested; he was examined by the Privy Council and subsequently found insane. For the next eleven years he was confined in Dr. Samuel Foart Simmons's asylum in Islington.

The charge against Brothers was one to disquiet any prophet against empire. According to *The Times* for 6 March 1795, 'The warrant on which *Brothers* was apprehended was grounded on the 15th of Elizabeth; and in which he stood charged with "Unlawfully, maliciously, and wickedly writing, publishing, and printing various fantastical prophecies, with intent to cause dissension and other disturbances within the realm, contrary to the Statute".' Perhaps coincidentally, one of Brothers's adversaries cited this very law in a satire published shortly before the arrest.

Blackstone hath ignorantly and unprophetically laid down the English Law with respect to *pretended Prophets* as follows, viz.

'False and *pretended Prophecies*, with intent to disturb the peace, are equally unlawful, and more penal, as they raise enthusiastic jealousies in the People, and terrify them with imaginary fears. They are therefore punished by our Law. . . . Now, by the Statute 5 Eliz. c. 15, the penalty for the first offense is a fine of ten pounds and one years imprisonment; for the second, forfeiture of all goods and chattels, and imprisonment during life.' Vol. IV, chap. ii.[7]

[5] D.N.B., s.v.; Cecil Roth, *The Nephew of the Almighty*, Edward Goldston, London, 1938.
[6] *A Revealed Knowledge of the Prophecies and Times*, London, 1794, ii. 19.
[7] Henry Spencer, *A Vindication of the Prophecies of Mr. Brothers*, London, 1795, pp. 19–20 n.

The actual wording of the statute, which was to remain law until 1863,[8] makes it even more clear that it could have been applied to Blake as well as to Brothers had the government wished to do so, especially as Blake had subtitled two of his Lambeth books 'a Prophecy'—*America* (1793) and *Europe* (1794):

An act against fond and fantastical prophesies

Soasmuch *as sithence the expiration and ending of the statute made in the time of King Edward the Sixth, intituled,* An act against fond and fantastical prophecies, *divers evil disposed persons, inclined to the stirring and moving of factions, seditions, and rebellion within this realm, have been the more bold to attempt the like practices in feigning, imagining, inventing and publishing of such fond and fantastical prophecies, as well concerning the Queen's majesty, as divers honourable personages, gentlemen and others of this realm . . . to the great disquiet, trouble and peril of the Queen's majesty, and of this her realm*:

II. For remedy whereof, be it ordained and enacted by the authority of this present parliament, That if any person and persons . . . do advisedly and directly advance, publish and set forth by writing, printing, signing or any other open speech or deed, to any person or persons, any fond, fantastical or false prophecy, upon or by the occasion of any arms, fields, beasts, badges or such other like things accustomed in arms, cognizances or signets, or upon or by reason of any time, year, or day, name, bloodshed, or war, (2) to the intent thereby to make any rebellion, insurrection, dissension, loss of life, or other disturbances within this realm or other the Queen's dominions: (3) That then every such person being thereof lawfully convicted according to the due laws of this realm, for every such offense shall suffer imprisonment of his body by the space of one year, without bail or mainprise, and shall forfeit for every such offense the sum of ten pounds.[9]

The statute goes on to specify life imprisonment and forfeiture of all possessions as the penalty for a second conviction. That such a law could be applied in 1795 should have been of particular interest to Blake, who, like Brothers, had prophesied the defeat of England by the forces of revolution. That Brothers was confined as a madman must have been far from reassuring to one who could write in his 'Public Address' (*c.* 1810) 'It is very true, what you have said these thirty two Years. I am Mad or Else you are so; both of us cannot be in our right senses' (K, p. 593).

There is little doubt that the motive for Brothers's incarceration was political. *The Times* on 4 March reported that 'He is daily visited by Ladies and Gentlemen, who want to have their fortunes told, by indigent French emigrants . . . and by different people, who delight in hearing, even from the mouth of a madman, invectives against the present Administration'. In this article Brothers is compared to 'other visionary dreamers' who sprang up in Paris under Robespierre. 'It seems, that there are men in this country, who propose to employ the same means to

[8] See Earl Jowitt and Clifford Walsh, *The Dictionary of English Law*, Sweet and Maxwell, London, 1959, i, 782.
[9] Danby Pickering of Gray's Inn, Esq., *The Statutes at Large*, Cambridge, 1763, vi, 207–8.

attain their end. . . . Brothers, appears to have been selected to act a prominent part in these scenes. . . .' On the following day, *The Times* commented on Brothers's arrest:

The sketch of the visions of the Prophet, given in our paper of yesterday, must clearly evince the necessity of confining him in a place, where the necessary remedies may be applied to cure his troubled imagination. His arrest seems the more urgent, as from the nature and object of his visions, he was become the tool of a faction, employed to seduce the people, and to spread fears and alarms. Government has therefore very properly secured the person of the prophet, in order to prevent this *Nephew of God* from doing the *work of a devil*.

In contrast, the Opposition *Morning Chronicle* thought the government had merely made itself look foolish:

The examination of Richard Brothers on Thursday, before the Privy Council, brought forth nothing satisfactory. The Lord Chancellor was the examiner; he tried what effect his large penetrating eye would have on the countenance of this extraordinary man; but after a rigorous examination of two hours, the Council owned that they could not exasperate, intimidate, nor disconcert him. He preserved that gentleness of deportment which is peculiar to him under the most biting harshness of rebuke, and he was never once deceived by the lures which were spread to throw him off his guard. . . . After two hours close examination he was remanded back to his apartment and the Council were left in considerable doubt whether to consider him as a madman or an impostor.

The most inexplicable thing in the conduct of this man, is, that with all the appearances of poverty in his manner of living, the Council have ascertained that he has actually given away pamphlets, the number and printing of which have cost him £250. The number who have inquired after him, and their prayers for his welfare, since his arrest, shew that his abominable nonsense has made converts, and the number is likely to be augmented by the stupidity of prosecution (Saturday, 6 Mar. 1795. Number 7924).

James Gillray, on the day after Brothers's arrest, published a caricature (Plate 65) depicting Brothers as a lunatic dressed as a sans-culotte[10] and bearing Charles James Fox and others of the Parliamentary opposition on his back in a *Bundle of the Elect*. He is leading the Jews toward the *Gate of Jerusalem*, at which he points with a fiery sword, but this Promised Land is in reality the triple gallows. He is treading down a most Blakean seven-headed beast of Revelation (cf. Plate 67) —one head is the pope's, another a king's—but the *assignats* in his pocket betray him to be a French agent. St. Paul's and the Monument collapse in flames, as in Brothers's prophecies; the sun, wearing the red cap of Liberty, drips blood.

It scarcely needs to be argued that Blake must have been aware of the controversy about Brothers from some of these public sources. In addition, he had

---

[10] For this and other details, see Mary Dorothy George, *Catalogue of Political and Personal Satires* Preserved in the Department of Prints and Drawings in the British Museum, 1793–1800, vii, London, 1942, 161–2.

The PROPHET of the HEBREWS, — the PRINCE of PEACE, conducting the JEWS to the PROMIS'D-LAND.

65. James Gillray: *The Prophet of the Hebrews,—The Prince of Peace,
conducting the Jews to the Promis'd-Land.* Engraving.
British Museum, Department of Prints and Drawings

friends and acquaintances who were interested in the Prince of the Hebrews. John Gabriel Stedman wrote in his journal for 5 June 1794: 'An earthquake prophesied by Brothers. Many leave town.' Four days later, Stedman 'gave a blue sugar cruse to Mrs. Blake' and 'Dined Palmer, Blake, Johnson, Rigaud, and Bartolozzi'.[11] It is hard to believe that under the circumstances this phenomenon was not discussed. Also, William Sharp, who, like Blake was at this time a political radical with links to the Johnson circle, as well as having been a Swedenborgian in the 1780s, was deeply involved in the Brothers movement.[12] Sharp, who was later to try to win Blake over to Joanna Southcott, seems to have been an inveterate proselytizer. He tried to convert Thomas Holcroft to Brothers and to persuade John Flaxman to act as Architect of Brothers's Promised Land.[13] On 16 April 1795 he published his engraving 'Richard Brothers, Prince of the Hebrews' (Plate 66) with the declaration: 'Fully believing this to be the man whom God has appointed, I engrave his likeness, William Sharp.' Moreover, Joseph Johnson himself displayed interest in Brothers at a time when he might well have been occupied with more personal concerns. Brought to trial in 1798 for selling the political writings of the Revd. Gilbert Wakefield, Johnson employed the famous Whig advocate Henry Erskine as his defence attorney. According to John Knowles,

the following anecdote respecting Lord Erskine, who subsequently was intimate with Fuseli, was told to me by Mr. Bonnycastle.[14] He and Johnson were, just previously to the trial, walking through Lincoln's Inn on their way to dine with Fuseli, and met Erskine there accidentally, who had several dogs with him, animals of which he was particularly fond. As soon as he saw them, he cried out, 'Johnson, I have something particular to say to you,' and then occupied him in close conversation, apart from Bonny-castle, for nearly a quarter of an hour.

At length Mr. Johnson took his leave; and when he joined Bonnycastle, said 'You cannot even guess the topic of our conversation.' 'Doubtless,' said the latter, 'your forth-coming trial.' 'Not a bit,' said Johnson; 'he never even alluded to it, and the time was wholly occupied with his opinions about Brothers the Prophet, and in asking questions respecting a book "on the Revelations," lately offered me for publication.'[15]

Strangely enough, Erskine would be Lord Chancellor in 1806, when Brothers's followers petitioned for his release. Brothers's chief supporter at this time, John Finleyson, writes that after 'Mr. Brothers' implacable enemy, Mr. Pitt . . . died

---

[11] *The Journal of John Gabriel Stedman*, ed. Stanbury Thompson, London, 1962, p. 382. See also Sir Geoffrey Keynes, 'William Blake and John Gabriel Stedman', *Blake Studies*, pp. 98–104; David V. Erdman, *Blake: Prophet against Empire*, 2nd ed., Princeton University Press, Princeton, N.J., 1969, pp. 230–1, 290–1.

[12] On Sharp, see W. S. Baker, *William Sharp, Engraver*, Gebbie and Barrie, Philadelphia, Pa., 1875.

[13] See Bentley, *Records*, p. 235 n. 2.

[14] John Bonnycastle, author of *An Introduction to Mensuration and Practical Geometry*, 1782, published by Johnson with a frontispiece engraved by Blake after Stothard.

[15] *The Life and Writings of Henry Fuseli, Esq., M.A., R.A.*, London, 1836, i, 203. I am indebted to Deirdre Toomey for bringing this passage to my attention.

RICHARD BROTHERS
PRINCE OF THE HEBREWS

Fully believing this to be the Man whom GOD has appointed:—I engrave his likeness, *WILLIAM SHARP.*

Published at Nº 8. Charles Street, Middˣ Hospital, London, April 16ᵗ 1795, by W. Sharp.

66. William Sharp:
Richard Brothers, Prince of the Hebrews. Engraving.
British Museum, Department of Prints and Drawings

broken hearted in the beginning of 1806',[16] proceedings were begun to obtain Brothers's freedom. Erskine heard the case on 14 April 1806 and, despite the opposition of Dr. Simmons, ordered Brothers's release. However, on being asked to supersede the verdict of lunacy, Erskine, according to Finleyson, 'took hold of me in the most familiar way, and said to me, that I, as his countryman, must not press him on that point, there were scruples to be got over in the King's mind'.[17] Finleyson took care of Brothers until 1824. Brothers died on 24 January of that year; his last words were addressed to Finleyson: 'Holding his right hand in my right hand, he asked me if my sword and hammer were ready?'[18]

In the same year that Blake wrote 'To defend the Bible in this year 1798 would cost a man his life' (Annotations to Watson, K, p. 383), Brothers declared: 'At present, it is so dangerous to mention the name of God, if it does not accord with the opinions of men and political principles of the times, that a man will most surely be used very ill, if not imprisoned and destroyed: so much is the human race fallen from a true knowledge of God, and a reverence for his mild precepts.'[19] May the case of Brothers have impressed Blake as a cautionary example? The fact that Blake, after publishing the Lambeth Books, issued no new illuminated works between 1795 and c. 1809 is usually explained by a shift of his energies to such pursuits as illustrating *Night Thoughts* and engraving for Hayley at Felpham. But what, in turn, caused this remarkable change in Blake's creative activities? May one of the reasons have been the instance of a man who, born like Blake in the year of the Swedenborgian new heaven, 1757, published two books of prophecies in 1794, was arrested on a charge of false prophecy, and confined to a lunatic asylum to (as *The Times* put it) 'cure his troubled imagination'? Although we are not now in a position to answer this question, there is a curious association of Blake and Brothers in Tatham's biographical essay. It is to be sure association by denial, yet the denial hardly need have been made some nine years after Brothers's death and six years after Blake's, if there were not some striking comparisons to be made between the two. Tatham writes:

These visions of Blake seem to have been more like peopled imaginations, & personified thoughts, they only horrified when they represented any scene in which horrors were depicted as a picture or Poem. Richard Brothers has been classed as one possessing this power, but he really was a decided madman, he asserted he was nephew to God the Father, & in a mad House he died as well indeed he might. Brothers is classed with Swedenborg in order to ridicule Swedenborg, & bring him into Contempt. Blake & Brothers therefore must not be placed together.[20]

---

[16] John Finleyson [Finlayson], *The Last Trumpet and the Flying Angel*, London, 1849 [1850], p. 15.
[17] Ibid., p. 16.
[18] Ibid., p. 17.
[19] *A Letter from Mr. Brothers to Miss Cott*, London, 1798, p. 120.
[20] 'Life of Blake', Bentley, *Records*, p. 520.

There are indeed some important differences between Blake and Brothers, and these must be considered, but a comparison of their writings also reveals a considerable community of interest. Both are Christian apocalyptists, seeing in the events of their own time parallels to the apocalyptic and Prophetic writings of the Bible, and both interpret these writings according to their own opposition to the war against France and the establishment of Britain's colonial empire. 'This Beast', Brothers writes of Rev. 13: 1, 'means the British Monarchy, and it is by ships and commerce that it has rose from the sea to such astonishing grandeur and magnitude. The Heads, Horns, and Crowns allude to the many departments of Government, and their splendid distinctions. The Blasphemer, means the title given to, and assumed by the King of England. . . .'[21] (Finleyson would later identify the seven-headed beast as George III himself.)[22] Blake, of course, uses the monster in a similar way, as, for example in *Night Thoughts* design 345 (Plate 67), where the seven heads represent the monarchic, ecclesiastical, legal, and military institutions of a fallen world.[23] Brothers's denunciation of 'ships and commerce' brings to mind Blake's 'Spirit, who lov'st Brittannia's Isle / Round which the fiends of Commerce smile . . .' (MS. Note-Book, K, p. 557) and also the activity of Urizen in *The Four Zoas*, Night viib:

> First Trades & Commerce, ships & armed vessels he builded laborious
> To swim the deep; & on the land, children are sold to trades
> Of dire necessity, still laboring day & night till all
> Their life extinct they took the spectre form in dark despair;
> And slaves in myriads, in ship loads, burden the hoarse sounding deep,
> Rattling with mental chains, the Universal Empire groans.
>
> (lines 12–17, K, p. 333.)

At the same time, neither Blake nor Brothers views commerce as evil in itself: in the prelapsarian world and in the millennial world to come, commerce has a positive function. In *Jerusalem* Albion tells Babylon

> 'Yet thou wast lovely as the summer cloud upon my hills
> 'When Jerusalem was thy heart's desire, in times of youth & love.
> 'Thy Sons came to Jerusalem with gifts; she sent them away
> 'With blessings on their hands & on their feet, blessings of gold
> 'And pearl & diamond: thy Daughters sang in her Courts.
> 'They came up to Jerusalem: they walked before Albion:
> 'In the Exchanges of London every Nation walk'd,
> 'And London walk'd in every Nation, mutual in love & harmony.'
>
> (24. 36–43, K, p. 647.)

---

[21] *A Revealed Knowledge*, ii. 95.

[22] Finleyson, op. cit., p. 22.

[23] See M. D. Paley, 'Blake's "Night Thoughts": An Exploration of the Fallen World', *William Blake: Essays for S. Foster Damon*, ed. Alvin H. Rosenfeld, Brown University Press, Providence, R.I., 1969, p. 154.

THE

COMPLAINT.

OR,

Night-Thoughts

ON

LIFE, DEATH, and IMMORTALITY.

NIGHT the EIGHTH.

VIRTUE's APOLOGY:

OR,

The MAN of the WORLD Answer'd.

In which are Confidered,

The LOVE of THIS LIFE;

The AMBITION and PLEASURE, with the WIT
and WISDOM of the WORLD.

LONDON:

Printed for G. HAWKINS, at Milton's Head, between the Two Temple-
Gates, Fleet-ftreet, near Temple-Bar.
And Sold by M. COOPER, at the Globe, in Pater-nofter Row.
MDCCXLV.

67. Design for Young's *Night Thoughts*, No. 345. Water-colour.
British Museum, Department of Prints and Drawings

Similarly, England has a special role to play in Brothers's millennial kingdom, because of her wealth:

England, situated in the sea beyond the straits of Ethiopia, is for Agriculture, and the abundance produced from it, the garden of the world: her daughters are all beautiful, and her sons are all brave: her extensive parks contain all the variety of prospect that can delight the eye, and enchant the mind! Her spreading downs are covered with sheep, her fields are full of corn, and her meadows are full of cattle! Her harbours are full of ships, and her cities are full of manufactures! the four corners of the world acknowledge her power, and receive her Commerce. Her capital for extent, trade, wealth, and such abundance of all things necessary for raising an empire from a desert waste to a fruitful soil, may very justly be stiled the queen of cities![24]

In Blake's millennial vision in Night ix of *The Four Zoas*, the repentant Urizen regrets '"burd'ning with my Ships the angry deep"' (K, p. 361) and is regenerated 'In radiant Youth' (K, p. 362); at the very end of the poem

> . . . Urthona rises from the ruinous Walls
> In all his ancient strength to form the golden armour of Science
> For intellectual War. The war of swords departed now,
> The dark Religions are departed & sweet Science reigns.
>
> (lines 852–5, K, p. 379.)

After the apocalyptic event, the weapons of war rise to their prelapsarian sources; the arts of death once more become arts of life. Brothers too imagines England's war machine as converted to peaceful purposes, in this case the settling and provisioning of Jerusalem:

. . . Ships of war of all nations may be converted to the necessary purposes of carriage: their thousands of unemployed water-casks will serve for beef-barrels; their cannon may be cast or beat into whatever articles are required; the musket-barrels, bayonets, and swords can easily be converted into plough-shares and reaping-hooks. Then will be fulfilled the prophecy of Micah in the 4th chapter and 3d verse relative to the approaching time of the world 'and he (meaning myself) shall judge among the people, and rebuke strong nations a far off; and they shall beat their swords into plough-shares; and their spears into reaping-hooks! nation shall not lift up sword against nation, nor shall they learn war any more.'[25]

The invasion of the French Republic by counter-revolutionary armies was of particular concern to Brothers, as it was to Blake. The King of Prussia, according to Brothers, was fulfilling the prophecy of Daniel, and 'when he entered France in 1792, the Proclamations which he issued at that time are full of *Blasphemy*

---

[24] *Letter to Miss Cott*, p. 122.
[25] Ibid., p. 123.

against God, presumption for his great Army, and violent threats, to destroy Cities, and cut innocent men in pieces'.[26]

> [Then Old Nobodaddy aloft
> Farted & belch'd & cough'd,
> And said, 'I love hanging & drawing & quartering
> 'Every bit as well as war & slaughtering.
> '(Damn praying & singing,
> 'Unless they will bring in
> 'The blood of ten thousand by fighting or swinging.' *del.*)
>
> Then he swore a great & solemn Oath:
> 'To kill the people I am loth,
> 'But if thy rebel, they must go to hell:
> 'They shall have a priest & a passing bell.' *del.*][27]

Both Blake and Brothers participate in a tradition in which the events of modern secular history are interpreted according to archetypal configurations found in the Bible, and these events are seen as having a particularly urgent meaning for the people of England, comprehending both 'unfallen' and 'fallen' possibilities. 'Thou shalt be called HEPZIBAH, and thy land Beulah', writes Brothers, applying Isaiah 62; 'For the Lord delights in thee, AND THY LAND SHALL BE MARRIED' (*Revealed Knowledge*, i. 19). Blake describes 'the Sleeping Man' as 'stretch'd on Albion's rocks . . . amidst his Twenty-eight / Cities, where Beulah lovely terminates in the hills & valleys of Albion . . .' (*J* 85. 24–6, K, p. 730). 'England is the spiritual Egypt' (*Revealed Knowledge*, ii. 51). 'And they left the pendulous earth. / They called it Egypt, & left it' (*Book of Urizen* 28. 21–2, K, p. 237). '"And the Lord will utterly destroy *the tongue of the Egyptian Sea*"' (*Revealed Knowledge*, ii. 51, citing Isa. 11: 15); the brain of the Covering Cherub 'incloses a reflexion / Of Eden all perverted: Egypt on the Gihon many tongued' (*J* 89. 14–15, K, p. 734). Brothers frequently uses Biblical prophecies about Edom as cautionary remonstrances to an aggressor nation: '"Egypt shall be a desolation, and Edom a desolate wilderness, for their violence against the children of Judah, and for shedding their innocent blood in the land"' (*Revealed Knowledge*, i. 32, from Joel 3: 19). In *Jerusalem* Albion asks Jesus: '"O Lord, what can I do? my selfhood cruel / Marches against thee, deceitful, from Sinai & from Edom / Into the wilderness of Judah, to meet thee in his pride"' (96. 8–10, K, p. 743). Again, both envision the imminent manifestation of Elijah in a new form. Brothers thought the prophet would shortly be revealed to the Hebrews to order their return to Jerusalem—'He will

---

[26] *A Revealed Knowledge*, ii. 32.

[27] Notebook, K, p. 185. For a detailed discussion of this poem, commonly known as 'Fayette', see Erdman, *Blake: Prophet*, pp. 182–8.

possess the spirit of God, and the power of fire, equal to Elijah' (*Revealed Knowledge*, i. 39). In *Jerusalem* this power is delegated to Los by the Divine Family:

> And feeling the damps of death, they with one accord delegated Los,
> Conjuring him by the Highest that he should watch over them
> Till Jesus shall appear; & they gave their power to Los
> Naming him the Spirit of Prophecy, calling him Elijah.
>
> (44 [39]. 28–31, K, p. 674.)

Among other resemblances are attacks upon a warmongering clergy which participates in public prayers 'Beseeching God to go forth with Fleets and Armies' (*Revealed Knowledge*, ii. 87).

> . . . The Prester Serpent runs
> Along the ranks, crying, 'Listen to the Priest of God, ye warriors:
> 'This Cowl upon my head he plac'd in times of Everlasting,
> 'And said, Go forth & guide my battles. . . .'
>
> (*The Four Zoas*, viib, 113–16, K, pp. 335–6.)

Brothers's vindication of the imprisoned reformers in 1794 (*Revealed Knowledge*, i. 39), his vision of the Treasury 'covered with thick darkness' (i. 19), his prediction of the annihilation of the English government, civil and ecclesiastical (ii. 91)—all these show how close in spirit he and Blake are at times. Most striking of all, perhaps, is the apocalyptic vision of each, involving the application of Biblical eschatology to the political world of the mid 1790s. Brothers says that Death on a pale horse in Rev. 6 *'relates to the present War—its progress—and* consequences; and its *destruction by the woeful, but just judgement of an offended God'* (*Revealed Knowledge*, ii. 84). In Blake's painting *Death on a Pale Horse*, virtually the same comment is made; here, as David Bindman remarks, 'Death is depicted as a king in armour, of the type of Urizen in the prophetic books of the Lambeth period . . . a warlike destructive tyrant.'[28] Just as Blake's prophetic writings lead to an apocalyptic Day of Wrath,[29] so Brothers says 'Therefore I warn all people in all nations—that the Terrible Day of the Lord—alluded to is nigh; it is not the Day of universal Judgment, but the Day which is to burn like an Oven, and which is to consume the wicked from the face of the Earth, like the Stubble of the Field' (*Revealed Knowledge*, ii. 83). Drawing on the same apocalyptic sources, Blake envisages the burning away of corrupt institutions followed by the regeneration of man's fallen Zoas:

> The books of Urizen unroll with dreadful noise; the folding Serpent
> Of Orc began to Consume in fierce raving fire; his fierce flames
> Issu'd on all sides, gathering strength in animating volumes,
>
> .   .   .   .

---

[28] *William Blake: Catalogue of the Fitzwilliam Museum, Cambridge*, Cambridge, 1970, p. 24 (Plate 11).

[29] See M. D. Paley, *Energy and the Imagination: A Study of the Development of Blake's Thought*, Clarendon Press, Oxford, 1970.

The morning dawn'd. Urizen rose, & in his hand the Flail
Sounds on the Floor, heard terrible by all the heavens.
Dismal loud redounding, the nether floor shakes with the sound,
And all the nations were threshed out, & the stars thresh'd from their husks.

(The Four Zoas, ix. 33–6, 650–3, K, pp. 358, 374.)

What is envisioned in these apocalypses is not the end of human existence but the end of human existence as we have known it, a transition to a new mode of being.

Yet, despite the common ground occupied by Blake and Brothers in the millenarian tradition—and we have yet to discuss one further parallel—there is ultimately a contrast to be made between them. The difference lies in their conception of the prophetic function. Brothers's is literal. He did believe he was the Nephew of the Almighty who would lead the Hebrews, 'visible' and 'invisible' (the latter referring to the vast number of people who, unknown to themselves, were descended from the Ten Lost Tribes) back to Jerusalem. He also attempted to predict the future in precisely the sense Blake denied a prophet could do: 'Every honest man is a Prophet; he utters his opinion both of private & public matters. Thus: if you go on So, the result is So. He never says, such a thing will happen let you do what you will. A Prophet is a Seer, not an arbitrary dictator' (Annotations to Watson, K, p. 392). Like all famous soothsayers, Brothers was sometimes astonishingly successful; for example, he had a vision of the throne of Sweden standing empty in 1792, and later that year the king was assassinated (*A Revealed Knowledge*, ii. 59). However, when his millennial prophecies failed to materialize, he lost the attention of the public. Again, for Blake the idea of having a special relationship to God, whether Son or Nephew, is 'Druidic'; Blake told Henry Crabb Robinson that Jesus 'is the only God' but then added 'And so am I and so are you.'[30] '"Thou art a Man"', says Blake's Jesus, '"God is no more, / Thy own humanity learn to adore"' ('The Everlasting Gospel', K, p. 752). This fundamental difference, as well as some attendant similarities, is best illustrated by considering the idea of Jerusalem in the works of each.

Blake can hardly have been unaware that in the years in which he was beginning to work on his own *Jerusalem*,[31] Richard Brothers published *A Description of Jerusalem* (London, 1801 [1802]) and *A Letter to the Subscribers for Engraving the Plans of Jerusalem, the King's Palace, the Private Palaces, College-Halls, Cathedrals, and Parliament-Houses* (London, 1805). The first of these was illustrated with engravings of the plans of the projected city. Most of the engravings are unsigned, but the 'Plan of the Holy City the New Jerusalem' (Plate 68) is signed 'Lowry Sc'

---

[30] Henry Crabb Robinson, in Bentley, *Records*, pp. 539–40.

[31] It is difficult to say when *Jerusalem* was begun, for although the title-page bears the date 1804 and some proof plates watermarked 1802 exist, much of the work seems to have been executed after these dates. Keynes remarks that 'none of the extant copies of the book can have been printed before 1818, the earliest date which appears in the watermarks of the paper used' ('New Lines from *Jerusalem*', *Blake Studies*, p. 115). Erdman suggests that the date 1804 may mark the division of 'the Grand Poem' into two—*Milton* and *Jerusalem* (E, p. 727).

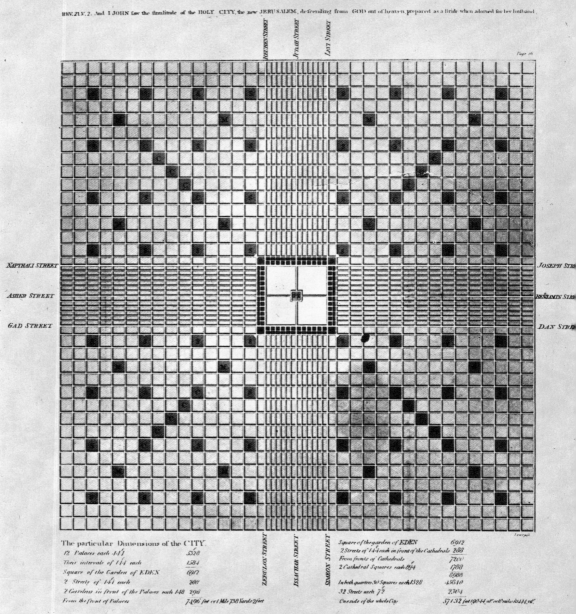

68. [Wilson?] Lowry: *Plan of the Holy City the New Jerusalem.*
Engraving for Richard Brothers, *A Description of Jerusalem.*
Edinburgh University Library

and is quite possibly by Wilson Lowry, whose portrait Blake was to engrave with John Linnell some two decades later.[32] (No other Lowry is recorded as a working engraver in London at this time, and Wilson Lowry specialized in architectural and mechanical subjects.) Only about half of *A Description* is devoted to the new Jerusalem, much of the rest being given over to an attack upon one of Blake's favourite villains in surprisingly Blakean terms: 'the great Sir Isaac Newton', whose calculations Brothers compares to 'the Babylonian priests that made a wonder of every lie they told, and of every fraud they committed, the better to secure the sanctity of their dragon, and conceal the fraudulent mysteries of their religion' (pp. 77, 130). Of course the most interesting aspect of both books is the model of Jerusalem, especially when we compare it to Golgonooza, Blake's spiritual fourfold London.

Just as Blake in his later writings affirms the precedence of Hebrew over classical art, so Brothers declares 'The Greeks were not sufficiently civilized to study the fine arts of sculpture, painting, etc., etc. until about 200 years after Solomon's reign'; the orders of classical architecture 'were copied from the buildings of Solomon' (*A Description*, p. 69). As for the temple itself, 'The regularity of Solomon's temple, in all its parts, is not to be equalled by any structure of similar designation in the world' (*A Description*, p. 50). The new Jerusalem will likewise be perfect because built according to Biblical specifications. Brothers's sources here are principally the same as Blake's—Revelation and Ezekiel. 'St. John in the 21st chapter of the Revelation, on seeing its similitude shewn him in a vision, says with pleasure & amazement in the 10th verse, "And then he shewed me that great city, the holy Jerusalem, descending out of heaven from God, having the glory of God, and her light was like unto a stone most precious"' (*A Description*, p. 42). Los, as he watches the Furnaces, sings: '"I see thy Form, O lovely mild Jerusalem, Wing'd with Six Wings / . . . Thy Bosom white, translucent, cover'd with immortal gems / . . . I see the New Jerusalem descending out of Heaven, / Between thy wings . . ."' (*J* 86. 1, 14, 19–20, K, pp. 730–1). Ezekiel provides the structural plan, though Brothers notes 'The measures I have reduced to the English standard, which, in future, shall become the Hebrew':

The form is planned by God himself; and as he has ordained the government shall be in a king. . . . His residence will be a noble palace, on the north side of the great central square that incloses the park, or Garden of Eden, for the public to walk in. The square is formed by a range of twelve private palaces on each side, including the king's, which makes forty-eight in all. Each palace is 444 feet long, with a space of 144 feet between each; to every one is a lawn in front, and behind is a spacious garden. What a noble square to excite admiration! Each side of it is near a mile and a half in length! Such is to

[32] See 'Wilson Lowry', reproduced in Keynes, *Engravings of William Blake*, Emery Walker, Dublin, 1956, Plate 44.

be the centre of the future Jerusalem, and round it the city is to be built.—The plan is divine.—It is glorious! The form is elegant, and fashioned so as to ensure health for its people. The palaces are to be built with stone, as are the other eminent structures either for residence, worship, or public business. I have delineated the whole under God's direction, as he ordered to be laid down about 2,360 years ago, in the last nine chapters of Ezekiel (*A Letter*, pp. 18–19).

Blake renders Ezekiel's vision according to his own symbolism:

> These are the four Faces towards the Four Worlds of Humanity
> In every Man. Ezekiel saw them by Chebar's flood.
> And the Eyes are the South, and the Nostrils are the East,
> And the tongue is the West, and the Ear is the North.
>
> .   .   .   .
>
> And every part of the City is fourfold; & every inhabitant, fourfold.
> And every pot & vessel & garment & utensil of the houses,
> And every house, fourfold; but the third gate in every one
> Is clos'd as with a threefold curtain of ivory & fine linen & ermine.
> And Luban stands in the middle of the City; a moat of fire
> Surrounds Luban, Los's Palace & the golden Looms of Cathedron.
>
> (*J* 12. 57–60, 13. 20–5, K, pp. 632, 633.)

In both instances, this city is the place where the millennial prophecies of the Bible are to be fulfilled. Blake says 'JERUSALEM IS NAMED LIBERTY / AMONG THE SONS OF ALBION' (K, p. 649); Brothers writes:

It shall be the land of true liberty! And no man in it shall say with justice that he was ever oppressed by the government through the influence of the Prince, or that he was wronged by the judge through the influence of the government. . . . Where the balance is even in any cause, the prince shall lose rather than the poor man. Honour is out of the question; his true dignity lies in being above captious trifles; it must always be shown in criminal matters too, in causing justice to be directed by the mild rule of humanity, instead of the iron one, of biting and oppressing . . . (*A Letter*, p. 41).

Brothers's plan of the new Jerusalem is, in one aspect, a beatific vision of a city as it might have been laid out by a heavenly town-planner of the period.

Look at London or Paris [he complains], those two great and wealthy cities, there are no such regular streets in either, or healthy accommodations as in ours. Their streets in general are narrow, and very crooked, their houses in many parts are confusedly crowded together, some high, some low, and very few with gardens except those of the most wealthy men. But with us every house throughout the city has its regular portion of ground for a garden, where the poorest families may walk and enjoy themselves—where their children may play in safety, to acquire daily fresh health and strength (*A Description*, p. 34).

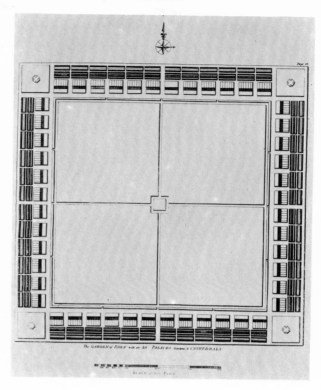

69. [Anon.] *The Garden of Eden with its 48 Palaces Gardens & Cathedrals.*
Engraving for Richard Brothers, *A Description of Jerusalem.* **Edinburgh University Library**

This idea of the perfect city is to some extent indebted to such plans as those of Samuel Pepys Cockerell, who proposed the building of Mecklenburgh Square and Brunswick Square in 1790, and the planners of the New Town of Edinburgh.[33]

Other buildings of a similar form exactly, are to be on each side of the other three squares for the Treasury and Mint, national Bank, Courts of Law, Registry, and for all other necessary uses. This one form is sufficient to be directed by; and the two in each square, instead of meeting at a point, or close to the angle of it, are to leave an opening between them into the square of 330 feet.—What a grand view from such a square to the Cathedral! And what a fine one also from the Cathedral into such a square! (*A Letter*, p. 36).

The central square is, of course, the Garden of Eden (see Plate 69), and 'All people, poor and rich, foreigner and native, who are in a cleanly dress, are always to have liberty to walk or sit in the garden' (*A Description*, p. 40). Blake's spiritual fourfold

[33] See John Summerson, *Georgian London*, rev. ed., Penguin Books, Harmondsworth, 1962, pp. 167–8; A. J. Youngson, *The Making of Classical Edinburgh, 1750–1840*, Edinburgh University Press, Edinburgh, 1966.

London is also imagined in architectural terms; it is the work of 'golden Builders', a city where

> Pancrass & Kentish-town repose
> Among her golden pillars high,
>   Among her golden arches which
> Shine upon the starry sky.   (*J* 27, K, p. 650.)

True to the spirit of the time, water-related amenities are provided even in millennial cities.

Had I my choice [says Brothers], on both sides of the Jordan, and near the lake, should be the place to build the future Jeursalem [*sic*]; for it is there that God and my understanding points as the most eligible place. On the lake, the gilded yatch [*sic*], with her colours proudly waving in the wind, might sail about with company, while elegant carriages filled with beauty lined the water side! I mention these things on purpose, that it may not be imagined the Hebrews on being restored are to become drones immediately after, like slothful hermits in a cave; nothing of the kind;—that must be the land of rejoicing (*A Letter*, pp. 39–40).

When the 'Mighty Temple' of Urizen is built in *Jerusalem*,

> Jordan sprang beneath its threshold, bubbling from beneath
> Its pillars: Euphrates ran under its arches: white sails
> And silver oars reflect on its pillars & sound on its ecchoing
> Pavements . . .   (58. 23–6, K, p. 690.)

So important is the idea of the building of Jerusalem to both that even a satire on this aspect of Brothers can remind us of Blake. One adversary, claiming to speak on behalf of the Jewish people, says that if Brothers were to perform a miracle such as walking on the Thames, 'We would all heart and hand, join you in the re-establishment of Jerusalem.'[34]

> In my Exchanges every Land
> Shall walk, & mine in every Land,
>   Mutual shall build Jerusalem,
> Both heart in heart & hand in hand.   (*J* 27, K, p. 652.)

Yet, again, despite the interesting similarities between Blake and Brothers, there is a fundamental difference in the mode of their conceptions. It is this that points up the distinction between them most poignantly. Brothers's Jerusalem remains an unrealized fantasy; lacking symbolic extension, it now lacks meaning except as a record of failed aspiration. In contrast Golgonooza, 'Continually build-

---

[34] Moses Gomez Pereira [pseud.?], *The Jew's Appeal on the Divine Mission of Richard Brothers and N. B. Halhed, Esq.*, London, 1795, p. 35.

ing & continually decaying desolate' (*J* 53. 19, K, p. 684) is a mental model of human reality. It is not tied down to literal predictions; rather it is what Blake calls a 'divine analogy'. What is unique about Blake's conception can be seen in the directions he gives to the builders:

> What are those golden builders doing? where was the burying-place
> Of soft Ethinthus? near Tyburn's fatal Tree? is that
> Mild Zion hill's most ancient promontory, near mournful
> Ever weeping Paddington? is that Calvary and Golgotha
> Become a building of pity and compassion? Lo!
> The stones are pity, and the bricks, well wrought affections
> Enamel'd with love & kindness & the tiles engraven gold,
> Labour of merciful hands: the beams & rafters are forgiveness:
> The mortar & cement of the work, tears of honesty: the nails
> And the screws & iron braces are well wrought blandishments
> And well contrived words, firm fixing, never forgotten,
> Always comforting the remembrance: the floors, humility:
> The cielings, devotion: the hearths, thanksgiving.
> Prepare the furniture, O Lambeth, in thy pitying looms,
> The curtains, woven tears & sighs wrought into lovely forms
> For comfort; there the secret furniture of Jerusalem's chamber
> Is wrought. Lambeth! the Bride, the Lamb's Wife, loveth thee.
>
> (*J* 12. 25–41, K, p. 632.)

It has been observed[35] that this passage (particularly the first twelve lines) is closely related to George Herbert's poem 'The Church-Floor':

> Mark you the floor? that square and speckled stone
> Which looks so firm and strong,
> Is Patience:
>
> And the other black and grave, wherewith each one
> Is checker'd all along,
> Humility:
>
> The gentle rising, which on either hand
> Leads to the quire above,
> Is Confidence:
>
> But the sweet cement, which in one sure band
> Ties the whole frame, is Love
> And Charity.[36]

What Blake has done in the *Jerusalem* 12 passage is a typical instance of the way

---

[35] By Harold Bloom, in E, p. 847.   [36] *The Temple*, London, 1844, p. 61.

his imagination works: he has applied Herbert's allegorical method but with a difference, embedding the allegory in actual building projects going on in early nineteenth-century London—excavation for new houses in Paddington, the consequent digging up of the bones of criminals executed at Tyburn,[37] the construction of an as-yet-to-be-identified house of mercy. Blake's habit of mind is to raise the perception of such details to a perception of the archetypes behind them. Here the subject is the 'terrible eternal labour' (*J* 12. 24) of building Golgonooza, of rendering human values concrete in the ultimate community. While it is true that this city can be represented in diagrammatic form,[38] such a diagram, unlike Brothers's ground-plans, is merely an aid to the imagination. 'Places' such as Cathedron and the Gate of Luban are not conceived as existing literally; they are symbols which are defined elsewhere in *Jerusalem* and in *Milton* and *The Four Zoas* as well.[39] London is 'a Human awful wonder of God', saying:

> 'My Streets are my Ideas of Imagination.
> 'Awake, Albion, awake! and let us wake up together.
> 'My Houses are Thoughts: my Inhabitants, Affections,
> 'The children of my thoughts walking within my blood-vessels. . . .'

> (*J* 38 [34]. 31–4, K, p. 665.)

The awakening of mankind in a regenerate community is as compelling in meaning today as it was when these lines were written. In the end, Tatham was right, despite the limitations of his own view: Brothers and Blake must not be placed together.

2

Joanna Southcott[40] (1750–1814) was a figure of a different cast from Richard Brothers. The Southcottian gospel is a type of salvation cult centring around a maternal virgin who eventually decided she was with child by the Holy Ghost. One may agree in a sense with E. P. Thompson's statement that 'authentic millenarialism ends in the later 1790s with the defeat of English Jacobinism, the onset of the Wars, and the confining of Richard Brothers in a madhouse'.[41] The Southcottians display little of the social fervour of the Brothers movement, and

---

[37] See Erdman, *Blake: Prophet*, p. 474; Michael J. Tolley, '*Jerusalem* 12: 25–29—Some Questions Answered', *Blake Newsletter*, iv (1970). A somewhat different interpretation of the building passages in *Jerusalem*, positing a relatively late date of composition, is advanced by Stanley Gardner, *Blake*, Evans Bros., London, 1968, pp. 142–3.

[38] S. Foster Damon, *A Blake Dictionary*, Brown University Press, Providence, R.I., 1965, p. 163. As Damon remarks, 'Golgonooza, being four-dimensional, cannot be reduced to a chart of three dimensions.'

[39] See M. D. Paley, 'The Figure of the Garment in *The Four Zoas*, *Milton*, and *Jerusalem*', in *Blake's Sublime Allegory*, ed. S. Curran and J. Wittreich, University of Wisconsin Press, Madison, 1973, pp. 119–39.

[40] See *D.N.B.*, s.v.; Ronald Matthews, *English Messiahs*, Methuen, London, 1936; G. R. Balleine, *Past Finding Out*, S.P.C.K., London, 1956.

[41] E. P. Thompson, *The Making of the English Working Class*, rev. ed., Penguin Books, Harmondsworth, 1968, p. 420.

Joanna's characteristic tone is often more petulant than prophetic. Still, if we take the term in a neutral sense, Southcott and her followers were millenarians: they believed the Millennium was about to come, and this belief was a central article of their faith. The Southcottian movement seems as appropriate in spirit to the early nineteenth century as Brothers was to the late eighteenth, the latter never losing an essential social optimism, the former withdrawing from the secular realm in order to spread the good news of an impending miracle.

Southcott was a farmer's daughter from Devonshire who, after a period of Methodism, began her career as a public prophetess with *The Strange Effects of Faith*, Exeter, 1801. She moved to London in 1802, and for a short time her following and Brothers's overlapped. Like Brothers, she drew heavily on the Book of Revelation, in her case to the extent of issuing seals of salvation to the faithful. (Estimates of the number sealed from 1802 to 1808 vary from ten thousand to one hundred thousand.) She and Brothers broke on doctrinal grounds in 1802, after Brothers asserted that the sealing in Revelation 'is only a metaphorical term', not referring to 'an artificial seal or the signing of names on paper', and that 'Besides, the 2nd verse of the 7th chapter says it's a HE, *not a She*.'[42] The South-cottians were especially discomfited by Brothers's view that there was no allegorical meaning to the seed of Eve in Genesis 3: 15, a passage which Joanna took as a prophecy referring to herself. The divine voice reassured her that Brothers's book 'was written under the influence of the Devil'; as for Genesis 3: 15,

> You know the Woman's seed must conquer all,
> Or else to My Bible you must give the Lie
> From first to last, and hear what John did say
> The SPIRIT and the BRIDE do bid you come.[43]

Among the former followers of Brothers who adhered to Southcott was William Sharp. Sharp, who remained a member of Joanna's inner circle until her death in 1814, wrote letters on her behalf, published pamphlets in her defence, and engraved her portrait (Plate 70). (Ironically, one thousand copies of his portrait engraving of Brothers with Sharp's declaration of faith were defaced by the Southcottians in 1806.) And he attempted to convert William Blake, as Henry Crabb Robinson reported after a conversation with John Flaxman:

He related some curious anecdotes of *Sharpe* the Engraver who seems the ready dupe of any and every religious fanatic & imposter who offers himself . . . Sh: tho' deceived by Brothers became a warm partisan of Joanna Southcoat [after June 1795]—He endeavoured to make a convert of Blake the engraver but as Fl: judiciously observed, such men as Blake are not fond of playing the second fiddle—Hence Blake himself a seer of visions

---

[42] 'A Dissertation on the Fall of Eve', in *A Letter to His Majesty and One to Her Majesty*, London, 1802, p. 64.
[43] *A Communication Given to Joanna In Answer To Mr. Brothers' Last Book*, London, 1802, pp. 16, 13.

Isaiah Ch. LXV & LXVI.   JOANNA SOUTHCOTT.   Jan.ʸ 1812.

Drawn and Engraved from life by Wᵐ Sharp.   Published by Jane Townley London.

Published according to Act of Parliament Jan.ʸ 12ᵗ 1812 by Jane Townley London.

70. William Sharp: *Joanna Southcott*. Engraving.

& a dreamer of dreams wo^d not do homage to a rival claimant of the privilege of prophecy—[44]

Blake may also have been subjected to the proselytizing of one other ardent South-cottian, his friend William Owen Pughe. Robert Southey, to whom Blake showed 'a perfectly mad poem called Jerusalem'[45] in 1811, says that Blake's *Descriptive Catalogue* passage about *The Ancient Britons* 'begins with a translation from the Welsh, supplied to him no doubt by that good simple-hearted, Welsh-headed man, William Owen, whose memory is the great storehouse of all Cymric tradition and lore of every kind'.[46] Elsewhere Southey gets his chronology confused, saying:

> My old acquaintance William Owen, now William Owen Pughe . . . found our Blake after the death of Joanna Southcote, one of whose four-and-twenty elders he was. Poor Owen found everything which he wished to find in the Bardic system, and there he found Blake's notions, and thus Blake and his wife were persuaded that his dreams were old patriarchal truths, long forgotten, and now re-revealed.[47]

Southey appears to have been right about the source of Blake's triad, which has been identified as the *Myrvian Achailogy*: according to Damon, 'Blake's friend . . . Pughe . . . who did most of the work on the *Archailogy*, was obviously the person who called Blake's attention to this passage.'[48] However, as the *Descriptive Catalogue* was published in 1809, it is clear that Blake and William Owen Pughe must have been acquainted years before Southcott's death, while Pughe was a disciple. Blake, then, had more than ample opportunity to hear of 'the woman clothed with the sun'.[49]

As in the instance of Brothers, one can find numerous resemblances between Southcott's millenarianism and Blake's. 'Is Jerusalem new-built?'[50] she asks, arguing for the continued existence of prophecy. The voice which inspires her dictates: '"When I my people do redeem / . . . Your houses I shall build anew / And palaces bring to your view; / . . . I've gold of ophir that shall come / To build Jerusalem up again."'[51] Our Redeemer 'will come riding in the chariot of his everlasting Gospel'.[52] Inspired by her prophecies, one of Southcott's 'Examiners' writes, 'Behold from Edom I appear with garments dipped in blood.'[53] In one of her own doggerel conversations with the spirit, Joanna exclaims 'Return, return,

[44] Bentley, *Records*, p. 235.
[45] Ibid., p. 229. This must have been a fragmentary version of the poem.
[46] Ibid., p. 226.
[47] Ibid., p. 399. Bentley, p. 400, comments that 'Southey's chronology is worthless'.
[48] *Blake Dictionary*, p. 443. The *Myrvian Archailogy* was published 1801–7.
[49] As Southcott frequently refers to herself; see for example her *Song of Moses and the Lamb*, London, 1804.
[50] *A Continuation of Prophecies*, Exeter, 1802, p. 50.
[51] Ibid., p. 15.
[52] *The Strange Effects of Faith; with Remarkable Prophecies*, Exeter, 1801, p. 29.
[53] *A Continuation*, p. 49.

oh! England / Return without delay / . . . And therefore I once more must try, / Oh, England now return!'[54] Blake in *Jerusalem* exhorts 'England! awake! awake! awake!' (K, p. 718) and 'Return, Jerusalem, & dwell together as of old! Return, / Return, O Albion!' (72. 34–5, K, p. 712). The account of inspiration given by each is strangely similar:

> This theme calls me in sleep night after night, & ev'ry morn
> Awakes me at sun-rise; then I see the Saviour over me
> Spreading his beams of love and dictating the words of this mild song.
>
> (*J* 4. 3–5, K, p. 622.)

I am awaked every morning between three and four o'clock; I sit up in my bed till the day breaks; and have communication given to me as soon as I awake.[55]

In 1803, at one of her 'trials', Southcott had her writings put on a table in a box tied with a cord. A little boy, 'Foley's son', was placed on the box; the Spirit 'ordered the cord to be cut, and to be cut in pieces . . . As they had cut the cord so would nations be cut . . . like the cord, the nation was cut in pieces, and the Jews scattered. . . .'[56] In *Jerusalem* 'the Four Sons of Los / Stand round him cutting the Fibres from Albion's hills / That Albion's Sons may roll apart over the Nations' (15. 22–4, K, p. 636). Contrastingly, the Spirit tells Joanna 'with cords of love have I drawn thee',[57] and the Saviour speaks to Blake of 'Fibers of love from man to man thro' Albion's pleasant land' (*J* 4. 8, K, p. 622). Again, as in the case of Brothers, a hostile parody of Southcott can sound almost astonishingly Blakean; Southey's resembles a pastiche of Blake's own writings.

'Thou knowest', he [Satan] says, 'it is written of God he is a consuming fire, and who can dwell in everlasting burnings? Our backs are not brass, nor our sinews iron, to dwell with God in Heaven. The Heaven therefore which men mistakingly desire, is in its very nature the very Hell of which they are themselves so much afraid; and it is sufficient proof of the truth of all this, that the Devil invites them to make themselves happy and lead a gay life, agreeably to his own cheerful disposition, whereas religion enjoins self-denial, penitence, and all things which are contrary to our natural inclinations.'[58]

> 'Why will you die, O Eternals?
> 'Why live in unquenchable burnings?'[59]

It indeed appear'd to Reason as if Desire was cast out; but the Devil's account is, that the Messiah fell, & formed a heaven out of what he stole from the abyss.[60]

---

[54] *The Book of Wonders, Marvellous and True*, London, 1813, pp. 83–4.

[55] *The Second Book of Wonders, More Marvellous than the First*, London, 1813, p. 3.

[56] *The Third Book of Wonders, announcing the coming of Shiloh, with a call to the Hebrew from Isaiah xi*, London, 1814, pp. 23–4. [57] Ibid., p. 45.

[58] 'Account of Joanna Southcott', *Letters from England by Don Manuel Alvarez Espriella*, 2nd ed., London, 1808, iii. 252–3. [59] *Book of Urizen*, 4. 12–13, K, p. 224 (Urizen speaks). [60] *MHH*, K, p. 150.

God out of Christ is a Consuming Fire.[61]

> 'Are these not the places of religion, the rewards of continence,
> 'The self enjoyings of self denial? why dost thou seek religion?'[62]

Flaxman maliciously insinuated that Blake resisted Sharp's indoctrination because one visionary would not play second fiddle to another.[63] Actually, we know why Blake could not accept Southcott as a genuine visionary: the evidence is in his epigram 'On the Virginity of the Virgin Mary & Johanna Southcott':

> Whate'er is done to her she cannot know,
> And if you'll ask her she will [tell you *del.*] swear it so.
> Whether 'tis good or evil none's to blame:
> No one can take the pride, no one the shame.

> (Note-book, K, p. 418.)

Blake's hostility derives from his lifelong opposition to the doctrine of the Virgin Birth, with its concomitant elevation of celibacy and denial of the erotic. His heroine Oothoon, though her 'virgin mantle' has been torn by the tyrannical Bromion, declares herself nevertheless 'a virgin fill'd with virgin fancies' in *Visions of the Daughters of Albion* (K, pp. 189, 194); the rebel Orc declares ironically that 'pale religious le[t]chery, seeking Virginity, / May find it in a harlot' (*America*, K, p. 199). To Blake true virginity is an inner attitude of innocence not to be confused with evading experience. The worship of literal virginity is the worship of 'Babylon the City of Vala, the Goddess Virgin-Mother' (*J* 18: 29, K, p. 640). This very doctrine was introduced in a new form by Joanna Southcott.

It was not until her *Third Book of Wonders* (1814) that Joanna Southcott announced to the world that she was indeed the virgin who was to give birth to the new Messiah, Shiloh. However, her earlier writings are full of veiled predictions which her followers were not slow to apply. (Sharp said he had bought the flannel for the accouchement fifteen years before the event.)[64] There is a certain disingenuousness in her statements on the subject: 'Yet I marvelled, how the 12th chapter of Revelations could be fulfilled, of the woman traveling in birth, and longing to be delivered. . . .'[65] In her first *Book of Wonders* (1813), she began to apply her earlier prophecies to herself, discovering with surprise that she herself was the woman. Precisely the parallel made in Blake's epigram is drawn, though

---

[61] From the inscriptions on the pictorial epitome of Hervey's *Meditations Among the Tombs* (Tate Gallery).

[62] *VDA* 7. 8–9 (Oothoon speaks).

[63] As Bentley notes, Robinson had not yet met Blake personally when this conversation was set down in 1815, and he later wrote 'I doubt whether Flaxman sufficiently tolerates Blake' (Bentley, *Records*, p. 235).

[64] Richard Reece, M.D., *A Correct Statement of the Circumstances That Attended the Last Illness and Death of Mrs. Southcott*, London, 1815, pp. 83–4. Reece found Sharp 'a plain honest man, of deep thought and great research . . . fully prepossessed that the child would establish the Millennium . . .' (p. 80).

[65] *Strange Effects of Faith*, p. 15.

in a positive sense, by the 'voice' that addresses Joanna: 'I have spoken to thee, though not understood by thee, nor any of the believers, before my visitation came to thee in a manner that astonished thee, that in the like manner I was born of the Virgin Mary, as she was visited from on high, so thy visitation is now the same. . . .'[66]

This announcement caused an enormous sensation, and when in November 1814 it was rumoured that she had recanted the *Sunday Monitor* reported:

> If the dome of St. Paul's had fallen in, or a quarter of the Metropolis had been swallowed up by an earthquake, it is scarcely possible that the awful event could have occasioned more general conversation. In every street, alley, court and house, nothing was heard but the name of Southcott, coupled with expressions of astonishment, disappointment, or profane ridicule.[67]

Meanwhile, Joanna lay in confinement, attended only by women, and guarded by the inner circle of her followers. A crib had been built at the cost of £200 and was displayed to large crowds in the shop in the window of its maker, Seddens of Aldergate Street; and the Temple of Peace in Green Park had been offered as a dwelling by a 'great personage'.[68] A number of doctors had visited her, and though she would not submit to a thorough examination, some of the medical men were astonished to find signs of pregnancy in a woman of sixty-five. Perhaps the most reliable of these witnesses was Dr. Richard Reece, who maintained an attitude of disinterested objectivity throughout. Reece wrote:

> The appearance of her breasts on inspection astonished me. They exhibited the picture of a young woman in the seventh month of pregnancy, being equally full, plump, and expanded. This fulness, on a close examination, consisted also of a real enlargement of the mammary glands, that part peculiarly destined for the secretion of milk. There was no appearance of disease or tendency to irregular enlargement, morbid hardness, or schirrosity. All was apparently healthy. The nipples also were elongated, but the skin around the areola or disk was not so red or so clearly marked as in common cases of pregnancy, circumstances which I considered as connected with her age, and with that scaly surface which is apt to cover it at an advanced period in life. . . .
>
> . . . I was next permitted to examine her belly. Here I discovered an alteration equally conspicuous and striking. In that part occupied by the womb, where its expansion equals what takes place in the seventh month of pregnancy, I felt a hard circumscribed tumor, not less than the size of a man's head, bearing the shape of the womb, and on tracing its edges round, I had no doubt of its being really the enlargement of that organ. It was peculiarly hard to the feel, and, she declared, acutely painful on the slightest pressure. This circumstance I attributed to the rigidity of fibre necessarily attendant on age. . . .

[66] *The Fourth Book of Wonders Being the Answer of the Lord to the Hebrews*, London, 1814, p. 38.
[67] 6 Nov. 1814 (from British Museum file of newspaper clippings 698/C 27).
[68] See Matthews, op. cit., p. 72; *D.N.B.*, xviii, p. 607.

I was allowed to keep my hand over the belly for the space of ten minutes, but in this time I felt no motion of a child, upon which she observed that it was always very quiet in the presence of a stranger in the room, but particularly troublesome and active when she took food. The experiment was accordingly tried, and on Mrs. Underwood putting a piece of a peach in her mouth, which she began to masticate, I felt something move under my hand, possessing a kind of undulating motion, and appearing and disappearing in the same manner as a foetus. The integuments or coverings of the belly I had occasion to observe were very flaccid; but this I considered as the natural effect of age.[69]

Although he was pilloried by caricaturists such as Cruikshank and Williams,[70] Dr. Reece never insinuated any belief in Joanna Southcott's prophetic role but confined his interest to the medical aspects of the case. Gradually, he became less convinced of the possibility of pregnancy (indeed, he decided after her death that she must have been a conscious fraud). Joanna was urged by another surgeon to submit to a complete examination, but she refused, saying 'that if she was not pregnant with a *human being*, there was some *living creature* within her . . .' (*The Times*, 2 Jan. 1815). On 25 December 1814 Joanna cried that the Child was making its way through her side. She died on 27 December.

Joanna Southcott had directed that her body be kept warm for four days; her followers, temporarily cheered by news of the end of the war with America, waited vainly for a resurrection. Dr. Reece, despite his impatience, had to wait until 31 December before an autopsy could be conducted.

On exposing the belly, it appeared much distended with air, which was evidently the consequence of putrefaction after death. . . . On dividing the teguments there was a considerable escape of putrid air, after which the contents of the cavity came into view. The first organ that immediately claimed attention was the womb, which contrary to all expectation was hid in the pelvis, and instead of being enlarged, appeared smaller than in the natural state. It was so small, I was obliged to introduce my hand into the pelvis, and to remove the whole contents, in order to bring it out for inspection. It was the size of a small pear. It was considered by the medical gentlemen present, as uncommonly small, but I thought not more so than what it ought to be in a virgin of sixty. On examining its substance, there appeared no mark of disease. . . . During the examination of the womb, a most interesting scene was presented. The believers were all on tiptoe to see Shiloh appear, and those who could not have a view themselves, were most anxiously making inquiries of the others. No promised child, however, appeared, which so confounded the rest that they gradually left the room abashed and dismayed. The state of the stomach was next examined . . . but the coats of this organ showed no sign of disease. On moving the liver, the gall-bladder was found full of calculi, or stones of a light colour,

[69] Reece, op. cit., pp. 8–10.
[70] For example, in 'The Imposter, or Obstetric Dispute' (Sept. 1814) and 'The Mock Delivery of Joanna!!!' (12 Dec. 1814), both by G. Cruikshank; and in 'Delivering a Prophetess' (1 Nov. 1814) by Williams, in which Reece is depicted examining the '*Living Water*' flowing from a tap hidden in Joanna's petticoats.

a proof they had been of long standing. The liver appeared dark and rather soft in its texture, which I considered to be the consequence of the disorganizing process taking place after death; it was not much enlarged. The mesentery was very much loaded with fat, and also the teguments of the belly.—The intestines were also distended with air . . . clearly the effect of a disengagement of air which had taken place since her dissolution. . . .

Thus on dissection of every part, no organic disease could be discovered to account for her death. . . .

The body was in so highly a putrid state, that it was thought unnecessary to examine the brain, where it was probable all the mischief lay, and which would have been discovered had the dissection taken place the day after her death. She certainly suffered from determination of blood to the head; and the sensations of giddiness and numbness of the extremities she experienced about a month before her dissolution, indicated compression of the brain from distension of blood vessels. When I saw her the day preceding her death, she was apoplectic, and in this state it may be said she died.[71]

One can understand the believers' dismay: there was, after all, to be no Millennium. 'Mr. Sharpe', according to Reece, 'was the only one that held out to the rest the balm of consolation. Life, he observed, was involved in mystery.'[72] (Ironically, one of the proofs Reece retrospectively found of Joanna's duplicity was the character revealed by Sharp's portrait engraving: 'Whoever accurately examines her portrait, as delineated by Mr. Sharpe, will perceive a certain archness of look about the eye, which tends to confirm this opinion.'[73]) Some of the most resolute of the faithful, however, maintained that an invisible Shiloh had made his way through Joanna's side. A Southcottian sect persists to this day and annually challenges the Bishops of the Church of England to open Joanna's box of sealed prophecies.

Joanna Southcott's attitude toward the Virgin Birth is precisely the opposite of Blake's. After hearing in 1797 that 'a dissenting minister had said, the Virgin Mary was a whore, and Our Saviour was a bastard', Joanna refuted 'this pernicious idea' in doggerel dictated by the divine spirit:

> I'll let them know with one accord,
> That I no *Bastard* did appear,
> My MOTHER no Adultress.[74]

Of course this is the very doctrine Blake promulgates in *The Everlasting Gospel*:

> Was Jesus Born of a Virgin Pure
> With narrow Soul & looks demure?
> If Jesus intended to take on Sin
> The Mother should have an Harlot been,
> Just such a one as Magdalen.   (K, p. 756, lines 1—5.)

[71] Reece, *A Correct Statement*, pp. 90—3.   [72] Ibid., p. 94.
[73] Ibid., p. 96. Joanna herself had regarded the Sharp portrait as an important proof of her identity, the divine voice having asked 'Will Sharp tell an imposter that he drew her likeness, if a woman, in any likeness of thee, should come forward?' (*Third Book of Wonders*, p. 55).   [74] *The Book of Wonders*, 1813, p. 62.

The contrast of true and false virginity is an important theme in *Jerusalem*, where Mary is set off against the would-be virgin mother, Gwendolen. Gwendolen pretends to have produced a man child unaided:

'Look! I have wrought without delusion. Look! I have wept,
'And given soft milk mingled together with the spirits of flocks
'Of lambs and doves, mingled together in cups and dishes
'Of painted clay; the mighty Hyle is become a weeping infant.'

(82. 5–8, K, p. 725.)

Holding 'A Falsehood' behind her loins, she addresses her sister Cambel, shown in the picture on plate 82 standing in the posture of the *Venus pudica*, one hand on her left breast, the other obscuring her genitals. Gwendolen continues:

'Look, Hyle is become an infant Love! look! behold! see him lie
'Upon my bosom; look! here is the lovely wayward form
'That gave me sweet delights by his torments beneath my Veil!'

(82. 37–9, K, p. 726.)

Triumphantly, 'She drew aside her Veil, from Mam-Tor to Dovedale' (line 45)—rock formations suggestive of the female breasts and vagina[75]—but she is no more able to produce an infant Love in this way than was Joanna Southcott. Despite Gwendolen's previous statement that 'Humanity is become / A weeping Infant in ruin'd lovely Jerusalem's folding Cloud' (81. 13–14, K, p. 724), all she produces is the monstrous worm pictured winding up the right hand margin of plate 82:

. . . She drew aside her Veil, from Mam-Tor to Dovedale,
Discovering her own perfect beauty to the Daughters of Albion
And Hyle a winding Worm beneath *her loom upon the scales*
Hyle was become a winding Worm & not a weeping Infant
Trembling & pitying she scream'd & fled upon the wind.
Hyle was a winding Worm and herself perfect in beauty.
The deserts tremble at his wrath, they shrink themselves in fear.

(82. 45–51, K, p. 726.)

Contrasting to this episode is that of Joseph and Mary on plate 61. It is interesting that both this plate and plate 82 display peculiarities that suggest afterthought on Blake's part. Plate 61 is clearly an insertion, the speech at the end of 60 being continued on 62, with the script of 61 being considerably larger and more flowery than that of 60 and 62. Plate 82, Erdman says, 'was prepared in a condition of unusual haste, or inattention, or illness'[76]—some of the evidence can be seen in

---

[75] See Damon, *Blake Dictionary*, p. 107.

[76] 'The Suppressed and Altered Passages in Blake's *Jerusalem*', *Studies in Bibliography*, xvii (1964), 31. The later the date of etching, of course, the more likely that the plate was put into final form after Joanna Southcott's death.

the two deleted half-lines in the passage quoted above. It seems at least possible that 61 and 82 are meant to counterpoise each other. Mary does not deny that she is 'a Harlot & an Adultress' (line 6), but she obtains forgiveness from Joseph, who has heard God's voice say:

'"There is none that liveth & Sinneth not! And this is the Covenant
'"Of Jehovah: If you Forgive one-another, so shall Jehovah Forgive You,
'"That He Himself may Dwell among You. Fear not then to take
'"To thee Mary thy Wife, for she is with Child by the Holy Ghost."'

(61. 24–7, K, pp. 694–5.)

There follows one of the most beautiful passages in *Jerusalem*, where Mary, 'lovely as a Virgin in his sight', becomes a river flowing through the surrounding lands. And in contrast to the Worm birth of 82, a human child is born. 'Mary leaned her side against Jerusalem: Jerusalem recieved / The Infant into her hands in the Visions of Jehovah' (47–8).

The idea of virginity here is antithetical to that of Joanna Southcott, whose divine voice was particularly concerned with the legitimacy of Shiloh. The truth had formerly been concealed because 'thousands of impostors would have arisen, to have said that they were visited like the Virgin Mary; and so the child would have appeared, in arts, by an impostor and a harlot. . . .'[77] The child had to be born of a new Immaculate Conception. 'If the visitation of the Lord to me now does not produce a Son this year, then Jesus Christ was not the Son of God, born in the manner spoken of by the Virgin Mary; but if I have a Son this year, then in like manner our Saviour was born.'[78] In order to legitimize the child, there had to be a wedding. Joanna was much agitated at the prospect, but the divine voice assured her 'so will thy friends all rejoice when marriage hath taken from thee thy reproach among women . . . to the surprise and astonishment of them all [that] . . . always judged thy awful trial was nothing but thy Trance'[79]—who judged, like William Blake, that 'Whate'er is done to her she cannot know.' The voice Blake hears is a quite different one:

> . . . And I heard the voice among
The Reapers, Saying, 'Am I Jerusalem the lost Adultress? or am I
Babylon come up to Jerusalem?' And another voice answer'd, Saying,
'Does the voice of my Lord call me again? am I pure thro' his Mercy
'And Pity? Am I indeed become lovely as a Virgin in his sight, who am
'Indeed a Harlot drunken with the sacrifice of Idols?'

(J 61. 34–9, K, p. 695.)

[77] *Third Book of Wonders*, p. 17.
[78] Ibid., p. 6.
[79] *Second Book of Wonders*, p. 10.

In order to ensure the respectability of the new Saviour, seven of Joanna's friends, under her direction, endorsed a document affirming the necessity of a marriage. Of the seven, one was William Owen Pughe and one was William Sharp. Joanna was married to one John Smith on 12 November 1814.

Shiloh himself appears as a figure of deliverance in Brothers's writings and in Blake's as well as in Southcott's. The Old Testament name, meaning 'peace', is that of the first resting-place of the Ark of the Covenant.[80] It figures in Jacob's deathbed prophecy: 'The sceptre shall not depart from Judah, nor a law-giver from between his feet, until Shiloh come; and unto him shall the gathering of the people be' (Gen. 49: 10). Brothers accordingly declared 'I am the Shiloh mentioned in the scripture for your restoration, the descendant of David that is to be your king to conquer all your enemies and give peace to the world.'[81] Joanna's Shiloh is announced in *The Third Book of Wonders*, which in addition to an engraving of 'Joanna Southcott. Prophetess' has another showing Shiloh's crib. The engraving of Joanna shows her as youthful, with the suggestion of a veil behind her head. The crib is surmounted by a dove with an olive-branch on top of a canopy. It seems likely that this is a deliberate counter to the celebrated Cradle of the King of Rome, which was originally surmounted by an 'eagle supporting a crown of stars, from which the cradle curtains were draped'.[82] That cradle, executed in 1811, was for a prince of this world, Shiloh's for a Prince of Peace.

The *Third Book* breaks off just where one would expect an explicit statement about Shiloh, but *The Fourth Book of Wonders* begins with a notice that Joanna had put into the *Observer* for 3 April 1814, saying that Shiloh is to fulfil Jacob's prophecy. The Spirit tells her that 'When I came there was no gathering of the people then; therefore I could not be the SHILOH there mentioned . . . the promise stands for the end, unto them that now shall be looking for the coming of SHILOH.'[83] From this point until the episode's pathetic conclusion, the Southcottian movement would live in expectation of a saviour who would be born to establish the Millennium. For Blake, in contrast, Shiloh is not a literal person but a figurative conception. He embodies the peaceful fruition that Blake wishes to see ensue after the end of the wars between England and France. Although far less important than Jerusalem as far as emphasis is concerned, Shiloh yet is parallel in meaning: both are 'Emanations', bringing together the creative and loving aspects of human endeavour.

> 'Shiloh, the Masculine Emanation among the Flowers of Beulah.
> 'Lo, Shiloh dwells over France, as Jerusalem over Albion.'
>
> (*J* 49. 47–8, K, p. 680.)

---

[80] See Damon, *Blake Dictionary*, pp. 371–2.   [81] *Letter to Miss Cott*, pp. 371–2.
[82] *The Age of Neo-Classicism*, Catalogue for the fourteenth exhibition of the Council of Europe, London, The Arts Council of Great Britain, 1972, p. 752.   [83] pp. 65, 66.

William Blake, The Prince of the Hebrews

> Nor can any consummate bliss without being generated
> On Earth, of those whose Emanations weave the loves
> Of Beulah for Jerusalem & Shiloh in Immortal Golgonooza
>
> (*J* 86. 42–4, K, p. 731.)

Even had Blake been less unsympathetic to Joanna Southcott, this fundamental difference would still remain, as it does with respect to Brothers. It is the difference between the external and the internal, between the unrealized promise of a failed messiah and 'Allegory address'd to the Intellectual powers'.[84]

The more we learn about William Blake, the more we see that far from being an isolated spirit living entirely in a private world, he was unusually responsive to the intellectual and social currents of his time. By studying Blake in relation to these currents, we do not diminish his stature or deny his uniqueness; we become all the more aware of them. This is particularly true when we consider an often misunderstood phenomenon such as millenarianism. As E. J. Hobsbawm has written,

It is not always easy to recognize the rational political core within millenarian movements, for their very lack of sophistication and of an effective revolutionary strategy makes them push the logic of the revolutionary position to the point of absurdity or paradox. They are impractical and utopian. Since they flourish best in periods of extraordinary social ferment and tend to speak the language of apocalyptic religion, the behaviour of their members is often odd by normal standards. They are therefore as easily misinterpreted as William Blake, who until quite recently was commonly regarded not as a revolutionary but simply as an eccentric other-worldly mystic and visionary.[85]

As we have seen, the pursuit of the millennium—to borrow Cohn's phrase—did not stop with the seventeenth-century antinomians. It continued into Blake's time and beyond.[86] Both visionary and radical, Blake conceived of a millennium that is in some ways related to the millennial conceptions current in his own day, but which is to be distinguished from them chiefly by its lack of literalism and by its imaginative wholeness:

> The Sun has left his blackness & has found a fresher morning,
> And the mild moon rejoices in the clear and cloudless night,
> And Man walks forth from midst of the fires: the evil is all consum'd.
> His eyes behold the Angelic spheres arising night & day;
> The stars consum'd like a lamp blown out, & in their stead, behold
> The Expanding Eyes of Man behold the depths of wondrous worlds!

[84] Letter to Thomas Butts, 6 July 1803, *The Letters of William Blake*, ed. Geoffrey Keynes, 2nd ed., Harvard University Press, Cambridge, Mass., 1968, p. 69.
[85] *Primitive Rebels: Studies in Archaic Forms of Social Movement in the 19th and 20th Centuries*, Manchester University Press, Manchester, 1959, pp. 59–60.
[86] On later millenarian movements, see Hobsbawm, *Primitive Rebels*.

and The Woman Clothed with the Sun

One Earth, one sea beneath; nor Erring Gloves wander, but Stars
Of fire rise up nightly from the Ocean; & one Sun
Each morning, like a New born Man, issues with songs & joy
Calling the Plowman to his Labour & the Shepherd to his rest.
He walks upon the Eternal Mountains, raising his heavenly voice,
Conversing with the Animal forms of wisdom night & day,
That, risen from the Sea of fire, renew'd walk o'er the Earth;
For Tharmas brought his flocks upon the hills, & in the Vales
Around the Eternal Man's bright tent, the little Children play
Among the wooly flocks. The hammer of Urthona sounds
In the deep caves beneath; his limbs renew'd, his Lions roar
Around the Furnaces & in Evening sport upon the plains.
They raise their faces from the Earth, conversing with the Man:

'How is it we have walk'd thro' fires & yet are not consum'd?
'How is it that all things are chang'd, even as in ancient times?'

(Four Zoas, ix. 825–45, K, p. 379.)

XIV

BLAKE, THE VARLEYS, AND THE PATENT GRAPHIC TELESCOPE

Martin Butlin

BLAKE'S Visionary Heads, although in one sense the most fantastic of all his works, had, or assumed, a strictly practical purpose. Drawn, it would seem, to humour the credulous John Varley they were then used to help illustrate his *Treatise on Zodiacal Physiognomy*, the first of four projected parts of which was published in 1828, the year after Blake's death.[1] This contained two plates engraved by John Linnell after Blake's famous drawing, now in the Tate Gallery, of 'The Head of the Ghost of a Flea', with open and closed mouth, and one of the 'Reverse of the Coin of Nebuchadnezzar'. At least one further plate after Blake, showing the head of 'Cancer' and the front of the Nebuchadnezzar Coin, was engraved by Linnell but never published,[2] and the prospectus for Varley's *Treatise* promised further plates of 'King Edward the First, Nebuchadnezzar, &c. &c.' to accompany 'a Memoir of the late William Blake, under the article "Cancer"'.[3]

Evidence exists that there was quite a little business preparing Blake's designs for the *Treatise*, though whether the work began during Blake's lifetime is uncertain. Most of the plates actually published in the first part were after Varley's own drawings, and a portfolio of his working sketches, sold by Linnell's great-grandson at Sotheby's on 10 June 1964 and now in the possession of Mr. Hugo Schwab, includes examples in which he modifies his zodiacal types and varies their placing on the page; some of these are on paper watermarked with the date 1825 (other sheets are watermarked 1813, 1817, and 1823).

However, one drawing from the portfolio, kindly given by Mr. Schwab to the present writer, bears, as well as an annotated sketch by Varley himself, a short note in his hand apparently addressed to Linnell criticizing the latter's engraving after Blake's 'Head of the Ghost of a Flea'. Varley ends, referring to the engraving,

---

[1] I am indebted to Mr. David Clayton-Stamm for the initial suggestion on which this paper is based and also for a copy of the patent specification of Cornelius Varley's Graphic Telescope. For a fuller discussion of the Visionary Heads as a whole see Martin Butlin, *The Blake–Varley Sketchbook of 1819*, 1969. The most complete anthology of contemporary accounts of the Heads is contained in Bentley, *Records*.

[2] Collection of Sir Geoffrey Keynes; see his *Bibliotheca Bibliographica*, 1964, p. 68, No. 611.

[3] Bentley, *Records*, p. 370.

'it has been compared with a tracing', presumably of the original, '& these remarks made'.[4]

No tracing is known in this case, though the original drawing, which comes from a sketchbook first used by Varley for landscape drawings and then handed over to Blake to record his visions when he visited Varley, must have been adapted for the two engravings, the second complete head being enlarged from Blake's sketch of the flea's open mouth alone.[5] There are, however, a remarkably large number of duplicates among the Visionary Heads as a whole, far more than can be explained by the normal usage of an artist making a finished drawing from a rough sketch and quite different in character, all being finished to more or less the same degree. There are three versions, for instance, of 'The Man who taught Blake painting in his Dreams', 'Solomon', 'Canute', and 'Wat Tyler', and two each of a greater number of subjects, including the 'Cancer' engraved for one of the later parts of Varley's *Treatise*. The original drawing of 'Cancer' was formerly part of the Blake–Varley Sketchbook already mentioned and there are duplicates of two of the other pages, 'Caractacus' and, it would seem, though the original sketchbook page is missing, 'The Man who built the Pyramids'.[6] The different versions are very close in draughtsmanship and it could be that some are replicas by Blake himself but, particularly in cases where one can be sure which drawing is Blake's original, as, for instance, when it is on a page from the Blake–Varley Sketchbook, one can sense a certain deadness in the other that betrays the hand of a copyist.

Some of the copies appear at first sight to be direct tracings on thin paper akin to present-day tracing paper. An example is that of 'Cancer' where even the inscribed title is closely followed though, significantly, Linnell's endorsement, 'original William Blake del', is not.[7] However, though close, the copy is not exact. Others are counterproofs, made by placing the original drawing face down on another sheet of paper and rubbing it vigorously on the back so that enough of the graphite adhered to the blank sheet to produce a reversed impression. These were then sometimes strengthened in pencil. Examples are the 'Caractacus' in the Huntington Library, done after the page from the Blake–Varley Sketchbook now in the collection of Sir Geoffrey Keynes, and one each of the three versions of 'Solomon' and 'Canute'.[8]

But there are further duplicates, not in reverse but with enough minor varia-

[4] Butlin, op. cit., p. 12, repr. Plate 6; the dimensions, given incorrectly, should read $4\frac{1}{2} \times 7\frac{1}{4}$ inches ($11 \cdot 5 \times 18 \cdot 5$ cm.).

[5] The original drawing is reproduced Martin Butlin, *William Blake, a Complete Catalogue of the Work in the Tate Gallery*, 2nd ed. 1971, p. 58; the engraving with the mouth open, in Butlin, op. cit., 1969, Plate 7.

[6] See Butlin, op. cit., 1969, pp. 23, 29–30, and, for 'The Man who built the Pyramids', Butlin, op. cit., 1971, p. 59, No. 50.

[7] The original is repr. Butlin, op. cit. 1969, facsimile volume; the copy in Geoffrey Keynes, *Drawings of William Blake*, 1970, No. 71.

[8] Huntington Library and Sotheby's 15 Mar. 1967, Lot 31, respectively.

tions from the original to prevent them from being exact copies or tracings. The most convenient example, two of the three versions being in the Tate Gallery, is 'The Man who taught Blake painting in his Dreams', though the position is complicated by the fact that the drawing that seems for reasons of quality to be the original, that in the collection of Sir Geoffrey Keynes, is in the reverse direction to the other two. Presumably the first of the Tate Gallery drawings began as a counter-proof from the original.

The sequence of the drawings and a possible reason for the existence of so many versions is suggested by the presence on the two Tate Gallery drawings of inscriptions written in John Linnell's hand. The Keynes drawing is not inscribed, but at the bottom of one of the Tate Gallery's versions (inventory no. 5187) Linnell began to write the title, starting more or less in the middle of the page: 'Imagination of A man who Mr Blake has rec^d instruct[ion]' (the last three letters were lost when the drawing was slightly trimmed round the edges). He then found that he had run out of space and was forced to squeeze in the rest of the title immediately above: 'in Painting &c from.' On the second Tate drawing (5186) Linnell's inscription is much tidier. On the left of the centre line made by the join down the front of the Instructor's garment, neatly written on two lines and correctly beginning on the upper one, is a new version of the title: 'The Portrait of a Man who instructed / M^r. Blake in Painting &c. in his Dreams.' Even the capitalization of initial letters is more orthodox. Similarly, on the right-hand side, again on two lines, is a variant of the title on the other drawing, perhaps written before that on the left: 'Imagination of a Man who^m Mr Blake has rec^d / instruction in Painting &c from.' It would seem that one reason for the duplicates was to try out alternative wordings and positions for the title, probably in preparation for an inscription on an engraved plate, though this was destined never to be published and, so far as is known, no engraving was made. The greater neatness of the inscription on the second drawing suggests that it was done after the first, and both presumably followed the untitled original.

There is another important difference between the two Tate drawings. In the first (5187) the proportion and relationship of the actual drawing to the complete sheet of paper is the same as on Sir Geoffrey Keynes's original (allowing for the slight difference in the size of the paper caused by subsequent trimming and the fact that the original is framed in a mount that covers some of the sheet). In the second of the Tate's drawings the figure looms much larger, even given the slightly smaller size of the sheet, $10\frac{1}{4} \times 8\frac{1}{8}$ inches as opposed to $11\frac{5}{8} \times 9\frac{1}{4}$ inches. In addition, the head is placed considerably higher on the page. Again one suspects that the change in the final version was, by giving it more presence, to make it more suitable for a projected engraving. Despite the change in scale, however, both lines and shading follow those on the other Tate drawing (and, though in

71. *The Man who taught Blake painting in his Dreams.* Pencil drawing.
Collection of Geoffrey Keynes

72. Copy of *The Man who taught Blake painting in his Dreams.* Pencil drawing. Tate Gallery, London (5187)

73. Copy of *The Man who taught Blake painting in his Dreams.* Pencil drawing. Tate Gallery, London (5186)

reverse, of the original), but there are slight variations in the precise placing of each stroke. This can be seen most clearly in details of the hair. Direct tracing is ruled out by the difference in size between the drawings and even the use of some such device as a pantograph seems highly unlikely on account of the slight divergences between them.

The somewhat dead quality of many of the copies, which is sometimes much more apparent than in the case of 'The Man who taught Blake painting', and the technical objections to other processes, suggest that Varley or Linnell, or both of them, used some device that was in part mechanical, to secure the degree of closeness to the originals, and in part done by hand, to account for the slight variations. Neither Linnell nor Varley seems to have been particularly practical: a number of anecdotes show that Varley was very much the reverse, though Linnell did in his later years earn a reputation for a very business-like approach to monetary affairs. Varley's younger brother Cornelius was, however, mechanic-ally inclined. Though a distinguished and perhaps more original landscape artist than John, he had been brought up, following his father's death when he was ten, by his uncle Samuel Varley, a watchmaker, jeweller, and instrument-maker under whom Cornelius had learnt such things as the preparation of optical lenses. On 4 June 1811 Cornelius had registered the Patent of 'A New Construction of a Tele-scope or Optical Instrument for Viewing Distant Objects, & for other Useful Purposes, with a suitable Table or Stand for the same' (Patent No. 3430). His invention consisted, as he wrote in his specification,

in combining one or two reflecting surfaces with a simple kind of telescope that inverts the object, and thereby gaining an erect image without any additional length to the telescope, placing the telescope out of the way of the image, and apparently projecting the said image flat on a table, so that it may be easily traced on paper, &c., the image being seen by one eye, and the pencil or tracer by the other, or by both eyes, and of a table or stand for supporting and using the same.

The projection of an erect image, in the same direction as the original, was done with the eyepiece mounted at the side of the telescope, but one could also place it at the end: '. . . by which means the image is shown reversed, and may be etched at once on copper or drawn on stone (in the German mode of printing) and printed the right way.' The specification was accompanied by detailed diagrams and there is an example of the finished instrument, lacking however its stand, in the Science Museum, beautifully engraved with the words 'Varley's Patent Graphic Tele-scope'.[9] It was one of a number of early-nineteenth-century developments of the

---

[9] One of the diagrams, giving a general view, and the Science Museum's telescope are reproduced by John Gage, *A Decade of English Naturalism 1810–1820*, the catalogue of an exhibition held in the Norwich Castle Museum and the Victoria and Albert Museum, London, November 1969–February 1970, on the cover and p. 17 respectively.

camera obscura which had been used by artists including Vermeer and Canaletto from the seventeenth century onwards.

The legs of the stand were adjustable so that 'the table may stand even upon any sloping or uneven ground', and the Graphic Telescope was probably designed primarily for drawing landscapes. An example is the pencil drawing, partly finished in water-colour, inscribed 'View from Ferry Bridge Yorkshire / C. Varley P.G.T.' (the initials standing for 'Patent Graphic Telescope') in the British Museum (1886-10-12-564).[10] But Cornelius seems to have used it more often for portraiture, there being ten examples in the British Museum including one of 'Miss Moncton / with Graphic Telescope C Varley' (1936-12-11-3) and one of an unknown man inscribed 'Drawn by Cornelius Varley in his patent Graphic Telescope Apl 9—1813' (1936-12-11-8); a drawing of John and Cornelius's Uncle Samuel is dated 1816 (1936-12-11-6). There is some evidence that he also did a drawing of Blake.[11]

John Varley also used the Graphic Telescope for portraits and may indeed have been the first to do so. A drawing of Miss E. Hayes that passed through the salerooms in 1970 was signed by John and inscribed 'Nov. 25 1811—The first Portrait Drawn in the Patent Graphic Telescope invented by C. Varley'.[12] Fourteen further examples are in the Victoria and Albert Museum as part of Dawson Turner's 'Collection of Original Portraits' by various artists. Those that are dated, four in number, are all of 1812 and include the portrait of his former patron Dr. Thomas Monro, 'The first Collector of Turner and Girtins Drawings / Done with the Graphic Telescope / April 12th 1812' (E. 1179-1927). This is also inscribed 'Dr Monro' in reverse, suggesting that John Varley was trying out the alternative placing of the eyepiece to produce a reversed image and perhaps even copying from another drawing, done in the opposite direction but bearing its sitter's name in normal writing.

One does not have to accept this supposition to see that the Graphic Telescope could be used for copying not only from the life but also from another drawing. The instrument was versatile enough even though the Patent Specification does not actually describe any special apparatus for holding a drawing to be copied. Certain characteristics of the duplicates of Blake's Visionary Heads are similar to those of the portraits done with the aid of the Telescope, for instance the frequent presence of rather heavy outlines, sometimes almost digging into the paper, and of mechanical-looking hatching or shading; an example is John Varley's portrait of J. Oliver (E. 1181—1927). Another of John Varley's portrait drawings at the

---

[10] Repr. *The Old Water-Colour Society's Club, fourteenth annual volume 1936—1937*, 1937, Plate 5.

[11] See Richard Seddon, 'Turner and Cotman: Two Portraits by Cornelius Varley', *Burlington Magazine*, lxxxvii (1945), 202–5, where two further examples, in the Graves Art Gallery, Sheffield, are reproduced.

[12] Christie's, 20 Oct. 1970, Lot 1.

74. Cornelius Varley: *View from Ferry Bridge, Yorkshire.*
Pencil drawing with water-colour.
British Museum, Department of Prints and Drawings

75. Cornelius Varley: *Miss Moncton.*
Pencil drawing.
British Museum, Department of Prints and Drawings

76. John Varley: *Dr. Monro*. Pencil drawing.
Victoria and Albert Museum

John Varley 1812

V. A. M.

J. Oliver

77. John Varley: *J. Oliver*. Pencil drawing.
Victoria and Albert Museum

Victoria and Albert Museum, showing the 'Revd. Mr. Cannon—well known in the fashionable circles who was once noticed by the king' (E. 1142-1927), is particularly close in its flat, slightly muzzy, silvery-grey pencilling to a version of 'Wat Tyler' now in the possession of a descendant of Fleetwood Varley (another brother).

That John Varley and Linnell made use of Cornelius Varley's Patent Graphic Telescope in making copies from Blake's Visionary Heads cannot be proved but there is enough evidence to suggest that this is likely. They certainly knew the Telescope and, although it would have been a rather cumbersome method, it had the advantage that the copy could be made larger in scale[13] and, if required, in reverse; by reversing the image it would even have been possible, as a final step, to etch the Visionary Heads directly on to the copper plates for the projected engravings. It would be paradoxical if an instrument designed as a mechanical aid towards achieving a greater objectivity towards visual reality had also been used in a project to perpetuate visions with so little claim to objective reality as those conjured up by Blake for his credulous friend.

[13] As well as the second Tate Gallery version of 'The Man who taught Blake painting', the Tate's 'Man who built the Pyramids' is also markedly larger than the putative original.

XV

REFERENCES TO BLAKE IN SAMUEL PALMER'S LETTERS

Raymond Lister

THE influence of William Blake on the group of young men calling themselves 'the Ancients' is now rightly taken for granted.[1] But it is also true that after his death his influence on them waned; this is especially apparent in the difference between the early and later work and thought of Samuel Palmer, Edward Calvert, and George Richmond, and is confirmed by several passages in letters written in later life by Palmer.

Although, when a young man, Palmer wrote enthusiastic passages about his meetings with Blake, and later passed on to Gilchrist fond recollections of the elder man,[2] his letters contain many cautious comments on Blake's philosophy and beliefs. So, despite the comment of his son, A. H. Palmer, that 'the influence of Blake . . . was part and parcel of Palmer's mental equipment',[3] we still find Samuel saying that 'Poor Mr Blake was "peculiar" on these subjects [i.e. wars and international politics]'. He continues, in an obvious reference to the poem, 'Then old Nobodaddy aloft',[4] to say that he 'made a remark which is more decorously preserved in memory than committed to writing'.[5] And his letters to Mrs. Gilchrist (who completed her husband's *Life of Blake* after his death) contain several warnings to her to be careful about such things as 'an indecent word in the text—or at least a coarse one' in *The Marriage of Heaven and Hell*.[6]

In some places Palmer shows more definite opposition to Blake's beliefs. In a letter to Leonard Rowe Valpy,[7] he says he disavows 'all adherence to some of the

---

[1] Cf. Laurence Binyon, *The Followers of William Blake*, 1925; Geoffrey Grigson, *Samuel Palmer, the Visionary Years*, 1947; Raymond Lister, *Edward Calvert*, 1962, *Samuel Palmer and his Etchings*, 1969.

[2] See, for example, A. H. Palmer, *Life and Letters of Samuel Palmer*, 1892, pp. 9–10, 13, 15–16; Alexander Gilchrist, *Life of William Blake*, 1942 ed., pp. 301–4, 306, and *passim*.

[3] Notebook in Ivimy MSS.

[4] 'Poems from the Note-book 1793', K, p. 185.

[5] Letter to George Richmond, 31 Dec. 1860; Mr. Anthony W. Richmond.

[6] Letter to Mrs. Anne Gilchrist, 27 June 1862, Yale University Library, New Haven, Conn. Probably Palmer refers to the first line from Plate 10: 'The head Sublime, the heart Pathos, the genitals Beauty, the hands & feet Proportion.' But there are other passages in the poem which might have offended Victorian morality, for example: 'Prisons are built with stones of Law, Brothels with bricks of Religion' (Plate 8, line 1).

[7] 1825–84. Valpy was John Ruskin's solicitor. He commissioned several works from Palmer.

doctrines put forth in [Blake's] poems, which seem to me to savour of Manicheism'.[8] In another letter, to the Revd. John Preston Wright,[9] Palmer refers to Swedenborg, and remarks: 'I doubt not that he saw and conversed with the spiritual world. But it may be that in the spiritual world there are spirits which are fallible—partly in error, though not malignant. Swedenborg thoroughly believed that our Lord came in the flesh, Blake was I think misled by erroneous spirits.'[10]

Notwithstanding all this, Palmer seems to have retained a genuine affection for Blake. In November 1863, for example, he wrote an enthusiastic letter to Mrs. Gilchrist on the publication of her husband's book, and described how, 'I could not wait for the paper knife but fell upon it, reading all in between:—now, I have cut the first volume,—and read wildly everywhere:—and now again I begin at the beginning, and meanwhile write to tell you how it has delighted me:—raising, however, a strange ferment of distressing and delicious thought.'[11]

And he included *Songs of Innocence* among the carefully selected books which he allowed his elder son, Thomas More, to read, though Blake must have turned in his grave to be bracketed with Thomas Day's simpering story of *Sandford and Merton*: 'If I had not taught you your letters every day—you could not now have read a chapter in the Bible nor the Pilgrim's Progress nor Sandford and Merton nor the Songs of Innocence nor any of your pretty story books.'[12] Incidentally, some of this reading would seem a trifle advanced for Thomas More, who at this date was only just over three and a half years of age.

It is possible that Palmer had Blake in mind in a passage that he wrote in a letter to George Richmond's wife, Julia, about his brother William's situation as an assistant at the British Museum.[13] William Palmer had taken continual periods of sick-leave between 1859 and 1861 and, as a result, it was resolved by the Museum Finance Committee in July 1861 that, if he was still unwell at the expiry of six months, his engagement should be terminated.[14]

Samuel was worried about his brother's superannuation and tried to obtain Richmond's help in soliciting members of the Committee to recommend some extra help for him. In the event, the superannuation was fixed (in January 1862)

---

[8] The original of the letter is untraced, but it is printed in Palmer, *Life and Letters*, pp. 254–6; dated June 1864.

[9] 1845–1927; he was vicar of Newborough, Staffs., 1877–81, rector of Oldbury, Salop, 1883–1927, and prebendary of Hereford 1916–27.

[10] Letter of Feb. 1869; Mr. John E. A. Samuels.

[11] Letter of Nov. 1863; Mr. Paul Mellon.

[12] Letter to Thomas More Palmer, 14 Sept. 1845; from a transcript owned by Mr. A. H. Palmer II, Vancouver, B.C.

[13] Letter of Oct. 1861; Mr. Anthony W. Richmond.

[14] British Museum, *Index to Minutes*, vol. v, Jan. 1858–Dec. 1865, pp. 371–2.

at £46 a year.[15] But, in the meantime, Palmer was seriously worried and wrote these lines in his letter:

> For, how wicked it is to be poor!
> How loathsome to hear the poor ask for help!
> How fawning if he ask compassion!
> How insolent if he ask for justice!

I think there can be little doubt that in writing these lines, Palmer was prompted, if only subconsciously, by something he may have seen in the manuscript of *The Four Zoas*:

> Compell the poor to live upon a Crust of bread, by soft mild arts.
> Smile when they frown, frown when they smile; & when a man looks pale
> With labour & abstinence, say he looks healthy & happy;
> And when his children sicken, let them die; there are enough
> Born, even too many, & our Earth will be overrun
> Without these arts.[16]

Palmer was never in doubt as to Blake's sanity or genius. He was quick to write to F. G. Stephens,[17] art editor of the *Athenaeum*, asking him to print a letter denying allegations made in an article in the *Cornhill Magazine*[18] that Blake was mad. Palmer's reply appeared in the *Athenaeum* of 11 September 1875, though it will be seen that, even here, Palmer seems to disavow Blake's writings:

Without alluding to his writings, which are here not in question, I remember William Blake, in the quiet consistency of his daily life, as one of the sanest, if not the most thoroughly sane man I have ever known. The flights of his genius were scarcely more marvellous than the ceaseless industry and skilful management of affairs which enabled him on a very small income to find time for very great works. And of this man the public are informed that he passed thirty years in a madhouse![19]

Of Blake's genius, Palmer wrote the following to George Gurney:[20] 'I certainly knew *one* man who was an Unity—but he was one of a thousand, of *Ten* thousand; —the greatest Art genius this country ever saw. Of course I allude to William Blake.' Again in a letter to William Abercrombie,[21] he paid tribute to Blake's genius and to the generosity of Thomas Butts who did so much to allow it to

---

[15] Ibid. [16] K, p. 323.

[17] Frederic George Stephens (1828–1907), art critic, artist, and collector.

[18] Vol. xxxii (1875), pp. 167–8. The article was in fact a general repetition of an earlier article by a Dr. Richardson, subtitled 'Hallucinations', and printed in *Chambers's Journal*, Series 4, No. 439 (1872), pp. 324–7.

[19] *Athenaeum*, No. 2498, 11 Sept. 1875, p. 649.

[20] Perhaps a relative of Joseph John Gurney (1788–1847), the philanthropist and religious writer. The letter, dated Oct. 1880, is in the Victoria and Albert Museum.

[21] 'One of the last entries in the second volume of [Palmer's] commonplace-book was this:—"Abercrombie William, of the Manor House, Ashton on Mersey (SALE) is illustrating BLAKE's Life."' Note by A. H. Palmer in *Victoria and Albert Museum . . . Catalogue of an Exhibition of Drawings, Etchings and Woodcuts by Samuel Palmer and other Disciples of William Blake*, 1926.

flourish: '[Mr. Butts] for years stood between the greatest designer in England and the workhouse,—that designer being, *of all men whom I ever knew*, the most *practically sane, steady, frugal* and *industrious*.'[22]

But the Palmer letters contain other fascinating references to Blake and his work. For instance, in a letter to Alexander Gilchrist, written probably in April 1861,[23] he says: 'I forgot I think to mention that in the late Sir R. Peel's copy of the *Europe* and *America* there is a pencil drawing by Mr Richmond—done soon after Blake's decease while the memory was fresh, and assisted by the cast of which I spoke, most probably this is the closest likeness existing.'

This poses some tantalizing problems. No recorded surviving copy of *Europe* or *America* has a Richmond portrait of Blake with it, nor can any copy of these works be traced to Sir Robert Peel. It is possible that the Peel copy may be one of the following:[24] *America* (Q) once bound with *Europe* (L); *America* (B) apparently once bound with *Europe* (C); *America* (G) bound with *Europe* (B) and *Jerusalem* (B); *America* (P) with *Europe* (M). Less likely is *America* (N) with *Europe* (I).

In another letter, 27 June 1862,[25] written to Gilchrist's widow, Palmer mentions the design in *The Marriage of Heaven and Hell* showing Nebuchadnezzar in the wilderness (Plate 24), and continues: 'I have very old German translations of Cicero and Petrarch in which among some wild and original designs, almost the same figure appears.' The design to which Palmer refers is on page lxxxi in a book, a copy of which is in the British Museum: *Officia M[arcus] T[ullius] C[icero]. Ein Buch . . .*, Augsburg, 1531. It shows Nebuchadnezzar crawling on the ground among trees. The figure and posture are much like those in Blake's design, but the king is facing the opposite way; unlike Blake's king he has no crown, and he appears to be wearing a suit made of feathers or fur, while Blake's is naked. The face is not horror-stricken like that in Blake's design, and the hands and feet are less bestial. It may be, indeed, an example of Blake borrowing a design, but giving it greater vitality and making it in the process completely his own.

Finally, on a lighter note, there is a reference to Blake's relationship with animals, but this occurs in a letter written by Mrs. Mary Ann Linnell, Palmer's mother-in-law, to her daughter Hannah, when the Palmers were in Florence.[26] Hannah had referred to the effusiveness of an Italian woman who had formed a friendship for her: 'We were amused with your account of the warmth of the

[22] Letter of 5 Feb. 1881; Sir Geoffrey Keynes.
[23] Yale University Library, New Haven, Conn.
[24] The references are to *William Blake's Illuminated Books, a Census* by Geoffrey Keynes and Edwin Wolf 2nd, 1953. I am indebted to Professor G. E. Bentley, Jr., for these suggestions of the possible identity of the Peel copy.
[25] Yale University Library, New Haven, Conn. Cf. Gilchrist, *Life of Blake*, 1942 ed., p. 77.
[26] Letter of 20 Aug. 1839; Mrs. Joan Linnell Burton.

Italian lady, but I should think such kissing and hugging must be troublesome. I thought of Mr. Blake who used to say how much he preferred a cat to a dog as a companion because she was so much more quiet in her expression of attachment, but I suppose climate makes a great difference in the feelings.'

This was something in which Palmer agreed with Blake. Palmer did in fact have a bull-terrier named Trimmer at the time of his marriage, and he once unsuccessfully adopted a dog for a short period, but it had fits and ran away. But he seems on the whole to have preferred cats. Writing to John Reed,[27] he remarks, of ideal evenings: '. . . there *must* be a cat upon the rug—a sedate well-conducted tabby—contemplative of temperament—shutting her eyes or blinking as she muses upon her last mouse—and not fidgetting about her next, like bristling dogs who dream they are after rabbits; whining and kicking in their sleep and wearing out the rug with their convulsive friction.'

Yet it was not always the quietness of the cat that attracted Palmer. In a letter to Charles West Cope R.A., written on 26 October 1880,[28] he wrote of how

the things I most miss in the country are the CATS, the improvised melodies and enharmonic delicacies of the pantiles. What varieties of tone, what richness in the 'instrumentation' of that furry orchestra. I regretted being kept awake here for *one* night by the nightingales in our garden, but should not in London have regretted *three* such nights, while the feline charmers—'All night long' their 'am'rous descant sung.'[29] It is the school and origin of *modern* music, it is nature's comic Opera, and what comedy was ever half so comic?

What Blake thought of the cat as an operatic performer, Palmer does not tell us, but perhaps we may see something of his preference if we compare the appealing cat in his water-colour illustrations for Gray's *Ode on the Death of a Favourite Cat* with the somewhat menacing and horrent dog in the engraving of the *Canterbury Pilgrims*. Mrs. Linnell's recollection is both an apposite confirmation of that preference and a reminder of one small point on which the two men agreed, even after Palmer's ideas had in several areas become remote from Blake's.

[27] A friend of Palmer; he was deaf and dumb. The letter is undated, but was probably written at the end of 1860; Mrs. Joan Linnell Burton.

[28] Mrs. Joan Linnell Burton.

[29] *Paradise Lost* iv. 603.

XVI

WILLIAM BLAKE IN THE WILDERNESS A CLOSER LOOK AT HIS REPUTATION 1827–1863

Suzanne R. Hoover

> With a heart of furious fancies,
>   Whereof I am commander;
> With a burning spear and a horse of air,
>   To the wilderness I wander.
>
> *Elizabethan Mad Song*

OVER the entrance to what is perhaps the most difficult long poem in English, the author inscribed a beguiling request: 'Dear Reader, forgive what you do not approve, & love me for this energetic exertion of my talent.' Some time after he had etched the Preface to *Jerusalem*, William Blake experienced a violent change of heart. In the sentence just quoted he scratched from the metal plate the words 'Dear', 'forgive', and 'love'. Other words, of self-confidence and of religious faith, were deleted from the Preface, including a long, dedicatory sentence in which the reader is reminded that 'the Ancients entrusted their love to their writing, to the full as Enthusiastically as I have who acknowledge mine for my Saviour and Lord . . .'.[1] The scratched-out spaces were never filled in with other words. Except for some particles, or 'crumbs', of letters, from which the deletions have been reconstructed,[2] the spaces remained disturbingly vacant—scars of Blake's suffering in his loves and wars with the public.

The subject of Blake's relation to the public was one of central concern to Blake himself. Along with his theories about art, written for the most part in defence of his own practice, it constitutes the chief subject-matter of his prose writings and overflows freely into the allegories of his later epic poems. His interest was not confined to the public response to his own work; it included the concern

---

[1] *J* 3, K, pp. 620–1.

[2] The reconstruction was accomplished by David V. Erdman, who has set forth the details in 'The Suppressed and Altered Passages in Blake's *Jerusalem*', *Studies in Bibliography*, xvii (1964), 1–54. With regard to the 'self-destructive' deletions on Plate 3 to which I refer, Erdman notes that 'the momentary effects of dismay upon the Preface of *Jerusalem* remain even in the most brightly-coloured copy, remained perhaps in his own will—for he could, after all, have made a new plate' (p. 10).

of the English public for art in general. And if Blake himself viewed his career in the light of 'Eternity' and allegorized his personal struggles as typical episodes in the general progress of art and intellect, perhaps we are entitled to see in the scratched-out spaces in the Preface to *Jerusalem* a sign, not only of the professional frustration and bitterness of one man, but also a sign of the times—an era of betrayed hopes and widespread despair.

The present study of Blake's reputation takes up the narrative after his personal battles with the public were closed by his death. It is a story that is often told, usually in a few words: after 1830 Blake was more or less forgotten, and significant interest in him was revived some thirty-three years later only by Gilchrist's biography with its companion volume of selections from Blake's work. Considering Blake's current standing, a surprising story. But such a simple statement of it will not do. Students who bring the received view to a fresh look at the evidence that has been accumulating must be struck by the number of expressions of interest in Blake during this period. Of course, neither during his life nor in the years that immediately followed his death, was Blake ever possessed of the wide public of a Byron—or a Stothard; but the words 'famous' and 'well known' were in fact used of him by several commentators. As the memory of him faded, so did the moderate fame; however, the evidence shows that it was never extinguished; indeed, there were always more than a few persons, generally notable names in the cultural life of their time, who, publicly or privately, expressed their interest in Blake and their sense of his extraordinariness. Most telling, perhaps, is the fact that there were those who were willing on occasion to pay large sums for his works. When all that is known of the history is examined, it becomes clear that, while Blake was in death even more than in life a wanderer in the wilderness—shockingly undervalued, misapprehended, and at times grossly neglected—he never was in actual danger of being forgotten. Moreover, as one follows the story step by step, there appears to be a certain inevitability about the making of Gilchrist's *Life*: the need for it was already distinctly present. And the great interest in Blake that it occasioned when it came—the 'Blake Revival'—tends to corroborate that judgement.

Several accounts of the posthumous, pre-Gilchrist phase of Blake's reputation have already been given in print,[3] but none of them has aspired to comprehensiveness. The longest of these, a chapter by Deborah Dorfman, is preliminary to her central concern, Blake's reputation as poet from Gilchrist to Yeats. It is a survey

[3] See, especially, G. E. Bentley, Jr., and Martin K. Nurmi, *A Blake Bibliography*, Minneapolis, 1964, pp. 10–12, and Deborah Dorfman, *Blake in the Nineteenth Century: His Reputation as a Poet from Gilchrist to Yeats*, New Haven, 1969, pp. 25–64. There are at least two unpublished dissertations partly about the period: Louis W. Crompton, 'Blake's Nineteenth Century Critics', doctoral dissertation, University of Chicago, 1954, and Valerie Rance, 'The History of William Blake's Reputation from 1806 to 1863', M.A. thesis, Reading University, 1965.

that looks at the main figures in the history, and the lesser ones only when they supplement information given by *A Blake Bibliography*. In the present essay I have attempted to avoid duplication of Dorfman's discussion whenever possible, while at the same time incorporating her contributions of fact.

'In the first few years after Blake's death', as G. E. Bentley, Jr., observes, 'there was more printed in praise of him than might have been expected.'[4] Of the seven obituaries that are known,[5] one is derisive, but the others are appreciative. True posthumous commentary on Blake (other than obituaries) begins, quite naturally, with biography. Only one year after his death, that is, in 1828, a sketch of Blake's life appeared in John Thomas Smith's *Nollekens and His Times*.[6] To his study of Nollekens (the most celebrated portrait sculptor of his day) Smith added 'Memoirs of several contemporary Artists, from the time of Roubiliac, Hogarth, and Reynolds, to that of Fuseli, Flaxman, and Blake'.

A more formal biography, although also a rather short one, was included in the second volume of Allan Cunningham's *Lives of the Most Eminent British Painters, Sculptors, and Architects*, in 1830.[7] Cunningham was a very minor poet, but a shrewd man of letters. While Blake would not have been considered by all at that time to be 'eminent', his inclusion in the *Lives* can be accounted for by the material itself: sensational visions, 'incomprehensible' poetry, touching domestic life, and so on. Cunningham probably did not know Blake personally. Smith had known Blake when they were both young. Unfortunately, it was Cunningham's account rather than Smith's that was to be considered for the next thirty-three years, on both sides of the Atlantic, to be the standard 'life' of Blake.

There is perhaps no better way to get a quick sense of the differences in their

[4] Bentley, *Records*, p. 348.

[5] Anon., 'William Blake: The Illustrator of The Grave, &c.', *Literary Gazette*, 18 Aug. 1827, pp. 540–1; Anon., 'William Blake', *The Literary Chronicle and Weekly Review*, 1 Sept. 1827, pp. 557–8; Anon., 'William Blake', *Monthly Magazine*, N.S. iv (Oct. 1827), 435; Anon., 'Mr. William Blake', *Gentleman's Magazine*, xcviii (Oct. 1827), 377–8; Anon., 'Mr. William Blake', *New Monthly Magazine*, xxi (1 Dec. 1827), 535–6; Anon., 'Biographical Index of Deaths, for 1827 . . .', *Annual Biography and Obituary for 1828*, xii (1828), 416–18; Anon., 'Deaths', *The Annual Register* [for 1827], lxix (1828), 253–4. All but the second of these obituaries were derived, or reprinted, from the first. (For William Paulet Carey's possible authorship of the *Literary Gazette* obituary, see Bentley, *Records*, p. 350.) Their texts are given in ibid., pp. 348–62. The *Annual Biography*'s account of Flaxman (who had died in the same year) contains a brief reference to Blake (ibid., pp. 361–2).

[6] John Thomas Smith, *Nollekens and his Times*, 2 vols., London, 1828, ii. 454–88. The complete text is reprinted in Bentley, *Records*, pp. 455–76. All references hereafter will be to that text. A second edition of *Nollekens* was published in 1829.

[7] Allan Cunningham, 'William Blake', *Lives of the Most Eminent British Painters, Sculptors, and Architects*, 6 vols., London, 1829–33, ii. 140–79; the second edition (also 1830) is reprinted, with variants, in Bentley, *Records*, pp. 477–507. All references hereafter will be to that text. The second edition, which leaves a more sympathetic impression of Blake and presents more of his poems, was not reprinted until 1880. The first edition was reprinted six times before 1863.

views of Blake, than to compare the opening paragraphs of the two accounts. They sound the same theme. First, Smith:

I believe it has been invariably the custom of every age, whenever a man has been found to depart from the usual mode of thinking, to consider him of deranged intellect, and not infrequently stark staring mad, which judgment his calumniators would pronounce with ... little hesitation. ... Cowper, in a letter to Lady Hesketh, dated June 3rd, 1788, speaking of a dancing-master's advertisement, says, 'The author of it had the good hap to be crazed, or he had never produced anything half so clever; for you will ever observe, that they who are said to have lost their wits, have more than other people.' (Pp. 455–6.)

As Smith had adverted to the sympathetic and poignant association of Cowper, Cunningham, who based his account on Smith's, countered with a quite different association—a name which was still the synonym for 'pernicious madman' in the English vocabulary:

Painting, like poetry, has its followers, the body of whose genius is light compared to the length of its wings, and who, rising above the ordinary sympathies of our nature, are, like Napoleon, betrayed by a star which no eye can see save their own. To this rare class belonged William Blake. (P. 477.)

Both of these openings sound the same theme, but Smith's genial woodwinds were to be drowned out by the brassy tones of Cunningham's sensationalism and philistinism.

A large part of Smith's sketch is devoted to a crude catalogue of some of the Illuminated Books, presumably in order to help Blake's widow sell the few copies that remained in her hands. Richard Thomson, the librarian of the London Institution, had compiled Smith's catalogue (p. 469), which consisted of detailed descriptions of the separate plates of *Songs of Experience*, and of some of the plates of *America*, *Europe*, and *The Book of Urizen*.

Of the *Songs of Experience* Smith says: 'The poetry of these songs is wild, irregular, and highly mystical, but of no great degree of elegance or excellence, and their prevailing feature is a tone of complaint of the misery of mankind' (p. 470). His comment on *America* is laconic and unjudging. The frontispiece to *Europe* seems to Smith to approach 'almost to the sublimity of Raffaelle or Michael Angelo' (p. 470), and some of the plates of *The Book of Urizen* 'are of extraordinary effect and beauty' (p. 472). It is interesting to notice that the word 'mystical' is used by Smith in a factual tone—an exceptional neutrality in Blake criticism. Less unusual at that time is the use of the word 'complaint' to describe Blake's concern with 'the misery of mankind', as if there were something both futile and tasteless in such a preoccupation.

It is difficult to believe that Smith had never seen the *Grave* designs, and yet in

313

his discussion of Blake's works he never mentions them except to say that they were commissioned by Cromek. He did, however, admire the *Night Thoughts* illustrations (p. 461); he thought the *Descriptive Catalogue* 'perhaps the most curious of its kind ever written' (p. 465); and the five-foot by seven-foot *Last Judgment* fresco, since lost, an 'extraordinary performance' (p. 468). Smith mentions both the Dante illustrations and the Job designs, with an absence of comment that suggests that he had not actually seen either series (pp. 475, 468). In his general estimate of Blake's treatment at the hands of booksellers and art patrons, Smith is determined to be generous to all sides. 'It is most certain', he says, 'that the uninitiated eye was incapable of selecting the beauties of Blake; his effusions were not generally felt' (p. 468). Similarly, in his appraisal of Blake's poetic gift, Smith steers a careful course, appreciative of the lyrics and equivocal about the Prophetic Books. One of the *Poetical Sketches*, 'How sweet I roam'd from field to field', is quoted, as well as two quatrains from *Jerusalem*. The last of several mysterious allusions to 'calumniators' and 'detractors' occurs as Smith considers the future of Blake's reputation: 'Whatever may be the public opinion hereafter of Blake's talents, when his enemies are dead, I will not presume to predict.' But he hazards a guess that 'the predictions of Fuseli and Flaxman may hereafter be verified—"That a time will come when Blake's finest works will be as much sought after and treasured up in the portfolios of men of mind, as those of Michael Angelo are at present"' (p. 467).

The present importance of Smith's memoir to Blake scholars lies in the first-hand picture it gives of Blake's youth, especially in the Mathew circle, including an account of the publication by Blake's friends of *Poetical Sketches* in 1783. (Unfortunately, those passages comprise less than one-tenth of the whole.) Smith also includes two interesting letters by Blake. In sum, Smith brought Blake's name, not unsympathetically, to a fairly wide circle of readers. He defended Blake against his 'detractors', too casually, perhaps, but like the rest of *Nollekens* the Blake memoir was primarily an entertainment—and, in that, how different from the intense, Carlylean spirit in which Gilchrist was to write thirty-five years later! Smith wrote of Blake once again, in 1845, remembering his youthful acquaintanceship with that man of 'original and extraordinary merit': 'A time will come when the numerous, though now very rare works of Blake . . . will be sought after with the most intense avidity.'[8]

An anonymous review of *Nollekens* in the *Athenaeum* singles out the notice of Blake as 'very interesting'. The author states, quite contrary to the fact, that Smith describes Blake as a 'very eccentric being, at times almost a madman'. The reviewer concedes that 'most of' Blake's pictures, whatever the source of inspiration,

---

[8] John Thomas Smith, *A Book for a Rainy Day; or, Recollections of the Events of the Last Sixty-six Years*, London, 1845, p. 81.

'certainly present the effect of an exceedingly grand imagination'.[9] A few weeks later, another reviewer of Smith finds that the account of Blake has 'pleased us most, inasmuch as we were not previously in possession of the facts, though well acquainted with that artist's works. Of his poetry we cannot speak favourably, and much of his invention in design is frigidly extravagant. But, amid much out-of-the-way rubbish, there are gleams of high conception and vigorous expression. . . .'[10]

In the first of these reviews of Smith the theme of 'Blake the madman' had surfaced, a theme intensified just at this time by the considerable attention paid to John Varley's attempts at publicizing Blake's 'spiritual' powers. The public was unfortunately inclined to write off Blake with Varley—if the one was a gull, the other was a lunatic. Under the title 'Literary Novelties', the *Literary Gazette* of 11 October 1828 takes notice of Varley's forthcoming *Treatise on Zodiacal Physiognomy*, in which there is to be an account of Blake's vision and drawing of the 'Ghost of the Flea'. Such a work, writes the journalist, is really 'too absurd' to be tolerated 'in the present age', and moreover 'the madness of poor Blake (sublime as in some remains of him which we possess, it was) is too serious a subject to be jested with'.[11] These words may have been written by Carey, who had praised the *Grave* designs eleven years earlier.[12] In the issue of 27 December, the *Literary Gazette*, at the end of a scathing review, reprinted the Blakean passage of Varley's *Treatise*.

It was Cunningham who gave the notions of Blake's fundamental sanity, and of coherence and purpose in his works, the *coup de grâce*. Varley had given Cunningham a detailed account of the 'Visionary Heads'. Through that glass Cunningham had seen Blake as, in Bentley's and Nurmi's words, 'a kind of Jekyll and Hyde, sanely engraving for the booksellers by day and madly writing Urizen by night'.[13] Over and over, Cunningham's praise and blame all but cancel each other out. With regard to the *Descriptive Catalogue* he even wonders that 'the man who could . . . write down . . . matter so utterly wild and mad, was at the same time perfectly sensible to the exquisite nature of Chaucer's delineations' (Bentley, *Records*, p. 494). Not that Blake had succeeded—his painting of the *Canterbury Pilgrims* was flatly pronounced 'a failure' by Cunningham (p. 492).

How are these contradictions to be explained? Cunningham's answer, although still moderate, places him securely with the moderns in its Romanticism. 'Imagination', he argues, 'is the life and spirit of all great works of genius and taste. . . .

---

[9] Anon., 'Nollekens and his Times', *Athenaeum*, No. 56 (Nov. 1828), 882. Cited in Bentley, *Records*, p. 625.

[10] Anon., 'Art. III. *Nollekens and his Times*: . . . by John Thomas Smith . . .', *Eclectic Review*, iii (Dec. 1828), 536–7. Cited in Bentley, *Records*, pp. 625–6.

[11] Anon., 'Literary Novelties', *Literary Gazette*, 11 Oct. 1828, p. 654.

[12] See *A Blake Bibliography*, p. 226, and Bentley, *Records*, p. 350 n. For Carey's comments on *The Grave*, see *A Blake Bibliography*, No. 988.   [13] *A Blake Bibliography*, p. 11.

Blake's misfortune was that of possessing this precious gift in excess.' He confused the unreal and the real, until he 'dreamed himself out of the sympathies of actual life' (p. 503). Although Cunningham admits that Blake's 'claims to the distinction of a poet were not slight' (p. 506) and that he was 'a man of genius, some of whose works are worthy of any age or nation' (p. 499), his ignorance of the assumptions and traditions Blake worked with leaves him baffled and disgruntled; he adopts a distant and condescending tone. Because he cannot imagine Blake to be responsible in practical matters, he must take sides with Cromek in the dispute over the *Grave* designs.[14] But in the end, to the obvious Romanticism of Blake's early lyrics he must give his Romantic approval: '—and this man's poetry obtained no notice, while Darwin and Hayley were gorged with adulation' (pp. 505–6).

Among the poems by Blake which were printed by Cunningham were 'I love the Jocund dance', 'To the Muses', 'Gwin, King of Norway' (in part), 'King Edward the Third' (in part), from *Poetical Sketches*; 'Introduction', 'Laughing Song', 'The Lamb', 'The Chimney-Sweeper', and 'Holy Thursday', from *Songs of Innocence*; and 'The Tyger' from *Songs of Experience* (mistakenly included by Cunningham among the *Poetical Sketches*). Lengthy passages from the *Descriptive Catalogue*, and descriptions of *Europe*, *America*, and *Urizen*—all probably copied from J. T. Smith— round out the picture of the Blake canon, from which Cunningham chooses the *Songs of Innocence*, *The Gates of Paradise*, and the *Job* illustrations as his 'happiest' work (p. 500). There are several passing references to Blake in other sections of Cunningham's *Lives*.[15] Finally, there is a curiously moving and witty Blake story (reminiscent of certain Jewish tales) told by Cunningham in 1833, in the midst of a discussion of Guercino's *Christ in the Sepulchre*.[16]

A review in the *Athenaeum* in 1830 of Cunningham's second volume of *Lives of the British Painters*, seems to accept Cunningham wholly, while also expressing deep interest in Blake's life and abilities, and noting with evident approval that 'he seemed literally to realize the idea of Fuseli,—that a painter, before he began his work, should hold his subject palpably depicted in his mind's eye'.[17] In the same month, Blake usurps an entire review: 'West, Barry, Blake, Opie, Morland, Bird, and Fuseli, are names to win attention from all lovers of their glorious art; but the memoir of Blake is so curious a sketch of a very extraordinary mind, that we cannot but choose it for our illustration. . . .' The rest of this comparatively long

---

[14] It should also be remembered that Cromek had been Cunningham's literary 'patron'. See the Preface by Peter Cunningham to Allan Cunningham, *Poems and Songs*, London, 1847.

[15] In *A Blake Bibliography* (p. 256) they are given and described as follows: 'There are three references to Blake in the biography of Flaxman (1st ed., vol. iii [1830], pp. 277, 283, 308), and a wonderful anecdote about Blake and the Virgin Mary in that of Fuseli (2nd ed., vol. ii [1830], p. 333).'

[16] Allan Cunningham, *Cabinet Gallery of Pictures*, 2 vols., London, 1833–4. i. 11–13. Reprinted in Bentley, *Records*, pp. 182–3.

[17] Anon., '*The Lives of the Most Eminent British Painters, Sculptors, and Architects . . .*', *Athenaeum*, No. 118 (6 Feb. 1830), 67.

review consists of quotation of Cunningham.[18] The reviewer for the *Gentleman's Magazine* mentioned Blake for the third time in the month, but evinced interest only in Blake's alleged mental abnormalities.[19]

In the *London University Magazine*, however, Cunningham was challenged. 'In our opinion, it was rather foolish of Mr. Cunningham to attempt the life of so extraordinary a man as Blake, the peculiar character of whose mind he could no more comprehend, than he could produce rival works in either poetry or painting.' The author is probably Blake's and Coleridge's Swedenborgian friend, Charles Augustus Tulk. Blake, Flaxman, and Coleridge, he says, are 'the forerunners of a more elevated and purer system' of art and philosophy.[20] Blake is perhaps the most difficult of the three to decipher, and yet 'we should endeavour rather to unlock the prison-door in which we are placed [*sic*], and gain an insight into his powerful mind than rail and scoff at him as a dreamer and madman',[21] because after all, 'every genius has a certain end to perform, and always runs before his cotemporaries, and for that reason is not generally understood'.[22] In Germany the response to Blake would have been 'of the highest order'; but England is devoted to 'natural knowledge' rather than 'works of the mind'.[23]

And yet, the author does not despair, because the English, to whom complete freedom of thought is allowed, have surpassed the ancients in the development of that principle in art which 'conducts from the merely sensual delight of form to a contemplation of the beauties of the soul'.[24] In his vigorous moralization of beauty, therefore, Blake is representative of his nation: 'He still remembered he was a moral as well as intellectual citizen of England, bound both to love and instruct her.' No great genius, insists the critic, writes 'without having a plan'. In one stroke he illuminates the moral plan and the poetic method of Blake by elucidating the figure of Albion (in Blake's epics *Milton* and *Jerusalem*): Albion embodies 'Blake's ideas on the present state of England', by which means he mourned 'the crimes and errors of his dear country'.[25]

The *London University Magazine* article is notable for several reasons. First, the author has made a modest effort to explain one of Blake's major symbols, the giant Albion, and has done it, moreover, with interest and respect. Further, he has not only quoted 'A Cradle Song' and 'The Divine Image' from *Songs of Innocence*, and

[18] Anon., 'The Family Library, No. X. The Lives of the most eminent British Painters . . .', *The Literary Gazette, and Journal of Belles Lettres, Arts, Sciences, &c.*, 6 Feb. 1830, pp. 85–6. Cited in G. E. Bentley, Jr., 'A Supplement to . . . A Blake Bibliography', *Blake Newsletter*, ii, 4, Part ii (Apr. 1969).

[19] Anon., 'The Lives of the most eminent British Painters, Sculptors, and Architects. By Allan Cunningham. Vol. ii. Murray, 1830', *Gentleman's Magazine*, c (Feb. 1830), 141–3. Cited in Bentley, *Records*, p. 626.

[20] Anon., 'The Inventions of William Blake, Painter and Poet', *London University Magazine*, ii (Mar. 1830), 318. Reprinted in part in Bentley, *Records*, pp. 380–6. For a convincing discussion of the authorship of this article, see Dorfman, op. cit., pp. 42–3.

[21] 'The Inventions of William Blake', p. 320.

[22] Ibid., p. 321.   [23] Ibid., p. 319.   [24] Ibid., p. 320.   [25] Ibid., p. 321.

317

'Introduction', 'The Poison Tree', and 'The Garden of Love' from the *Songs of Experience*, but also he has printed, for the first time in letterpress, part (exactly one-third) of *The Book of Thel*. Most remarkable is the author's grasp of Blake's idea of the artist as a prophet. (Even his most enthusiastic admirers of the Revival of the sixties would not have such a sympathetic insight into Blake's moral purposes; they would tend rather to read his Prophecies as a new kind of psychological or aesthetic experiment—or an attempt *épater les bourgeois*.) For all of these reasons, the *London University Magazine* article may rightly be said to be 'in most respects . . . the most important criticism of Blake's poetry to appear before the 1860s'.[26] As if that were not enough, it gives us, in a footnote, the only evidence we have, besides a brief statement by Crabb Robinson, that Blake and Coleridge had talked together.[27]

Another article devoted exclusively to Blake was inspired by Cunningham's sketch. Entitled 'The Last of the Supernaturalists', it appeared in 1830 in *Fraser's Magazine*, which, like the *London University Magazine*, was then only in its second year. This puzzling piece has been called 'pretentious' and 'empty', and has been attributed to a number of persons, including Carlyle.[28] Blake, says the writer, was thought by the world to be a madman, but was in fact not mad; rather, his brain had become 'fevered' through adversities which caused him to take refuge in a belief in the supernatural (hence the title of the article). The article's routine biographical information and its uncommonly long and frequent quotations all come directly from Cunningham, but the author's own novel conclusion is that Blake was a 'glorious piece of mortality',[29] whose disabilities were imperfect mental health, poor education, and the lack of a friend who was a man of the world, to advise and sustain him.[30] Three of Blake's lyrics are given, and a fragment of 'King Edward the Third'. The article ends with a challenge to all those who would sneer at Blake: 'CAST OUT THE BEAM OUT OF THINE OWN EYE.'

Most readers of Cunningham did not respond vehemently to the picture of Blake that was painted in the 'Life', but many were interested. Felicia Hemans was moved to write a poem, 'suggested by the closing scene in the life of the painter Blake; as beautifully related by Allan Cunningham'.[31] In a letter to her future husband, Robert Southey, Caroline Bowles registers a sympathetic, passing interest of a kind that began during Blake's lifetime and continued through

---

[26] *A Blake Bibliography*, p. 11.

[27] 'The Inventions of William Blake', p. 323.

[28] *A Blake Bibliography* describes the article thus and discusses the attributions (p. 225). For a further discussion of attributions see Dorfman, op. cit., pp. 41–2.

[29] Anon., 'The Last of the Supernaturalists', *Fraser's Magazine*, ii (Mar. 1830), p. 220.

[30] Ibid., p. 231.

[31] 'The Painter's Last Work—A Scene', *Blackwood's Edinburgh Magazine*, xxxi (Feb. 1832), 220–1. For the editions and transformations of the poem, see *A Blake Bibliography*, p. 284.

three decades after his death—a polite and loyal opposition to the general impression that 'poor Blake' was mad and that it was best to leave it at that. Her letter, written in delightfully genteel prose, is dated April 1830:

I am longing to see some of Blake's engravings from his own extraordinary designs, of which I first heard from yourself. . . . They are certainly not generally known. Cunningham's life of him . . . has strengthened the interest for Blake and his works with which your account first inspired me. Mad though he might be, he was gifted and good, and a most happy being. I should have delighted in him, and would fain know how it fares with the faithful affectionate partner of his honourable life. I hope she is not in indigence. Have I ever told you that I have lost my kind and valuable neighbours the Dalrymples?...[32]

Southey replies, looking across the eighteen or twenty years that had intervened since his meeting with Blake:

I have nothing of Blake's but his designs for Blair's *Grave*. . . . His still stranger designs for his own compositions in verse were not ready for sale when I saw him, nor did I ever hear that they were so. [Southey is probably referring to *Jerusalem*, which he had seen in 1812] . . . I came away from the visit with so sad a feeling that I never repeated it.

He recalls the private exhibition held by Blake in 1809:

Some of the designs were hideous, especially those which he considered as most supernatural in their conception and likenesses. In others you perceived that nothing but madness had prevented him from being the sublimest painter of this or any other country. You could not have delighted in him—his madness was too evident, too fearful. It gave his eyes an expression such as you would expect to see in one who was possessed.[33]

 Southey's final comments on Blake were published posthumously in the mid forties in the last two volumes of *The Doctor*. In the first, Blake is identified as the author of the *Descriptive Catalogue* and of a poem about madness—'Mad Song', from *Poetical Sketches* (given by Southey in its correct form, implying the use of a copy in which typographical errors had been corrected by Blake himself).

My regard for thee, dear Reader, would not permit me to have left untranscribed this very curious and original piece of composition. Probably thou hast never seen, and art never likely to see either the 'Descriptive Catalogue' or the 'Poetical Sketches' of this insane and erratic genius, I will therefore end the chapter with the *Mad Song* from the latter . . .[34]

Although he calls Blake an 'insane and erratic genius', Southey may have had a more complex view, as has been suggested in a discussion of the strange Spanish

[32] Robert Southey, *The Correspondence of Robert Southey with Caroline Bowles*, ed. Edward Dowden, London, 1881, p. 191.   [33] Ibid., pp. 193–4.   [34] Robert Southey, *The Doctor*, vi, London, 1847, p. 126.

quotation that he uses to introduce the poem.[35] Southey's other published reference to Blake concerns Varley's engraving of *The Ghost of a Flea*, with some remarks on Blake from Varley's *Zodiacal Physiognomy*.[36] With these comments, however equivocal, Southey, who was himself to go mad, must have contributed some share to the legend of Blake's insanity.

It was a legend that could generate new documents as if from its own substance, and enlarge itself by so doing. Mona Wilson recorded the most sensational of these 'births' in her biographical study of Blake: an English article of 1833, containing two separate accounts, one of Blake-as-visionary, and the other of an inhabitant of Bedlam named Martin, was homogenized, in a French article claiming to be a translation of the English one. Blake rises up across the Channel, and behold! he is an inhabitant of Bedlam![37] In 1854, a Frenchman writing on hallucinations quite naturally tucked Blake into Bedlam, in a book that came out in an English translation in 1859.[38]

The original fuel for most accounts of Blake's madness seems to have come from Cunningham, who, in the abundance of his detail concerning Blake's visions and the creation of the Visionary Heads, provided abnormal psychologists of the day with one of their most useful documents. Robert Macnish, a member of the faculty of physicians and surgeons at Glasgow, published a study entitled *The Philosophy of Sleep* in 1830; as its writing antedated Cunningham's account, it contained no mention of Blake. In 1834 Macnish brought out a second, virtually rewritten edition (revised along phrenological lines) in which, not surprisingly, Blake appeared:

Perhaps the most remarkable visionary, of whom we have any detailed account, was Blake the painter. This extraordinary man not only believed in his visions, but could often call up at pleasure whatever phantasms he wished to see; . . . The greater part of his life was passed in beholding visions and in drawing them. . . . No conception was too strange or incongruous for his wild imagination, which totally overmastered his judgement, and made him mistake the chimeras of an excited brain for realities.[39]

[35] Michael Phillips raises this point in 'The *Poetical Sketches* of William Blake: A Definitive Text, the Reputation of the Poems from 1783 to the Present, and an Interpretation of their Meaning', doctoral dissertation, University of Exeter, 1968, pp. 158–60.

[36] *The Doctor*, vii, 1847, pp. 161–2.

[37] The articles, in the *Monthly Magazine* and *Revue Britannique*, both appeared in 1833. See Mona Wilson, *Life of William Blake*, 2nd ed., London, 1948, pp. 347–50. The author of the *Monthly Magazine* piece writes of having been present at the sittings that produced the Visionary Heads.

[38] A. Briere de Boismont, M.D., *On Hallucinations: A History and Explanations*, 1854, trans. R. S. Hulme, F.L.S., London, 1859, pp. 83–5. Cited in Dorfman, op. cit., pp. 40–1.

[39] Robert Macnish, *The Philosophy of Sleep*, New York, 1834, pp. 227–8. I quote from a (presumably) pirated American edition, because I have been unable to see the British edition of 1834, the story of which is told by D. M. Moir in the biography included in Robert Macnish, *The Modern Pythagorean*, 2 vols., Edinburgh and London, 1838, i. 321. Moir also mentions an 1835 Boston edition, for which the author sent corrections (p. 337). Neither Moir nor Macnish appear to have known of the first American edition.

Walter Cooper Dendy, in *The Philosophy of Mystery*, London, 1841, also comments on Blake as visionary

America's response to Cunningham's Blake was immediate, but shallow and sentimental. (The great majority of American references before 1863 can be studied in articles by S. Foster Damon, T. O. Mabbott, and Stephen A. Larrabee.[40] The following is an attempt to summarize the available material.) Before 1830 there are no known references to Blake in American publications; within several months of the publication of Cunningham's second volume in London, those parts of the 'Life' which describe Blake's visions and his idyllic marriage were reprinted or paraphrased in three magazines issued in Philadelphia and Hartford.[41] An American edition of Cunningham appeared in 1831. Even into the 1850s, his biography colours American accounts of Blake. These may be found in the *American Monthly Magazine* and the *New Jerusalem Magazine* of 1832, in a treatise, for 'young readers', on the fine arts in 1833, in the widely read *Atkinson's Saturday Evening Post* in 1835, in Whittier's *Supernaturalism of New England* in 1847, in T. S. Arthur's *The Brilliant: A Gift Book for 1850*, and in Shearjashub Spooner's anecdotes of artists in 1853.[42] In most of what was written about Blake, emphasis was laid on his powers of visualizing, which had the effect of classing him as a psychological curiosity. And yet, as Damon observes, 'nobody seems to have called him mad: Swedenborgianism had prepared America for such marvels'. The New World also reacted to Blake in verse. Americans wrote poems about Blake's marriage, his visions, and his lovely death.[43]

Some of Blake's early lyrics were printed in American magazines and anthologies. Among these, in the pre-Gilchrist period, are: 'On Another's Sorrow',

in a chapter on 'Poetic Phantasy, or Frenzy'. Shakespeare's relation to his 'fairy mythology' is compared to Blake's 'reverie' in which he witnessed a fairy's funeral. This interesting passage is reprinted in Bentley, *Records*, p. 489 n.

[40] S. Foster Damon, 'Some American References to Blake Before 1863', *Modern Language Notes*, xiv (1930), 365–70; Thomas Ollive Mabbott, 'Blake in America', *Notes & Queries*, cxlii (1922), 128; 'Blake's American Fame', *Times Literary Supplement*, 23 Feb. 1933, p. 127; 'More American References to Blake before 1863', *Modern Language Notes*, xlvii (1932), 87–8; 'More Early Publications of Blake', *Notes & Queries*, clxv (1933), 279; Stephen A. Larrabee, 'Some Additional American References to Blake, 1830–1863', *Bulletin of the New York Public Library*, lxi (1957), 561–3.

[41] The Philadelphia *Casket, Flowers of Literature, Wit and Sentiment*, v (May 1930), 231–2; *New-England Weekly Review*, Hartford, 3 May 1830; *Philadelphia Literary Port Folio: A Weekly Journal of Literature, Science, Art and the Times*, 13 May 1830, pp. 19, 150. All cited by Larrabee, op. cit., p. 561.

[42] *American Monthly Magazine*, Boston, iii (June 1831), 155–74; *New Jerusalem Magazine* [Swedenborgian], Boston, Jan. 1832, pp. 192–9; [Josiah Holbrook], *A Familiar Treatise on the Fine Arts, Painting, Sculpture, and Music*, Boston, 1833, pp. 96–7; *Atkinson's Saturday Evening Post*, Philadelphia, 28 Feb. 1835; [John Greenleaf Whittier], *The Supernaturalism of New England*, New York, 1847, pp. 25–6; T. S. Arthur, ed., *The Brilliant: A Gift Book for 1850*, New York, 1850, pp. 120–6; Shearjashub Spooner, *Anecdotes of Painters, Engravers, Sculptors and Architects, and Curiosities of Art*, 3 vols., New York, 1853, i. 3–4, ii. 79. The American edition of Whittier's *Supernaturalism* is noted in Merle Johnson's *American First Editions*, 4th ed., New York, 1942. The English edition, usually cited, appears to have been made up from American sheets.

[43] See Mabbott, 'More American References to Blake Before 1863', Damon, op. cit., and Larrabee, op. cit. As the poems do not have literary merit, they are not particularlized here. The one on 'The Fairy's Funeral', in the *New-York Mirror* for 21 June 1834, was inspired by 'Macnish's very interesting volume on the "Philosophy of Sleep". [The poet] was much struck with his brief but very characteristic account of the painter Blake.'

'Night', and 'The Little Black Boy', in Mrs. Anna Cabot (Jackson) Lowell's *Poetry for Home and School*, 1843; 'A Cradle Song', in Mrs. S. Colman's *Little Keepsake for 1844*; 'The Little Boy Lost' and 'The Little Boy Found', in Mrs. S. Colman's *Child's Gem*, 1845; 'On Another's Sorrow', in the *Harbinger* for 31 October 1846; 'The Tyger' (in the six-stanza version) and 'The Little Black Boy' in Longfellow's *The Estray*, 1847; 'To the Evening Star', 'To Morning', 'How Sweet I Roam'd', 'My Silks and Fine Array', 'Love and Harmony Combine', 'To Spring', 'To Summer', 'To Autumn', and 'To Winter', in the *Harbinger* in 1848;[44] 'The Tyger', in T. S. Arthur's *The Brilliant: A Gift Book for 1850* (already mentioned); 'The Tyger', 'The Little Black Boy', 'My Silks and Fine Array', 'The Garden of Love', and 'On Another's Sorrow', in Charles A. Dana's *Household Book of Poetry*, 1857. This last, which was reprinted many times and enlarged, added 'The Chimney Sweeper' to its edition of 1858.

The early American reader was also given a sample of Blake the artist. In 1847 appeared a New York edition of Blair's *Grave* with the Blake designs. The publisher was A. L. Dick and the plates, re-engraved in reduced size after the originals, bear Dick's name as engraver.[45] The plates were used again in 1858 by another New York publisher, though the date on the *engraved* title-page remains '1847'. This is very much a Blakean production. It contains Phillips's portrait (signed 'Wm. Blake del'!), Cromek's advertisement, Fuseli's puff, the essay 'Of the Designs', and a new Cunningham-derived biography of Blake (pp. v–vi). The plates are crudely executed and are notable chiefly for the addition of Victorian drapery (see Plate 78). Presumably the rather fleshly greetings of 'The meeting of a Family in Heaven' could not be dealt with by a flounce, and the plate was omitted.

The last of this group of American items also concerns Blake's art: a short passage in an *Outline History of the Fine Arts*, 1840.[46] The *Outline*, written from an American point of view, contains a short passage, in a section devoted to a history of engraving techniques, on '*metallic relief engraving*. The first attempts in this style were made by William Blake, an Englishman, in 1789.' The explanation that follows might have been taken straight out of Cunningham—or Smith—except that the secret liquid is casually identified as 'a kind of varnish'. The treatment of Blake is followed by a technical discussion of later attempts—English, Scottish, and American—at relief etching in metal.

Cunningham could serve a variety of interests, as shown by Mrs. D. L. Child (*née* Lydia Maria Francis) in her account of Mrs. Blake in 1833 in a book entitled

---

[44] The *Harbinger* reprintings are discussed below, p. 335.

[45] Archibald L. Dick, born and trained in Scotland, was working in New York by the 1830s and appears to have died about 1855. See George C. Groce and David H. Wallace, *The New-York Historical Society's Dictionary of Artists in America*, New Haven, 1957.

[46] Benson J. Lossing, *Outline History of the Fine Arts*, New York, 1840, pp. 301–3.

THE

GRAVE

A Poem

BY

BLAIR,

With Illustrations from Designs

BY

WM BLAKE.

1847.

Wm Blake. del.

A.L.Dick. sc.

78. *The Grave*, title-page.
Engraving by Archibald L. Dick, after Blake, for Blair's *Grave* (1847).
Kerrison Preston Blake Collection, Westminster City Library, 1858 reprint.

Good Wives.[47] Mrs. Child was an American journalist and abolitionist, whose *Appeal in Favor of that Class of Americans called Africans*, published in the same year as *Good Wives*, caused her membership in the Boston Athenaeum to be cancelled, and a periodical that she had started in 1826, the *Juvenile Miscellany*, to fail. *Good Wives* went through six editions before 1863; the fourth of these, in 1849, was published in London and Glasgow, the rest in America.

Meanwhile, reverberations of the 'Life' continued in Britain. A long notice of it in the *Edinburgh Review* in 1834 identified Blake as 'the able, but alas! insane author of some very striking and original designs, who could scarcely be considered a painter—. . .'.[48] It was a decidedly unfavourable climate for the efforts of Blake's old friend and patron, Linnell, who was still occupied with the promotion of the engraved set of *Illustrations of the Book of Job*.[49] Linnell's careful records in his 'subscription book' show that by 1834 only forty-four copies of the *Job* had been sold, about twenty-five of these while Blake was still living. Linnell eventually recouped about £168 of the nearly £250 he had advanced for the commission, copyright, and publishing expenses of the series, but the work was in no sense a popular success. Most of the copies were sold at the discounted trade price, to artists, booksellers, and friends. One set of proofs was subscribed by the King for ten guineas.[50]

The illustrations to Dante had an even gloomier fate; they remained virtually unknown. None of the drawings or copperplates of the series was sold until the present century—owing partly to a dispute over their ownership which arose after Blake's death between Frederick Tatham, who claimed that he was acting for Mrs. Blake, and Linnell, who considered the series to be his property and did in fact retain possession. When the dispute arose Linnell discontinued his efforts to dispose of the material.[51]

[47] Mrs. D. L. Child, *Good Wives*, Boston, 1833, pp. 128–33. The book was reviewed in Anon., 'Art. ii—Works of Mrs. Child', *North American Review*, xxxvii (1833), 138–64, with an anecdote from the life of Mrs. Blake. This review is cited in Suzanne R. Hoover, 'Fifty Additions to Blake Bibliography: Further Data for the Study of his Reputation', *Blake Newsletter*, v (Winter 1971–2), 167–72.

[48] [T. H. Lister], 'Art. iii. *Lives of the Most Eminent British Painters . . .*', *Edinburgh Review*, lix (Apr. 1834), 53. There is a second Blake reference in this article, on p. 64, which *A Blake Bibliography* fails to note: 'Those artists are most safe who can grapple with subjects which scarcely any have ventured to figure to themselves,—who can far outsoar the imaginations of others, and leave spectators wondering at a distance. But these are the possessors of a rare gift,—exceptions in art, and not to be circumscribed by common rules. Such were Fuseli and Blake. . . .' See Hoover, No. 5.

[49] See Bernard Barton's letter to Linnell of 12 Apr. 1830, in which he thanks Linnell for having sent a copy of *Job* for possible purchase. Cited in Joseph Anthony Wittreich, 'William Blake and Bernard Barton', *Blake Studies*, i (Autumn 1968), 91–4.

[50] The facts concerning the *Job* illustrations are given in Edwin Wolf 2nd, 'The Blake–Linnell Accounts in the Library of Yale University', *Papers of the Bibliographical Society of America*, xxxvii (1943), 1–22. See also 'The Blake–Linnell Documents', in Keynes, *Blake Studies*, 2nd ed., Oxford, 1971, pp. 205–12, and *The Letters of William Blake*, 2nd ed., London, 1968, pp. 144 ff.

[51] A full account of this sad postscript to the relationship between Blake and Linnell is given in Keynes, *Blake Studies*, pp. 224–8.

A few persons did take an interest in Blake's other works after his death, and sought out purchasable copies. Some of these are mentioned by Keynes and Wolf in their *Census of the Illuminated Books*:[52]

> Soon after [Blake's] death, and about the middle of the nineteenth century [N.B. there are two distinct periods suggested here], there appeared several eager collectors of Blake's books. William Beckford acquired many of them, including most of Cumberland's copies. Benjamin D'Israeli inherited his father's and may have acquired others. Frederick Locker-Lampson bought a number for the Rowfant Library. Francis Palgrave was the owner of several now in the British Museum, and a significant collection was formed by Thomas Gaisford.

This very partial list is capped by one of the worldliest names in mid-century London: 'The most important collection of all was that gathered by Richard Monckton Milnes, first Lord Houghton, who acquired among others several of the Butts copies when these were sold in 1852.' 'Songs of Innocence and of Experience', as Keynes and Wolf observe, surveying the evidence, 'was . . . by far the most popular, and it seems to have attracted many customers who did not buy copies of Blake's other works.' The *Songs* held the first place in popularity among Blake's works after his death as well as before—indeed, from the time they were first 'published' to the present day.

At least two quasi-biographies of Blake were written in the early 1830s, but neither of them was published until the twentieth century. One of these, recently discovered in the British Museum by G. E. Bentley, Jr., is merely an encyclopedia entry written by a London printseller and auctioneer named Thomas Dodd, whose birth and death dates are virtually identical with Wordsworth's. Dodd, who Bentley believes 'may very well have known Blake', published between 1825 and 1831 the first six volumes of *The Connoisseur's Repertorium: or a Universal Historical Record of Painters, Engravers, Sculptors, and of their Works*. 'Public support', Bentley tells us, 'subsided before Dodd got beyond "Barraducio".' The Blake entry remained in manuscript. Its information was taken from Cunningham's 'Life', and its brief mention of Blake's poetry is Cunninghamesque: 'most sublimely obscure, if not absolutely unfathomable.'[53] It was Blake's engraved work that interested Dodd and claimed his historical attention. For all that, the notice is no more than routine.

Another unpublished biography, longer and much more authoritative than Dodd's, was written by Frederick Tatham, the young sculptor who knew Blake during the last two or three years of his life. It was Tatham who had gained

[52] Geoffrey Keynes and Edwin Wolf 2nd, *William Blake's Illuminated Books: A Census*, New York, 1953, p. xviii.

[53] See G. E. Bentley, Jr., 'An Unknown Early Biography of Blake', *Times Literary Supplement*, 16 Mar. 1962, p. 192. Both here and in *A Blake Bibliography* Bentley gives Dodd's first name as 'Robert'.

possession of the works remaining in Blake's studio at his death—by Blake's own wish, according to Tatham's story. Blake's wife, Catherine, had stayed with the Linnells as housekeeper for nine months after her husband's death, then moved to Tatham's house, and finally to rooms of her own, where in 1831, in the presence of Mr. and Mrs. Tatham, she had died. Tatham's 'biography'—really a sketch, similar to Smith's memoir of Blake in *Nollekens*—was found bound up with the only whole coloured copy of *Jerusalem*, and first published in 1906.[54] The date of its composition by Tatham is some time in 1832; part of it may have been written earlier. Apparently, Tatham had been trying to sell the *Jerusalem*, and wrote the 'Life of William Blake' for that purpose. That the sketch of Blake was written specifically in order to be bound up with the *Jerusalem* is at least suggested by a reference in the sketch to the unintelligibility of Blake's poetry written 'in the manner of the present work]'—a remark more apologetic than critical. There is also an allusion, in another passage, to 'the following Work'.[55] Tatham may have thought that it would be easier to sell a volume as unusual and expensive as the *Jerusalem* if it were accompanied by a sympathetic biographical account.

With the exception of several small anecdotes, Tatham's 'Life' does not contribute much new information about its subject.[56] For the facts of Blake's early life the author draws on Malkin. Like Malkin, he quotes several poems from *Poetical Sketches* and *Songs of Innocence and of Experience*. When Gilchrist was doing research for the Blake biography he interviewed Tatham, from whom he learned Blake's method of producing his colour prints;[57] Tatham's interest in Blake's technical experiments is also apparent in his 'Life of Blake', in which he spends over 1,300 words justifying Blake's rejection of oil as a vehicle for paint.

Perhaps the most interesting passages in the sketch are those in which Tatham defends Blake's character against the charge of oddness:

... there is sufficient evidence to prove that many of his Eccentric speeches, were thrown forth more as a piece of sarcasm, upon the Enquirer, than from his real opinion. If he thought a question were put merely for a desire to learn, no man could give advice more reasonably & more kindly but if that same question were put for idle curiosity ... he then made an enigma of a plain question. Hence arose many reports of his oddities. He was particularly so upon religion.[58]

Swedenborg himself, who 'was not a madman, nor does he appear to have been considered so, by his contemporaries', is put forward by Tatham as an example of the respectability of vision; but 'all that is necessary to prove ... is, that other

---

[54] In Archibald G. B. Russell, ed., *The Letters of William Blake*, London, 1906, pp. 1–49. The text is reprinted in Bentley, *Records*, to which all citations hereafter will be made.

[55] Bentley, *Records*, pp. 531, 532.

[56] And in fact, some of his information is inaccurate. See ibid., p. 508.

[57] Alexander Gilchrist, *Life of William Blake*, 'Pictor Ignotus', 2 vols., London, 1863, i. 421.

[58] Bentley, *Records*, pp. 529–30.

men, other sensible men, such as scarcely could be designated as mad or stupid, did see into an immaterial life denied to most—'. Indeed, the visionary power is not so unusual: the author 'has known others besides Blake, on whose veracity & sanity he could equally well rely, who have been thus favoured'.[59]

From an unexpected quarter came another appreciative glimpse of Blake, in a book published in 1839. Lady Charlotte Bury told of meeting 'an eccentric little artist, by name Blake' at a dinner party given by Lady Caroline Lamb in about 1818. 'He appeared to me to be full of beautiful imaginations and genius; . . . He appeared gratified by talking to a person who comprehended his feelings. I can easily imagine that he seldom meets with anyone who enters into his views; for they are peculiar, and exalted above the common level of received opinions.'[60] But Lady Bury's appreciation was buried in a long and little-read book and Tatham's remained unpublished. Meanwhile, Cunningham's legend of 'mad Blake' was embroidered by others. A popular connoisseur of literature and art, who had known Blake slightly, the Revd. Thomas Frognall Dibdin, described Blake as 'amiable but illusory', and 'far beyond my ken or sight. In an instant he was in his "third heaven"—flapped by the wings of seraphs . . . the sublime and the grotesque seemed, somehow or the other [*sic*], to be forever amalgamated in his imagination; . . .'[61] A more learned indictment of Blake appeared in passing in a review of John Martin's *Illustrations of the Bible*: '. . . [Martin] must have a world of his own to paint. His pictures are opium dreams, a plantasmagoria of landscape and architecture, as Fuseli's and Blake's designs were of human beings.'[62]

It is especially interesting to follow the younger generation of literary men as they discovered Blake for themselves in the 1830s. In 1833 Edward FitzGerald, who knew Malkin, Southey, and Crabb Robinson, wrote in a letter to W. B. Donne (later librarian of the London Library) that he had just bought 'a little pamphlet which is very difficult to be got, called the Songs of Innocence'. He described the author as mad, 'but of a madness that was really the elements of great genius ill-sorted . . . to me there is a particular interest in this man's writing and drawing, from the strangeness of the constitution of his mind'.[63] Bulwer-Lytton found Blake the most remarkable of 'enthusiasts', whose madness was 'delightful' and whose verses were 'exquisite'. Like FitzGerald, he had just come across a work of Blake's, in this case the *Night Thoughts* engravings, which seemed to him strange

[59] Ibid., p. 519.

[60] [Lady Charlotte Bury], *Diary Illustrative of the Times of George the Fourth*, ed. John Galt, 4 vols., London, 1838–9, iii. 345–8.

[61] Revd. Thomas Frognall Dibdin, D.D., *Reminiscences of a Literary Life*, London, 1836, pp. 786–7.

[62] Anon., 'Art. xi. Illustrations to the Bible', *The Westminster Review*, xx (1 Apr. 1834), 452–65. The quotation is taken from p. 464. Cited in G. E. Bentley, Jr., 'A Supplement to . . . A Blake Bibliography'.

[63] Edward FitzGerald, *Letters and Literary Remains of Edward FitzGerald*, ed. William Aldis Wright, 2nd ed., London, 1894, i. 25–6.

and new. His description of the work is intense but nevertheless not particularly fresh: '. . . so grotesque, so sublime—now by so literal an interpretation, now by so disconnected a train of invention', that its over-all effect is of 'one of the most astonishing and curious productions which ever balanced between the conception of genius and the ravings of insanity'. For the purpose of periodical literature this 'romantic' description by Bulwer-Lytton was good copy, and was published accordingly in the *New Monthly Magazine* in 1830.[64]

A minor literary man who knew many major ones, R. H. Horne, writing in 1838, found that 'William Blake's estimate of himself as a man of genius (visions inclusive) was a just one'.[65] Walter Savage Landor's interest in Blake was robust rather than intense. As his biographer notes, under the year 1836, Landor found some of Blake's writings at a Bristol bookseller's,

and was strangely fascinated by them. . . . He protested that Blake had been Wordsworth's prototype [for the *Lyrical Ballads?*], and wished they could have divided his madness between them; for that some accession of it in the one case, and something of a diminution of it in the other would very greatly have improved both.[66]

In a manuscript notebook of Landor's there is an undated comment, which reads, 'Blake: never did a braver or a better man carry the sword of justice.'[67] Unfortunately, Landor was given to such extravagant praise of Blake among his companions, and at the expense of other poets—and given, as well, to perverse judgements of the most shocking kind—that his real appreciation of Blake's moral position was not communicated to his contemporaries. Crabb Robinson reports on two literary breakfast parties at which Landor was present in 1838, one given by Robinson himself on 20 May, and the other, two days later, given by Richard Monckton Milnes. We may infer, incidentally, from what Robinson says, that Carlyle probably already knew of Blake.

May 20th.—My breakfast party went off very well indeed as far as talk was concerned; I had with me Landor, Milnes, and Serjeant Talfourd. A great deal of rattling on the part of Landor. He maintained Blake to be the greatest of poets, that Milnes is the greatest poet now living in England, and that Scott's *Marmion* is superior to all Wordsworth and Byron, and the descriptions of the battle better than anything in Homer! but Blake furnished chief matter for talk. . . .

---

[64] [Edward Bulwer-Lytton], 'Conversations with an Ambitious Student in Ill Health', *New Monthly Magazine*, xxix (Dec. 1830), 511–19.

[65] [Richard Henry Horne], 'British Artists and Writers on Art', *British and Foreign Review*, vi (1838), 610–57. Cited in H. B. de Groot, 'R. H. Horne, Mary Howitt, and a Mid-Victorian Version of The Ecchoing Green', *Blake Studies*, iv (1971), 81–8. For two minor references to Blake in comments by younger writers, see C. C. Abbott, *The Life and Letters of George Darley*, London, 1928, p. 165, and J. W. and A. Tibble, eds., *The Prose of John Clare*, London, 1951, p. 228. (Both noted in Dorfman, op. cit., pp. 35–6.)

[66] John Forster, *Walter Savage Landor*, London, 1869, ii. 322–3.

[67] Keynes, *Bibliography of William Blake*, New York, 1921, p. 335.

May 22nd.—A delightful breakfast with Milnes, Rogers, Carlyle, who made himself very pleasant indeed, Moore, Landor—a party of eight. . . . Talk very good, equally divided. Talleyrand's recent death and the poet Blake were the subjects. Tom Moore had never heard of Blake—at least not of his poems. Even he acknowledged their beauty. . . .[68]

At about this time Milnes was apparently thinking of Blake between breakfasts, as well as during them. In a letter to Aubrey De Vere, which has been conjecturally assigned to this year (1838),[69] Milnes asks, 'Have you ever seen any of Blake's poetry? I think of publishing some selections from him which will astonish those who are astoundable by anything of this kind.' But he never did, and it fell to another young man, three years his junior, to edit the first book of poems by Blake in regular letterpress since the *Poetical Sketches* of 1783. It was the *Songs of Innocence and of Experience*, without illustration of any kind, published jointly by Pickering and Newbury in 1839.[70]

The editor—Blake's first—was James John Garth Wilkinson, a twenty-seven-year-old Swedenborgian who was to become a well-known medical doctor and homeopathist, as well as a Fourierist, the translator and biographer of Swedenborg, the highly regarded friend of such men as Emerson and Henry James, Sr., and an acquaintance of Browning, Longfellow, Hawthorne, and Carlyle. It was undoubtedly through his interest in Swedenborg's works and his closeness to the Swedenborgian Society, which date from about 1836, that Wilkinson had met Charles Augustus Tulk. This old friend of Blake, who was at that time a Member of Parliament for Poole, showed his copy of the *Songs* (the same he had shown to Coleridge twenty years earlier)[71] to Wilkinson, who determined to print the book (edited anonymously) in the regular manner. Money to publish it was obtained from his brother William, and the edition appeared in 1839, with a twenty-one page Preface by Garth Wilkinson.

Perhaps as a consequence of his new interest in Blake, Wilkinson was introduced, in the November preceding the publication of his book, to Tatham.[72] To Wilkinson, who had known only the *Songs*, the violence of some of Blake's other work, shown to him by Tatham, came as a shock:

It was indeed a—*not* a treat, but an astonishment to me. The first painting we came to realized to me the existence of powers which I did not know were had in it [i.e. in the art of painting]. 'Twas an infernal scene, and the only really infernal thing I ever saw—. . . . It was most unutterable and abominable—a hopeless horror. . . . On the whole . . .

[68] Edith J. Morley, ed., *Henry Crabb Robinson on Books and Their Writers*, 3 vols., London, 1938, ii. 549–50.
[69] T. Wemyss Reid, *The Life, Letters, and Friendships of Richard Monckton Milnes, First Lord Houghton*, 2nd ed., London, 1891, i. 220.
[70] [James John Garth Wilkinson, ed.], *The Songs of Innocence and of Experience*, London, 1839. The volume concludes with Blake's dedication 'To The Queen' from *The Grave*.
[71] See Earl Leslie Griggs, ed., *Collected Letters of Samuel Taylor Coleridge*, 6 vols., Oxford, 1959, iv. 835–8.
[72] Clement John Wilkinson, *James John Garth Wilkinson*, London, 1911, p. 29.

giving me an idea that Blake was inferior to no one who ever lived, in terrific tremendous power, also gave me the impression that his whole inner man must have been in a monstrous and deformed condition. . . .[73]

Some months later Wilkinson saw Blake's designs again, and again was 'puzzled what to say of the man who was compounded of such heterogeneous materials'— his example, here, of an inexplicable combination of sympathies in Blake is a revealing one—'as to be able at one time to write the "Songs of Innocence" and at another "The Visions of the Daughters of Albion"'. As *The Visions of the Daughters of Albion* pleads for freedom and honesty in relations of sex and love, its difficulties for a young Victorian are not hard to find. But *The Book of Thel* is hardly more accessible to Wilkinson,[74] and when he came to write the Preface to his edition of the *Songs*, he felt quite able to state that 'the present volume contains nearly all that is excellent in Blake's poetry'.[75]

A part of Wilkinson's Preface is an attack on Allan Cunningham that recalls the similar, briefer charges made, probably by Tulk, in the *London University Magazine* in 1830. Disdainfully, Cunningham is called 'clever', and 'incapable, by Nature, or by Will, of dealing with the Spiritual phenomena' exhibited by Blake. Wilkinson uses Cunningham's biographical material gladly, but rejects his materialist 'tone of feeling' and 'style of thought'.

But the true villain of Wilkinson's Preface is not Cunningham—it is Blake. 'In thus condemning the superficial canons by which Blake has been judged', writes the Swedenborgian novice, he must yet withhold from Blake 'any approbation of the spirit in which he conceived and executed his later works'. For although Blake, correctly, 'naturalized the spiritual, instead of spiritualizing the natural', he was too likely 'to prefer seeing Truth under the loose garments of Typical, or even Mythologic, Representation, rather than in the Divine-Human Embodiment of Christianity'. In turning from the evils of scientism, materialism, and realism Blake's imagination 'found a home in the ruins of Ancient and consummated Churches', instead of in the New Spiritualism.[76] Carefully, he distinguishes between Blake's hell and Byron's: 'He embodies no Byronisms,—none of the sentimentalities of civilized vice, but delights to draw evil things and evil beings in their naked and final state.' It is an evil that gathers to itself weariness and desolation such as accumulate in *Macbeth*:

We have the impression that we are looking down into the hells of the ancient people, the Anakim, the Nephilim, and the Rephaim. Their human forms are gigantic petri-factions, from which the fires of lust and intense selfish passion, have long dissipated what was animal and vital; leaving stony limbs, and countenances expressive of despair, and stupid cruelty.[77]

---

[73] Clement John Wilkinson, *James John Garth Wilkinson*, pp. 29–30.   [74] Ibid., pp. 30–1.
[75] Wilkinson, ed., *Songs*, p. xx.   [76] Ibid., pp. xiv–xvii.   [77] Ibid., p. xviii.

For the first time in print, Blake is compared with Shelley. Both were led to find their materials in 'the ages of type and shadow which preceded the Christian revelation'. But this took quite a different form in each of the poets: Shelley's 'metaphysical irreligion took him . . . to the Philosophy and Theology of the Greeks . . . [where he could have] liberty to distribute Personality at will to the beautiful forms of the visible creation'; by contrast, Blake's visionary tendencies, his mysticism, his unformalistic, expansive genius led him to 'the mythic foundations of an elder time', where he 'entered into . . . the Egyptian and Asiatic perversions of an ancient and true Religion'.[78] This last phrase is probably the first reference to Blake's 'Satanism'—an aspect of Blake which was not to engage commentators again until Swinburne emphasized and championed it in the late 1860s. Shelley's taste for subversion and heresy—which brought him to a 'Satanic' reading of *Paradise Lost* that was rather similar to Blake's—brings him also to judgement with Blake. They both imagined, says Wilkinson, 'that they could chop and change the Universe, even to the confounding of Life with Death, to suit their own creative fancies'.

Of all Blake's works, only the *Songs* escaped these errors, and of these, especially the poems of *Innocence*. Instead of the 'ancient hells', the *Songs of Innocence* give us glimpses of the Golden Age, with its holy and pastoral simplicity—and will therefore, Wilkinson hopes, by being now available in print, give an added impulse 'to the New Spiritualism which is now dawning upon the world'.[79]

There is no record of communication about Blake between Wilkinson and Robert Browning, and yet some communication on that subject may well have occurred. The two men were acquainted (they had met some time in 1836 or early in the next year; Wilkinson had been present at a private reading of Browning's *Strafford* before its opening on 1 May 1837, and present at the opening as well).[80] Moreover, there is a poem entitled 'Transcendentalism', written by Browning in the forties (it is not known exactly when), which may be about Blake and poetry. Mr. Thurman Los Hood has argued that 'Transcendentalism' is not written as an address by Browning himself to some unidentified poet, but rather, it is 'a dramatic monologue, exemplifying, expounding, and illustrating aspects of Browning's poetics, in the form of a remonstrance to William Blake by the shade of his dead brother Robert against the abandonment of lyric form and essence in Blake's Prophetic Writings'. If Hood's interesting reading is accurate, the poem should also be considered to be the first expression of concern with Blake's poetics.[81]

[78] The comparison occurs on pp. xviii–xix, from which all the quotations in the present paragraph are taken. (For a possible earlier linking of the poets' names, although not a comparison, see Stuart Curran and Joseph Anthony Wittreich, Jr., 'Some Additions to *A Blake Bibliography*', *Blake Newsletter*, iii. 1 (15 June 1969), 4–6.)

[79] Wilkinson, ed., *Songs*, pp. xx–xxi.   [80] Clement Wilkinson, op. cit., p. 31.

[81] Thurmon L. Hood, 'Browning and Blake', *Trinity Review* [Hartford, Conn.], N.S. ii (Mar. 1948), 42–3.

There is at about the same time a very familiar reference to Blake by Browning in a letter to Elizabeth Barrett. Writing on 9 July 1846 of Benjamin R. Haydon, who had recently committed suicide, Browning observes that 'even a smaller strip of land was enough to maintain Blake . . . in power and glory through the poor, fleeting "sixty years" . . .'.[82] It is just possible that Browning's use of Blake's phrase for the human lifetime—'sixty years'—may indicate an acquaintance with some of the Prophetic Books. Where might Browning have seen them? One of the likelier possibilities is the home of Monckton Milnes. The two men were acquainted sufficiently for Browning to call on Milnes on 3 and 21 March 1846, about four months before he wrote the letter that mentions Haydon and Blake.[83]

In the absence of stronger evidence, connections and readings such as those suggested with regard to Browning, must remain very tentative. Carlyle's connections with Blake are similarly meagre, but they are more direct. Carlyle has already been seen at Milnes's breakfast party in May 1838, when the conversation was of Blake. According to Wilkinson's biographer, a copy of the 1839 edition of *Songs of Innocence and of Experience* was sent to Carlyle by Wilkinson, who received a reply in thanks, which has presumably been lost.[84] A closer association with Blake scholarship awaited Carlyle when his new friend Gilchrist began to write Blake's biography. It may have been at Carlyle's house that Gilchrist first saw the Job designs, for Carlyle owned a copy.[85] And yet, for all of this cross-pollination, Carlyle never mentioned Blake in his published work, or evinced an interest in him.

Emerson, on the other hand, was interested. Like Carlyle, he read at least the *Songs* and Gilchrist's *Life*. His copy of the *Songs* in Wilkinson's edition was inscribed to him as a gift from Elizabeth Palmer Peabody.[86] Unfortunately, the inscription is undated, and the few endpaper and marginal annotations which were made in pencil by Emerson himself are virtually useless in determining his response to the poems. Several references to Blake were made by Emerson in the period before Gilchrist's *Life*, in his 'Journals', which are at the present time being edited for publication by the Harvard University Press from manuscripts in the Houghton Library. None of the volumes of *Journals* published so far, contains a notation on Blake.

In my examination of the 'Journals' I found three entries that were of interest and some insignificant notations of Blake's name. In 1848 Emerson wrote, 'I cannot remember J.[ones] Very without being reminded of Wordsworth's remark on

---

[82] Elvan Kintner, ed., *The Letters of Robert Browning and Elizabeth Barrett Barrett* (*1845–1846*), 2 vols., Cambridge, Mass., 1969, ii. 861. The editor conjectures that the 'sixty years' 'must be Haydon's reference to himself; Blake died at the age of seventy'.   [83] *Letters*, i. 512 and 548.

[84] Clement Wilkinson, op. cit., p. 35.

[85] See Herbert Harlakenden Gilchrist, *Anne Gilchrist, Her Life and Writings*, 2nd ed., London, 1887, p. 59.

[86] This copy belongs to the Houghton Library of Harvard University. The annotations are given in Edward J. Rose, 'The 1839 Wilkinson Edition of Blake's *Songs* in Transcendental America', *Blake Newsletter*, iv. 3 (1971), 79–81. Rose also notes that Thomas Wentworth Higginson read this edition in 1842.

William Blake, "There is something in the madness of this man that interests me more than the sanity of Lord Byron and Walter Scott." '[87] The private papers of Henry Crabb Robinson, from which this remark appears to have been quoted verbatim, were not published until after his death in 1867. Emerson and Robinson became acquainted in 1848. It would seem that Robinson had given Emerson his diaries to read. When in 1862 Emerson remarked on Blake once again, again he quoted from Robinson. A third time, in 1863, Robinson was quoted on Blake, with two Proverbs of Hell from *The Marriage of Heaven and Hell*.[88] Except for one or two casual references, Emerson, like Carlyle, did not mention Blake in any of his published works.[89]

The early and middle forties seem to mark a lull before a new surge of interest in Blake. An edition of the *Songs*, numbering only twelve copies, was printed privately by Charles Augustus Tulk, on paper watermarked 1843.[90] The printing consisted of letterpress alone, but spaced as in the original, in order that the illustrations might be copied in.

In 1843 Keats's old friend Charles Wentworth Dilke, now editor of the *Athenaeum*, and said to be an early collector of Blake's works,[91] visited Linnell to see his Blake collection. Dilke arranged for Henry Cole,[92] who was writing an article for the *Athenaeum*, to see the Virgil's *Pastorals* wood-blocks which were in Linnell's possession. Linnell permitted one of the woodcuts to be reproduced for Cole's article. A review of Mulready's illustrations for *The Vicar of Wakefield*, the article contains a long digression on the necessity for the work of engraving to be done by the designer himself, rather than by another hand. The one print from the Virgil series is reproduced beside an engraving by another artist of the same design. (It had been engraved before the series was first published, because of fear the public would react against Blake's style.) Of the 'few wood-engravings which that wonderful man cut himself' Cole observes: '. . . Blake's rude work, utterly

[87] 'Journal GULISTAN 1848', Houghton Library MS. No. 108, p. 136. Cited in Hoover, 'Fifty Additions . . .', No. 6. Quotation by permission of the Harvard College Library. Jones Very (1813–80) underwent a period (*c.* 1837–8) of religious ecstasy, in which he took dictation from the Holy Ghost and composed religious sonnets. Elizabeth Palmer Peabody, a family friend, introduced him to Emerson, whose short-lived enthusiasm induced him to help Very in the publication of a volume entitled *Essays and Poems*.

[88] 'Journal WAR 1862', Houghton Library MS. No. 79, pp. 244–6, Hoover, No. 16; 'Journal FOR 1863', Houghton Library MS. No. 79, p. 284, Hoover, No. 17.

[89] For a late reference in an essay entitled 'Poetry and Imagination', see Rose, op. cit., pp. 80 f.

[90] This edition bears no title-page, and no indication as to the date and place of printing. The pertinent facts and history of the edition are given in Geoffrey Keynes, 'Blake, Tulk, and Garth Wilkinson', *Library*, 4th series, xxvi (1945), 190–2.

[91] Sir Charles Wentworth Dilke, ed., *The Papers of a Critic*, selected from the writings of Charles Wentworth Dilke, 2 vols., London, 1875, i. 51.

[92] Later Sir Henry Cole (1808–82), administrator and artist, chiefly remembered for his part in organizing the Great Exhibitions of 1851 and 1862 and in founding the Victoria and Albert Museum and the Royal Albert Hall.

without pretension . . . the merest attempt of a fresh apprentice—*is* a work of genius; whilst the latter is but a piece of smooth tame mechanism.'[93] Cole's view was now in the ascendent, although for a while still it was to be only infrequently expressed.

A very minor mention of Blake was made in 1847 in *Howitt's Journal*, edited by William Howitt, in the form of a note which accompanied the 'illustration for this present week', a reproduction of 'Death's Door', from *The Grave*. The text of this (presumably editorial) note was taken from Cunningham, more or less verbatim, and is notable only in that it identifies Blake as 'one of the most spiritual-minded and original men that ever lived'.[94] A similar article, with the same plate (reversed) engraved in wood by W. J. Linton, was put together several years later in a large and elegant picture-magazine.[95]

A new aspect of Blake's art was introduced for consideration in Anna Brownell Jameson's *Sacred and Legendary Art* in 1848. Mrs. Jameson observes that 'the most original, and, in truth, the only new and original version of the Scripture idea of angels which I have met with [in recent painting and sculpture] is that of William Blake'. 'His adoring angels float rather than fly, and with their half liquid draperies, seem about to dissolve into light and love: and his rejoicing angels—behold them —sending up their voices with the morning stars, that "singing, in their glory move!"'[96] A close friend of the Brownings from about 1845, Mrs. Jameson was given most of the materials for her book by the (later) President of the Royal Academy, Sir Charles Eastlake. Her remarks on Blake are illustrated with reversed engravings of three Blake angels, which appear to have been selected from Plates five, fifteen, and sixteen of the *Illustrations of the Book of Job*.

One evening in that same year (1848) Wilkinson dined out and met Crabb Robinson. He wrote afterward:

The said Crabb Robinson is one of the most entertaining and interesting old gentlemen I have ever met. He is one of the Council of University College, an old friend of Mr. Tulk's and one of the executors of Flaxman. He knew Blake well. After tea, he singled me out by miracle, and entertained me beyond measure about the great artist. It was he who gave

---

[93] [Henry Cole], 'Fine Arts. *The Vicar of Wakefield* . . .', *Athenaeum*, No. 795 (21 Jan. 1843), 65. The author of this article is identified in *A Blake Bibliography*, p. 253.

[94] Anon., 'Death's Door', *Howitt's Journal*, ii (Nov. 1847), 322.

[95] Anon., 'Death and Immortality', *The Illustrated Exhibitor and Magazine of Art*, i (Jan. 1852), 369–71. At the close of 1852 Linton's version of Blake's design was reproduced in the *Ladies' Drawing Room Book* (Dec. 1852), pp. 14–16. The volume was 'intended to demonstrate . . . the great perfection to which the art of engraving upon wood can be brought . . .'. A two-page discussion, mostly of Blake, includes this statement concerning his current standing in the marketplace: '. . . his works have long since found their value in the market: most of them have become scarce, and are now bought up at prices double and treble those at which they were originally published.' Both articles are cited in Bentley, 'A Supplement to . . . A Blake Bibliography'.

[96] [Anna Brownell] Jameson, *Sacred and Legendary Art*, 2 vols., London, 1848, i. 50. Blake is mentioned in a review of this work in *Blackwood's Edinburgh Magazine*, lxv (Feb. 1849), 175–89. Cited in Bentley, 'A Supplement to . . . A Blake Bibliography'.

Blake 25 guineas for the 'Songs of Innocence'. He warmly invited me to call on him, when he will show me several of Blake's originals, both poems and pictures.[97]

(It is interesting to note that when Wilkinson offered three books by Blake to Robinson in 1850, Robinson declined to buy them because of the price, which was five pounds. Keynes thinks it likely that these three books were the *Songs of Innocence and of Experience*, *America*, and *The Book of Thel*.)[98] At the same dinner Wilkinson met Emerson, who was lecturing in England. There is a curious coincidence in dates, between that meeting of Wilkinson, Crabb Robinson, and Emerson in England on 17 April and the subsequent appearance in New York, in the 24 June and 8 July issues of the *Harbinger*, of a total of nine poems by Blake. The *Harbinger* had been the unofficial organ of Brook Farm, and was currently being published from New York. It was financed and strongly influenced by Henry James, Sr., a Swedenborgian, who was a friend of Emerson and who, as it happens, had corresponded intensively with Wilkinson since the early forties. Before June 1848, only one Blake poem, 'On Another's Sorrow', had been printed in the *Harbinger*. That little poem, printed in 1846, belongs to the *Songs of Innocence*; all the poems printed in the *Harbinger* in 1848 were from *Poetical Sketches*. It would therefore seem that a copy of *Poetical Sketches* had crossed the Atlantic during the spring of 1848. By whom was it sent?

On 2 May Robinson took Emerson to dinner at the Antiquarian Society. Eleven days later Robinson spent 'a considerable time' with Wilkinson, whose 'love of Blake is delightful'.[99] There were certainly many matters to be discussed besides Blake, but it is likely that Robinson persuaded either Wilkinson or Emerson (or both) of the exceptional quality of the *Poetical Sketches*, and that one of them sent the book (or some of its contents) to Henry James, Sr., in America. If this guess is correct, it shows us another instance of Robinson's important efforts to make Blake known during the dark ages of the poet's reputation.[100]

A year later, in August, 1849, Henry James, Sr., made the first significant reference in print to Blake's social concerns—his 'striking humanitary strain', as James called it. James's extremely short article appeared in the form of a letter to the editor on the front page of Channing's *Spirit of the Age*.[101] The interest of the article, which concerns only one poem, 'The Little Vagabond', from *Songs of Experience*, is twofold, inasmuch as it discusses the idea behind the poem—'True worship is always spontaneous, the offspring of delight, not duty; and it cannot be spontaneous so long as the native passions or susceptibilities of the worshippers

[97] Clement Wilkinson, op. cit., p. 52. (*A Blake Bibliography* omits this reference from its list of Blake references in this book.)

[98] Keynes, 'Blake, Tulk, and Garth Wilkinson', pp. 191–2.

[99] Morley, ed., *Henry Crabb Robinson on Books and Their Writers*, ii. 675–6.

[100] See Phillips, op. cit., pp. 191–2.

[101] [Henr]Y. [Jame]S., 'William Blake's Poems', *Spirit of the Age*, i (25 Aug. 1849), 113–14.

are unsatisfied' by a society which permits poverty and oppression—not only is there serious consideration given to this idea, but also we are struck by the choice of that particular poem. James chose (could it have been deliberately?) the single poem omitted by Wilkinson from his 1839 edition of the *Songs*. (There are two issues, one with the poem, and one without. Keynes conjectures that the poem was printed in the first issue and later cancelled. Dorfman states that 'The Little Vagabond' was dropped from the first printing and restored in the 'second printing' but does not give evidence for this.)[102] Was it the poem's contempt of organized religion that frightened Wilkinson in England? For James in America, it seemed 'that this curious *morceau* involves much useful truth'. He said, 'I agree with this clear-eyed little vagabond.' Not until 1868 was there mention again of Blake's social ideas, when Swinburne discovered Blake's revolutionary spirit.[103]

Several pieces of evidence, also from 1849, give an uncertain, even contradictory, impression of the state of Blake's fame at the mid-century mark. First, there is Bryan's *Biographical Dictionary of Painters and Engravers*. The facts and tone of the article are from Cunningham, e.g., 'it may be lamented that his genius was not restrained by judgment; but had that been the case, the world would have lost those wonderful . . . etc.' And yet, what in other respects is a routine account concludes with the astonishing assertion that Blake's 'published works are now sufficiently known to render description or criticism unnecessary'.[104]

But that was not at all true, either of the *Songs*, or of the published graphic work; indeed, contemporary neglect of Blake's graphic work seems to have disturbed Ruskin deeply at just this time. In a passage from *The Seven Lamps of Architecture* (1849) which was cancelled before publication, perhaps because it was too much of a digression from the main path of setting forth an architectural programme for the future, Ruskin comments ruefully on the English neglect of art:

We have had two in the present century, two magnificent and mighty—William Blake and J. M. W. Turner. I do not speak of the average genius . . . but of the Great Pharoses of the moving wilderness, those towering and solitary beacons. . . . We have had only two of these built for us; two men who if they had been given to us in a time of law, and of recognized discipline, if they had had either teaching in their youth, or reverence in their manhood, might have placed our age on a level with the proudest periods of creative art.[105]

---

[102] Keynes, *Bibliography*, pp. 265–7; Dorfman, op. cit., p. 47.

[103] Algernon Charles Swinburne, *William Blake, A Critical Essay*, London, 1868, *passim*.

[104] Michael Bryan, *A Biographical Dictionary of Painters and Engravers*, London, 1849. Blake was not included in the 1816 edition of this work.

[105] John Ruskin, *The Works of John Ruskin*, Library Edition, ed. E. T. Cook and Alexander Wedderburn, viii, London, 1903, p. 256. This edition of Ruskin will hereafter be cited as Cook and Wedderburn.

Blake's influence, says Ruskin, 'is felt as much as the weight of last winter's snow'.

Another bit of evidence from 1849 points in a direction from which changes were to come. When young William Allingham came to London in that year to be a literary man, he obtained through Henry Sutton an introduction to Coventry Patmore, who helped him to look up Blake at the British Museum.[106] They were disappointed to find that the Museum had 'nothing of his'. (The Print Room had, in fact, acquired a copy of *Jerusalem* and of the *Job* in 1847, but these were probably not listed in the catalogue they consulted.) Allingham was planning 'a new edition of Blake's poems', in which he had already interested a publisher named Slater. The edition was never printed—was probably never prepared for the press. But the idea indicates a high regard for Blake in the mind of a young man who might be considered representative of his generation: a few days before going to the British Museum he had made a pilgrimage to Coleridge's grave at Highgate, then to the Gilman house where Coleridge had spent his last years ('Out of one window looks a black cat, perhaps belonging to the Witch of Cristabel')—and all this with a copy of Poe's poems under his arm.[107] He wrote an article on Blake this year for *Hogg's Weekly Instructor*; it contained nothing new, merely warmed-over Cunningham.[108]

Allingham was a friend of Dante Gabriel Rossetti who, two years earlier, in 1847, had bought Blake's Notebook from Samuel Palmer's brother for the price of ten shillings. For the small and gifted group of young men gathered around the Rossetti brothers Blake was to become a heroic figure; the full story of their involvement with Blake would take us into the Gilchrist period and so is alluded to here only in passing.

However important Blake's influence might have been on an older generation—Palmer, Linnell, Richmond, Calvert, *et al.*—while he was still living, curiously few traces of Blake remained in the later work of these men, who in any case appear to have felt more affinity with the woodcuts for Virgil's *Pastorals* than with any of his other, landscapeless works. But the 'Ancients' were still involved in Blake matters from time to time. George Richmond had helped Ruskin to purchase some Blake drawings in 1843.[109] Palmer had acquired, possibly through Tatham, a

---

[106] Allingham gives an account of his introduction to Patmore in a letter to Ralph Waldo Emerson, dated 12 Oct. 1851. H. Allingham and E. Baumer Williams, eds., *Letters to William Allingham*, London, 1911, p. 47. Henry Sutton (1825–1901) wrote poetry early in his life, later theology. Although deeply influenced by his friends Patmore and Emerson, he joined the Swedenborgians in 1857. His last work (1900) was a book on Swedenborgian phrenology.

[107] William Allingham, *A Diary*, ed. H. Allingham and D. Radford, London, 1908, pp. 52–3. Cited in Dorfman, op. cit., p. 62.

[108] William Allingham, 'Some Chat about William Blake', *Hogg's Weekly Instructor*, N.S. ii (1849), 17–20.

[109] Cook and Wedderburn, xxxvi, London, 1909, pp. 32–3.

z

number of Blake's effects, including annotated books. He had several of Blake's 'finest panel pictures', which, according to his son A. H. Palmer, 'were stored away in the basement with a lot of rubbish; and it was barely possible to see that they were pictures'.[110]

When the large collection of Blake's early and long-standing patron Thomas Butts was sold at Sotheby's in 1852, much of it was bought by Richard Monckton Milnes, whose interest in Blake went back at least fourteen years, when he had spoken of bringing out an edition, and possibly even further. In the year of the Butts sale, Crabb Robinson notes near the conclusion of his 'Reminiscences of Blake' that 'Monkton Milne [*sic*] talks of printing an edition'—perhaps just of the *Songs of Innocence and of Experience*, Robinson does not specify. The edition was never made. Access to Blake's works remained limited to a few owners and their friends. 'I have a few coloured engravings', Robinson continues, 'but B[lake] is still an object of interest exclusively to men of imaginative taste & psychological curiosity.' The 'Reminiscences' of 1852 draw to a close with the following note, which not only characterizes Robinson in its measured cheerfulness, but also captures the contradictory quality of Cunningham's essay: 'I have been reading . . . the life of Blake by Allan Cunningham [writes Robinson] . . . It recognizes perhaps more of Blake's merit than might have been expected of a Scotch realist.'[111]

A new biography by someone born into Romanticism was necessary before the circle of persons interested in Blake could widen beyond the few men 'of imaginative taste & psychological curiosity'. Materials were still to be found at first hand. The difficult task of gathering all available data and re-examining Blake in the light of it was undertaken in about 1855 by Alexander Gilchrist, a young lawyer, the adulator of Carlyle, and already at twenty-seven the author of a life of the painter, William Etty.

Meanwhile, throughout the middle and late 1850s, as Gilchrist's biographical inquiries were jogging the memories of an older generation that had known and admired Blake, the artist's name was being uttered increasingly often by the newer generation of Blake admirers—the Rossetti brothers, William Bell Scott, Ruskin, and Swinburne—in their disputes with contemporary taste in art and poetry. In 1856 Ruskin, for example, in his reforming *Modern Painters*, considered Blake in the same breath with Dürer, as a master, especially of 'the etched grotesque'.[112]

[110] Letter from A. H. Palmer to Martin Hardie, 29 Apr. 1920. Quoted in Geoffrey Grigson, *Samuel Palmer: The Visionary Years*, London, 1947, p. 143.

[111] Edith J. Morley, ed., *Blake, Coleridge, Wordsworth, Lamb, etc.*, Manchester, 1932, p. 27. In the same year, a review of a biography of Stothard reopened the case of Blake *v.* Cromek. Here for the first time was printed a letter from Cromek to Blake supplied by Allan Cunningham's son, Peter. Anon., 'The Life and Works of Thomas Stothard, R.A.', *Gentleman's Magazine*, n.s. xxxvii (1852), 149–50.

[112] Cook and Wedderburn, v, London, 1904, pp. 137–8.

In *The Elements of Drawing* in the following year, under the section entitled 'Things to be Studied', Ruskin includes Blake, observing that

The *Book of Job*, engraved by himself, is of the highest rank in certain characters of imagination and expression; in the mode of obtaining certain effects of light it will also be a very useful example to you. In expressing conditions of glaring and flickering light, Blake is greater than Rembrandt.[113]

Ruskin's admiration for Blake's technical powers was expressed again in a letter of thanks to Flaxman's sister-in-law, Maria Denman, who had lent him her copy of *Songs of Innocence and of Experience*. In reaction to the 'invaluable little volume' Ruskin says, 'I had, before, the deepest respect for the genius of Blake—yet I was quite ignorant of his fine feeling for colour—which is one of the ruling & lovely qualities of these noble designs— . . .'[114]

The introduction of an article on Blake in the 1854 *Encyclopaedia Britannica* (8th edition) points to some fresh talk about Blake in art circles even before Gilchrist began his researches for the biography.[115] In previous years there had been encyclopaedia notices, but they had been less frequent after the thirties: in *Biographical Sketches of Eminent Artists . . . from the Earliest Ages to the Present Day* in 1834; in the *Lives of Eminent and Illustrious Englishmen from Alfred the Great to the Latest Times* and *The British Cyclopaedia of Biography* in 1837; in *The Biographical Treasury, A Dictionary of Universal Biography . . .* in 1838; in the *General Dictionary of Painters*, which Cunningham revised in 1840; in Michael Bryan's *Biographical Dictionary of Painters and Engravers* (already referred to) in 1849. That was about to change. In addition to the entry in the *Encyclopaedia Britannica* in 1854, there would be articles on Blake in Knight's *English Cyclopaedia* in 1856, in Allibone's *Critical Dictionary* in 1859, and in *Chambers' Encyclopaedia* in 1861.[116]

---

[113] Ibid., xv, London, 1903, p. 223.

[114] The letter, which is undated, and apparently has never been published, is kept with Mrs. Anna Flaxman's copy of the *Songs* (Copy O in the Keynes and Wolf *Census*) in the Houghton Library of Harvard University. Maria Denman died on 23 Dec. 1859, at the age of eighty, which gives us the latest possible date for the letter. (Cited in Hoover, No. 10.)

[115] The author of this frequently inaccurate piece is not known.

[116] John Gould, *Biographical Sketches of Eminent Artists . . . from the Earliest Ages to the Present Day*, London, 1834, pp. 49–50; George Godfrey Cunningham, *Lives of Eminent and Illustrious Englishmen from Alfred the Great to the Latest Times*, viii (1837), p. 310 (there is no separate Blake entry—the reference noted here is part of the life of Flaxman); Charles F. Partington, *The British Cyclopaedia of Biography*, i (1837), p. 223; Samuel Maunder, *The Biographical Treasury. A Dictionary of Universal Biography intended as A Companion to The 'Treasury of Knowledge'*, London, 1838; Matthew Pilkington, *A General Dictionary of Painters*, revised by Allan Cunningham, London, 1840, pp. xcii–xciii, 52–3; Michael Bryan, op. cit.; Charles Knight, ed., *The English Cyclopaedia*, i (1856), cols. 716–17; S. Austin Allibone, *A Critical Dictionary of English Literature and British and American Authors*, i, London, 1859, p. 203; *Chambers' Encyclopaedia*, ii (1861), p. 142.

The first, second, and fourth of these entries are cited in Bentley, 'A Supplement to . . . A Blake Bibliography'. There are several articles on Blake in Continental reference works of the period which I do not report on here because they are not properly part of the present narrative.

The inclusion of Blake in these standard, general reference works would suggest that by about 1860 Blake had begun to be more widely known. And yet, in two periodical pieces of this period it is implied that the writer's knowledge of Blake runs counter to public ignorance. For a series entitled the 'Tombs of English Artists' Frederick William Fairholt did a brief *reprise* of Cunningham which concluded that Blake's 'works are now exceedingly rare, the illustrated books of poetry particularly so; but there is so much beauty, fancy, and simplicity in them, that they deserve to be known'.[117] In the same cause George Walter Thornbury wrote, 'Blake was the Hell-Breughel, the Kaulbach, the Doré of English art, and it shames us that he should still be unknown. . . .' Thornbury's tone—he was writing in 1861—is light and indulgent, admiring of Blake and scornful of those unable to appreciate him. 'For he anticipated Wordsworth, rivalled our old dramatists in sustained majesty and dignity, and at times vied with Shelley in nervous fire. . . .' Perhaps the chief strength of this popularizing piece is its assumption of intellectual sophistication on the part of Blake: an enthusiast and idealist, yes, but one still capable of complex, adult commentary on life. For example, Blake's 'Demon Flea' is 'worthy of a Rabelais Cruikshanks', and his *Urizen*, 'which even his wife could not fully understand', is 'full of purgatorial horrors and Dantesque thought, and probably [was] intended to represent the effects of the fall, and the efforts of evil to corrupt man'.[118] There is something rather new in this sort of explication (except, of course, for the piece in the *London University Magazine* some thirty years earlier), and in the linking of Blake's name so securely with that of Wordsworth.

These writers raise a crucial question. For an artist's or poet's works to be known, they must be seen. In practical terms, this means the works must either be published or reprinted in books, or (in the case of art) they must be exhibited. And original prints, drawings, and hand-made books must be available for consultation in libraries. All of these conditions were in fact slowly being met with regard to Blake—hastened, perhaps, by such proddings as those of Fairholt and Thornbury. Towards the end of the decade it is possible to see the figure of Blake, like Milton's vision of England in *Areopagitica*, begin 'to rouze himself like a strong man after sleep'.

Coincidentally with the initial phase of Gilchrist's work, the British Museum began to add works by Blake to its Print Room collection. By the end of the

[117] F. W. Fairholt, 'Tombs of English Artists', *Art-Journal*, xiv (1858), 236. Fairholt mentions *Jerusalem* 'the maddest of all his inventions'. Other subjects of the series were Bewick, Cosway, Etty, Flaxman, Gainsborough, Hogarth, Reynolds, Woollett (an engraver for Boydell who engraved the 'Death of Wolfe'), and Wyatt.

[118] George Walter Thornbury, *British Artists from Hogarth to Turner*, 2 vols., London, 1861, ii. 26–44. At the end of his chapter on David Scott, Thornbury quoted Blake's dedication 'To the Queen' from *The Grave*, which William Bell Scott had quoted earlier in his book on his brother. (See below, p. 346.) Cited in Hoover, No. 7. Thornbury was an extremely prolific author, whose most important work, a *Life of J. M. W. Turner*, 2 vols., London, 1861, was published in the same year as the *British Artists*.

1850s the Print Room possessed all of the major illuminated books and most of the minor ones, and a representative number of engravings by Blake, including the engraved illustrations to Dante. By the time Gilchrist's biography appeared in the late autumn of 1863 the Blake holdings of the Print Room had been still further augmented by the engraved *Night Thoughts*, Flaxman's *Hesiod*, *For Children : The Gates of Paradise*, and other works. The Library of the Museum began its own collection of the illuminated books after the opening of the present Reading Room in 1857.[119] Compared with private collections, of course, the Museum's acquisitions were late and few. Swinburne wrote to Monckton Milnes as late as 1862 that the Museum 'has not a tithe of what you have in the way of Blakes; and we know of no other accessible place that has.'[120] The Museum acquisitions were nevertheless the first steps toward the recognition of Blake as a national asset. That those steps were taken before Gilchrist's biography rather than after, suggests that there was a new interest in Blake 'in the air' in the 1850s, of which the biography itself was only one instance—although certainly the most extensive and important.

Not only was Blake being collected for public institutions, but also he was being exhibited. Gilchrist himself recorded the fact that 'at the Manchester Art Treasures Exhibition of 1857, among the select thousand water-colour drawings hung two modestly tinted designs by Blake, of few inches size: one of the *Dream of Queen Catherine*, another *Oberon and Titania*'.[121] (See Plate 79.) Five years later, in the great International Exhibition of 1862 held in the Crystal Palace in London, five pictures by Blake were shown: the tempera of the *Canterbury Pilgrims*, lent by William Stirling, later Stirling-Maxwell, a group of three early water-colours on the subject of Joseph and his brothers, which had been exhibited by Blake at the Royal Academy in 1785 (see Plates 80, 81, 82), and an oil or tempera, *Christ in the Lap of Truth*. J. D. Coleridge (John Duke Coleridge, son of a nephew of Samuel Taylor Coleridge, later created Baron Coleridge and lord chief-justice of England) was listed as owner of the Joseph paintings in the International Exhibition *Catalogue*. *Christ in the Lap of Truth* was lent by Milnes.[122] One of the authors of the *Catalogue*, Francis Turner Palgrave, brought Blake and Stothard together in the article on 'The British School of Water Colour Painting'.[123] They were, wrote Palgrave, '. . . two men singularly contrasted in their life and in their genius, gifted respectively with exquisite fancy and intense imagination, and to whom

[119] The dates of these acquisitions may be found in the Keynes and Wolf *Census* and in 'A Handlist of Works by William Blake in the Department of Prints and Drawings of the British Museum', *Blake Newsletter*, v. 4 (1972), 226–57.　　　　　[120] Cecil Y. Lang, ed., *The Swinburne Letters*, 6 vols., New Haven, 1959, i. 62.

[121] Gilchrist, i. 3. He goes on to say they went 'unnoticed'.

[122] For catalogues to the Exhibitions see Hoover, Nos. 8 and 11. For earlier proveniences of the *Joseph* pictures, see David Bindman, ed., *William Blake. Catalogue of the Collection in the Fitzwilliam Museum, Cambridge*, Cambridge, 1970, pp. 13–14.

[123] Francis Turner Palgrave, 'The British School of Water Colour Painting', *Official Catalogue of the Fine Art Department, International Exhibition*, London, 1862, p. 46.

79. *Oberon and Titania*. Water-colour.
Private collection

80. *Joseph's Brethren Bowing Before Him*. Water-colour.
Fitzwilliam Museum, Cambridge

81. *Joseph Ordering Simeon to Be Bound.* Water-colour.
Fitzwilliam Museum, Cambridge

82. *Joseph Making Himself Known to His Brethren*. Water-colour.
Fitzwilliam Museum, Cambridge

England is indebted for a long series of works, which, take them all in all, no other water-colourists in this style have equalled.' Palgrave charged Stothard with the lack of 'depth and impressiveness', and with domination by 'Fancy'. By contrast, Blake is charged with domination by a 'morbid Imagination':

But it is hardly as art that the strange creations of the visionary Blake appeal to us; the drawings and execution are rarely successful; it is in the force of the penetrative imagination that their value lies,—in their almost painful intensity,—in their sublime suggestions of some earlier world of patriarchal days, or the mysteries of spiritual and ecstatic existence.

In his statement Palgrave echoes one of the dominant notes in earlier Blake criticism—a note that would be heard less frequently later in the nineteenth century, but never entirely forgotten. It might be described as a note of awe.

That there were *any* works by Blake exhibited in 1862 imports some public interest; its significance must be balanced, however, against the almost incredible fact that the section of the fine arts exhibit devoted to engravings contained work by virtually every known British engraver but Blake. In any case, Blake's work was exhibited on these two occasions, to vast audiences, for the first time since 1812, that is, the first time in forty-five years. Being exhibited, it was singled out and commented upon, either with admiration or contempt, in at least six separate instances. In a *Handbook* to the Manchester Exhibition Blake is paired with Richard Dadd 'as examples of painters in whom a disordered brain rather aided than impeded the workings of . . . fancy'. Palgrave's *Handbook* to the fine arts exhibit in 1862 brings Blake and Stothard together once more, in a passage very similar to the one (already mentioned) written by Palgrave for the *Catalogue* in the same year. There were two more notices of Blake at the International Exhibition, in the *Athenaeum* and the *Art-Journal*—the first too brief to signify, the second a comparison, favourable to Stothard, of his *Canterbury Pilgrimage* with that of Blake.[124]

In contrast to these displays of his art, there were few printings of poems by Blake in the 1850s. At the beginning of the decade, William Bell Scott, one of the founders of the Pre-Raphaelite Brotherhood just two years before, quoted the dedication ('To the Queen') from *The Grave* in his memoir of his late brother,

[124] Anon., *A Handbook to the Water Colours, Drawings, and Engravings, in the [Manchester] Art Treasures Exhibition*, London, 1857, pp. 12–13; Francis Turner Palgrave, *Handbook to the Fine Arts Collections in the International Exhibition of 1862*, London, 1862, pp. 65–6; Anon., 'International Exhibition. The English Water-colour pictures', *Athenaeum*, 17 May 1862, p. 663, reprinted in Robert Kempt, *What Do You Think of the Exhibition?*, London, 1862; Anon., 'International Exhibition, 1862: Pictures of the British School', *Art-Journal*, i (July 1862), 149–52. All of these references are cited in Hoover, Nos. 9, 12, 13, 14, and 15. In his 'Supplement' Bentley cites Tom Taylor, *Handbook of the Pictures in the International Exhibition of 1862*, London, 1862, as containing a reference to Blake. (I have not seen this work.) For a full discussion of Blake's part in the Exhibitions and contemporary reactions, see my 'Pictures at the Exhibitions', *Blake Newsletter*, vi. 1 (Summer 1972).

David Scott.[125] Mary Howitt (the wife of William Howitt) quoted 'The Ecchoing Green' in *The Pictorial Calendar of the Seasons* in 1854.[126] In America, as has been noted (see p. 322 above), six poems were printed in the fifties. One of these, 'The Tyger', was printed twice.

In 1860 William Allingham printed four lyrics in an anthology entitled *Nightingale Valley*.[127] The four he chose were the 'Introduction', 'The Angel', and 'The Blossom', from the *Songs of Innocence*, and 'The Tyger', from *Experience*. In 1862 Coventry Patmore printed 'The Tyger', and the 'Introduction' to *Innocence* (he retitled it 'The Child and the Piper') in a collection of poems for children, *The Children's Garland*.[128] In sum, I count sixty instances of poems printed in letterpress (excluding Wilkinson's edition of the *Songs* in 1839 and Tulk's privately printed edition of 1843) between the time of Blake's death and the appearance of Gilchrist's biography in 1863. In this count are included seven fragments, or excerpts, of poems. It should be remembered, however, that these sixty instances do not represent sixty different poems; in fact, only thirty-seven different poems were printed. Of these, 'The Tyger' was the most popular, having been printed as many as seven times. Next came the 'Introduction' to *Innocence*, which was printed six times. The sixty printings of poems just mentioned is about four times the number of Blake's poems printed in letterpress during his lifetime, excluding, of course, the volume of *Poetical Sketches*.

Looking back over the large terrain just travelled, the main features emerge quite clearly. First, a renewal of interest in Blake at his death and for a few years thereafter. As first-hand knowledge of him faded, the sensationalism and crude 'human interest' of Cunningham's 'Life' helped to keep Blake's name alive for reasons that had little or nothing to do with his poetry or art. And, in fact, by suggesting that Blake's more difficult works were mere madness, Cunningham may actually have postponed a true recognition of Blake's genius.[129] In the development of such a 'true' estimate of Blake, a few land-mark figures stand out—Crabb Robinson for his ceaseless promotion of Blake among his friends, Linnell for his

---

[125] William Bell Scott, *Memoir of David Scott, R.S.A.*, Edinburgh, 1850, p. 334. Hoover, No. 7. Bell Scott culls the following from David Scott's notes: 'Blake touched the infinite in expression or signification, without distraction from lower aims, and in a kind of Christian purity. He is very abstract in style or meaning, but very defective in execution' (p. 238).

[126] Noted in Carl Woodring, *Victorian Samplers: William and Mary Howitt*, Lawrence, Kansas, 1952, p. 61. For an interesting description of the use to which Mary Howitt put the poem, see H. B. de Groot, op. cit. De Groot also gives a letter of 1830 in which Mary Howitt, evidently reacting to Cunningham, chats enthusiastically about Blake.

[127] Giraldus [William Allingham], ed., *Nightingale Valley*, London, 1860.

[128] Coventry Patmore, ed., *The Children's Garland*, London, 1862.

[129] Peter Cunningham, in the Preface to his father's volume of poems (see above, n. 14), suggests that the 'Life' of Blake was one of the works by which Allan Cunningham had hoped to be remembered. This, of course, has come to pass.

continuing efforts to find purchasers for the *Job* illustrations, Wilkinson for the mere fact of editing the *Songs* and putting them before a wider public, Ruskin for his high seriousness when speaking of Blake's art, and Dante Gabriel Rossetti for his deepening identification with Blake as artist–poet.

If the main features are clear, how shall the total history be described? The great accumulation of data that we have just considered is proof enough that it is never literally correct to say that Blake's reputation was 'moribund', nor to speak of 'the great silence'. It is, undoubtedly, truer to say that the data are numerous, but their significance is contradictory and often difficult to assess; that much of what one makes of the evidence depends on one's frame of reference. If it is plausible to emphasize the notice given to Blake, as I have done here, it is equally plausible to make much of the frailty of the attention he received; for many of these instances are indeed frail. As often happens in life, a closer look leaves us with knowledge that is both truer to fact, and more elusive to the generalizing mind, than we had earlier supposed. But of certain aspects of the history we can be certain. Never is Blake forgotten. The low point in the fortunes of his fame is probably in the early and middle forties; thereafter, interest gathers, and when Gilchrist's sympathetic full-length biography arrives in the early sixties, its time has come.

XVII

GEOFFREY KEYNES'S WORK ON BLAKE
FONS ET ORIGO
AND A CHECKLIST OF
WRITINGS ON BLAKE
BY GEOFFREY KEYNES, 1910–72

G. E. Bentley, Jr.

Energy is Eternal Delight.[1]

GEOFFREY KEYNES first began working actively on Blake about 1909, when he was a medical student in his early twenties. For over sixty years he has been presenting new texts and designs of Blake to an increasingly enthusiastic world, a world learning to share his enthusiasm. He has been responsible for over forty books on Blake (some of them by now in up to seven printings), most of them editions of Blake's writings and designs, and he has written about eighty separate essays on Blake. He has made uniquely valuable contributions to Blake studies in at least five areas: as Bibliographer, as Editor, as 'Publisher', as Discoverer, and as Collector.

1. *The Bibliographer*

What is now proved was once only imagin'd

The vicissitudes of Keynes's work on his Blake bibliography from about 1909 to its publication in 1921 are given in his '*Religio Bibliographici*' (1953).[2] *A Bibliography of William Blake* is one of the landmarks in Blake studies. Before this there had not even been a complete list of Blake's writings, much less a detailed bibliographical description of each of his works in manuscript and in print, a census of every known contemporary copy, and a responsible list of works about Blake. All this Keynes included, together with quotations of many of the less-accessible documents about Blake and handsome illustrations of the more important of his designs, including *All Religions are One* for the first time. A great many of the

---

[1] Unidentified quotations here and elsewhere are from *The Marriage of Heaven and Hell*.

[2] Keynes's writings on Blake, identified here by date, are given in more detail in the chronological 'Checklist of Writings on Blake by Geoffrey Keynes' below. (See also 1949.)

problems he faced were unique and formidable, for no other books have been published by Blake's process of Illuminated Printing. The 1921 *Bibliography* is the foundation of all modern Blake studies.[3]

He has made many further contributions to Blake bibliography, many of them bringing up to date the corresponding sections of the *Bibliography*. For the coloured works in Illuminated Printing, these contributions were incorporated in *William Blake's Illuminated Books*: A Census (1953), in which Edwin Wolf, 2nd, assisted with the descriptions of copies in the United States. For all Blake's works in Illuminated Printing, the standard description is in the Census (1953), plus, for *There is No Natural Religion*, his edition (1971) authoritatively altering the order of the plates; for *Thel*, Miss Bogen's report in her edition (1971) of a previously unnoticed variant; for *For Children* and *For the Sexes*, the Keynes edition (1968) with the corrected and expanded census of copies; and, for *Jerusalem*, the revised census in his *Blake Studies* (1971) and D. V. Erdman, 'The Suppressed and Altered Passages in Blake's *Jerusalem*', *Studies in Bibliography*, xviii (1964), 1–54.[4] For works in conventional typography, the best description of *The French Revolution* is still that in the *Bibliography* (1921), while for the *Poetical Sketches* and *Descriptive Catalogue* we must turn to Keynes's *Blake Studies* (1971).[5] For Blake's manuscripts, few textual or bibliographical scholars even glanced at them for thirty years after the *Bibliography* was published, and still Keynes's first volume on Blake (1921) is the only place where a description of all of them may be found. For the *Island in the Moon*, there is still no more detailed description than that in the *Bibliography*, though many of the other manuscripts have received more minute attention in the last two decades, particularly in D. V. Erdman's text of 'Wo cried the Muse' and 'Then she bore Pale desire' in the *Bulletin of the New York Public Library*, lxii (1958), 191–201; in the edition of *Tiriel* (1967) ed. G. E. Bentley, Jr.; in Keynes's edition of the *Notebook*[6] (1935); in his editions of the letters (1956, 1968); in editions of *Vala* (1956) ed. H. M. Margoliouth, and of *The Four Zoas* (1963) ed. G. E. Bentley, Jr.; and in G. E. Bentley, Jr., 'The Date of Blake's Pickering Manuscript or The Way of a Poet with Paper', *Studies in Bibliography*, xix (1966), 232–43. And of course Keynes has added to our knowledge of the physical properties of each of Blake's works in his editions of Blake down to 1972.

Further, unlike the authors of most pioneering works, he has with justice escaped fundamental attack from younger followers in his field. One may perhaps feel that he sometimes expresses opinions with the certainty of fact or neglects to point out the links of evidence which led him to a conclusion. Many a student has

---

[3] It may be supplemented by *A Blake Bibliography* (1964; second edition forthcoming).

[4] Perhaps to this list should be added G. E. Bentley, Jr., 'The Printing of Blake's *America*', *Studies in Romanticism*, vi (1966), 46–57.

[5] See also Michael Phillips, 'Blake's Corrections in *Poetical Sketches*', *Blake Newsletter* (Fall 1970).

[6] An elaborate edition of the *Notebook* prepared by D. V. Erdman is now in the press.

said to himself, 'Since Keynes presents no evidence for that conclusion, it may not be true', only to discover, after months of search, that the evidence, when found, solidly supports Keynes's conclusion. One may diagnose a tendency to supplement his own works rather than to revise them, occasionally preserving even the misprints of the earlier edition (e.g. in the description of *Urizen* [copy E, called D in 1921] in the *Bibliography* [1921] and the Census [1953]). Sometimes he quotes a work through an intermediary source without identifying the intermediary, as in his account of the ghostly '1843' sale of *Milton* (D) or of the sale of *Ahania* (A) 'at Sotheby's in 1855'. Such slips may be greeted almost with gratitude; they give the student, if not authority, at least precedent for his own mistakes.

We owe Keynes one important bibliographical debt beyond what was attempted in his 1921 *Bibliography*. In his *Engravings by William Blake*: The Separate Plates (1956), he not only provided a description, census, and history of each copy of each work, but he reproduced most of the plates, a number of them in several states. The Separate Plates is, therefore, important both as an edition and as a bibliography (or rather as a chalcography).

2. *The Editor*

Keynes's efforts as an editor have been yet more long-lasting and influential than his work as a bibliographer. The first new Blake text he presented was the 'Laughing Song' (1910), and the last to date (I believe) was the previously unpublished letter of 27 December 1826 in the second edition of the *Complete Writings* (1966). Since 1925, anyone who has wanted a reliable and truly comprehensive text of Blake has had to turn to those prepared by Keynes.[7]

After the publication of his *Bibliography of William Blake* in 1921, the next obvious step was an edition incorporating the discoveries he had presented in the *Bibliography*. The state of Blake editions in 1920 was on the whole deplorable, for the only reliable editor of Blake was John Sampson, whose *Poetical Works* (1905, 1914) omitted the prose and most of *The Four Zoas*, *Milton*, and *Jerusalem*. Other editors, such as W. M. Rossetti and Ellis and Yeats, had persistently shaken up Blake's text and tidied it to fit modern sensibilities. There was a crying need for an edition of Blake's writings which would be both comprehensive and meticulously accurate.

Keynes's problems and triumphs as a Blake editor are recorded in his essay 'On Editing Blake' (1964). The results appeared in a remarkably handsome three-volume Nonesuch edition of the *Writings* in 1925. This included not only reliable

[7] D. V. Erdman's edition of Blake's *Poetry and Prose* (1965) is admirably reliable but omits some of Blake's work in prose.

texts of all Blake's writings but reproductions of a number of them and careful annotations of a kind worthy of Sampson. This edition, together with the *Biblio- graphy* (1921), assembled all the available information about Blake's texts in a way that was far in advance, not only of what had been done for Blake before, but of what had then been done for most great English authors. The 1925 *Writings* is one of the great accomplishments of literary scholarship in the 1920s or indeed in the first half of the twentieth century.

Succeeding generations of scholars (including inevitably the evergreen Keynes himself) have, however, found ways of improving upon it. For example, the manifold complexities of the more puzzling manuscripts could only be demon- strated through facsimiles such as that of the *Notebook* which Keynes edited in 1935. Further, Keynes had carefully regularized Blake's often exceedingly puzzling and opaque punctuation, with no more than a blanket statement that he had done so. Since much often turns upon the punctuation (as in the last lines of *Tiriel*), succeeding editors and critics have often found that, as Blake wrote in the *Marriage*, 'Improve[me]nt makes strait roads; but the crooked roads without Improvement are roads of Genius'.[8]

The 1925 *Writings* was a very bulky and expensive work which most students could consult only in institutional libraries. To make it more widely available, Keynes purged it of many of the variants and scholarship, and Nonesuch published the resulting *Poetry and Prose* first in 1927. This was confessedly a simplified edition, but it was wonderfully compact and accessible, not to mention being the only one (besides the 1925 *Writings*) to contain everything Blake wrote. For thirty years, from 1927 to 1956, it was deservedly the text of Blake most widely used.

To accommodate changes in knowledge of Blake and in sophistication of his readers during these thirty years, Keynes published a revised edition of Blake as the *Complete Writings* in 1957, with most if not 'All the Variant Readings'. So uniformly satisfactory to scholars has this edition of the *Complete Writings* (1957) proved, that it was made the basis of the *Concordance* produced by D. V. Erdman and a host of assistants in 1967. Incidentally, the *Concordance* had the effect of stabilizing the text of the *Complete Writings*; subsequent editions of the *Complete Writings* (1966, 1969, 1971) have had to preserve the same page-numeration as in 1957 so that they may be used in conjunction with the *Concordance*, and sub- stantial additions (such as a newly discovered letter) had to be added in an appendix.

Keynes has also made more minute contributions to presenting the text of Blake. For example, his facsimile of the *Letters . . . to Thomas Butts* (1926) remains

---

[8] An alternative, to present Blake's apparently anarchic punctuation as Blake left it, has been presented notably in D. V. Erdman's edition (1965). Another possibility, to emend Blake's punctuation where necessary but to indicate exactly where and how this has been done, has not yet been attempted in print.

the only volume of reproductions of Blake's letters. Keynes's typographical editions of Blake's *Letters* (1956, 1968) present most of the minutiae of postmarks, histories of the manuscripts, and addresses that scholars in the 1950s came to expect for great authors. And his reproduction of Blake's *Notebook* (1935) made the complexities of that crucial work apparent for the first time to Blake students.

3. The 'Publisher'

One of Keynes's most important roles has been to be, as it were, Blake's 'Publisher', to make widely known to the literary and artistic worlds Blake's extraordinary capacities as poet and designer. He has repeatedly helped with exhibition catalogues, he has reported news about Blake (e.g. 1924, 1928, 1957), and since 1910 he has reviewed books about Blake. He has made contributions about Blake to reference books such as the *Encyclopaedia Britannica* (1929) and *The Cambridge Bibliography of English Literature* (1940, 1957), and he introduced a dramatization of *Jerusalem* for the B.B.C. in 1970.

> A fool sees not the same tree that a wise man sees

Most important in this respect have been his editions reproducing Blake's designs. Not only has he made popular collections of designs (1945, 1965), but he prepared the only comprehensive collection of Blake's designs for Milton's poems (Nonesuch, 1926), the only extensive series of *Night Thoughts* designs in appropriate size (1927), by far the most complete set for *Job* (1935), the best series for Virgil (1937), the first and best set for Bunyan (1941), by far the largest series of pencil drawings (1927, 1956, 1971), a comprehensive set of reproductions from his Biblical designs, with a catalogue (1957), and the most extensive series of reproductions from his engravings (1950). Whenever we want to see reproductions of Blake's designs, in any medium from pencil to water-colour to tempera to engravings, we are likely to turn to the publications of Sir Geoffrey Keynes.

Keynes's most important action as a 'Publisher' was his fostering of 'The William Blake Trust', the story of which he told in his essay for the Foster Damon Festschrift (1969). He feared that 'some catastrophe might happen' to the unique coloured copy of *Jerusalem* (E), and he determined therefore that the book should be reproduced to preserve it. Money from the sale of the late Graham Robertson's Blake collection in 1949 became part of a sinking-fund, depleted to produce a given facsimile and refilled from the proceeds of its sale to make possible the publication of the next facsimile. All the Blake Trust facsimiles have been meticulously produced by the Trianon Press in Paris, by a combination of printed

A a

collotype and hand-coloured stencils which produces a result extraordinarily faithful to Blake's engraving-plus-water-colour.

The Blake Trust facsimiles are not only remarkably fine facsimiles of Blake's originals,[9] but (like many other Keynes books) they are exceedingly handsome in their own right, with beautiful marbled endpapers and boards, morocco spines, and matching slip-cases. The prices (£6 to £1,200) are suitable for collectors of beautiful books rather than for impecunious students. For each of these editions of Blake's writings, Keynes has produced a Bibliographical Statement, usually with a Description as well, and the Blake Trust series now comprehends most of Blake's works in Illuminated Printing, plus the *Illustrations to the Bible* (1957), the *Blake–Varley Sketchbook* (1969), and Blake's Gray designs (1972), plus a few other works. The works presently in hand are *The Song of Los, Ahania, Jerusalem* (copy B), and *Job*. The most important work of scholarship fostered by the Blake Trust will be the *catalogue raisonné* of his art by Martin Butlin, based partly on work by Geoffrey Keynes and Ruthven Todd. When these works are completed, Keynes will have been responsible for reproducing every major series of Blake's designs except for Dante, *The Four Zoas*,[10] and the 500 *Night Thoughts* designs which have still not been reproduced together.

4. *The Discoverer*

Keynes has also been remarkably energetic as a discoverer of facts concerning Blake's life and writings. The more important of his discoveries are incorporated in the *Bibliography* (1921), the Census (1953), The Separate Plates (1956), and *Blake Studies* (1949, 1971), but some of them are still uncollected.

He has a keen eye for new truths. For example, he recognized that the plates of *There is No Natural Religion* (copy L) catalogued as facsimiles at their sale in 1953 were in fact unique Blake originals previously unknown (Census, 1953), and he was thus enabled to acquire the plates himself and to establish with their crucial assistance that the order of the plates of *No Natural Religion* had previously always been misapprehended. He also has a keen eye for the spurious. He identified the colour-forgery—and the colour-forger—of *America* (Q) and *Europe* (L) in the Census (1953); he detected that two of the drawings in Figgis's *Paintings of William Blake* are not by Blake, and he demonstrated that the poet is *not* the Blake who paid Flaxman £100 (1945), as M. R. Lowery had claimed.

Almost everywhere we explore in Blake studies, we will find that Keynes has been there before us.

---

[9] A pedant might, however, complain that in the black-and-white *Jerusalem* (1952), every even page-number has been moved from the right-hand side (where Blake put it) to the left side (to be in the outer corner); in *The Gates of Paradise* (1968), the imprints are sometimes outside the facsimile-indentation of the copper plates; and in the three reproductions of the Gray title-page for the exhibition (1971), 'Drawings by William Blake' appears in several different hands and places. [10] Plus *Tiriel*, if these form a 'major' series.

5. *The Collector*

Keynes has been indefatigable, judicious, and deservedly fortunate in collecting works by Blake and by many others.[11] While he could not compete financially with the Titans such as Lessing Rosenwald or Paul Mellon for the long-known treasures among the Illuminated Books, his energy and judgement have brought to his collection works so diverse, so little known, and so fascinating, that they frequently possess greater interest for the scholar than those in collections apparently more spectacular. There are among his treasures one of two known copies of the frontispiece to *Ahania*, a copy of the *Songs* (G) which he has assembled plate by plate over forty years, two drawings for *Tiriel*, a manuscript title-page for 'For Children The Gates of Hell', a number of unique or very rare separate plates such as 'The Ancient of Days', six copies in different contemporary boards of the rare *Remember Me!* with Blake's plate, and a proof of Blake's engraving for Hayley's *Designs to A Series of Ballads* (1802) with, on the verso, a transcript by Blake of a poem by Sheridan.[12]

To this collection in Suffolk, Keynes has warmly welcomed many scores of Blake scholars, from graduate-students to those who should know better than to intrude upon the time of such a busy man. I have been there in both capacities and have always found treasures in the collection and in the knowledge of its owner of which I had not dreamt before. One always comes away intellectually breathless, dazzled, and a little unsteady on one's scholarly legs from such a display.

All Blake scholars, if they are concerned to see and hear the best of Blake, must look, with his help, through his shelves and drawers and listen at his dining-table and desk. The tracks of such pilgrimages may be traced in the prefaces and notes of virtually every important scholarly book on Blake within the last fifty years. In Blake studies, all roads lead to Keynes.

[11] J. T. C. Oates, 'Contemporary Collectors XXXIX: Sir Geoffrey Keynes', *Book Collector*, xiii (1964), 473–80, calls him 'the foremost English collector of our time'; 'I account Sir Geoffrey the complete bibliophile'.

[12] Most of the Blake collection is promised to the Fitzwilliam Museum, Cambridge.

A Checklist of Writings on Blake by
Geoffrey Keynes, 1910–72

This checklist contains four conventions which should be especially remarked:

§   means I have not seen a copy of this work, chiefly reviews.

*   means the work bears Blake illustrations.

A B   Capital letters in alphabetical order are used to indicate editions and reprints of a given book or essay.

Plates 1–18   I count the plates of a work by Blake (e.g. *Europe*) uniformly in arabic numerals (e.g. 1–18), whereas Keynes and Wolf in their standard Census sometimes use roman numerals as well (e.g. i–iii, 1–15).

            The details concerning numbers of copies printed derive from the 'Bibliography of Writings by Geoffrey Keynes on Blake' in *Blake Studies* (1949).

1910

A. 'William Blake's "Laughing Song": A New Version.' *N & Q* cxxii [11th Ser., i] (1910), 241–2. B. Separately printed in Edinburgh, 1969.

     A transcript of Blake's MS. poem in *Poetical Sketches* (copy F), first printed here (1910).

§ Review of Joseph Wickstead, *Blake's Vision of the Book of Job* and of G. K. Chesterton, *William Blake*, in *Cambridge Review*, 1 Dec. 1910, pp. 169–70.

1919–20

H. J. C. Grierson, John Sampson, Geoffrey Keynes, G.B., Thomas J. Wise. 'A Textual Point in Blake.' *TLS* 9, 16, 23, 30 Oct. 1919, pp. 548 (Grierson), 572 (Sampson), 591 (Keynes and G.B.), 611 (Wise); 12 Feb. 1920, pp. 105–6 (Keynes again).

     A debate as to whether 'Mad Song' l. 7 should read 'beds' (as printed in 1783) or 'birds' is settled by Keynes through reference to Blake's MS. alterations in the Butts and Flaxman copies of *Poetical Sketches*.

A. **A Bibliography of William Blake*. N.Y., 1921. B. * N.Y., 1921 [i.e. 1969].

     There are 66 reproductions (including all of *All Religions are One*) and 973 entries. 250 copies were printed. The important Blake references from a number of early books are reprinted here. B is a photographic reprint of A.

Keynes's massive and monumental bibliography for the Grolier Club vastly increased our knowledge and understanding of Blake. The undertaking and the difficulties were enormous and the accomplishment splendid. Only gradually, as new information and techniques have become available, has the work been superseded in half a dozen separate books, mostly by Keynes (see below under 1923, 1942, 1943, 1945, 1949, 1953, 1956, 1968, 1971). The 1921 *Bibliography* is still of very great importance for independent judgement. It was largely translated, reprinted, and somewhat extended, by Bunsho Jugaku in his *William Blake Shoshi* (1929).

1922

'The Bibliography of Blake.' *TLS* 23 Mar. 1922, p. 196.

An attempt to answer the criticism that 250 copies of the *Bibliography* are not enough.

1923

'Blake's Milton.' *TLS* 13 Dec. 1923, p. 875.

Bibliographical information.

On the Morning of Christ's Nativity. Milton's Hymn with [six] Illustrations by William Blake and a Note by Geoffrey Keynes. Cambridge, 1923.

'Note on the Illustrations' is on pp. 31–2. 150 copies.

1924

'The Macgeorge Blakes.' *TLS* 26 June 1924, p. 403.

A description of Macgeorge's Blakes to be sold at Sotheby's.

Max Plowman and Geoffrey Keynes. 'A Text of Blake.' *TLS* 16, 23 Oct. 1924, pp. 651, 667.

Plowman inquires whether anyone is producing a text of Blake (16 Oct.), and Keynes replies that he is (23 Oct.).

1925

'Blake Drawings.' *TLS* 17 Dec. 1925, p. 883.

Two drawings reproduced in Figgis, *Paintings of William Blake* (1925), are not by Blake.

The Writings of William Blake. In Three Volumes. Ed. Geoffrey Keynes. London, 1925.

The 'Editor's Preface' is in Vol. i, pp. xi–xviii. 1,575 copies were printed.

The 1925 *Writings* is the first reliable comprehensive edition of Blake. It was revised and superseded in the *Complete Writings* (1957 ff.) and condensed in the *Poetry and Prose* (1927–56).

1926

'The Nonesuch Milton.' *Nation and Athenaeum*, xxxix (1926), 697.

> Blake's 'Satan, Sin, and Death' reproduced with Milton's *Poems* (below), is very like Hogarth's.

A. 'William Blake and Josiah Wedgwood.' *TLS* 9 Dec. 1926, p. 909. B–C. *Revised and reprinted in *Blake Studies* (1949, 1971).

> Gives an account of the relationship and prints some letters.

§'William Blake.' With a Selection from his Poems. Pp. 114–20 of *Great Names*: An Anthology of English and American Literature. Ed. W. J. Turner. N.Y., 1926.

A. *Letters from William Blake to Thomas Butts 1800–1803*. Printed in Facsimile with an Introductory Note by Geoffrey Keynes. Oxford, 1926. B. §*Folcroft, Pennsylvania, 1969.

> The introduction is pp. vi–ix. 350 copies of A were printed. Blake's letters and the debtor–creditor account are in facsimile, while the letter *from* Butts is a transcript. B is a facsimile of the facsimile.

*John Milton. *Poems in English with Illustrations by William Blake*. [2 vols.] London, 1926.

> The 'Notes on Blake's Illustrations to Milton's Poems' (Vol. i, pp. 271–9) and 'Notes on Blake's Illustrations to Paradise Lost' (Vol. ii, pp. 355–9) are by Geoffrey Keynes. There were 53 plates and 1,540 copies.

1927

A. *Poetry and Prose of William Blake*. Complete in One Volume. Ed. Geoffrey Keynes. London and N.Y., 1927. B. § London and N.Y., 1927. C. § London and N.Y., 1932. D. § London and N.Y., 1939. E. London and N.Y., 1943. F. London and N.Y., 1948. G. London and N.Y., 1956.

> 'The Editor's Preface' is 2 pages, and the 'Preface to the Fourth Edition' (1939) is 1 page. The first edition had 6,500 copies, and the second (1927) and third editions (1932) were corrected. The work was reset, and the pages renumbered, in the editions of 1939 and after. *The Gates of Paradise* is reproduced in full. The *Poetry and Prose* is a simplified version of the scholarly *Writings* (1925) and was the most widely used text of Blake until it was

superseded by the *Complete Writings* in 1957. The text is used in pp. 493–1045 of *The Complete Poetry and Selected Prose of John Donne & The Complete Poetry of William Blake*. With an Introduction by Robert Silliman Hillyer. N.Y., 1941. A Modern Library Giant.

Pencil Drawings by William Blake. Ed. Geoffrey Keynes. London, 1927.

'Blake's Pencil Drawings' is on pp. vii–xvi; there are 82 plates (including the 22 *Job* sketches), 27 of which are reproduced in the 1970 *Drawings*. 1,550 copies were printed. For the Second Series, see *Blake's Pencil Drawings* (1956).

Illustrations to Young's Night Thoughts, Done in Water-Colour by William Blake. Thirty pages, five reproduced in colour and twenty-five in monotone from the original water-colours. With an introductory essay by Geoffrey Keynes. Cambridge [Mass.] and London, 1927.

Keynes's 'Introductory Essay' is 8 pages (reprinted in *Blake Studies* [1949, 1971]). 500 copies.

A. *Burlington Fine Arts Club Catalogue: Blake Centenary Exhibition*. London, 1927. B. 1927.

In his 'Introductory Note' (pp. 11–15 in A, pp. 7–11 in B), L. B[inyon] says that the 91 entries are 'in most cases reprinted (with some alterations) from the Catalogue' made by A. G. B. Russell for the National Gallery exhibition (1913). G. L. K[eynes], 'Books and Prints, Chiefly in Illuminated Printing: Introduction' is pp. 54–6 in A, pp. 50–2 in B. The chief difference between A and B is that there are 49 plates in A.

1928

*'A Gift to the Nation. Blake Drawings from the U.S.A. "Ninepence Each".' *The Times*, 28 July 1928, pp. 13, 16.

The 537 water-colour drawings for *Night Thoughts* have been given by Frances White Emerson to the British Museum.

1929

'Blake, William.' *Encyclopaedia Britannica*. London and N.Y., 1929. Vol. iii, pp. 694–6. [No attempt has been made to record issues of the *Encyclopaedia Britannica*, but it may be useful to note that there were printings in 1929, 1930, 1932, 1936, 1937, 1938, 1940, 1941, 1942, 1943. . . .]

A replacement for the article by J. Comyns Carr.

1930

A. 'William Blake and the Portland Vase.' *TLS* 3 July 1930, p. 557. B–C. *Revised and reprinted in *Blake Studies* (1949, 1971).

> On the basis of a letter from Joseph Johnson to Erasmus Darwin (23 July 1791), we may be confident that Blake engraved the plate of The Portland Vase for Darwin's *Botanic Garden* (1791).

'Blake and Hayley: A New Letter.' *TLS* 31 July 1930, p. 624.

> Text of the letter of 7 Oct. 1803.

?1931

Geoffrey Keynes and Gwendolen Raverat. *Job: A Masque for Dancing* Founded on Blake's Illustrations to the Book of Job. Music by R. Vaughan Williams. Pianoforte arrangements by Vally Lasker. London, N.Y., Leipzig, Amsterdam [?1931].

> The Masque was first performed at the Norwich Festival in 1930 and is now a regular part of the repertoire of the Royal Ballet.

1933

T[homas] O. M[abbott] and Geoffrey Keynes. 'The Text of Blake's "A Fairy Stepd upon my Knee".' *N & Q* clxiv (1933), 388–9; clxv (1933), 302.

> T. O. M. corrects Swinburne's transcription of the poem from a facsimile of the MS. in a sale catalogue; Keynes corrects the text and points out that he had already printed a careful version.

§'Description of Blake's Entombment.' *The Vasari Society for the Reproduction of Drawings by Old and Modern Masters*, 2nd Ser., Part xiv (Oxford, 1933).

1935

A. **The Note-Book of William Blake Called the Rossetti Manuscript*. Ed. Geoffrey Keynes. London, 1935. B. *N.Y., 1970.

> The 'Introduction' is pp. v–xiii (reprinted in *Blake Studies* [1949, 1971]). This is both a facsimile and a transcript of the MS. 650 copies were printed of A. B is a photographic facsimile of A, a facsimile of a facsimile.

**Illustrations of the Book of Job by William Blake*: Being all the Water-colour Designs Pencil Drawings and Engravings Reproduced in Facsimile. With an introduction by Laurence Binyon and Geoffrey Keynes. N.Y., 1935.

> 'The History of the Designs' (pp. 3–15, revised and reprinted in *Blake Studies* [1949, 1971]), 'The Interpretation' (pp. 16–19), 'The Water-Colours, the

Pencil Drawings, and the Engravings' (pp. 50–4), 'Reproductions of the Engravings' (pp. 55–7), and 'The Stage Version' (pp. 58–61, revised and reprinted in *Blake Studies* [1949, 1970] are by Keynes; 'The Place of the New Zealand Set' (pp. 47–9) is by Binyon; and 'The Variations in the Designs' (pp. 20–46) is by Binyon and Keynes. 500 copies were printed.

The 134 plates of this excellent Pierpont Morgan edition include Blake's drawings, water-colours, and proofs. For the genesis of *Job* it is of crucial importance.

1937

The Illustrations of William Blake for Thornton's Virgil with the First Eclogue and the Imitation by Ambrose Philips. The Introduction by Geoffrey Keynes. London, 1937.

The 'Introduction' is pp. 7–19 (revised and reprinted in *Blake Studies* [1949, 1971]). Besides facsimiles of Blake's designs printed from electrotypes, there are 8 proof plates from the first state and 16 reproductions of the pencil designs. Inserted in a pocket is a set of the prints printed one to a page. 1,000 copies were printed.

1939

'William Blake (1757–1827) Bibliographie Générale.' *Messages*, i (1939), 63–8.

A contribution to a special Blake issue.

1940

'William Blake (1757–1827).' Vol. ii, pp. 347–50 of *The Cambridge Bibliography of English Literature*. [5 vols.] Ed. F. W. Bateson. Cambridge, 1940.

A checklist, supplemented by Keynes in 1957.

1941

*John Bunyan. *The Pilgrim's Progress*. Illustrated with 29 watercolor paintings by William Blake now printed for the first time. With a new introduction by Geoffrey Keynes. N.Y., 1941. Limited Editions Book Club.

The 'Introduction' is pp. vii–xxxii (revised and reprinted in *Blake Studies* [1949, 1971]).

Songs of Innocence and of Experience. Sixteen designs printed from electrotypes of the original plates for Ruthven Todd and Geoffrey Keynes. London, 1941.

1942

A. 'Engravers Called Blake.' *TLS* 17 Jan. 1942, p. 36. B–C *Revised and reprinted in his *Blake Studies* (1949, 1971).

On William Staden Blake, the writing-engraver.

A. 'Blake's Copper Plates.' *TLS* 24 Jan. 1942, p. 48. B–C. *Revised and Reprinted in his *Blake Studies* (1949, 1971).

Describes Blake's engraving techniques.

A. Geoffrey Keynes and Ruthven Todd. 'William Blake's Catalogue: A New Discovery.' *TLS* 12 Sept. 1942, p. 456. B–C. *Revised and reprinted in his *Blake Studies* (1949, 1971).

A new advertisement leaf found; description and census of copies of the *Descriptive Catalogue*.

1943

A. 'New Blake Documents: History of the Job Engravings.' *TLS* 9 Jan. 1943, p. 24. B–C. *Revised and reprinted in his *Blake Studies* (1949, 1971).

A summary from Linnell's receipts and account books of the financial history of *Job*.

A. 'William Blake's Brother.' *TLS* 6, 13 Feb. 1943, pp. 72, 84. B–C. *Revised and reprinted in his *Blake Studies* (1949, 1971).

An account of Robert Blake.

A. 'New Lines from Blake's "Jerusalem".' *TLS* 10 July 1943, p. 336. B–C. *Revised and reprinted in *Blake Studies* (1949, 1971).

Deleted lettering on Plate 1 is legible on an early proof, plus a census.

1944

Max Plowman. *Bridge into the Future*. Letters of Max Plowman. Ed. D[orothy] L. P[lowman]. London, 1944.

Many of the letters to Keynes discuss Blake.

§Review of J. Bronowski, *William Blake, 1757–1827*: A Man Without A Mask in *Time and Tide*, 3 June 1944.

1945

A. 'Blake's Poetical Sketches.' *TLS* 10, 17 Mar. 1945, pp. 120, 132. B–C. Revised and reprinted in *Blake Studies* (1949, 1971).

Description of the circumstances of publication, corrections, punctuation, and a census of copies. (H. J. C. Grierson, 'Blake and Macpherson', *TLS* 7 Apr. 1945, p. 163, commented on Keynes's essay.)

C. F. Bell and Geoffrey Keynes. 'Blake and Flaxman.' *TLS* 31 Mar. 1945, p. 151.

> The Flaxman receipt for £100 from Blake was misattributed to the poet by M. R. Lowery, *Windows of the Morning* (1940), instead of to Robert Blake of 14 Essex Street.

'Blake, Tulk, and Garth Wilkinson.' *Library*, 4th Ser., xxvi (1945), 190–2.

> The edition of the *Songs* described by John Sampson (*N & Q* [1906]) was printed by G. A. Tulk, as the recently acquired British Museum copy demonstrates.

A. **Blake*. Ed. G. Keynes. London [1945]. The Faber Gallery. B. **N.Y.*, 1949. C. **London, 1954.

> The 'Introduction by Geoffrey Keynes' is on pp. 2–5, 24; the ten colour-plates are the *raison d'être* of the book.

1947

*William Blake, 1757–1827. Catalogue de l'Exposition organisée par la Galerie René Drouin et The British Council. Paris, 1947.

> There were editions of this catalogue in English (London, The Tate Gallery), French (the edition above and another at Brussels, Musée royal des Beaux-Arts), and in German (Zurich, Kunsthaus). To the Paris edition, Keynes contributed a 'Bibliographie' (pp. 39–42).

§Review of Northrop Frye, *Fearful Symmetry*: A Study of William Blake in *Time and Tide*, 27 Dec. 1947, p. 1394.

1948

§Review of J. G. Davies, *The Theology of William Blake* in *TLS* 20 Nov. 1948, p. 658.

1949

§Review of Mona Wilson, *Life of William Blake*, in *Time and Tide*, 26 Feb. 1949, p. 206.

Catalogue of Original Works by William Blake the property of the late Graham Robertson, Esq. which will be sold by Christie, Manson & Woods, Ltd., July 22, 1949.

> Geoffrey Keynes, 'Preface', is on pp. 3–4, and he prepared the descriptions of the 90 Blake entries.

§Review of Bernard Blackstone, *English Blake*, in *Listener*, 4 Aug. 1949, pp. 202–3.

A. *'A Newly Discovered Painting by William Blake.' *Country Life*, 11 Nov. 1949, p. 1427. B. 'Condensed' in *A Newly Discovered Painting by William Blake lent by The National Trust*. The Arts Council of Great Britain, 4 St. James's Square, S.W. 1. 16th December 1949–14th January 1950.

> The article reproduces and comments on the Arlington Court Picture.

A. *'Job.' pp. 24–34 of Joan Lawson, James Laver, Geoffrey Keynes, Frank Howes. *Job and The Rake's Progress*. London, 1949. Sadler's Wells Ballet Books, No. 2. B–C. *Revised and reprinted in his *Blake Studies* (1949, 1971).

> On the genesis of the Job masque for dancing (see 1931).

A. *Blake Studies: Notes on his Life and Works in Seventeen Chapters. London, 1949. B. *Blake Studies: Essays on his life and work. Second Edition. Oxford, 1971.

> *Blake Studies* is a collection of essays (17 in 1949, 29 in 1971), most of which first appeared elsewhere. 'None of the papers is here reproduced exactly as it first appeared; all have been revised and most of them extended' (1949, p. xiii); further revisions were made in 1971. The work consists of:

	1949		1971		*Original*
Title	*Chapter*	*Pages*	*Chapter*	*Pages*	*printing*
William and Robert	I	3–12	I	1–7	1943
Blake's Notebook	II	13–20	II	8–13	1935
The Engraver's Apprentice	IV	41–9	III	14–30	
Poetical Sketches	III	23–39	IV	31–45	1945
Engravers Called Blake	V	50–5	V	46–9	1942
Blake's Illustrations to Young's *Night Thoughts*	VI	56–66	VI	50–8	1927
Blake and the Wedgwoods	VII	67–75	VII	59–69	1926
A Descriptive Catalogue	VIII	76–83	VIII	66–73	1942
William Blake with Charles Lamb and his Circle	IX	84–104	IX	74–89	1943[1]
William Blake and Sir Francis Bacon			X	90–7	1957
William Blake and John Gabriel Stedman			XI	98–104	1965
'Little Tom the Sailor'			XII	105–10	1968
Blake's Miniatures			XIII	111–12	1960
Blake's Trial at Chichester			XIV	113–14	1957
New Lines from *Jerusalem*	XI	110–18	XV	115–21	1943
Blake's Copper-Plates	X	105–9	XVI	122–9	1942

[1] Read at the Lamb Society, 9 Oct. 1943.

A Checklist of Writings on Blake by Geoffrey Keynes, *1910–1972*

Title	1949		1971		Original printing
	Chapter	Pages	Chapter	Pages	
Blake's Visionary Heads and the Ghost of a Flea			XVII	130–5	1954
Thornton's *Virgil*	XV	157–66	XVIII	136–42	1937
Remember Me!	XVII	186–90	XIX	143–6	
Blake's Copy of Dante's *Inferno*			XX	147–54	1957
Blake's Library			XXI	155–62	1959
The Pilgrim's Progress	XVI	167–85	XXII	163–75	1941
The History of the *Job* Designs	XII	119–34	XXIII	176–86	1935
Blake's *Job* on the Stage	XIV	146–56	XXIV	187–94	1949
The Arlington Court Picture			XXV	195–204	1954
The Blake–Linnell Documents	XIII	135–45	XXVI	205–12	1943
William Blake and John Linnell			XXVII	213–20	1958
John Linnell and Mrs. Blake			XXVIII	221–9	1958
George Cumberland and William Blake			XXIX	230–52	1970

There are 48 plates in A and 81 reproductions in B. The 1949 edition has an incomplete 'Bibliography of the writings of Geoffrey Keynes on Blake' (pp. 193–9); see also 'A List of the Writings by Sir Geoffrey Keynes Compiled by permission from his own register by W. B. Le Fanu', pp. 27–61 (esp. pp. 41–7) of *Geoffrey Keynes*: Tributes on the Occasion of his Seventieth Birthday [in 1957] with a bibliographical check list of his publications (London: Rupert Hart-Davis for The Osler Club, 1961).

1950

'Blake's "Jerusalem".' *TLS* 16 June 1950, p. 373.

An announcement that the subscription dates for the Blake Trust facsimile have been extended.

*William Blake's Engravings. Ed. Geoffrey Keynes. London, 1950.

The 'Introduction' is on pp. 7–22; there are 142 plates, including all those for Virgil, *Job*, and *For Children*.

1951

§Review of Morchard Bishop, *Blake's Hayley*, as 'Bad Poet: Good Friend' in *Spectator*, 24 Aug. 1951, p. 248.

*_Jerusalem_ [copy E]. A [colour] Facsimile of the Illuminated Book. [Five fascicles.] London [1951]. The William Blake Trust.

> The 'Preludium' by Joseph Wicksteed is on pp. v–vi; Geoffrey Keynes, 'Bibliographical Statement', is on pp. vii–ix.

*_The Tempera Paintings of William Blake_: A Critical Catalogue. Arts Council of Great Britain. London, 1951.

> Geoffrey Keynes, 'Introduction', is pp. 5–11; there are 30 Blake entries in this exhibition catalogue.

1952

§Review of _The Blake Collection of W. Graham Robertson_, ed. Kerrison Preston, in _TLS_ 15 Aug. 1952.

A. _Jerusalem_ [copy C]. Foreword by Geoffrey Keynes. London, 1952. B. N.Y., 1955. C. London, 1955. The William Blake Trust.

> The 'Foreword' is one page; the black-and-white facsimile is accompanied by a transcript of the poem.

1953

A. '_Religio Bibliographici_.' _Library_, viii (1953), 63–76. B. Reprinted in pp. ix–xxiii of his _Bibliotheca Bibliographici_ (1964).

> Includes a history of his _Bibliography_ (1921).

A. *_William Blake's Illuminated Books_: A Census compiled by Geoffrey Keynes and Edwin Wolf, 2nd. N.Y., 1953. B. §N.Y., 1969.

> Keynes's 'Preface' is on pp. vii–xix; the Grolier Club Census brings up to date the comparable section of the _Bibliography_ (1921). The 1969 reissue is a photographic reprint.

1954

§Review of A. S. Roe, _Blake's Illustrations to the Divine Comedy_, in _TLS_ 9 May 1954.

§Review of Bunsho Jugaku, _A Bibliographical Study of William Blake's Notebook_, in _TLS_ 21 May 1954.

A. *'Blake's Vision of the Circle of the Life of Man.' pp. 202–8 of _Studies in Art and Literature for Belle Da Costa Greene_. Ed. Dorothy Miner. Princeton, [N.J.] 1954. B. *Revised and reprinted in his _Blake Studies_ (1971).

> A history and interpretation of the picture called the 'Circle of the Life of

Man' discovered in 1947 at the Arlington Estate (see 1949, above), the interpretation radically revised in 1971.

*Joseph Wicksteed. *William Blake's Jerusalem.* Foreword by Geoffrey Keynes. London, 1954.

> The 'Foreword' is pp. ix–x. The book was written to accompany the Blake Trust facsimiles of *Jerusalem* (1951–5).

Songs of Innocence [copy B]. London, 1954. The William Blake Trust.

> Geoffrey Keynes, 'Bibliographical Statement', is 2 pages.

1955

'Blake's Letters to Hayley.' *TLS* 25 Mar. 1955, p. 181.

> Lists lost letters.

Songs of Innocence and of Experience [copy Z]. London, 1955. The William Blake Trust.

> Geoffrey Keynes, 'Bibliographical Statement', is 3 pages.

1956

A. *The Letters of William Blake.* Ed. Geoffrey Keynes. London, 1956. B. §N.Y., 1956. C. London, 1968. D. *Blake no Tegami* [*The Letters of Blake*]. Tr. Narumi Umetsu. Tokyo, 1970.

> A–C include fairly full notes, some related documents such as receipts, and provenances; is a revised edition. The Japanese translation (D) includes a chronological history of Blake's life.

Engravings by William Blake: The Separate Plates: A Catalogue Raisonée. Dublin, 1956.

> The 'Preface' is pp. xi–xiii; there are 44 entries (not counting varying states and impressions) and 45 plates. This is an extremely important catalogue.

Blake's Pencil Drawings Second Series. Ed. Geoffrey Keynes. London, 1956.

> 'Blake's Pencil Drawings Second Series' is on pp. vii–xi (for the first series, see *Pencil Drawings* [1927]); there are 57 plates, 39 of which are reproduced (darker) in the 1970 *Drawings*.

1957

A. 'William Blake and Sir Francis Bacon.' *TLS* 8 Mar. 1957, p. 152. B. *Revised and reprinted in his *Blake Studies* (1971).

> The newly discovered copy of the *Essays* with Blake's annotations.

George Harris Healey and Geoffrey Keynes. 'Blake and Wordsworth.' *TLS* 5, 12 Apr. 1957, pp. 209, 225.

> Healey says that Blake's annotations in the copy of Wordsworth's *Poems* now at Cornell have never been published in full; Keynes replies that they were printed and adds information on the ownership of the book.

'William Blake's Notebook: An American Generosity to the British Museum.' *The Times*, 16 Apr. 1957, p. 11.

A. 'Blake's Copy of Dante's "Inferno".' *TLS* 3 May 1957, p. 277. B. *Revised and reprinted in his *Blake Studies* (1971).

> The annotations in the newly discovered book.

Frederick W. Bateson and Geoffrey Keynes. 'Selections from Blake.' *TLS* 26 Apr., 10 May 1957, pp. 257, 289.

> Bateson objects to the review of his edition of Blake's *Selected Poems*; Keynes points out that both Bateson and the reviewer are wrong in saying there was no final order for the plates of the *Songs*, for the order was fixed in seven out of eight copies he completed after 1815.

'The Nonesuch Blake.' *TLS* 8 Nov. 1957, p. 673.

> In his 1927 and 1957 editions of Blake's *Writings*, 'off his own tail' in the *Marriage* should read 'off of his own tail'.

'Kidnapping Blake.' *Spectator*, cxcix (13 Dec. 1957), p. 833.

> Answer to a review of his *Complete Writings* on 6 Dec.

§'Blake's Illuminated Books.' *Books*, No. 314 (1957), 231–3.

'Blake and Wesley.' *N & Q* ccii (1957), 181.

> On Blake's copy of Wesley's *Hymns* (1782).

A. 'Blake's Trial at Chichester.' *N & Q* ccii [N.S., iv] (1957), 484–5. B. *Revised and reprinted in his *Blake Studies* (1971).

> Two new documents: the indictment of Blake, and the recognizance entered into by his accusers to ensure their presence at the trial.

'William Blake (1757–1827).' pp. 425–8 of Vol. v (Supplement: A.D. 600–1900. Ed. George Watson) of *The Cambridge Bibliography of English Literature*. Ed. F. W. Bateson. [5 vols.] Cambridge, 1957.

> A supplement to the 1940 *CBEL*.

A. *The Complete Writings of William Blake* with All the Variant Readings. Ed. Geoffrey Keynes. London and N.Y., 1957. B. *The Complete Writings of William

Blake with Variant Readings. Ed. Geoffrey Keynes. London, N.Y., Toronto, 1966. C. §1966. D. *1967. E. *London, Oxford, N.Y., 1969. F. §*1971.

> In A and B, 'The Editor's Preface' is pp. ix–xv, 'The Notes' pp. 883–927, and the plates include those of *For the Sexes: The Gates of Paradise*. In B, the 'Preface to this Edition' (p. viii) says the page-references are the same as in the 1957 edition, in order to make the work usable with the *Concordance* of Erdman *et al.* (1967). Corrections from the *Concordance* have been made on 124 pages of text (though not including all known variants) and in some notes. A 'Supplement' of new material (pp. 928, 939–44) includes some of the matter which had come to light since 1957.
>
> *N.B.* In the *Writings* (1925) from which this edition derives and in the *Complete Writings* (1957–71), Blake's works are intermingled in chronological order, though in the *Complete Writings*, the letters are gathered in one place (not scattered through the text as in the 1925 *Writings*). The *Complete Writings* (Nonesuch, 1957) contains a significant number of minor additions to the *Writings* (1925) and is in turn slightly extended in B–E (Oxford).

William Blake's Illustrations to the Bible: A Catalogue compiled by Geoffrey Keynes. London, 1957. The William Blake Trust.

> George Goyder's 'Introduction' is pp. x–xi. There are 208 entries in this 'list [of] all the tempera and water-colour paintings Blake is known to have made in illustration of the Bible'. All the paintings presently locatable (174) are reproduced in small dimensions, with nine also of enormous size and lovely colour.

1958

§Review of George Wingfield Digby, *Symbol and Image in William Blake*, in *Apollo*, Mar. 1958, pp. 94–5.

A. 'William Blake and John Linnell.' *TLS* 13 June 1958, p. 332. B. *Revised and reprinted in his *Blake Studies* (1971).

> Extracts from A. H. Palmer's transcriptions of portions of John Linnell's journal.

A. 'John Linnell and Mrs. Blake.' *TLS* 20 June 1958, p. 348. B. Revised and reprinted in his *Blake Studies* (1971).

> A supplement to 'William Blake and John Linnell' describing the bickering between Linnell and Tatham, from evidence in the Ivimy MSS.

§Review of Martin Butlin, *William Blake (1757–1827): A Catalogue of the Works of William Blake in the Tate Gallery*, in *TLS* 14 Feb. 1958, p. 89.

The Book of Urizen [copy G]. London, 1958. The William Blake Trust.

> It concludes a 2-page 'Bibliographical Statement' by Geoffrey Keynes and another unpaginated, untitled, and unsigned statement.

1959

A. 'Blake's Library.' *TLS* 6 Nov. 1959, p. 648. B. *Revised and reprinted in his *Blake Studies* (1971).

> Prints a letter from Tatham (8 June 1864) about Blake's reading and gives a list of books Blake is known to have owned.

A. *Blake's Poems and Prophecies*. Ed. Max Plowman. Supplementary note, select bibliography, and revisions to the notes by Geoffrey Keynes. London and N.Y., 1959. B. *London, 1970.

> Keynes advised Plowman extensively on the preparation of the original text of *The Poems & Prophecies of William Blake* (1927, 1934, 1950, 1954, Everyman), particularly on *The Four Zoas* (see Plowman's letters to Keynes in his *Bridge into the Future* [1954]), and to the editions of 1959 and 1970 he contributed a 'Supplementary Note' to Plowman's introduction (pp. xxvii–xxviii) and textual 'Notes' (pp. 435–9); 'The text of the writings remains exactly as it was.'

Visions of the Daughters of Albion [copy C]. London, 1959. The William Blake Trust.

> The Bibliographical Statement by Geoffrey Keynes is 4 pages.

1960

A. 'Blake's Miniatures.' *TLS* 29 Jan. 1960, p. 72. B. *Revised and reprinted in his *Blake Studies* (1971).

> Quotes a letter from Hayley to David Parker Coke of 13 May 1801 referring to a miniature by Blake which has not been traced.

'Blake's "Holy Thursday" in Anne and Jane Taylor's *City Scenes*.' *Book Collector*, ix (1960), 75–6.

> Blake's poem was reprinted in editions of 1818 ff.

A. *'Blake's Visionary Heads & the Ghost of a Flea.' *Bulletin of New York Public Library*, lxiv (1960), 567–72. B. *Revised and reprinted in his *Blake Studies* (1971).

> Amplifies and illustrates the source suggestion made by Charles Singer, 'The first English microscopist: Robert Hooke (1635–1703)', *Endeavor*, xiv (1955), 12–18.

The Marriage of Heaven and Hell [copy D]. London, 1960. The William Blake Trust.

> Geoffrey Keynes, 'Descriptive and Bibliographical Statement', is 4 pages.

§Review of Anthony Blunt, *The Art of William Blake*, in *Criticism*, iii (1960), 306–8.

1962

§Review of Kerrison Preston, *Notes For a Catalogue of the Blake Library at The Georgian House Merstham*, in *Library*, 5th Series, xvii (1962), 192–3.

1963

*'A Blake Engraving in Bonnycastle's *Mensuration*, 1782.' *Book Collector*, xii (1963), 205–6.

> Bibliographical details.

America a Prophecy [copy M]. London, 1963. The William Blake Trust.

> Geoffrey Keynes, 'Description and Bibliographical Statement', is 5 pages.

1964

'On Editing Blake.' *English Studies Today*, ed. G. I. Duthie, 3rd Ser. (1964), 137–53.

> A history of his texts of Blake.

Kerrison Preston and Geoffrey Keynes. 'Blake's America.' *TLS* 5, 19 Mar. 1964, pp. 195, 238.

> Corrections of a review (6 Feb., p. 111) of the Blake Trust 'facsimile' of the 'Andrew [i.e. Paul] Mellon' copy of *America*.

Bibliotheca Bibliographici: A Catalogue of the Library Formed by Geoffrey Keynes. London, 1964.

> 'Religio Bibliographici' (1953) is reprinted on pp. ix–xxiii. The important collection of Blake works and Blakeana comprehends especially nos. 467–783. Of these, nos. 467–500, 506–9, 511–14, 516–20, 522–3, 551–2, 555, 558–60, 563–77, 579, 582–4, 588–610, 612–727 are to go to the Fitzwilliam Museum, according to the Fitzwilliam Catalogue (1970), below, which reprints the more important entries here.

A. *An Exhibition of the Illuminated Books of William Blake Poet · Printer · Prophet* Arranged by The William Blake Trust. A Commemorative Handbook with a study by Geoffrey Keynes and a foreword by Lessing J. Rosenwald. Clairvaux, 1964.

The William Blake Trust. B. Geoffrey Keynes. *A Study of the Illuminated Books of William Blake Poet · Printer · Prophet*. London and Paris, 1964.

> In A, the 'Foreword' is pp. 7–8 and 'The Illuminated Books' (a general explanation, not a catalogue of the exhibition) is pp. 11–55; there are 27 colour plates.

> B seems to differ from A in the omission of Mr. Rosenwald's 'Foreword', the relocation of the plates so that the unchanged study of 'The Illuminated Books' is on pp. 11–27, the addition of some 34 new plates, and cursory bibliographical descriptions of each book reproduced.

1965

A. 'William Blake and John Gabriel Stedman.' *TLS* 20 May 1965, p. 400. B. *Revised and reprinted in his *Blake Studies* (1971).

> A résumé of the Blake passages in Stedman's recently published diary.

Review of G. E. Bentley, Jr., and M. K. Nurmi, *A Blake Bibliography*, in *Book Collector*, xiv (1965), 250–1.

Blake. London, 1965. The Masters 6.

> Geoffrey Keynes, 'William Blake 1757–1827', is pp. 2–6; there are 38 plates.

The Book of Thel [copy O]. London, 1965. The William Blake Trust.

> Geoffrey Keynes, 'Description and Bibliographical Statement', is 5 pages.

1966

*'William Blake.' Vol. iv, p. 247 of *Collier's Encyclopedia*, N.p., 1966.

John E. Grant, Our Reviewer [Kathleen Raine]; Geoffrey Keynes. 'Illuminations.' *TLS* 2, 9 Nov. 1967, pp. 1045, 1069.

> Grant corrects a review (of 14 Sept., p. 820) in fact and interpretation, and the Reviewer replies with an attack on all Blake scholars; Keynes defends himself for having cited the views of Damon.

1967

Milton, a Poem [copy D]. London, 1967. The William Blake Trust.

> Geoffrey Keynes, 'Description and Bibliographical Statement', is 13 pages.

A. *Songs of Innocence and Of Experience* [copy Z]. London, 1967. B. *N.Y., 1967. C. Oxford, 1970.

> A facsimile 'printed in 6- and 8-colour offset', with facing transcript and

following explication by Keynes. The 'Publisher's Note' by Arnold Fawcus is pp. vii–viii, and the 'Introduction' by Geoffrey Keynes is pp. ix–xvii. (The Blake Trust facsimile [1955] of the same copy by the same firm used a different process of reproduction.)

C. Reprinted as an Oxford Paperback.

1968

A. *'Blake's *Little Tom the Sailor.*' *Book Collector*, xvii (1968), 421–7. B. *Revised and reprinted in his *Blake Studies* (1971).

Bibliographical description and census of copies.

Review of *Tiriel*, ed. G. E. Bentley, Jr., in *Library*, 5th Ser. xxiii (1968), 172–3.

The Gates of Paradise: For Children, For the Sexes. Introductory volume by Geoffrey Keynes with Blake's preliminary sketches. [3 vols.] London, 1968. The William Blake Trust.

Vol. i is the Introductory volume, with A. D. F[awcus], 'Publisher's Note', and Geoffrey Keynes, 'Introduction' (pp. 1–5), 'Commentary' (pp. 7–22), list and reproduction of the drawings for the *Gates* (pp. 23–46), and an important 'Census' (pp. 47–51) of *For Children* and *For the Sexes*. Vol. ii is a facsimile of *For Children* (copy D) and Vol. iii reproduces *For the Sexes* (copy F).

1969

'The William Blake Trust.' Pp. 414–20 of *William Blake*: Essays for S. Foster Damon. Ed. Alvin H. Rosenfeld. Providence [R.I.], 1969.

A history of the Blake Trust.

§'Talking about Jerusalem.' *Cambridge Review*, xci (1969), 24–5.

Review of Kathleen Raine, *Blake and Tradition*.

Europe, a Prophecy. London, 1969. The William Blake Trust.

Geoffrey Keynes, 'Description and Bibliographical Statement', is 6 pages. The colour facsimile reproduces copy B (Plates 1, 6, 13–15, 17–18), copy G (Plates 2, 4–5, 7–12, 16), and copy K (Plate 3).

William Blake: A Loan Exhibition [21 August to 30 September 1969] in the National Library of Scotland, Edinburgh, 1969.

Geoffrey Keynes, 'The Blake Trust' (pp. 3–4), remarks that 'The exhibition has been organized primarily to bring to general notice the work . . . of the

William Blake Trust'. The essay was expanded in the Damon *Festschrift* (1969) and revised and reprinted in the 1971 Gray catalogue.

William Blake Engraver: A Descriptive Catalogue of an Exhibition by Charles Ryskamp with an Introductory Essay by Geoffrey Keynes. Princeton University Library [December 1969 to February 1970]. Princeton, [N.J.], 1969.

Charles Ryskamp, Preface, is pp. vii–x; Geoffrey Keynes, 'Introduction', is pp. 1–18; the 129 entries are described with great care.

1970

A. *'Some Uncollected Authors XLIV: George Cumberland 1754–1848.' *Book Collector*, xix (1970), 31–65. B. *Revised and reprinted in his *Blake Studies* (1971).

'This study of George Cumberland's books and more particularly of his relations with William Blake' (p. 31) points out evidence that Blake engraved the map for Cumberland's *Attempt to Describe Hafod* (1796). A includes a checklist of Cumberland's books which is omitted in B.

'Correspondence.' *Blake Studies*, ii (1970), 63–4.

Corrections to the article (i. 139–90) by Karl Kiralis on Blake's 'Canterbury Pilgrims'.

William Blake: Catalogue of the Collection in the Fitzwilliam Museum, Cambridge. Ed. David Bindman. Cambridge, 1970.

In the 'Foreword' (p. vii), David Piper explains that the catalogue was compiled about 1953 by Sir Geoffrey Keynes, 'added to by many hands, notably those of Mr Carlos van Hasselt, Mr J. W. Goodison, Mr Malcolm Cormack and Mr Martin Butlin', and then 'entirely recast' by Mr. David Bindman. 'The History of the Fitzwilliam Blake Collection' is on p. 1. There are 64 entries and 74 plates.

The 'Appendix' (pp. 65–84) reprints Keynes's *Bibliotheca Bibliographici* (1964), nos. 467–500, 506–9, 511–14, 516–20, 522–3, 551–2, 555, 558–60, 563–77, 579, 582–4, 588–610, 612–56, 721–6, and announces that Sir Geoffrey has 'promised to bequeath to the Museum these' plus nos. 657–76, 678–720.

The publication of the catalogue was accompanied by an exhibition of all 64 Fitzwilliam Blakes, extended by works described in a flyer: '*William Blake* (1757–1827) [*12*] Additional items on exhibition, 13 January–28 March 1971'.

Drawings of William Blake: 92 Pencil Studies. Ed. Sir Geoffrey Keynes. N.Y., 1970.

The 'Introduction' is pp. v–xi. Most of the drawings are repeated, rather darker, from the *Pencil Drawings* of 1927 (27) and 1956 (39).

All Religions are One [copy A]. London, 1970. The William Blake Trust.

Geoffrey Keynes, 'Description and Bibliographical Statement', is 5 pages.

1971

*Mona Wilson. *The Life of William Blake*. Ed. Geoffrey Keynes. London, Oxford, N.Y., 1971.

The first edition of Mona Wilson's biography (1927) was printed and bound to range with Keynes's edition of Blake's *Writings* (1925). In the second edition of her book (1932), all the notes and appendices were omitted; the third edition (1948) was revised, the notes and appendices were restored, and some notes and appendix material were added. In the 1971 edition, Keynes checked her references, added numerous new footnotes, retained Appendices III, V, and VI ('Blake's Calligraphy', 'Extracts from Varley's *Zodiacal Physiognomy* and *Urania*', and 'Extracts from *Revue Britannique*'), and added the 'Editor's Preface' (pp. ix–x).

Miss Wilson's biography scrupulously used contemporary accounts of Blake, a number of which had not appeared in print before. This is a very full, accurate, and reliable work, and is sometimes called the 'standard' biography of Blake.

The Oxford edition was issued in both paperback and §hardcover.

There is No Natural Religion. London, 1971. The William Blake Trust.

The work is in two volumes, Series a in a small volume, Series b in a large one. Geoffrey Keynes, 'Description and Bibliographical Statement', is on 10 pages in the larger volume. The facsimile is eclectic, reproducing parts of Copy F (Plate a1, a3), copy C (Plate a2, a4, a8–a9), Copy G (Plate a5–a7), and Copy L (Plate b1–b4, b6–b12). In his essay, Keynes alters the identification and order of the plates as follows:

1971	designation:	a1—a2—a3—a9;	b1, b3–b10—b11—b12
1953	Keynes and Wolf designation:	a2, a1, a3–a9;	b2, b3–b10, a10, b11.

A. *William Blake's Water-Colour Designs for the Poems of Thomas Gray* with an Introduction and Commentary by Geoffrey Keynes Kt. London, 1971. B. *William Blake's Water-Colours Illustrating the Poems of Thomas Gray* with an Introduction and Commentary by Sir Geoffrey Keynes. Chicago and Paris, 1972. C. §*William Blake's Water-Colour Designs for the Poems of Gray*. Introduction and Commentary by Geoffrey Keynes Kt. London, 1972. The William Blake Trust.

A is 'a Commemorative Catalogue to accompany the exhibition arranged by the William Blake Trust . . . at the Tate Gallery, London [Dec. 1971–Jan. 1972] and at . . . Yale University [Spring 1972] and at other [unspecified] museums' (p. iv), as well as 'an introductory handbook' to the (then still-unpublished) Blake Trust facsimile of Blake's water-colours (p. viii). The text of A consists of Geoffrey Keynes, 'The William Blake Trust' (pp. vii–viii, reprinted with minor changes but without acknowledgement from his essay in the 1969 Edinburgh exhibition catalogue), Arnold Fawcus, 'Acknowledgements' (p. ix), Keynes's 'Introduction' (pp. 1–6) and 'Commentary' (pp. 41–71), the last mostly descriptive. The 137 plates (including the covers) comprehend the 116 Gray designs in black-and-white mostly reduced 4-to-a-page plus 19 large ones in colour.

B is like A except for the omission of the Keynes essay on 'The William Blake Trust' and small revisions to the 'Acknowledgements' (pp. ix–x).

C is the full-size set of colour reproductions.

1972

Pierre Leyris and Geoffrey Keynes. 'Blake.' *TLS* 28 Apr., 5 May 1972, pp. 496, 521.

Leyris suggests that in the *Poetical Sketches* 'Song' beginning 'Fresh from the dewy hill, the merry year', the terminal word in l. 1 would make better sense if it were 'dawn' rather than 'year'; Keynes replies that such a change 'is surely unnecessary for the sense'.

A. *'Blake's Engravings for Gay's Fables.' *Book Collector*, xxi (1972), 59–64.
B. *Reprinted as pp. 47–52 of *To Geoffrey Keynes*: Articles Contributed to The Book Collector to Commemorate his Eighty-Fifth Birthday. London, 1972.

A comparison of Blake's plates with those of the same designs by preceding engravers.

BLAKE INDEX

An asterisk indicates that the subject is illustrated on that page.

C C

GENERAL INDEX

Abbott, C. C., 328 n.
Abrams, Harvey N., 135 n.
Abyssinia, 246, 250, 255, 256 n., 257
Accidie, sin of despair, 209–12
Aders, Charles and Elizabeth, 146 n.
Aeneas, 40, 47, 59
Aeschylus, 50
Agrippa, Cornelius, 51
Akenside, Mark, 104 and n., 231
Allingham, William, *Diary*, 337; *Hogg's Weekly Instructor*, 337; *Nightingale Valley*, 347
Altdorfer, 146
Amaurians, 260
American Monthly Magazine, 321 and n.
American Revolution, 231, 233
Anchises, 59
'Ancients, The', 337–8
animal magnetism, 233
Antal, F., 251 n.
Antiquarian Society, 335
Antoinette, Marie, 121
Aphrodite, 251
Aquinas, St. Thomas, 212 n., 214
Armstrong, John, 238
Arthur, T. S., *The Brilliant*, 321 and n., 322
Art-Journal, review, 346
Athenaeum, 307, 333; reviews, 314, 316, 346
Atkinson's Saturday Evening Post, 321 and n.
Augustan influences, 70

Bacon, Sir Francis, *Advancement of Learning*, 1
Baker, W. S., 265 n.
Balleine, G. R., 280 n.
Barbauld, Mrs. Anna Letitia, 106
Barry, James, 42, 52 and n., 65, 316
Bartolozzi, Francisco, 265
Barton, Bernard, 324 n.
Bartram, W., *Travels*, 255
Basire, James, 1, 29, 31, 33
Bateson, F. W., 104
Bazin, Germain, 145 n.
Beattie, James, 2; *The Minstrel*, 3
Beckford, William, 325
Beer, John, 51 n., 197 n., 232, 233 n., 236 n., 244 n., 256 n., 257 n.; *Blake's Humanism*, 81
Benthall, G., 44 n.
Bentley, G. E., jr., 50 and n., 59, 150 n., 243 n., 244 n., 285 n., 308 n., 311 n., 312, 315, 317 n., 325 and n., 326 n., 327 n., 334 n., 339 n., 346 n., 350 and n.; *A Blake Bibliography*, 312
Bethlam Hospital, 8

Betz, Paul F., 257 n.
Bindman, David, 52 n., 61 n., 272, 341 n.
Binyon, Laurence, 305 n.
Bird, Edward, 316
Blair, Robert, *The Grave*, 29–30, 322
Blake, Mrs. Catherine, 35, 265, 322–4, 326, 340
Blake, Jerry S., 162 n.
Blake, Robert, 37, 48, 331
Blakey, 41
Bland, David, 227 n.
Bloom, Harold, 1 n., 10, 65 n., 99 n., 101 n., 146, 279 n.
Bloomfield, Morton W., 212 n., 213 n., 215
Blunt, Sir Anthony, 31 n., 33 n., 145 n., 250 and n.
Boehme, Jacob, 1, 80, 84, 238
Bogen, Nancy, 51, 236 n., 350
Boismont, A. Briere de, 320 n.
Bonaparte, Napoleon, 313
Bonnycastle, John, 265 and n.
Bowles, Caroline, 318–19
Boydell, John, 41
Brion, Marcel, 129
Bristol, 239
British historians, 40–1, 49
Brook Farm Movement, 335
Brooks, Cleanth, 1 n.
Brothers, Richard, 261–80, 281, 284, 291; *Description of Jerusalem*, 273, 275, 276, 277; 'Dissertation on the Fall of Eve', 281; *Letter from Mr Brothers to Miss Cott*, 267, 270, 277, 278, 291; New Jerusalem, 275–80; *Revealed Knowledge*, 261, 268, 270–2, 273; vision of throne of Sweden, 273
Browning, Elizabeth Barrett, 332, 334
Browning, Robert, 329, 332 and n., 334; *Strafford*, 331; 'Transcendentalism', 331
Bruce, James, 246, 250; *Travels*, 253, 255
Brucker, Ronnie, 162 n.
Brutus, 40, 44, 47
Bryan, Michael, *Biographical Dictionary*, 336 and n., 339
Bryant, Jacob, 51, 250; *A New System, or, an Analysis of Ancient Mythology*, 6, 247
Bulwer-Lytton, Edward, 327–8
Bunyan, John, 213, 221; *Pilgrim's Progress*, 219, 306
Burke, Edmund, *A Philosophical Enquiry into the Origin of our Ideas of the Sublime and Beautiful*, 1
Burton, Richard, *Anatomy of Melancholy*, 213
Bury, Lady Charlotte, *Diary*, 327
Butlin, Martin, 47 n., 58 n., 212 n., 221 n., 294 n., 295 n.